Mental Health and Well-Being
IN THE
Learning and Teaching
Environment

EDITOR-IN-CHIEF

Colin R. Martin
RN BSc PhD MBA YCAP FHEA CPsychol AFBPsS CSci MSc

EDITORS

Mick P. Fleming
RMN PhD MA BA(Hons) Adv Dip PSI YCAP FHEA

Hugh Smith
MEd DipEdTech Dip(CE) LTCL(CMT) LLCM(TD) FHEA

Published by Swan & Horn

First edition 2016

ISBN 978-1-909675-02-5

British Library Cataloguing in Publication Data:
A catalogue record for this book is available from the British Library

Swan & Horn | Auchtermuchty | Fife | Scotland
Telephone: +44 1337 827 397
Email: info@swanandhorn.co.uk

Publisher's Disclaimer: Every effort has been made to ensure the accuracy of information contained in this publication, particularly with respect to medicines and other inverventions, their therapeutic efficacy, precautions to be observed and side effects, and government recommendations and regulations, however no guarantee can be given that all errors and omissions have been excluded. The Publisher and Editors accept no responsibility for loss occasioned to any person acting or refraining from action as a result of the content of this book.

Production by Shoreline BioMedical, UK.

Editorial assistants Sophie O. Hampshire and Bethany R. Hampshire. Cover art by Bethany R. Hampshire.

Printed by Ashford Colour Press Ltd, UK.

Contents

PART I: SETTING THE SCENE

PART II: THE WELL-BEING OF LEARNERS

PART III: THE WELL-BEING OF LEADERS OF LEARNING

PART IV: CONTEMPORARY ISSUES

PART V: THE WAY FORWARD

Foreword

Professor Gabriel Kirtchuk

Traditionally, education and mental health have been seen as separate and independent of each other – conceptually and operationally unrelated. Fortunately, the important and influential relationship between education and mental health has become increasingly recognised, within the context of the well-being of both students (in terms of the educational process) and teachers (in terms of the educational environment). For those of us who work in the clinical environment, it is clear that many significant mental health problems that permeate into adulthood have their origins in the experiences in childhood across a range of environments, including family, peers and school. Understanding this complex relationship is incredibly important, not simply from a philosophical or research perspective, but from a strategic, policy and sometimes interventionist standpoint. Engaging, and where appropriate intervening, early in the development of a mental health issue may not only reduce the extent, or even negate the development, of a mental health problem, but also foster a sense of coherence, comprehensiveness, comfort and care within the educational environment.

It is worth reflecting that modern classrooms resemble an extended family environment; they are dynamic places where relationships are fundamental to growth and maturity, both intellectually and behaviourally. This dynamism is complex, comprising a myriad processes and contexts that interplay uniquely to influence, facilitate, and sometimes obstruct, everyone enmeshed within that environment. Teachers thus have one of the most challenging and most important jobs imaginable, being key influencers in the development, growth and achievement of the students in their care. These challenges often present a significant emotional burden for teachers in achieving their objectives with their students. Stress-related illnesses in the teaching profession are – historically and contemporarily – concerning for all those involved in the educational and care systems, as well as policy-makers.

Teachers, of course, encounter a broad range of students in the educational environment and are generally successful at accommodating their wide spectrum of abilities and characteristics. However, the interaction of this diversity with the developing character and personality of each student can manifest as a 'sub-clinical' or overt mental health problem.

Within the overarching agenda of equity and inclusivity in education, children with challenging or concerning behaviours are more likely to remain in mainstream education than be excluded or taught in a special setting. This pursuit of inclusivity, desirable though it is, can produce a high-stress, high-emotion environment for both educators and fellow students.

The current political landscape is one of austerity, with scarce resources. And in this context, teachers find themselves striving to provide high-quality education to students with very diverse abilities and behaviours, with limited support. It is no surprise that perhaps this 'noblest' of professions is increasingly vulnerable to significant stress-related disorders, particularly depression and anxiety.

Colin Martin, Mick Fleming and Hugh Smith have done a superb job bringing together an excellent set of contributors, including key academics and practitioners in the education and mental health fields, to explore the discourse between mental health and education in an applied and translational way. *Mental Health & Well-Being in the Learning and Teaching Environment* is the first book that considers the relationship between mental health and education in an evidence-based and practice-focused way, and discusses the mental health needs of both teachers and students contextually anchored in the learning environment. The book is a practical and useful resource for teachers, and for all professionals whose work brings them into this environment, for example, educational psychologists and school nurses.

It is my hope that the key messages contained in this exciting new book may not only contribute to enhancing and improving the quality of experience of both students and teachers, but also reduce the occurrence of significant mental health problems by facilitating early identification and intervention. Nurturing an environment of positive mental health and well-being is instrumental to such an aspiration and this impressive volume holds that ideal as a central tenet and core value throughout.

London 2015

Professor Gabriel Kirtchuk is a consultant psychiatrist in psychotherapy for West London Mental Health NHS Trust and a fellow of the British Psychoanalytical Society. He has worked in forensic settings for more than two decades and established a forensic psychotherapy department at the Three Bridges Unit. He has been the lead clinician of the National Forensic Psychotherapy Training and Development Strategy and Chair of the Forensic Psychotherapy Society at the British Psychoanalytic Council. He is also Visiting Professor at Buckinghamshire New University and an honorary clinical senior lecturer at Imperial College London. His interests include the development of psychotherapeutic approaches within forensic mental health, as well as multidisciplinary educational programmes in the field.

Profiles of contributors and editors

Stuart Blythe

Reverand Dr Stuart Blythe MA BD MTh was a lecturer at the Scottish Baptist College at the University of the West of Scotland for ten years. He is currently the Rector of the International Baptist Theological Study (IBTS) Centre in Amsterdam in the Netherlands, which offers an MA as an approved partner with the University of Manchester, and a PhD as a collaborative centre within the faculty of theology of the VU University Amsterdam. He is also the Moderator for the Consortium of European Baptist Theological Schools. He is a practical theologian, and his current research interests include the nature of theological education, ethnography as a theological approach, and theological belief as a convictional commitment.

Tim Bradshaw

Tim Bradshaw started his career in mental health nursing in 1987 and currently works as a senior lecturer in the School of Nursing, Midwifery and Social Work at the University of Manchester. For the last fifteen years, he has undertaken research on improving the physical health and well-being of people with serious mental ill health, and published numerous articles. Tim has recently been an applicant on two large clinical trials which are now completed and their findings published; these are HELPER InterACT which studied weight management in early psychosis, and SCIMITAR which was the first randomised controlled trial of smoking cessation for people with serious mental ill health conducted in the UK. He is now an applicant on SCIMITAR-Plus – beginning in September 2015, this is the largest randomised controlled trial of smoking cessation in people with serious mental ill health in the world.

Maria Carter

Before obtaining an honours degree in biomedical sciences from Westminster University, Maria Carter assisted for two years at a school for adolescents with developmental and mental health disorders. She conducted postgraduate research at St Thomas's Hospital in neuropharmacology and pursued a career in clinical education, medical communications and academic publishing. She is currently a biomedical information analyst, editor, writer and publisher (e.g. *Patient Safety: Cognitive Factors in Healthcare* by Mitchell P. *et al.*) and works for organisations such as the MRC, NHS, NIHR and NICE, as well as British and European medical societies and the WHO. She has recently written a major report for HTA Programme on diagnostic technology in primary care. Her interests relate to mental health, neurological disease and trauma, and translational research.

Bill Colley

Bill Colley worked his way up to head-leadership of an independent school for pupils unable to manage mainstream learning environments, and has held several with key positions in special education since then. He was a member of the UKAP ADHD Partnership, the National Autism Strategy Reference Group for Scotland, and the Tayside Autism Assessment Pathway & Complex Kids Panels, Chair of the Perth & Kinross Autism Network, and Depute of the Training and Cross-agency Collaboration ASD group. He has also worked at local education authority level, and held advisary positions on autism and attention disorders with Mindroom (Perth & Kinross) and the governments of Scotland and United Arab Emirates. He now runs Caledonia Learning & Care.

Stephen P. Day

Dr Stephen Day is a Lecturer in Education within the School of Education at the University of the West of Scotland, where he is the programme leader for the MEd Enhanced Educational Practice. Prior to joining the university, he worked for ten years as a secondary school biology teacher. His current research interests focus on the handling of controversial socioscientific issues in the classroom and how Initial Teacher Education programmes prepare teachers to handle socioscientific discussion.

Mick P. Fleming

Dr Mick Fleming is an Associate Professor of Mental Health at Napier University in Edinburgh. After many years in mental health nursing, he began research into schizophrenia and psychosis and has published extensively on these subjects. He has received national awards for his work on evidence-based psychosocial interventions.

Christine Forde

Christine Forde is Professor of Leadership and Professional Learning at the University of Glasgow, mainly working in leadership and teacher professional development. She teaches across a range of postgraduate programmes for experienced professional practitioners, and works regularly with national bodies on issues of leadership and teacher development. Her research focuses on two areas: on leadership and professional development, and on gender and equality in education. She publishes widely in these areas and is currently co-editor of the *Scottish Educational Review*.

Jim Gibson

Jim Gibson currently works as a psychotherapist with NHS Ayrshire and Arran, where he specialises in cognitive behavioural therapy (CBT). Jim is an accredited CBT clinician, supervisor and trainer with the British Association of Behavioural and Cognitive Psychotherapies (BABCP), and previously lectured in CBT and mental health nursing at the University of the West of Scotland. He has published several papers on CBT.

Mark Gillespie

Mark Gillespie worked for twenty years in NHS mental health services, with experience in a variety of clinical settings. His main area of focus was in the treatment of psychosis. The experience he gained in developing his own practice encouraged him to get involved in the educational development of others, leading to him to become a lecturer in mental health at the University of the West of Scotland. He is currently a programme lead and lecturer in mental health, with research interests in the influences on clinical development of pre-registration mental health nurses.

James Gordon

Reverend Dr James M. Gordon MA is currently Honorary Lecturer within the School of Divinity, History and Philosophy at the University of Aberdeen, where he supports research and training within the Centre for Ministry Studies. From 2002 to 2013 he was Principal of the Scottish Baptist College, which works in a collaborative partnership within the University of the West of Scotland. He has experience of theological education in the context of intellectual and spiritual formation for pastoral ministry. His current research interests and writing focuses on theology, disability and autism; kenosis as model of ecclesial and pastoral care; theology and wisdom; these are integrated and applied to such social and human experiences as welcome and hospitality, reconciliation and peace-making, pastoral care and presence, generosity and gift, community and disability.

Vivienne Grant

Viv Grant BEd MA has been in the education profession for over twenty seven years. She is a former headteacher and a passionate advocate for the promotion of coaching in schools. An expert in the field, she is the Director of Integrity Coaching, the UK's leading provider of coaching support for head teachers and senior school leaders. Her work with school leaders focuses on the development of emotional awareness and resilience through coaching. She is the author of a seminal work in the field, *Staying A Head: The Stress Management Secrets of Successful School Leaders.* Her contributions have been featured in *The Guardian*, *London Live*, Radio Four's *Woman's Hour* and *World at One*. She has also worked as a lead consultant for the Institute of Education at the University of London, the National College, the National Union of Teachers (NUT) and the Department for Education on a wide range of leadership and school improvement initiatives.

Lynne Grant-McMahon

Dr Lynne Grant-McMahon is a lecturer in the School of Education at the University of the West of Scotland. She is the programme leader for the MEd Leadership for Learning and the Professional Graduate Diploma in Education (Primary). Before joining the university, she was a primary school-teacher and worked at local-authority level. Her research interests currently include assessment, teachers' perceptions of the learning and teaching process, social capital in education, and quality assurance and improvement.

Ben Greer

Ben Greer is currently working towards his BSc undergraduate degree at the University of Bath, and is also a student research assistant in the Forensic Research & Development Domain (FRED) at Broadmoor Hospital, where he is involved in a large-scale project on the multimodal classification of mentally disordered offenders, and its relation to treatment outcome. He is also conducting research on the prevalence of hyperactive, inattentive and impulsive traits in this population. He has a broad interest in the areas of clinical and forensic psychology, with particular interest in topics such as ADHD, juvenile offending, developmental psychopathology, psychopathy and personality disorder.'

Bethany R. Hampshire

Bethany Hampshire has a first-class degree in BSc Psychology from Glasgow Caledonian University, with qualitative research experience of gender issues and identity construction in a male-dominated environment. She has worked with young adults with range of learning disabilities and was part of a peer-mentoring scheme for young learners of mixed backgrounds and attainment levels in low-achieving primary and secondary schools. She is currently tutoring children of various ages who have autism spectrum disorder (ASD), including the use of behavioural analysis techniques, gaining experience before postgraduate studies in child and adolescent mental health.

Cliff Jones

Cliff Jones studied Political Theory and Institutions and Education in Political Contexts at university. He has taught young people and prison inmates, and experienced three reorganisations. As a local government advisor specialising in alternative curriculum and assessment, he helped prepare teachers for dramatic changes introduced by central government, and spent 22 years as a national public examiner. He was part of a movement promoting political education in the curriculum and was Director of Continuing Professional Development (CPD) in education at the University of Liverpool. He chaired the CPD Committee of the Universities Council for the Education of Teachers and the International Professional Development Association, contributed to national initiatives, and editing a monthly journal for school-teachers. He visits many universities that work with teachers, writes on politics and education, and directs Critical Professional Learning (see www.criticalprofessionallearning.co.uk).

Ken Jones

Professor Ken Jones taught in London for thirteen years before returning to Wales to work in Higher Education and is currently Senior Consultant for Professional Learning and Development at University of Wales Trinity Saint David, based in Swansea. He has been involved in the continuing education of teachers and headteachers, nationally as a consultant in the field of school leadership, and internationally through his position as Managing Editor of the journal Professional Development Education and as one of the founding members of the International Professional Development Association (IPDA). He has worked extensively in Wales on professional programmes for middle and senior leaders, supply teachers and School Business Managers. His international work has included the organisation of symposia on professional learning in many European countries, in the USA and in India. Recent publications include K. Jones and J. O'Brien (eds) (2014) *European Perspectives on Professional Development in Teacher Education,* London: Routledge.

Hilary Mairs

Hilary Mairs PhD MSc BA(Hons) DipCOT is an occupational therapist and chartered psychologist. She is currently a Reader and the Director of Postgraduate Education in the School of Nursing, Midwifery and Social Work at the University of Manchester, and the Chair of the Board of Trustees for Connect Support, a Manchester-based charity that supports the friends and families of people with mental ill health. She has worked in a range of NHS settings as an occupational and cognitive–behavioural therapist. Her research and teaching interests focus on the reduced levels of expression and activity (negative symptoms) often observed in psychosis.

Colin R. Martin

Colin Martin is Professor of Mental Health at Buckinghamshire New University, where he drives a clinically meaningful research agenda and works in collaboration with West London Mental

Health NHS Trust as Director of the Institute of Mental Health. He is a registered mental health nurse, chartered health psychologist, chartered scientist and an Honorary Consultant Psychologist to The Salvation Army (UK and Eire), for whom he formulated an addictions policy to foster high-quality clinical care and services. Former Chair in Mental Health at the University of the West of Scotland and Editor for the *Journal of Reproductive and Infant Psychology*, his national and international research activities have attracted over £5 million in funding. His longstanding interests include psychobiology (he developed a psychobiological model of alcohol dependency), brain injury (developmental and acquired) and neurocognitive impairment, including the clinical features common to dementia and Alzheimer disease. With around 200 research papers and book chapters to his name, his own books include the *Handbook of Behavior, Food and Nutrition* (2011), *Nanomedicine and the Nervous System* (2012), *Perinatal Mental Health: A Clinical Guide* (2012), *Scientific Basis of Healthcare: AIDS and Pregnancy* (2012), *Comprehensive Guide to Autism* (2014) and *Diet and Nutrition in Dementia and Cognitive Decline* (2015).

Amanda McGrandles

Amanda McGrandles is currently a Lecturer in Mental Health and Programme Lead for the Masters (MSc) in Vulnerability Programme at the University West of Scotland. She has held a variety of posts within higher education, clinical practice in adult psychiatric settings, and primarily in child and adolescent mental health services. She also previously served as a Police Officer in Edinburgh with a particular interest in domestic violence and child protection. After completing an MBA she developed her knowledge in business management and ran her own small business. Her current interests are anxiety, depression, cognitive–behavioural therapy and relationship counselling. She is a member and registered teacher with the Nursing and Midwifery Council and Fellow of the Higher Education Academy.

David McMurtry

Dr David McMurtry is a Senior Lecturer in the School of Education at the University of Aberdeen. He is Programme Director for the MSc in Studies in Mindfulness and a Director of Inspired By Learning.

Graeme Nixon

Dr Graeme Nixon is a Senior Teaching Fellow in the School of Education at the University of Aberdeen. His teaching and research interests include initial teacher education; religious, moral and philosophical studies; critical thinking in schools; philosophy for children; and mindfulness. Since 2010 Graeme has taught on the University's Studies in Mindfulness MSc programme and has supervised students undertaking masters and doctorate degrees in this area.

Jim O'Brien

Jim O'Brien is Professor Emeritus at the University of Edinburgh and an Associate of the Robert Owen Centre for Educational Change, University of Glasgow. He continues to write and research and is a Managing Editor of the journal Professional Development in Education (Routledge). He has published numerous articles, chapters and papers as well as several books focusing on leadership and professional learning. He is currently preparing with colleagues the third edition of School Leadership, published by Dunedin Academic Press in Edinburgh.

Fiona Patrick

Fiona Patrick is a lecturer in the Interdisciplinary Science Education Technologies and Learning group in the School of Education, University of Glasgow. She works in the area of initial teacher education (principally on the PGDE programme). Her recent publications have focused on teacher professionalism and education policy in Scotland, understanding music talent development, and education policy in Saudi Arabia. Her most recent research has included participation in the Assessment at Transition project, the Literature Review on Teacher Education in the 21st Century (for the Donaldson Committee), and Professional Culture Among New Entrants to the Teaching Profession (for the GTCS and the Scottish Government).

Jean Rankin

Professor Jean Rankin, PhD, MMedical Science, PGCert LTHE, BSc (Hons), RN, RSCN, RM works in maternal, child and family health at the University of the West of Scotland. She has been involved in research for over 15 years in nursing and midwifery and is currently involved in the supervision and support of postgraduate research students.

David Rawcliffe

David Rawcliffe has been nursing since 1977 and for the last nine years has been a senior lecturer at Buckinghamshire New University. In two of those years he was nominated by the students for the most inspirational tutor award – which he won. David holds degrees in mental health nursing, education, and applied positive psychology and until recently was a clinical director for Irlen syndrome. His publications cover subjects such as mentorship in nursing and service user and staff experiences of restraint and depression. He has given presentations at international research conferences on restraint and the use of simulation in education. Among his research interests are the experiences of students with disabilities and autoethnographic studies of the flourishing continuum. He has worked with people on the autistic spectrum and has supported staff caring for those with challenging behaviours. He is also a member of an autism support group.

Graham Sloan

Dr Graham Sloan PhD, BSc (Hons) RMN RGN is a consultant nurse in psychological therapies for NHS Ayrshire and Arran, a psychological therapies training coordinator with NHS Education for Scotland, and an accredited psychotherapist and clinical supervisor (cognitive behavioural psychotherapy; interpersonal psychotherapy, cognitive behavioural analysis system of psychotherapy). With extensive experience of supervising psychological therapists and other mental health practitioners, he has contributed to the development of NHS Education for Scotland's clinical supervision training for psychological therapists and his direct involvement in training substantial numbers of clinical supervisors. Graham is the author of *Clinical Supervision in Mental Health Nursing* and has numerous additional scholarly publications on clinical supervision. Currently, his research is focused on the development of a scale for self-efficacy of clinical supervision and a competency framework for clinical supervision in nursing.

Hugh Smith

Hugh Smith is formerly Head of Career-Long Professional Learning at the School of Education, University of the West of Scotland. His learning and teaching experience spans over three decades, fourteen of these, as a teacher educator supporting initial and post training of teachers. He is now involved in consultancy, research and writing activities and continues to support the professional learning of learning, teaching and training colleagues. He is a practising educational technologist and has diverse research interests covering technology enhanced learning approaches to supporting pedagogy; professional development and learning and the professional learning of teacher educators. He peer reviews academic papers for the Journal: Professional Development in Education and presents at national and international conferences on a range of themes relating to his diverse research interests. He champions the synergies between mental health and well-being within learning, teaching and contexts.

Suzanne Thomson

Suzanne Thomson is a member of the mental health lecturing team at the University of the West of Scotland. With a career history including roles as health visitor, child and adolescent mental health team leader, and infant mental coordinator for an NHS board area, she has a keen interest in early parent–child relationships and their impact on future developmental and mental health outcomes. As well as teaching on mental health programmes, she contributes to the undergraduate degree in midwifery and an MSc in public health nursing (Health Visitor). Early relationships are the subject of her research dissertation for an MSc in vulnerability. Suzanne has a BSc in health studies (community health nursing), a first-class honours degree in mental health practice (children and young people), and postgraduate certificates in therapeutic skills and teaching and learning in higher education.

Alison Toner

Alison Toner MEd BSc RGN RMN LPE HEA (Fellow) has been a nurse for 28 years, mostly within the field of mental health nursing in acute admissions and addictions. She was a lecturer in mental health nursing from 2003 at the University of the West of Scotland and is currently Deputy Programme Leader for the BSc course in Mental Health Nursing. Her main areas of interest are skills development for mental health nurses, dual diagnosis and physical health care. She has taught in pre-registration programmes and postgraduate studies.

Deirdre Torrance

Dr Deirdre Torrance is Co-Director of Teacher Education Partnerships and Director of the Masters in Educational Leadership and Management in the Moray House School of Education at the University of Edinburgh. Deirdre has a substantial professional background both as a teacher working in a range of posts across primary, secondary and special education, and as a local government officer, developing important perspectives in the areas of educational leadership and leadership development. Deirdre joined the School of Education in 2004 where she is a senior member of staff and lead expert in the field of educational leadership theories, research and practice. She is engaged in a number of collaborative research and writing projects around issues of leadership policy and development. Her primary research interests include leadership preparation, school leadership and management, teacher leadership, middle leadership, distributed leadership (PhD focus), social justice leadership, and school improvement processes. Deirdre has considerable experience in leadership preparation, developing innovative programmes through various collaborations at university, local authority and national levels.

Susan J. Young

Professor Susan Young is a Clinical Senior Lecturer in Forensic Clinical Psychology at the Centre for Mental Health, Imperial College London, and Visiting Professor at Reykjavik University. She is an Honorary Consultant at Broadmoor Hospital and Director of Forensic Research and Development for West London Mental Health Trust. She has extensive experience in the assessment and treatment of youths and adults with mental disorder, specialising in forensic neuropsychology and neurodevelopmental disorders. She was a member of the National Institute for Health and Clinical Excellence (NICE) ADHD Clinical Guideline Development Group (2009; 2013). She is President of the UK ADHD Partnership (www.UKADHD.com) and Vice-President of the UK Adult ADHD Network (www.UKAAN. org) and a member of the European Network in Adult ADHD. Professor Young has published numerous articles in scientific journals, three psychological intervention programmes and three books. Her work has been translated into Icelandic, Hebrew, Polish, Danish, Spanish, Chinese, Japanese and Swedish (see www.psychology-services.uk.com).

Synonymous terms used throughout this book

Leaders of learning

educators ▪ tutors ▪ instructors ▪ pedagogues ▪ schoolteachers ▪ experts academics
coaches ▪ trainers ▪ lecturers ▪ professors ▪ educators ▪ departmental heads ▪ dons
fellows ▪ readers ▪ guides ▪ mentors ▪ professors ▪ headteachers ▪ support staff
supervisors ▪ deputes ▪ team leaders ▪ guidance counsellors ▪ class teachers
form teachers ▪ heads of year ▪ school principals ▪ educationalists

Learners

students ▪ pupils ▪ freshers ▪ schoolchildren ▪ trainees ▪ beginners
apprentices ▪ mentees ▪ novices ▪ newcomers ▪ starters ▪ initiates
recruits ▪ supervisees ▪ probationers

Learning and teaching environments

kindergartens ▪ universities ▪ colleges ▪ primary schools ▪ institutions
secondary schools ▪ classrooms ▪ centres of learning ▪ faculties ▪ academies
boarding schools ▪ training establishments ▪ conservatoires ▪ nurseries
institutes ▪ workshops ▪ university departments ▪ seminaries ▪ preparatory schools

Professional support and other concerned parties

teaching assistants ▪ educational psychologists ▪ clinical psychologists
clinical nurse specialists ▪ hospital consultants ▪ developmental psychologists
psychiatrists ▪ inclusion coordinators ▪ occupational therapists ▪ lunchtime supervisors
care-givers ▪ playground supervisors ▪ school nurses ▪ special educational needs
coordinators ▪ SENCOs ▪ social workers ▪ occupational therapists ▪ psychotherapists
paediatric neurologists ▪ guidance counsellors ▪ healthcare professionals
speech and language therapists ▪ SALTS ▪ carers ▪ general practitioners
parents ▪ guardians ▪ community members ▪ family ▪ siblings
policy makers ▪ educational shareholders ▪ physiotherapists

List of illustrations

List of abbreviations

ABA	applied behaviour analysis
ADHD	attention–deficit hyperactivity disorder
AIE	Autism in Education
ALICE	Assessment of Locus of Control in Industry, Commerce and Education
APSEA	Atlantic Partnership in Autism in Education
ASD	autism spectrum disorder
ASN	additional support needs
BABCP	British Association of Behavioural and Cognitive Psychotherapies
CAMHS	Child and Adolescent Mental Health Services
CAS	complex adaptive system
CBT	cognitive–behavioural therapy
CDC	Centres for Disease Control and Prevention
CLASP	Cardiovascular Limitations and Symptoms Profile
COSLA	Convention of Scottish Local Authorities
COWAT	Controlled Oral Word Association Test
CPD	continuing professional development
CPLD	continuing professional learning and development
CPT	continuous performance task
CSR	corporate social responsibility
CT	computerised tomography
DBD	disruptive behaviour disorder
DfE	Department for Education
DUP	duration of untreated psychosis
ECF	executive control function
EI	emotional intelligence
EIS	early intervention services
EWB	emotional well-being
FAE	fetal alcohol effects
FAS	fetal alcohol syndrome

HPA	hypothalamic–pituitary–adrenal (axis)
HSE	Health and Safety Executive
IAPT	Increasing Access to Psychological Therapies
IEP	individualised education programme
IWM	internal working model
JMSC	Joint Management–Stakeholder Committee
KT	knowledge translation
LINK	Local Involvement NetworK
MOOC	massive open online course
MRI	magnetic resonance imaging
NASUWT	National Association of Schoolmasters Union of Women Teachers
NEET	not in education, employment or training
NES	NHS Education Scotland
NUT	National Union of Teachers
OCD	obsessive–compulsive disorder
OfSTED	Office for Standards in Education
PAR	Participatory Action Research
PATOSS	Professional Association of Teachers of Students with Specific Learning Difficulties
PECS	picture exchange communication system
PSHE	personal, social, health and economic
PMR	progressive muscle relaxation
PTS	practising teaching standards
SALT	speech and language therapist
SCERTS	social communication, emotional regulation and transactional support
SENCO	special education needs coordinator
SLCN	speech, language and communication needs
SNAP	Special Needs and Autism Project
SSA	school support assistance
TDA	Training and Development Agency (now Department for Education)
WHO	World Health Organization

PART I
Setting the scene

CHAPTER 1

The need for an interdisciplinary perspective

Colin R. Martin

Why is there a need for a book covering what seem to be two distinct areas of interest, namely mental health and education?

Answering this question is not easy if you believe these two domains to be distinct and unrelated. However, the compelling evidence – as summarised so elegantly by the many experts and practitioners who have written in this book – is that the areas are highly related and that the relationship between them is complicated and sophisticated; moreover, it represents a complex gestalt of conceptual synthesis.

The importance of this synthesis to the educational process and achievement of educational milestones cannot be underestimated. The learning context represents a microcosm of the human developmental process, whereby we learn, we grow, we learn further and we grow further – the process and the interrelationships between education and key psychological dimensions of mental health (such as stress, anxiety, depression, low mood, self-esteem, self-efficacy, confidence and indeed, personality formation) being inseparable.

Consequently, understanding the relationships between these factors not only gives both educationalists and practitioners insights into the relationships between education and mental health within a normal developmental context, but also facilitates understanding when a deleterious impact on the educational process occurs and how it might be influenced by these interrelationships.

Examples are very useful for illustrating both the subtle and obtuse effects within these relationships. A high-achieving student, for instance, who always does well in his or her coursework and passes examinations with high marks, may be expected to have a relatively high degree of confidence, self-efficacy and motivation and an absence of depression.

However, what if this characteristically exemplary performance falters? A myriad of influences may be the cause of the decline, but for the student outlined above, there may be a corresponding reduction in their confidence, self-efficacy and motivation, and possibly an increase in performance anxiety and even low mood. A further example are colleagues engaged within educational practice – the leaders of learning – who begin to experience their work with learners as extremely stressful. They may not only perceive themselves as being unsupported, but may develop issues of anxiety and depression, alongside negative effects on their personal social milieu and engagement with their students.

These two examples represent just two brush-strokes on the canvas of complexity that represents mental health in education. Critical issues are:

- How do we support both students and colleagues who experience difficulties within the educational setting?
- How does this affect their learning and wider relationships?
- What can we do, as colleagues and educators, to help?

The purpose of this book is to address these issues by presenting the key concepts and critical principals in an easily accessible and (most importantly) evidence-based manner. The key issues affecting the aspirations and performance of people involved in the formal educational setting are explored in depth including, policy, motivation, attachment theories, staff support, expectations and life skills, mindfulness, faith, culture, supervision and engagement with stakeholders.

To address this 'melting pot' of synthesis of so many significant factors requires addressing practical aspects of where one may engage, for example, understanding of the principles of intervention and the problems of stress, anxiety, depression and burnout. Fostering a culture of inclusivity – as opposed to exclusivity – students with specific conditions that may be related to a formal diagnosis are discussed in depth, including autism spectrum disorders (ASD) and attention deficit hyperactivity disorder (ADHD), as well as less well-defined but equally important phenomena, such as the development of symptoms of early psychosis within the classroom setting.

In marked contrast to scientific papers, which (arguably) represent little more than academic voyeurism, the purpose of this book is to engender knowledge and understanding in order not only to gain a strategic oversight of the fundamental issues, but also to enable anyone working in educational practice to proactively engage at the level of the learning environment, to identify problems related to the relationship between mental health and education, to support students and colleagues experiencing difficulties in this context, and to transform the educational experience to one in which all students and leaders of learning can look forward to their experience within the learning environment with vim, vigour and optimism while fostering a context of inclusivity.

CHAPTER 2

The synergistic nature of mental health and education

Stephen P. Day, Mick P. Fleming and Colin R. Martin

The view underpinning this book is that education as a profession has much to learn from mental health professionals about adopting a more holistic view of issues that greatly impact upon the mental health and wellbeing of everyone in education. The interface between health in general (mental health in particular) and education has been brought into sharp focus because of the austerity agenda in the UK, and the weight of education reforms. A shared understanding of the issues faced by education is needed; health professionals may learn something from the way educational research is conducted and education professionals conceptualise, problematise and resolve issues that have a health dimension. The desire to foster a culture of mutual understanding between the disciplines of mental health and education was the overarching driving factor behind this book.

When most people think about education, they are drawn to the notion that the related (yet distinct) processes of teaching and learning are what lie at the heart of education. To a certain extent this is true, but when we view education through an academic lens, our concept of what constitutes 'education' necessarily expands beyond the narrow view of the centrality of teaching and learning. Education is a dynamic, sociocultural entity that functions as a complex adaptive system, purposed with the development of young people, and equipping them to make a positive contribution to the life and prosperity of the nation as active citizens. Unfortunately, this lofty goal has seen education become something of a political toy, used to measure the relative success or failure of the government. Arguably, it is this political dimension that provides the external pressure which drives the prevailing neoliberal agenda of the education system, and the concomitant managerialism and accountability culture through which the system is stewarded. Most governments (regardless of their political persuasion) follow the logic that *since* they are accountable to the electorate, in terms of the relative health of the education system, *then* they expect the education system to perform within set parameters as outlined within their electoral manifesto.

The influence of government and policy

The impact of government control over education is complicated by the fact that the UK government only has direct control over the English education system. Education as an area of government policy is devolved to the Scottish Parliament and the Welsh and Northern Irish Assemblies. Each nation exerts control over its own education system through a network of inspectors such as Education Scotland and OfSTED (in England). These inspectors are tasked with assessing the quality of education within schools, colleges, universities and local authorities; they have powers to monitor and track 'failing' schools and make recommendations to local authorities on issues such as leadership and management, quality of the learning environment, and attainment and achievement.

Stresses and strains – and their devastating impact

The manner in which these inspections are implemented leads to significant levels of stress and strain in schools. Unfortunately, some members of school staff experience such stress because of the inspection process that they commit suicide.

The following three case histories represent the extreme end of the mental health and wellbeing spectrum, and are relatively few in number, but they highlight the enormous pressures felt by teaching staff during the inspection process.

Case history I

Irene Hogg was headteacher of Glendinning Primary School in Galashiels for 18 years. Contemporary accounts suggest that she was disappointed and visibly distressed when she received critical feedback from a school inspection visit. She took her own life in March 2008. This case is noteworthy for two reasons. First, it is believed to be the first suicide of a headteacher in Scotland that is linked to the stress of a school inspection. Second, shortly after this incident (possibly even as a result of this incident), Her Majesty's Inspectors of Education Scotland began a review of school inspections, which lead to the introduction of a new model of school inspection, with slimmed-down procedures and a shift in emphasis from inspection *of* the school to inspection *with* the school. Public interest was high and a fatal accident inquiry was held. Evidence was produced that suggested Ms Hogg was not coping with her workload and intended making an appointment with an occupational therapist after the inspection. The inquiry also heard that she was 'very stressed before the inspection, very stressed during it and very stressed after it'. Sheriff James Farrell suggested '... there can be no doubt that Irene Hogg's death is inextricably linked to the outcome of the Glendinning school inspection on March 2008'. This was the first high-profile case in Scotland, but it is by no means a new phenomenon in England, where there have been a number of similar cases.

Case history II

In 2013, Helen Mann, aged 43, was appointed as headteacher of the village primary school, Sytchampton Endowed First School in Worcestershire. A month later, she was distraught after being told that the school's OfSTED-awarded 'outstanding' status was at risk. On the day she returned to work, she hanged herself in a stairwell at the school. The local newspaper (Kidderminster Shuttle) reported that she had taken an overdose of prescribed sleeping pills ten days previously. She had been receiving counselling and was on antidepressants for work-related stress.

> ### Case history III
>
> Fifty-three-year old Jed Holmes took his life on the eve of an OfSTED inspection, by carbon monoxide poisoning. He had been the headteacher at Hampton Hargate School in Peterborough for seven years. His health had suffered because of the work-related stress and had been taking antidepressants for several months. The coroner reported evidence that he was concerned about the inspection, and concluded: 'We can't exclude the proximity of the OfSTED inspection at the date of his death. It was that impending inspection that triggered off the action he decided to take.'

The spectre of burnout

A study on occupational stress by Nübling *et al.* (2011) spanning the whole of Europe revealed that UK teachers had:

- The highest levels of burnout.
- The second highest levels of cognitive stress.
- Above-average levels of lesson disturbances and verbal abuse.
- Above-average numbers of conflicts with parents.

The Health and Safety Executive (2012) confirms that teachers continue to suffer more than other professions. They report that most sectors manage to reduce stress levels, but education and teaching professionals 'continue to report higher levels than other industries and occupations.' Average suicide rates among teachers in Britain are 40% higher than those for other occupations'. FIGURES 2.1–2.2 present data from the Office for National Statistics for England and Wales on the number of deaths of indeterminate cause (attributed to suicide) by teachers over a six-year period. Between 2007 and 2012 there were more suicides among men aged 35-64 than women. Between 2008 and 2009 the number of deaths among men doubled, and that among women increased five-fold. While we recognise that the number of deaths is small relative to other causes, they represent the tip of the iceberg with regards to the ongoing mental health of the teaching profession.

Several surveys provide evidence of the increasing incidence and prevalence of stress, burnout, physical health issues such as high blood pressure, and mental health issues such as depression, within the teaching profession (Association of Teachers and Lecturers 2014; National Association of Schoolmasters Union of Women Teachers 2015; Teachers Assurance 2013). There is also emerging evidence about organisational and personal factors that influence the development of stress that leads to burnout due to excessive job demands.

The complex, dynamic nature of education

Classrooms are complex environments, and this fact, in many respects, explains why teaching as a profession is so psychologically demanding. Teachers must balance cognitive, affective

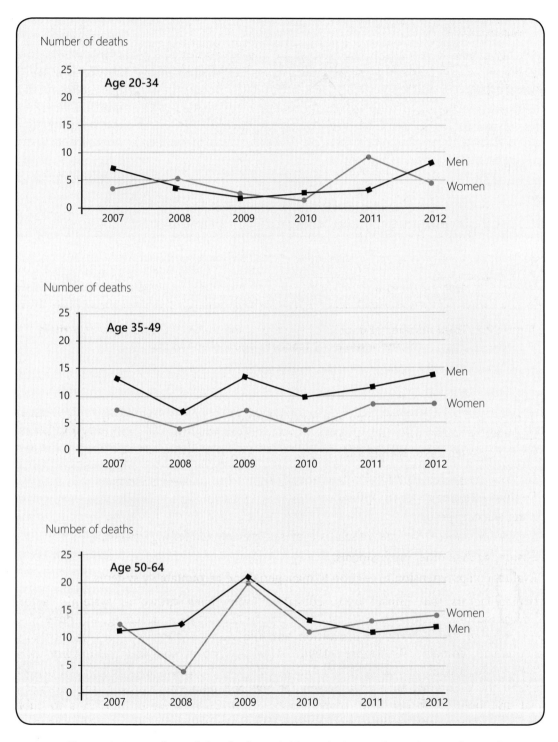

Figure 2.1: Number of deaths by suicide or indeterminate intent for male (■) and female (●) teachers in different age groups.

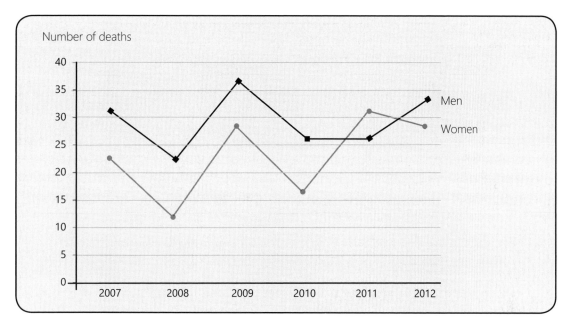

Figure 2.2: Total number of deaths by suicide or indeterminate intent among male (■) and female (●) teachers aged 20–64 years.

and social domains while planning and implementing lessons. They also have to be cognisant of many intrinsic and extrinsic factors that impact on teaching practice (Male and May 1998; Pithers and Soden 1998; Travers and Cooper 1997). Intrinsic factors include:

- Increasing workload (particularly role overload).
- Dealing with classroom discipline.
- Long working hours.
- Poor status (related to issues of self-esteem, self-efficacy and feeling valued).
- Lower pay than other professionals.
- Evaluation apprehension in relation to managerial and accountability systems.

Extrinsic factors that impact upon education (sometimes known as systemic factors) are organisational factors that are not intrinsic to the nature of teaching, but depend on the culture of the educational institution and the wider context of education, including the political domain. Blackmore (1996) suggests that a complex relationship exists between educational institutions, the individuals within those institutions, and society, whereby the emotional state of a person (at any one moment) is largely the product of social and political forces. The unpredictable nature of this relationship leads to subtle variations between educational establishments and departments within establishments. In cultural terms, these variations are emergent properties. At the institutional level, factors such as social support (or lack of it) from colleagues – related to the concepts of collegiality and leadership style – appear to be important factors that affect teacher stress levels.

To adequately discuss the role that the leadership culture plays in the mental health of teachers, we must make a technical distinction between how we view leadership – as opposed to management. We would argue that leadership and management are not interchangeable constructs. Smircich and Morgan define leadership in the following terms:

> *... leadership is realised in the process whereby one or more individuals succeed in attempting to frame and define the reality of others [...] leadership situations may be conceived as those in which there exists an obligation or a perceived right on the part of certain individuals to define the reality of others. (Smircich and Morgan 1982)*

In other words:

- **Leadership** is about setting the direction or defining the vision for a group to follow, where the leader is the spearhead for that new direction.

- **Management** controls or directs people or resources in a group according to established principles or values.

In education, both leadership and management functions are often performed as part of the same role (e.g. by a head of department or depute head) because there is a need for continual adjustment of the direction (leadership) and controlling resources to achieve that direction (management). The leadership culture within a school impacts on its staff and teachers at both departmental and whole-school levels. In a survey of teachers in England, Hoel *et al.* (1999) found that 35% reported being bullied by one of their line manager (who may also have a curriculum leadership role) in the last five years – this compares with an average of 24% across other occupations. Nash (2004) found that conflict with a colleague was the most common problem for which teachers seek counselling (24% of cases) and that 66% of conflicts were with line managers. These figures might be a sign of increasing stress and pressure within the system as a whole, or they might indicate that some 'managers' are failing to cope with their workload and are experiencing stress themselves, thereby resorting to bullying as a maladaptive coping strategy. It could also be argued that middle managers, such as principal teachers or department heads, are particularly vulnerable to systemic stress because their management roles combine high levels of accountability with low levels of control, that may conflict with their leadership role in curricular terms. It is possible that the prevailing neoliberal culture of managerialism and accountability is at the root of many of the mental health issues faced by teachers today.

This suggestion has some merit: Nias (1996) suggests there has been a shift in the emphasis placed the source of stress, from intrinsic factors to extrinsic factors; teachers used to attribute stress to problems with learners, but now report that their most negative emotions arise in response to contact with other adults and from having to interact more closely with policy.

Concluding comments

The evidence available to date highlights the complex relationships between mental health and the learning environment. Much of this chapter focused on this complexity in relation to teachers, or leaders of learning. However, as will be seen in later chapters of this book, this complex relationship manifests itself in a myriad of often poorly understood ways for learners themselves. Understanding the complex relation between mental health and education is not easy, not least because the current evidence base is at an early stage of development; it is even harder because there is a 'silo' philosophical position that deems mental health and education as intrinsically distinct and unrelated fields. This fallacy needs to be redressed, and this will challenge some widely held attitudes, opinions and beliefs; the process must, therefore, be systematic, incremental and methodologically rigorous, in order to demonstrate relevance, importance and application to practice in an understandable and accessible way, and to foster inclusivity, awareness and evidence-based practice development. Embracing such principles with a strategic perspective for accommodating the education–mental health gestalt will contribute enormously to improving the experiences of learners and leaders of learning across a range of educational environments – indeed beyond – by influencing policy and strategy at the level of government.

KEY MESSAGES FROM THIS CHAPTER

The evidence supporting a relationship between mental health and education – both in specific instances and more generally – is incontrovertible.

Mental health is of critical concern to education practice and outcomes for both learners and leaders of learning.

There are significant consequences of impoverished mental health for both leaders of learning and learners, including the potential for self-harm and suicide.

The learning environment is a complex organisational structure in which mental health is significantly implicated. Lack of awareness of the role of mental health in this context can influence educational practice and outcomes negatively.

The evidence base linking mental health and education is currently under-developed and it is now of paramount importance to forward a coherent and strategically-aligned policy to tackle the stress and strain that adversely affect those involved within education.

Supporting evidence and further reading

Association of Teachers and Lecturers (2014) *Pressures on teachers causing rise in mental health issues*. Press Release 14 April 2014 ahead of Annual Conference of the Association of Teachers and Lecturers, Northumberland Street, London.

Blackmore J (1996) Doing emotional labour in the education market place: stories from the field of women in management. *Discourse: Studies in the Cultural Politics of Education* 17, 337–349.

Health and Safety Executive (2012) *Stress and psychological disorders*. Available at: www.hse.gov.uk/statistics/causdis/stress/stress.pdf (accessed June 2015).

Hoel H, Rayner C, Cooper CL (1999) Workplace bullying. In: CL Cooper, IT Robertson (eds) *International Review of Industrial and Organisational Psychology*. Chichester: John Wiley,

Jennings C, Kennedy E (1996). *The Reflective Professional in Education*. London: Jessica Kingsley.

Male D, May D (1998) Stress and health, workload and burnout in learning support coordinators in colleges of further education. *Support for Learning* 13, 134–38.

Nash (2004) *The teacher support network*. Presented at: Improving Employee Effectiveness in Public Sector Conference, University of Stirling, UK, September 2004.

National Association of Schoolmasters Union of Women Teachers (2015) *A dreadful assault on teachers' mental health and well-being*. Available at: www.nasuwt.org/uk/Whatsnew/NASUWTNews/PressReleases/NASUWT_013973 (accessed April 2015).

Nias J (1996) Thinking about feelings: the emotions in teaching. *Cambridge Journal of Education* 26, 293–306.

Nübling M, Vomstein M, Haug A, Nübling T, Adiwidjaja A (2011) *European-Wide Survey on Teachers' Work-Related Stress – Assessment, Comparison and Evaluation of the Impact of Psychosocial Hazards on Teachers at Their Workplace*. Brussels: ETUCE.

Pithers RT, Soden R (1998) Scottish and Australian teacher stress and strain: a comparative study. *British Journal of Educational Psychology* 68, 269–79.

Smircich L, Morgan G (1982) Leadership: the management of meaning. *Journal of Behavioural Science* 18, 257–73.

Teachers Assurance (2013) *Teachers Assurance stress and well-being research*. Available at: www.teachers assurance.co.uk/money–news/teachers–stress–levels–affecting–performance (accessed April 2015).

Travers C, Cooper C (1997) Stress in teaching. In: D Shorrocks-Taylor (ed.) *Directions in Educational Psychology*. London: Whurr.

CHAPTER 3

The dynamics of the learner and the leader of learning

Hugh Smith

Learning does not take place in a vacuum. Successful outcomes rely on the context of the learning and the environment. Learners and leaders of learning – or educators – bring a rich tapestry of learning experiences as part of their continued learning. What is often overlooked is the preparedness of learners to engage with effective learning experiences – learners as well as the leaders of learning must be mentally receptive of such experiences. This chapter explores the conceptual underpinnings of what it is to be a learner and touches on some of the thinking and theories relating to learning. Non-managerialism ideology relating to the definition of leaders of learning is also explored, touching on the philosophical complexities required to support and encourage learners through the notion of leading from behind. The interaction between learners and leaders of learning depends on being aware of the challenging complexities of context, environment and the mental processes of learning that can influence mental health and well-being.

Debate continues among educationalists and researchers about the traits of learners and leaders of learning, about why tension is perceived about the form, type and effectiveness of both informal and formal learning and, in particular, where and with whom the most effective learning takes place. Even in the womb, the developing baby engages in certain aspects of the learning process. Learning theorists provide a rich tapestry on which the emergence of a definition of a learner emerges. For example, Jarvis explores the concepts of 'learning to be me' and 'to be a person', while Heron explores life cycles and learning cycles (Gardner *et al.* 1995; Heron 1992; 2009; Jarvis 2006; 2009) and Gardner explores the multiple aspects of intelligence, understanding and the education of the mind (Gardner 2006; 2009). The traits of leaders of learning are more complex. Definitions support mainly a managerialism ideology as applied to education management within a societal, political, economic and governance context. The popular terminology – such as teacher leadership (Forde 2011), leadership for learning (O'Brien 2011), leading learning (O'Donoghue and Clarke 2010) and distributed leadership (Harris 2008) – includes terms that operate mostly, but not exclusively, within governance in education contexts. The term 'leader of learning' is applied to learning within an education or training context and is characteristic of organisational learning; it is operational rather than managerial and strategic. The origin of the term has roots embedded within situated cognition and pedagogue concepts.

This chapter explores and contextualises the concepts of the terms 'learner' and 'leader of learning' and attempts to highlight the dynamics of both in relation to their potential impact on mental health and well-being within a learning or training environment.

The concept of 'learner'

Newborn babies are extremely vulnerable and require nurturing in order to survive, while most newly born animals stagger to their feet and very quickly find their way around their environment. Newborn babies do not quickly engage with their physical environments, but they do develop cognitive capacity. Lindon (2006) and Featherstone and Williams (2007) explain that newborn babies engage with learning before they are born and this continues from the first days of birth. Newborns are interested in faces and sounds (particularly voices) and some clearly recognise an individual adult, often a parent, and can soon copy facial expressions and remember them. Repetition plays a large part in the early stages of learning, as does exploring different approaches to achieving the same outcome. Cognitive connections can be established and developed by young babies as they make their own sounds, explore objects with their mouth, and make their first tentative attempts at crawling (leading to supported and unsupported movements). Babies are sociable and like to engage with other people, so the extension of their world through early-years activities at toddler groups and nurseries is important. From these early stages of learning, three distinct types of learning evolve: non-formal, informal and formal.

TYPES OF LEARNING

(i) Non-formal learning

Colley *et al.* (2002) provide a helpful discourse in relation to mapping the conceptual aspects of non-formal learning. This is voluntary learning that takes place within a range of environments. Learners may only engage with these environments in the short term, with activities led by family members, friends, professional learning facilitators or volunteers (such as youth trainers and youth leaders). Hobbies such as collecting fossils and developing an understanding of the prehistoric world, may be classed non-formal learning.

(ii) Informal learning

Greenfield and Lave (1982) offer a useful cognitive perspective on informal education, while Hodkinson *et al.* (2003) suggest that the terms 'non-formal' and 'informal' are largely interchangeable and difficult to differentiate between. However, informal learning takes place in out-of-school settings, community centres and within the home, through regular interactions and shared relationships among members of society. Many learners learn language, cultural norms and manners through informal learning.

(iii) Formal learning

Misko (2008) describes formal learning in terms of engagement with recognised qualifications, leading eventually to employment; Choi and Jacobs (2011) consider formal learning in the context of a supportive learning environment, highlighting subsequent implications for practice. Formal learning is the engagement with tasks that are explicitly designated as learning tasks within structured organisational learning systems that lead to formal recognition or credentials. This involves a curriculum with learning and teaching objectives (primarily intentional), content, specific methods and assessment related to intentional learning and explicit knowledge that can be verbalised. This is provided in primary school, secondary school and further education (college and university) settings. Similar systems exist in business through technical or professional training. A learner, at any stage of development, engages with all three types of learning – non-formal, informal and formal – but the specific focus depends on a range of external factors relating to context and setting. The particular mix of learning, alongside family, social and other environmental factors, can have an impact on the person's physical and mental well-being. FIGURE 3.1 illustrates how each type of learning might be engaged by a learner placed at the centre of activities. The learning types interconnect and may overlap, with the learner controlling the weighting of the interconnectivity according to context and setting.

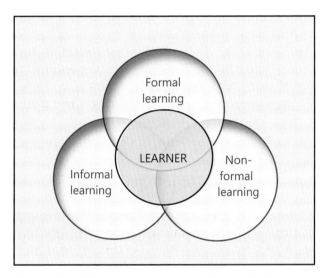

Figure 3.1: The learner's interaction with learning.

The concept of leader of learning

The popular understanding of the term 'leader of learning' is expressed through contexts such as teacher leadership, leadership for learning, leading learning, and distributed leadership, all of which are embedded within the management of education, supporting mainly a managerialism ideology. Fitzsimmons (1999) and Preston (2001) provide useful definitions of managerialism within education contexts, and Hoyle and Wallace (2005) discuss the rhetoric of managerialism and leadership. The work of Greenleaf (1998; 2002) on servant leadership was developed in the early 1970s, whereby the notion of leadership emerges from the desire to help others. In this chapter, the focus is on non-managerialist interpretation, with roots in both situated cognition and pedagogue application and theory.

Situated cognition (cognitive apprenticeship) relates to learning or knowledge based on actions embedded within a social, cultural and environmental context. Aspects include situated action, communities of practice, learning as active participation, knowledge in action, interactionism and identities of construction of self (Wilson and Myers 2000). Roth (2007) discusses distributed cognition (knowledge that lies within the individual and the individual's social and physical environment), embodied cognition (an individual's cognition that is strongly influenced by aspects of the body beyond the brain) and situated cognition (knowing is inseparable from doing) in the terms of how and why we understand knowing as situated. An underpinning theory for situated cognition is provided by Hung *et al.* (2004) who address its foundations, the interconnectedness of mind, body and external reality, and concepts such as meaning of action, physical coordination of perception, conception and action, and behaviour in spaciotemporal contexts (Clancey 1997; Heidegger 1962).

PEDAGOGY

Pedagogue application and theory dates back to the ancient Greece, where learners engaged with humanistic values and were recognised as competent human beings by those who were gifted with sharing and nurturing knowledge and skills. Successful pedagogues did not lead learners, but created an environment where learners could immerse themselves and solve contextualised problems, using their existing knowledge and skill while acquiring new knowledge and skill.

Petrie *et al.* (2009) discuss pedagogy (delivered by a pedagogue) as a holistic approach to a learner's experiential learning, intertwining cognitive (thinking) with feelings, emotions and practical engagement and application. The European Social Pedagogy movement provides a holistic approach to contextualised learning based on a conceptual framework of sociology, psychology, education and philosophy. Key influences in this area are described below:

- **Johann Heinrich Pestalozzi (1746–1827)** believed that pedagogues should ensure an appropriate balance of the head, heart and hands. This social pedagogue belief systems links with the Petrie *et al.*'s (2009) intertwined elements of cognition and feeling.

- **Paul Natorp (1854–1924)** focused on the relation between education and social conditions, seeking opportunities for those people without access to education and developing a sense of morality and renewal of a community.

- **Maria Montessori (1879–1952)** believed that children develop and think very differently from adults and are competent learners with a capacity for self-directed learning in a range of contexts and environments.

- **Janusz Korczak (1878–1942)** believed that children have rights and are entitled to respect, and should be involved in the development of self-governing approaches to learning.

- **Kurt Hahn (1886–1974)** developed the concept that learning impacts on the formation of personality and that education develops compassion and character-forming qualities. His concept of learning extended to service to the community, outward-bound learning and fitness. This philosophy contributed to the development of the Duke of Edinburgh Award Scheme.

Situated cognition and pedagogue theory have influenced other education (learning) philosophies such as child-centred learning (Darling 1994; Entwistle 2012) and student-centred learning (O'Neill and McMahon 2005). Irrespective of the background of leaders of learning, their personal philosophies are continually shaped by a multitude of researched and established philosophies. FIGURE 3.2 illustrates the type of pedagogical concepts and theories that a leader of learning might engage in for supporting learners. The theories fall into three categories: constructivist, cognitivist and behaviourist. Engagement with these theories depends on the extent to which learning activities are leader-centred or learner-centred. Leaders of learning evolve out of philosophical complexity to support and encourage learners through motivation, investigation, guidance and leading, not from the front, but from behind. This is an important shift away from the managerialism perspective and is the point of reference for all who engage with learners, irrespective of age, stage or context. FIGURE 3.3 shows how leaders of learning might engage with learners. The interconnectivity between learning types still link with the leader of learning through the learner.

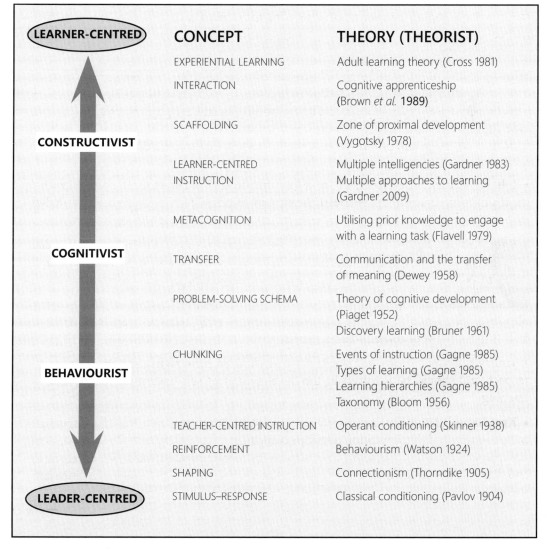

Figure 3.2: Pedagogical concepts, theories and theorists in the context of approaches along the spectrum from learner-centred to leader-centred.

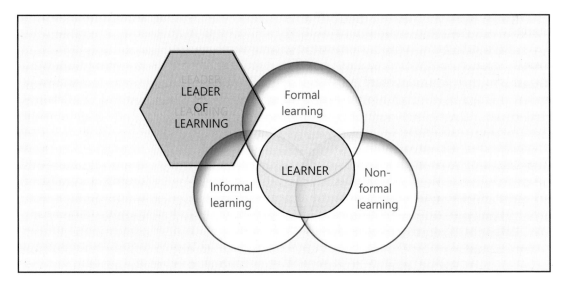

Figure 3.3: Interactions between leaders of learning and learners.

Mental processes of learning

Illeris (2008) considers that the mental process of learning is based within our bodies, and has evolved to include learning embedded in the brain and nervous system, thus going beyond the established understanding of the relationship between the body and mind. This idea was based on the thinking of philosophers such as Descartes (1596–1660), who was responsible for the precept 'Cognito, ergo sum' (I think therefore I am), whereby the centrality of our mental (cognitive) capacity is intertwined with our existence; others consider this to be successful only within the context of learning in an environment that is meaningful to both the learner and the leader of learning. The mental process of learning in society (and for life) occurs naturally and is placed at the centre of our existence. The balance of both mental and physical engagement with learning is crucial for ensuring motivation and sense of purpose. Brain research confirms the link between learning, our bodies and our (learning) environment, and how we respond to changes in our environment. However, learners can engage with learning without being conscious of these facts. Demaggio (1999) describes the fundamental differences between human and animal interactions in terms of language and consciousness. We engage with 'conscious learning' on a regular basis through contexts such as advertising, which may seem insignificant at the point of contact, but is significant enough to have an impact through 'influence'. Illeris (2008) contextualises learning within society in three dimensions, in the context of learning as a 'competence development'. These dimensions are:

- **Content**: knowledge, understanding and skills that provide functionality through meaning and ability.
- **Incentive**: motivation, emotion and volition that provide sensitivity through mental and bodily balance.
- **Interaction**: actions, communication and co-operation that provide sociality through integration.

Jarvis (2009) explores the notion of 'learning to be me' within a societal context and defines learning as:

A combination of processes throughout a lifetime whereby the whole person–body (genetic, physical and biological) and mind (knowledge, skills, attributes, values, emotions, beliefs and senses) experiences social situations, the perceived content of which is then transformed cognitively, emotively or practically (or through any combination) and integrated into the individual person's biography, resulting in a continually changing (or more experienced) person.

This highlights the complexity of learning for learners (even over very short timeframes) and also how complex the contextualisation of learning is when leaders of learning engage with the needs of different learners. Heron's definition of the processes of living and learning derive from his 'theory of the person' (Heron 2009). This identifies four kinds of learning:

- **Experiential learning**: knowledge acquired through participation.
- **Presentational (imaginal) learning**: knowledge acquired though intuition, perception and imagination.
- **Propositional learning**: knowledge acquired through the intellect.
- **Practical learning**: knowledge acquired through the practice of a particular skill.

Illeris (2008) addresses situations in which intended learning does not happen and discusses attributes associated with mislearning, mental defence against learning, ambivalence, and resistance to learning. Mislearning occurs when learning does not match what was intended; it includes the wider manifestations of misunderstanding and misconception. Mental defence against learning is a curious state relating to forms of stress and strain; learners may reject learning and teaching for various reasons and require reassurance (security), permissiveness and motivation, and may also display prejudice based on a mistaken belief. Ambivalence occurs in learners who both want and do not want to engage in learning, and is common in society, when learners perceive pressure from external sources to involve themselves in learning. An example is the drive to obtain qualifications for work, with the uncertainty of securing job employment as a result. Resistance to learning is very interesting to educationalists, whereby resistance can be activated through contexts that learners find unacceptable or uncomfortable. Gardner (1983, 2009) developed a theory of multiple intelligencies in the 1980s that is still being debated today. It explored learning styles, on the basis that learners engage with or prefer a specific style of learning. He classified these as:

- Linguistic.
- Logical–mathematical.
- Musical.
- Bodily–kinaesthetic.
- Spatial.
- Interpersonal.
- Intrapersonal.

Gardner proposed that learners do not all learn in the same fashion, engaging with combinations, or avoidance, of some of the classifications. In his more recent thinking, multiple approaches to understanding further aligns his multiple intelligence theory with that of learner understanding, reaffirming that learners already possess knowledge and skills based on biological, cultural and personal contexts and therefor develop different types of minds. Understandably, this poses yet more challenges for leaders of learning. Learning, being a learner, and leading learning cannot be explored without an awareness of historical development and contextualisation. Those who present themselves within a learning environment (either as learner or leader of learning) bring with them a contextualised complexity that can be very challenging and affect the mental health and well-being of both learners and leaders of learning. FIGURE 3.4 illustrates the contextualised complexity between a learner and leader of learning who is also a learner, engaged with the interconnectivity of the three types of learning. The interconnectivity of the three learning types also links with the leader of learning through the learner.

Concluding comments

The processes, complexity and contextualisation of learning continue to fascinate learning theorists, educationalists and practitioners. It is fascinating because learning is what defines us as human beings. However, the diversity of both learners and leaders of learning is enormous within a given learning situation and effective learning is dependent on a range of factors – both internal and external – and is challenging for both learners and leaders of learning. The mental health and well-being of both is crucial for successful outcomes, and an important role for leaders of learning is to recognise when they and others in their environment are not mentally receptive to learning or the learning environment. Engaging with suitable interventions or implementing effective strategies should therefore be explored.

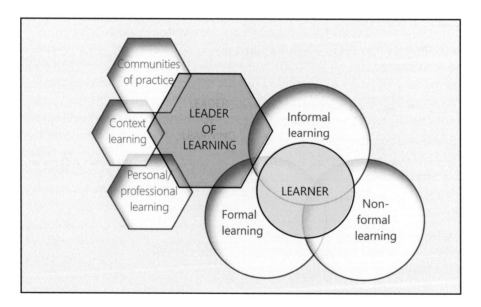

Figure 3.4: Contextualised complexity of the interaction between the learner and the leader of learning.

KEY MESSAGES FROM THIS CHAPTER

Learners engage with three types of learning – non-formal, informal and formal – with a specific focus for each context and setting.

Leaders of learning support and encourage learners through motivation, investigation and guidance and lead learning from behind.

Mental processes of learning are based within our bodies, but are embedded in the brain and nervous system. A balance between mental and physical engagement is crucial for achieving successful learning outcomes.

The mental health and well-being of both learners and leaders of learning is vital for successful outcomes within the learning and/or training environment.

Contextualisation of learning is complex, especially when leaders of learning engage with the individual needs of different learners.

Leaders of learning should be aware when they and others might not be mentally receptive to learning or to the learning environment and implement effective strategies and/or interventions to support effective outcomes.

Supporting evidence and further reading

Bloom BS (1956) (ed.) *Taxonomy of Educational Objectives. Vol. 1: Cognitive Domain.* New York: McKay.

Brown JS, Collins A, Duguid P (1989) Situated cognition and the culture of learning. *Educational Researcher* 18(1), 32–41.

Bruner JS (1961) The act of discovery. *Harvard Educational Review* 31(1), 21–32.

Choi W, Jacobs R (2011) Influences of formal learning, personal learning orientation and supportive learning environment on informal learning. *Human Resource Development Quarterly* 22(3), 239–57.

Clancey W (1997) *Situated Cognition.* Cambridge: Cambridge University Press.

Colley H, Hodkinson P, Malcolm J (2002) *Non-Formal Learning: Mapping The Conceptual Terrain. A Consultation Report.* Leeds: University of Leeds.

Cross KP (1981) *Adults as Learners.* San Francisco: Jossey-Bass.

Darling J (1994) *Child–Centred Education and its Critics.* London: Paul Chapman.

Demaggio A (1999) *The Feeling of What Happens: Body, Emotion and the Making of Consciousness.* London: Vintage.

Dewey J (1958) *Experience and Nature.* New York: Dover.

Entwistle H (2012) *Child–Centred Education.* Abingdon, Oxon: Routledge.

Featherstone S, Williams L (2007) *Baby and Beyond.* London: A & C Black.

Fitzsimmons P (1999) *Managerialism and Education. Encyclopaedia of Philosophy of Education.* Available at: eepat.net/doku.php?id=managerialism_and_education (accessed September 2015).

Flavell JH (1979) Metacognition and cognitive monitoring: A new area of cognitive–developmental inquiry. *American Psychologist* 34(10), 906–11.

Forde C (2011) Being a teacher leader. In: M McMahon, C Forde, M Martin (eds) *Contemporary Issues in Learning and Teaching*. London: Sage.

Gagné RM (1985) *The Conditions of Learning and Theory of Instruction*. New York: Holt, Rinehart & Winston.

Gardner H (1983) *Frames of Mind: The Theory of Multiple Intelligencies*. New York: Basic Books.

Gardner H (2006) *The Development and Education of the Mind: The Selected Works of Howard Gardner*. Oxon: Routledge.

Gardner H (2009) Multiple approaches to understanding. In: K Illeris (ed.) *Contemporary Theories of Learning: Learning Theorists. In Their Own Words*. Oxon: Routledge.

Gardner H, Kornhaber M, Wake W (1995) *Intelligencies: Multiple Perspectives*. Belmont, CA: Wadsworth.

Greenfield P and Lave J (1982) Cognitive aspects of informal education. In: Wagner D and Stevenson H (eds) *Cultural Perspectives on Child Development*. San Francisco, CA: Freeman & Co.

Greenleaf RK (1998) *The Power of Servant Leadership*. San Francisco. CA: Bennett-Koehler.

Greenleaf RK (2002) *Servant Leadership: A Journey into the Nature of Legitimate Power and Greatness*. Mahwah, NJ: Paulist Press.

Harris A (2008) *Distributed School Leadership: Developing Tomorrow's Leaders*. Oxon: Routledge.

Heidegger M (1962) *Being and Time*. Oxford: Blackwell.

Heron J (1992) *Feeling and Personhood: Psychology in Another Key*. London: Sage.

Heron J (2009) Life cycles and learning cycles. In: K Illeris (ed.) *Contemporary Theories of Learning: Learning Theorists. In Their Own Words*. Oxon: Routledge.

Hodkinson P, Colley H, Malcolm J (2003) The interrelationships between informal and formal learning. *Journal of Workplace Learning* 15(7/8), 313–18.

Hoyle E, Wallace M (2005) *Educational Leadership: Ambiguity, Professionals and Managerialism*. London: Sage.

Hung D, Bopry J, Looi C, Koh T (2004) Situated cognition and beyond: Martin Heidegger on transformations in being and identity. In: JL Kinchekoe, RA Horn (eds) *The Praeger Handbook of Education and Psychology. Volume 4*. Westport, CT: Praeger.

Illeris K (2008) *How We Learn: Learning and Non-Learning in School and Beyond*. Oxon: Routledge.

Jarvis P (2006) *Towards a Comprehensive Theory of Human Learning*. London. Kogan Page.

Jarvis P (2009) Learning to be a person in society: Learning to be me. In: K Illeris (ed.) *Contemporary Theories of Learning: Learning Theorists. In Their Own Words*. Oxon: Routledge.

Lindon J (2006) *Care and Caring Matter: Young Children Learning Through Care*. London: Early Education.

Misko J (2008) *Combining Formal, Non-Formal and Informal Learning for Workforce Skill Development*. Adelaide, SA: National Centre for Vocational Education Research.

O'Brien J (2011) Leadership for learning in the United Kingdom: Lessons from the research. In: Townsend T and McBeath J (eds) *International Handbook of Leadership for Learning*. London: Springer.

O'Donoghue T, Clarke S (2010) *Leading Learning. Process, Themes and Issues in International Contexts*. Oxon: Routledge.

O'Neill G, McMahon T (2005) Student-centred learning: what does it mean for students and lecturers? In: O'Neill G, Moore S and McMullin B (eds) *Emerging Issues in the Practice of University Learning and Teaching*. Dublin: All Ireland Society for Higher Education.

Pavlov IP (1904) Classical conditioning. In: J Malone (ed.) *Theories of Learning: A Historical Approach*. California: Wadsworth.

Petrie P, Boddy J, Cameron C *et al.* (2009) *Pedagogy: A Holistic, Personal Approach to Work with Children and Young People, Across Services. European models for Practice, Training, Education and Qualification*. London: Thomas Coram Research Unit, University of London.

Piaget J (1952) *The Origins of Intelligence in Children*. New York: International University Press.

Preston DS (2001) *The Rise of Managerialism*. Available at: eepat.net/doku.php?id=the_rise_of_managerialism (accessed September 2015).

Roth WM (2007) Situating situated cognition. In: JL Kinchekoe, RA Horn (eds) *The Praeger Handbook of Education and Psychology. Volume 4*. Westport, CT: Praeger.

Skinner BF (1938) *The Behavior of Organisms: An Experimental Analysis*. Oxford: Appleton Century.

Thorndyke E (1905) *The Elements of Psychology*. New York: Mason Press. Available at: ia802300.us.archive.org/27/items/elementspsychol01goog/elementspsychol01goog.pdf (accessed September 2015).

Vygotsky LS (1978) *Mind in Society: The Development of Higher Psychological Processes*. Cambridge, MA: Harvard University Press.

Watson JD (1924;1970) *Behaviourism*. London: WW Norton & Co.

Wilson BG, Myers KM (2000) Situated cognition in theoretical and practical context. In: DH Jonassen, SM Land (eds) *Theoretical Foundations of Learning Environments*. Mahwah, NJ: Lawrence Erlbaum.

CHAPTER 4

Educational policy and issues of ownership

Cliff Jones

This chapter addresses issues central to the well-being of learners and leaders of learning: their roles as receivers and implementers of policy and their exclusion from its conception and construction. The language and concepts of education are, the chapter argues, controlled centrally and because the values inherent in policies have not been arrived at inclusively, the damage to well-being extends to society itself. The current touchstones for educational policy are league tables. This discussion suggests that we could do better and we must do better.

The central argument of this chapter is that when policy-making is based on an inclusive and consensual process of arriving at shared values it is better for the well-being of learners, leaders of learning and society in general and better than policy-making that excludes the concerns, interests, anxieties, experience, expertise and values of learners and leaders of learning. The meaning of politics and, its polar opposite, alienation, are explored, as well as the concepts that form the basis of fought-over educational narratives. These are progress, reform, improvement and modernisation. Obtaining the power to define such concepts is important to policy-makers. Losing the power to dispute those definitions is not good for learners, leaders of learning or society.

There is a strong government urge to measure learners and educators and demonstrate improvements in their performance compared with previous years and with other countries. The reasons given usually involve a link between education and economic performance. As a consequence, the educational emphasis is increasingly on setting and hitting targets but this is not confined to education. The influence of people such as Michael Barber has not been confined to the UK. He came into the UK government in 1997, first to effectively direct education policy, then to drive forward the 'delivery' of government policy in general. His writings and his work have become very influential throughout the world. As a way of carrying out the business of government, the approach he now advocates still places the emphasis on instruction, delivery, performance management and a shift of accountability from the government to the governed. The fountainhead for all of this is policy thought up, designed and handed down by government, sometimes with carefully managed consultation processes. We cannot (must not, in my view) disconnect learning and the leading of learning from our thinking about society, from our notions of democracy, or from our fundamental human values. Other supporters of this view include John Dewey from the USA, Stephen Kemmis from Australia and Nurit Peled-Elhanen from Israel, all of whom will be discussed later in the chapter. The serious consequences of excluding learners and leaders of learning from the process of educational policy-making cannot be overstated. Educational narratives are social narratives that help form our views of ourselves and other human beings. These views can disparage, disadvantage and demonise others; they can also celebrate and support; they can include and they can exclude. Forming policy on a narrow basis reduces its legitimacy and calls for stronger measures of enforcement. An officially sanctioned narrative can be an un-noticed enforcement measure – un-noticed because, while policy targets are being chased, there is no time for inclusive discussion and we lose the habit of questioning anything except how to implement what is required. The creativity of learners and leaders of learning does not extend to the shaping of policy: it is devoted to its delivery.

Towards the end of the chapter, I categorise the threats to the well-being of learners, leaders of learning and society that arise from an exclusive approach to policy-making. The ultimate threat is, I believe, social fracture and, at present, in much of Europe and the USA, I see few possibilities of preventing it. That education, standing for growth and fulfilment, could be recruited to contribute to social fracture is difficult to contemplate or accept. Attempting to change the situation is like picking up a few bricks to re-build a house that a bulldozer is in the process of demolishing. However, I do not think we should stand idly by. I have also included discussion points that I hope will elucidate what the text has obscured; they are intended to develop arguments further, provide examples and offer more perspectives.

Background

The well-being of learners and leaders of learning is affected by how public policy is formed and implemented. The effects can be direct in terms of education policy and indirect in as much as social and economic policies set the contexts for education. Policy decides what learners and leaders of learning do; it also decides its value, and even their value as members of society. The process is interactive and how learning takes place affects the nature, the well-being and even the publicly declared purpose and values of the societies in which we live. The means by which this happens can be confusing, contradictory and contentious – even hidden from view. To make critical sense of the changing interactions between learners and leaders of learning on the one hand, and makers of policy on the other, we need to discuss a number of relevant concepts, the values with which they are associated, and the effects they can produce when turned into policy. We also need to look at who, at various times and to varying extents, is permitted to contribute to the making of policy and the ascribing of value. Bernard Crick published *In Defence of Politics* in 1962 with the intention of restoring the meaning of politics: to remind us that it is about public values. Fifty years after the book went on sale, Michael Flinders, a successor of Crick's at the University of Sheffield, published *Defending Politics* with a similar intention. Why, we should ask, is it necessary from time to time for us to have to be reminded that politics is an inclusive public activity and not one exclusively limited to the few people making policy?

Politics and alienation

It might be thought that politics is what politicians do as they manoeuvre to acquire and keep power. The phrase 'playing politics' and the accusation of being 'politically motivated' contribute to this impression. They actually refer to partisan behaviour and manipulation. In fact, politics is the inclusive and collective process of arriving at agreed values. Crucially for the subject of this chapter it is a process that should take place before policies are established: political process first, policy making second. If education policies are constructed without prior agreement about values, the effect on learners and leaders of learning is to reduce them to reacting to the values and decisions of those with power: it disempowers them. There remains, of course, the question of how inclusive or exclusive the political process can sometimes be. It changes. When Karl Marx used the concept of alienation, it was to help him describe how workers could be reduced to commodities and excluded from any discussion of values as a prelude to decision-making on matters of great importance to them – namely the conditions of their lives and work. Alienation can lead to dehumanisation. If learners and leaders of learning are estranged and excluded from decision-making about their roles, value and purpose, the consequences can be stressful and counterproductive socially, and individually damaging. Taken together, the concepts of politics and alienation represent varying opposites. The smaller the group that agrees on values and goes on to make policy, the greater the group that is alienated. Setting the ratio for the two groups is the problem.

Governance without politics: the delivery of policy

Possibly the clearest exposition today of the belief that politics is subordinate to governance comes from Michael Barber. Partly self-deprecatingly and partly proudly, he adopted the word 'deliverology' to describe his central belief of how to do government by setting clear targets and hitting them as a sign of success. In 2005, he left his UK government job to become a partner and head of McKinsey's Global Education Practice. While there, he co-authored a short work in 2007 entitled *How the World's Best-Performing School Systems Come Out Top*. The word 'instructor' replaces 'teacher' in this text. Now he is Chief Education Advisor at Pearson, a profit-making company with a huge global educational reach. He has been described as 'the control freak's control freak'. Two concepts dominate his approach to education and the business of government.

- **Instruction**: this implies a manual, an authorised text, transmission of an approved orthodoxy.
- **Delivery**: this implies performance management and inspection.

Put these two together and we can see how policy-makers set about their business by instructing others to deliver. *Instruction to Deliver* is the title of Barber's major book. For an antidote to this book, and an understanding of how governments may fail to work efficiently (and often work extremely inefficiently) – especially when they fail to do politics inclusively – take a look at *The Blunders of Our Governments* (2013) by Anthony King and Ivor Crewe. The majority of the blunders they describe and analyse took place in the UK, but their sections on human errors and system failures are relevant globally. Readers may find themselves repeatedly asking the following questions:

> — *How on earth do the devisers of disastrous policies manage to (a) escape the blame?*
> — *And (b) give all the difficult jobs to others?*

Previously we may have thought of accountability as something that governments owe its people. In the instruction and delivery model, the burden of accountability is borne by those that are managed. Whether talking about schools or universities, or hospitals or businesses, the effect is the same – policy-makers decide the targets for others to hit. This approach can backfire because targets may not be hit if they were badly chosen or in conflict with other targets; even when targets are hit, there can be unforeseen and undesirable consequences. The question is:

— *Who takes the blame when things go wrong?*

In Volume III of *Man and Society* (1963 and 1992), John Plamenatz offers an authoritative disquisition on the idea of 'progress': how at times it has been taken as a law governing history; how much it is associated with the growth of knowledge; how much it has been associated with happiness. Progress is not a straightforward concept. As I discuss below, to hold its meaning captive is, however, to give the impression that it is. Another effect of the rigorous application of this model is that receivers (implementers) of policy can spend their time ironing out problems, complaining and resisting. I suggest that in an educational context this takes the joy out of learning. And learning without some joy is not, I believe, good for well-being.

A cluster of four concepts and control of their use

Four concepts that should be taken together are: progress, reform, improvement and modernisation. Although their meanings may appear (and can be) close, dispute over their definition results in them being used, sometimes simultaneously, in contrary ways. They can dominate policy dis-course in education, so it is always important to unpick the current meanings. They also represent highly desirable and sometimes fought-over labels.

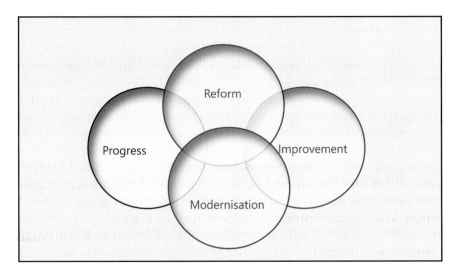

Figure 4.1: Four key concepts that need careful consideration in policy discourse in education.

(i) Progress

Progress is a problematic concept because the assumption is that it takes place in a particular manner or direction, and it implies that countries, groups and people who develop in different and unapproved ways and directions do not progress. So-called developing countries, for example, are expected to make progress according to the values of other more powerful countries, to fit an economic and administrative template drawn up by others. This can mean a country has to earn the right – granted by others – to be labelled as a 'democracy', but of a particular kind. In the classroom setting it can mean having to demonstrate only such knowledge, understanding and skill that has been officially established as worthy of being awarded grades. The psychologist Jerome Bruner generated lots of terms that gained currency, especially in the 1960s, '70s and '80s; terms such as 'scaffolding', 'discovery learning' and 'the spiral curriculum'. He was interested in how learning takes place as a human activity and how it can be re-visited in differing contexts over time. Like Dewey and others, he also takes account of cultural links and contexts. His ideas may be interpreted as simply allowing children to do as they like, but this disregards the need for careful planning and observation required by his approaches. What continues to puzzle me is why educators and psychologists such as Bruner in the USA use the word 'instruction' to describe what educators do. Its meaning seems totally counter to his approach.

Personal reflection

THE SHEEP AND THE PIG

Some years ago, in a Liverpool Nursery School, the headteacher was very keen on Records of Achievement. A four-year-old child asked the headteacher if she could put one of the two pictures she had drawn that day into her portfolio. The answer was 'Yes, which one?'. Now the child had done one picture of a sheep and one picture of a pig. The picture of the pig was really very good: clearly a well-delineated and recognisable pig. The picture of the sheep, on the other hand, was not very good at all. When she asked the child which picture should be included, she was surprised to be told: 'The sheep, of course'. Being an experienced teacher, and remembering that the purpose of Records of Achievement was that the child should own the decision about what went into the portfolio, the head refrained from intervening. She did, however, when the parent came to collect the child, ask why she thought her child had chosen the poor sheep rather than the much better pig. The mother replied, 'Well, you see, she's been doing pigs for months – our house is full of her pictures of pigs. That's her first sheep'. In other words, the achievement identified by the child as worthy of celebration represented a step towards new learning.

The story of the sheep and the pig has stuck with me for a long time and I often wonder what happened to that four-year-old girl as she 'progressed' through a school system that required her to submit the equivalent of better and better pictures of pigs rather than her pictures of sheep. The idea that learning includes recognition of tentative steps to new, sometimes unexpected (and often self-directed and unpolished) learning is not itself new. Bruner's ideas of discovery learning and Lawrence Stenhouse's encouragement of teachers to be researchers, for example, support this approach and give it value. However, national anxieties to perform well in international educational league tables, work against it. The competition to produce better pictures of pigs means that the poor sheep don't get much of a look in. These national anxieties are transmitted, via the leaders of learning, to the learners. In whatever context the concept of progress is used – the performance management of school-teachers, the development of nations or the acquisition of knowledge, skills and understanding – the danger is that failure to fit the approved criteria defining progress results in negative labelling that might be somewhat unfair, especially if the criteria are not well and inclusively chosen.

In 1975, Lawrence Stenhouse produced *An Introduction To Curriculum Research And Development*. It was a set book for the Open University. *The Times Educational Supplement* called it 'a profoundly important book' and predicted that it would be read widely. That was at a time when thinking and experimenting about what and how to teach and what and how to assess were regarded as proper activities for professional educators, when universities appointed professors of curriculum development and when at least some educational policy was made on the ground. Bruner began and carried out much of his work in Scotland, but it was in England, when the Teaching Council was dominated by educators, that he became part of and a positive force for professional research activity. He even saw school inspectors as collaborators with (and enablers of) school-teachers undertaking research. We have moved far away from that position and now, monitored by inspectors, with must-hit targets set up by others.

(ii) Reform

Taken literally, reform simply means change. Yet this simple concept is very powerful because it is associated with so many measures that have gained approval over so many years: abolition of slavery, extension of the franchise, welfare, free medical care and education for all, for example. It is easy to understand why politicians are so keen to apply the word to their policies. The question to ask is this:

— *If we believe that the use of the word reform confers approval, are we tacitly accepting that when a policy is presented to us with that label it cannot be challenged?*

As with *improvement* (below), once policy-makers capture and control the use of the concept of reform, its critics can be made to appear to be opposed to a well-thought-of concept of high value. That is not a good position from which to make an argument.

(iii) Improvement

The international standards for quality assurance (produced by the International Standardisation Organisation or ISO) make much use of this word. A business should, they assert, always be seeking to improve its performance. To do better what it seeks to do. The following questions should be asked, however.

— *Is what a business seeks to do a good thing in and of itself?*
— *Who or what might be affected when a business pushes harder to achieve more?*
— *How is improvement to be measured?*

Imagine a government writing a national curriculum that concentrated on drawing pictures of pigs. Would that be a good thing? If the government says it is a good thing, then it is – especially if no one outside government has the opportunity to contribute their views or the power to change things. If you cannot change a policy, you have to work to the values placed on it by those that made it. What might be affected if this policy were enforced? For one thing, there would be no pictures of sheep – or of anything else. All the resources of schools, especially human resources, would be devoted to teaching children to draw pictures of pigs. The curriculum would be very narrow, making it much easier to measure and inspect performance. It will be very simple to identify which children and teachers improve and which fail to hit target.

Then there is the issue of assessing and evaluating the pictures. Standards and expectations need to be established. Who should do this and on what basis? The government could ask the learners and the leaders of learning to take a lot of time to research this before making any decisions, but the politicians will have made pledges to the people that (unlike the previous government) they would 'drive up standards'. In general, politicians prefer microwaved policies to slow-cooked ones. Quick decisions are, therefore, likely to be made about what a picture of a pig should look like and teachers will be sent on courses to learn how to instruct children to draw them properly. Continuing professional learning would be timed, tidy and targeted, with tangible evidence making it easy to carry out value-for-money analysis. It certainly would not be untimed, untidy or untargeted with intangible evidence – no chance for the accidental discovery of professional penicillin. As for standards, how, we should ask, can they be driven up? Or, for that matter, *down*? They are only standards if they stay still so that measurements can be made against them. They are, however, part of the rhetoric of educational policy-makers today. Learners and leaders of learning are now required to be fluent in a language that is essentially that of quality assurance. My argument is that when the meaning given to standards keeps shifting, without serious research and merely at the whim of a politician, the language is being misused to the detriment of both learners and leaders of learning.

The ISO has a family of standards documents that are derived firstly from a set of British quality assurance standards, but ultimately from the USA, which some years ago realised that if a soldier aims a gun at a target and pulls the trigger, the bullet should go on its way as intended. Becoming qualified to wear an ISO label is important for many businesses: it means that other label wearers accept them; it means they can advertise to customers that they only deal with or subcontract to fellow label wearers. This becomes a quality-assured family, all of whom are dedicated to doing better what they already do. Asking awkward questions about their central purpose is not part of the accreditation process. It is also not part of the audit process. Is education going this way? And so we come to our next concept.

(iv) Modernisation

As with progress, we could go back a while to trace and discuss the concept of modernisation: back to the encyclopaedists and the sociologist, social psychologist and philosopher, Emile Durkheim, and many others. It is not a recently introduced concept. It is, however, often a sloppily deployed concept. To say that it means that something is 'new' is an insufficient and possibly misleading explanation. There can be times when the human spirit seems to want to put names to periods of history such as the 'age of enlightenment' in the eighteenth century or the 'new Elizabethan age' in Britain when Queen Elizabeth II came to the throne. It can be part of wanting to feel both new and, by implication, modern. Even refreshing and inspiring. To give names to ages like this is to satisfyingly categorise them and set them out as steps we take in the modernisation process. By subscribing to this approach, we can make ourselves feel that *every day in every way we are getting better and better*. The French psychologist Emile Coué (1857–1926) gave us this phrase, suggesting it should be repeated as a mantra. Autosuggestion and psychotherapy are not my fields, but maybe he was right – that there are great benefits for our health in being optimistic. I borrow the saying here to suggest that it can be unwise to accept history uncritically when it is presented to us complete with some rather grand labels that suggest the future will be better than the past. To be referred to as 'old-fashioned' is generally regarded as something of an insult unless, of course, someone wishes to label part of the past as a 'golden age' in order to disparage the present. When they do so, it brings out some of the contradictions inherent in a captured concept because the rhetoric uses an idealised past to legitimate devising policies for a preferred future. The major point about modernisation is that it tries to bring together and unify the other three concepts described above, so that they appear to represent a totally unchallengeable set of values. To march behind the banner of modernisation is to march in the approved direction. It is labelled 'progress' and all change can be called 'reform' leading to 'improvement'. This is a very powerful cluster of concepts, each one of which has to be engaged with in order to alter or influence the policy discourse or chosen narrative. The debilitating task is obtaining permission to meaningfully engage with the concepts and participate in policy-making. Without this participation, fulfilment for learners and leaders of learning can be limited to implementing received policy. A phrase in widespread use nowadays is 'best practice'. Professionals are supposed to discover, learn, follow and disseminate the best way of doing something. Two questions arise here:

— *Who decides the 'something' they should be doing?*

— *Who has the power to identify the best way of doing it?*

And we could ask a third:

— *Once best practice has been identified, does it close down experimentation to find other ways of doing things?*

In the late 1960s and '70s, the government of El Salvador, in the name of modernisation, attempted to make a radical change to the role of school-teachers: all lessons were to be designed and broadcast via television from the capital city into the classroom. Alienated is probably too mild a word to describe how teachers felt. Protest was violently suppressed and blood was spilt. *Modernizing Minds in El Salvador: Education Reform and the Cold War* (2012) was written by Lindo-Fuentes and Ching. It describes how, in the name of modernisation (supported by lots of money and designed by very clever people) the military regime of the country managed to create an educational policy that helped start a civil war. Failing to include school-teachers at the policy-making stage was a contributory factor. Some think it was the key factor.

So far, the introduction of Massive Open On-line Courses (MOOCs) has not involved bloodshed, but it will be interesting to see what issues are raised as people debate this initiative. Are critics who assert that learning is a social activity to be silenced by peremptory use of the word modernisation and made to feel out-of-date? MOOCs are discussed frequently on the professional network LinkedIn™. On one hand, there are arguments about MOOCs being the only way forward and warnings that universities and countries that stay out of the game will lose out somehow; on the other are arguments about the social nature of learning. Squeezed into the arguments are points about practical problems and low completion rates.

What I think is detectable is fear, by some, of a disturbing future that challenges us to adapt to new technologies and threatens certain long-held beliefs. When 'change' seems to signify a combined threat – to competence and values – there is the potential to get lost in a modernisation maze, and a need to find something solid to cling onto, at least until professionals find their bearings.

Themes and issues

The major themes of this chapter so far are as follows.

- Exclusion from the articulation and discussion of values prior to policy-making.
- Restriction of the creativity of learners and leaders of learning to the implemented policy.
- Control by policy-makers of language, discourse, narrative and value.

We might conclude that there are no issues here at all: if the purpose of learners is to 'do what the teacher says' and if the purpose of leaders of learning is to teach 'what they are told to teach in the way they are told to teach it' then what is the problem? I want to introduce three witnesses.

(i) John Dewey

Dewey began to articulate his educational philosophy in the USA before the First World War. He saw education as part of what made democracy work. Schools were for communities. Now I have a confession to make. In the late 1960s, when I was qualifying as a schoolteacher, we were given a lot of Dewey to study. At the time, I lumped him together with all the other people, such as Rousseau, our teachers had chosen to burden us with. They were simply yet more 'stuff' we had to wade through to qualify. But having had to experience formal education as it entered the cul-de-sac of instrumentalism, I began to find him inspiring. Although he was born in 1859 and died in 1952, he could be said to have represented the Spirit of 1968. There are far too many books and articles for me to recommend a single one, and I'm not suggesting total acceptance of everything he said or wrote, but to be reminded that education is about far more than passing examinations is important; it is part of what makes a democratic society. For this reason, he has to be revisited.

(ii) Stephen Kemmis

Kemmis and his colleagues in Australia provided us with the notion of a socially critical school – not a school that passively conforms to social structures and norms but one that plays an interactive, even proactive, role in society. In 1983, Kemmis and his coworkers, published *Orientations to Curriculum and Transition: Towards the Socially Critical School*. This argues that schools can do better than simply preparing young people for a world of work or for life as individuals; they underline the idea that schools are not simply preparers for society but are participants in society, which has implications for how they approach what they do. The book was written in Australia, but I have used it with educators in Israel and the UK for many years. It helps me show leaders of learning that there are other perspectives, and that there is a valid educational language that is somewhat different from the language of quality-assured pursuit of targets.

(iii) Nurit Peled-Elhanen

Peled-Elhanen offers a disturbing perspective on the socially critical roles of learners and leaders of learning. Her close analysis of the treatment of Palestinian people in school textbooks in Israel reveals what is essentially a dehumanisation of 'others'. It also dehumanises the learners and the leaders of learning that are drawn into a scarcely challenged national narrative. Published in 2012, Peled-Elhanen's *Palestine in Israeli School Textbooks*: *Ideology and Propaganda in Education* confronts an issue that is not confined to Israel. It is the issue of establishing an official national narrative that suppresses the narratives of others. However, unless it is revealed, there can be no issue. To be dehumanised and devalued is to be dismissed from discussion. If you are one of the 'others' then your maps, your place names, your customs and your celebrated events are not allowed into the classroom.

Policies do not have to come in the form of laws. They can be so culturally embedded that they cannot escape from the dominant discourse to be identified and disputed. There are no issues about well-being if the policies cannot be 'seen'. To look at the work of Dewey, Kemmis and Peled-Elhanen is to be reminded that education is not just about preparation for measurement: it is about growth as a human in relation to other humans. Educational policies, whether formal or informal, extrinsic or intrinsic, affect the terms within growth takes place. They can be positive. They can also be negative. And they can wobble in between.

Personal reflection

FAILURE TO LEARN FROM THE LEARNERS *–OR–*
WHO SHOULD WRITE SCHOOL REPORTS?

For some time I had been trying out different ways of producing school reports, attempting to escape from the eternal set of variations on the word 'satisfactory' combined with 'very', 'quite', 'un-', 'not', 'not very' and so on. Remember them? My idea was that all the children were entitled to three things that so far had been kept from them: first, they were entitled to a framework and language that could help them make overall sense of their learning; second, they were entitled to tell their teachers how they made sense of their learning; third, they were entitled to be listened to before a teacher made any statement that passed judgment on them. There was a fourth entitlement: they had the right to contribute to the shape, nature, scope and language of the sense-making evaluation framework. So I drafted a framework and, mostly with my own registration class, got it into a shape that we thought would work throughout the school.

The next task was to persuade colleagues to accept it. Here I made a classic error. I thought that the members of staff who did not object to it had accepted it. Having persuaded senior management to extend registration each Friday morning to evaluate the learning of the week, we embarked on what I believed was a journey into that socially and educationally fulfilling world called 'comprehensive education'. But guess what? When it came to writing reports, half the staff ignored everything the kids had written. I ought to have taken more care and more time to 'embed' the project. The key to gaining consent was the sharing of ownership and after more than thirty years, the feeling of having persuaded the kids to come to a dance at which teachers failed to take the floor with them continues to gnaw at me.

The relationship between learners and leaders of learning

We could place together the interests of learners and leaders of learning and view them as joint receivers of policy with a median role for leaders of learning as transmitters of policy. This would neglect the dynamic of their relationship, and devalue the extent to which leaders of learning also learn when they collaborate as joint participants with learners. In that dynamic also lies potential for disappointment and a lack of respect. On the opposite page is another story. I call it 'Failure to learn from the learners' or 'Who should write school reports?'. It is my own story from the early 1980s. These are my questions today.

— *What kind of a hearing do we give to what is now often called the 'student voice'?*

— *Are learners at the bottom of a triangle, with policy-makers at the top and leaders of learning acting as their agents?*

— *In what aspects of learning are their voices to be heard?*

— *Is it the job of leaders of learning to quieten those voices, especially when they are discomforting?*

— *Is it the job of policy-makers to quieten the voices of leaders of learning, especially when they are discomforting?*

CATEGORIES OF THREATS TO WELL-BEING

A danger when describing and categorising threats to well-being is that we might engage in that well-known practice of re-defining as medical or social conditions the ordinary ups and downs of life. If grief over the death of a friend, for example, is categorised as a medical condition, we can apply medication to treat the 'problem'. This is to visualise grief as something wrong with us that has to be cured.

> In the book *Cracked: Why Psychiatry is Doing More Harm Than Good* (2013), James Davies looks very closely at how respected medical academics and famous pharmaceutical companies so easily medicalise everyday sufferings, hide research failings and build up false categories of conditions in order to meet the targets sustaining a massive industry. Is it possible that the education industry might do the same in response to policy imperatives?

If to be a little bored or to daydream or simply feel a bit fed up in a classroom is categorised as 'abnormal' behaviour, then we can develop an industry of educational consultants equipped with the latest ideas and gadgets to make the learner return to an approved normality. We may even accuse teachers who fail to deal with such abnormalities of professional shortcomings that must be corrected by means of special training sessions. I suggest that a bit of boredom and fedupness, from time to time, are normal for human beings; and as for daydreaming – it can be very stimulating. They usually represent no serious threat to our well-being and it is seldom necessary to make an issue of them. Bearing in mind these caveats, and also that no teacher enjoys hearing the phrase 'This is boring', I think we can, nevertheless, identify some real and strong threats to well-being that arise from the interaction between policy-makers and those engaged, in whatever role, in organised learning. From a long list of many candidates I have a short list of three. I see them as a sequence.

(i) The threat of abnormalisation

Abnormalisation is a very strong word but I consider it to be an appropriate one. I chose it because it signifies the difference between approved and non-approved beliefs and behaviours. Having the power to label people as abnormal when they disagree with you destroys not only their arguments but also their self-esteem. Many cultures have a history of making fun of and disrespecting people because they are different. If the people who are considered different have similar power then they can retaliate in kind; if they do not, all that is left is resentment. Our subject here is the interaction between learners and leaders of learning on one hand, and policy and policy-makers on the other. The threat is that policy establishes what we might call an official educational religion. Believers in the religion are normal; non-believers are abnormal and must take the consequences of wearing a negative label. Powerful official educational religions not only have the liturgy but also the equivalent of bishops and priests. School-teachers and lecturers who wish for promotion must demonstrate that they are confirmed members of a church that is strongly organised, with the power to excommunicate.

(ii) The threat of exclusion

This threat – a consequence of abnormalisation – is very subtle. Learners and leaders of learning who have never known what it can be like to articulate and discuss their concerns, interests, beliefs, anxieties and values as part of a process leading to policy-making might not expect or hope for inclusion in the process. What you never had you never miss, after all. So who or what is being threatened by exclusion? There are three layers to this threat. First, learners who are excluded from contributing to decisions about what and how they learn. Second, leaders of learning with deep and long professional experience are not allowed to bring it to the policy-making party. And the third layer is the threat of social fracture.

(iii) The threat of social fracture

Ultimately it is the well-being of society that is being threatened. When unorthodox learners and leaders of learning are deemed to be abnormal, the different perspectives they draw to our attention are ignored or devalued. When both unorthodox and orthodox are excluded from discussion of values before policy-making, the policies that emerge have a narrower and more fragile base. The ownership of policies is confined to a small group who are liable to change as elections take place and ministers are reshuffled. When we talk about the well-being of learners and leaders of learning we are, surely, also talking about the well-being of society. Dewey, Kemmis and Peled-Elhanen did not confine their writings on education to what happens in classrooms; they were fully aware that learning – how it is organised, the values that shape it, and the human beings closely involved in formal educational systems–is part of a societal ecology. But that ecology can malfunction.

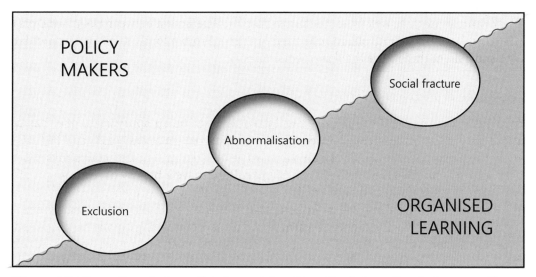

Figure 4.2: Three threats to well-being arising from the interaction between policy-makers and those engaged in organised learning.

I am thinking here of the work of Fred W. Riggs. In 1964 he produced *Administration in Developing Countries: The Theory of Prismatic Society*. He introduced readers to so many newly minted terms (a tendency of structural functionalists), making the book, although short, a struggle to read. The irony is that this new language was part of an attempt to make his work accessible. He saw society and administration in ecological terms and in order to get us to see this clearly he used the concept of a prism: a fused light beam indicated a society administered by means of very simple administrative structures, but a refracted light beam, split into its component colours, represented societies generating multiple structures. He was careful not to view this simplistically as a transition from traditional agrarian societies to 'modern' industrial ones; rather, he demonstrated a way of looking at the shifting inter-relationships between administrative structures and society. Why choose the word 'fracture'? Because two forces are at work: one creating distance between makers and implementers (or receivers) of policy, and the other creating turmoil as it rotates policy-makers. I am not proposing an oppressively enforced harmony between the two groups nor a sterile stability with little change; I am arguing that learning should be fulfilling and that without fairness and inclusion the fulfilment of some will come at the expense of others, thus creating an unequal distribution of well-being.

In the last few years there have been several books that argue in favour of a fairer, less unequal society. Some of the arguments are made on moral grounds – it is simply wrong that some people are exploited while others are privileged; powerful economic arguments in favour of fairness and equality are also made. In 2012, Stewart Lansley published *The Cost of Inequality: Why Economic Equality is Essential for Recovery*. Based on considerable and very thorough research, his point is that if we wish for a good economy we must narrow the gap between the rich and the poor. Concentrating mostly on the UK and the USA, he highlights the social, individual and economic damage in those countries since the end of the 1970s when the gap began to widen. Joseph Stiglitz, concentrated mostly on the USA when making similar points in *The Price of Inequality* (2010). Lansley quotes Wilkinson and Pickett's book of 2009 *The Spirit Level: Why More Equal Societies Almost Always Do Better*. They show, supported by a great deal of evidence, that not only does inequality increase illness and stress for individual people, but that society at large, including the rich and privileged, will enjoy greater well-being in a more equal society.) We may mend our fracture with a temporary weld here and there from time to time. However, unless learners and leaders of learning are respected as having something to contribute to discussions before educational policy is made, the resulting damage to well-being will not be confined to them but will extend to society.

The interests closing the door to policy-making are driven by beliefs that only a single-minded approach to education – one that involves targeting high attainment in specific subjects – will bring about economic success. They have the power. The interests behind attempts to open the door not only appear weak (because it is more difficult to gain a hearing for complex arguments from different perspectives) but actually are weak because, having no control over discourse, so many of them are now conditioned to accept the simplistic. There are not enough shoulders pushing at the door. When it comes to policy-making, the act of exclusion damages individual and societal well-being. For this reason, I take my stand on inclusion. A more general ownership of policies, and a growing habit of taking part, will enable a more equal and a more fair social interaction – that is, if we ever contrive the chance to try it out.

Concluding comments

The many points made in this chapter bring us to a single question:

— *How might it be possible to make the formation of policy a more inclusive process?*

If, in particular, education policy-makers gave a more than desultory hearing to the interests, anxieties, concerns and values of learners and leaders of learning, policies might be more widely owned and, I assert, become more effective in achieving fulfilment – not only for learners but also for leaders of learning. Essentially, however, this is about the well-being of the kind of societies in which we wish to live. The arguments we hear about the world of learning should not be confined to examining techniques of teaching, learning and assessing. We must look to the likes of Dewey, Kemmis and Peled-Elhanen to create touchstones against which we can examine policies for the social and human values that they represent. Who now, when attempting to qualify as a teacher, is encouraged to think, for example, about the work of Plato, Aristotle and Rousseau? Coming from so long ago does not make what they wrote irrelevant; the questions they posed and mused over were about what it means to be a human being interacting with other human beings.

Today's touchstones are league tables. Rational argument and appeals evoking fairness and humanity are unlikely to alter the habits of politicians who are addicted to forming policies on an exclusive basis and expecting to hold to account those charged with their delivery. Without the inclusive and consensual articulation, by both learners and leaders of learning, of social and human values against which we can critique policies, we shall remain reactors to what is given. Assuming that we wish to, where shall we begin to do this and obtain a hearing? In many countries today I am not so sure that the process of qualifying to be a teacher makes much space for discussion of professional values. And to be inducted as a new professional to a school, college or university is to very quickly learn, adopt and internalise the means by which those institutions have come to respond to governmental imperatives. The starting point may have to be during the post-qualification and induction stage: continuing professional learning. When this is called 'in-service training' we may expect it to be biased towards instruction on how to implement new policy. When it is called 'continuing professional development', or CPD, the risk remains that the development is still according to an approved template. Witness the widespread advertising by publishers and consultants offering CPD 'toolkits' that are matched to policy. I advocate the word 'learning' because it is less constrained; there are more possibilities. It is therefore open to be given meaning by learners and leaders of learning. I would like to suggest three things.

1. That we need more and more international conversation about the experience of leading learning and what that means in terms of values.

2. That the experience of learners be given voice.

3. That, by every means possible, policy-makers are drawn into the conversation.

If learners and leaders of learning wait for policy-makers to open the door to dispute, discussion and debate they will grow cobwebs. I have no detailed plan to persuade them to open the door and what I suggest might generate lots of hot air. What can be guaranteed, however, is that silenced voices persuade no one; furthermore, my professional prejudices lead me to believe that the hot air of learners and leaders of learning is preferable to the hot air of certain policy-makers.

KEY MESSAGES FROM THIS CHAPTER

Politics is a process of inclusively and consensually arriving at values prior to policy-making. Devising and implementing policies without following a political process threatens not only the well-being of learners and leaders of learning but also that of society as a whole.

The urge to 'deliver' policy is spreading and there is increasing pressure to hit targets that are imposed rather than consensually agreed.

The concepts of progress, reform, improvement and modernisation dominate educational discourse. It is in the interests of policy-makers to control how they are defined, and so create a narrative that serves them. The power of learners and leaders of learning to dispute these definitions is diminished.

The creative powers of learners and leaders of learning are confined to the delivery of educational policy that it is assumed will be the key to economic performance.

The threats to well-being include the categorisation and dismissal as abnormal of anyone with other perspectives and values.

The consequences of policy that is made exclusively rather than inclusively will be social fracture.

Supporting evidence and further reading

Acemoglu D and Robinson J (2012) Why Nations Fail. *The Origins of Power, Prosperity and Poverty.* London: Profile Books.

Barber M (2012) *Instruction To Deliver, Fighting to Transform Britain's Public Services.* York: Methuen.

Barber M, Mourshed M (2007) *How the World's Best-Performing Education Systems Come Out On Top.* London: McKinsey.

Crick B (1962) *In Defence of Politics.* London: Pelican.

Davies J (2013) *Cracked. Why Psychiatry is Doing More Harm Than Good.* London: Icon Books.

Flinders M (2012) *Defending Politics. Why Democracy Matters In The Twenty-First Century.* Oxford: Oxford University Press.

Keane J (2010) *The Life and Death of Democracy.* London: Pocket Books.

Kemmis S, Cole P, Suggett D *et al.* (1983) *Orientations to Curriculum and Transition*: *Towards the Socially-Critical School.* Melbourne: Victorian Institute of Secondary Education.

King A and Crewe I (2013) *The Blunders of our Governments.* London: Oneworld Publications.

Lansley S (2012) *The Cost of Inequality: Why Economic Equality is Essential for Recovery.* London: Gibson Square.

Lindo-Fuentes H, Ching E (2012) *Modernizing Minds in El Salvador. Education Reform and the Cold War 1960–1980.* Albuquerque: University of New Mexico Press.

Peled-Elhanen N (2012) *Palestine in Israeli School Books. Ideology and Propaganda in Education.* London: IB Taurus.

Plamenatz J (1992) *Man and Society. Volume III: Hegel, Marx and Engels, and the Idea of Progress.* London and New York: Longman.

Riggs FW (1964) *Public Administration in Developing Countries*: *The Theory of Prismatic Society.* Boston MA: Houghton Mifflin.

Riggs FW (1973) *Prismatic Society Revisited.* New Jersey: General Learning Press.

Stenhouse L (1975) *An Introduction to Curriculum Research and Development.* London: Heinemann.

Stiglitz J (2012) *The Price of Inequality.* London: Allen Lane.

Wilkinson RG and Pickett K (2009) *The Spirit Level*: *Why More Equal Societies Almost Always Do Better.* London: Allen Lane.

Wilson E (1972) *To the Finland Station*: *A Study in the Writing and Acting of History.* London: Phoenix.

CHAPTER 5

Optimistic professional learning for teachers

Ken Jones

At a recent conference on professional development coordinators in schools, a useful model was proposed for embedding professional learning in their institutions. It elicited the following response from one of the participants, the deputy headteacher of a large secondary school: *'Oh no! Not another good idea!'*. The reason for this reaction was understandable. If the suggestion had been impractical, she could have dismissed it as unworkable. However, because it was 'a good idea' there was a moral obligation not to ignore it; she had to add it to her ever-growing list of things to be done. The suggested model had pricked her professional conscience. To ignore it would lead to professional guilt for turning her back on something that ''good' schools should do; If she set out to adopt it, it would need to be 'sold' to senior leaders in the school and to the staff, many of whom would have the same reaction.

So, how can the development of new ideas be enacted sensitively, with due care for the mental health and well-being of those involved? The introduction of any change can be seen from three perspectives (Jones 2010): the political perspective, the professional perspective, and the pragmatic alternative.

The political perspective

The political perspective has an element of compulsion underpinning the rationale for change: this is what you must do. In the scenario above, the deputy headteacher could have taken this approach; with the support of her colleagues in the senior leadership team, she may have justified the introduction of the new initiative on the basis that it had been fully discussed by the senior leadership team and would be adopted in the school, that it would improve teaching and learning in the school, that it would ultimately improve pupil performance and achievement, and that it would be seen in a positive light when the school was next inspected. Then the staff would have to engage with it, and the new approach would become school policy. Its implementation would be monitored and form part of the performance management review. Whether or not they agreed with the initiative, the staff are relieved of the burden of choice and the dilemma of decision-making. They may blame the decision-makers themselves, but that is what senior leaders get paid for. Ultimately, it is easier to be a follower than a leader.

The professional perspective

The professional perspective carries more professional guilt for individual members of staff. It builds on the concept of staff as professionals who want to achieve the best for the pupils in their care, who will go the extra mile to introduce something that improves teaching and learning. DiPaola and Hoy (2005) apply this concept of 'organisational citizenship' to schools, the principles of which are stated or implied in most published lists of professional standards for teachers. It relates to professional trust and the fundamental ethics of professional practice that include, often implicitly, the assumption of altruism in doing the best for one's pupils. It assumes that teachers will take on new ideas when, as professionals, they have assessed the potential influence on their pupils. Where that impact is likely to be in the pupils' best interests, it is assumed that positive professional behaviour will ensue. It is underpinned by the mantra 'This is what you *should* do'. Not to do so would be letting down both oneself and one's pupils.

The pragmatic alternative

This is a frequent outcome of the two forces for change – political and professional – whereby pragmatism is used as a shield to resist both. The pragmatic response to political pressure is to hold back action until absolutely necessary; by that time, logically, the imperative may have softened or even gone away if it has its aegis in political dogma. The pragmatic response to professional pressure is to disown the idea – 'It wouldn't work in my school' – or its source – 'Another theoretical contribution from universities' – or claim that workload or other priorities will mean a slower-than-desired introduction of the change. There is often active resistance to political imperatives, but the action of ignoring 'good ideas' from professional sources is more difficult to justify and can affect professional well-being. If the strategy for change is not directive, therefore, the need to work with staff in a supportive way through measured and strategic implementation through professional learning programmes is paramount.

Continuing professional learning and development (CPLD)

A fundamental principle of what is now referred to as CPLD is that good professionals are continuously improving (Day 1999; Timperley 2011; Wells 2013). In fact, the term 'continuous' is sometimes used in place of the more common 'continuing' as in the 'C' in CPLD. Continuous – by definition – means unbroken. Taken as career-long professional learning, the implication is that a professional cannot allow professional standards to lapse, so the maintenance of these standards is unbroken. However, when taken as active learning, or the enactment of new initiatives, it would be unrealistic for there to be no stepping back to reflect on engagement with professional learning and development. The term 'continuing' is therefore much more important. A number of education systems define and emphasise the continuity of professional expectation through the publication and cyclical monitoring of practice against listed professional standards. In Wales, at the time of writing, the performance management process that aligns with the Practising Teacher Standards requires that:

> *... teachers must meet the Practising Teacher Standards (PTS) at the end of the induction period and continue to meet them throughout their teaching career. (Welsh Government 2011)*

There is clearly an expectation that the implicit and explicit adoption of these Standards will be 'continuous'. The revised Practising Teacher Standards are designed to 'clarify the expectations at each stage of a practitioner's career' and to 'raise standards of teaching and improve learner outcomes'. They are intended to be used as part of an annual performance management cycle, and practitioners are required to:

> *... reflect on and assess their practice against the backdrop of the relevant professional standards. (Welsh Government 2012)*

Similar sets of standards exist in England, Scotland and in many other countries. Again they apply to all stages of a teacher's career.

> *Following the period of induction, the standards continue to define the level of practice at which all qualified teachers are expected to perform. (Department for Education 2013)*

> *Having attained the Standard for Full Registration, teachers will continue to develop their expertise and experience across all areas of their professional practice through appropriate and sustained career-long professional learning. (General Teaching Council for Scotland 2012)*

One highly positive aspect of the use of professional standards is to make explicit the importance of professional development (or, in Scotland, professional learning). This reinforcement of the centrality of CPLD cannot be underestimated. In Wales, the Practising Teacher Standards state that teachers should:

> *... value the improvement of practice through reflection and taking responsibility for continuing professional development. (Standard 10)*

In Scotland, teachers are expected to sustain and develop professional learning in a number of ways, including through the development of:

> *... skills of rigorous and critical self-evaluation, reflection and enquiry, including how to investigate and evidence influence learners and professional practice.*

They should also:

> *... commit to ongoing career-long professional learning, including postgraduate study as appropriate [and] lead and contribute to the professional learning of all colleagues, including students and probationers. (General Teaching Council for Scotland 2012)*

The use of Standards helps to define the key professional principles on which teaching and learning in schools is based. They are not only 'good ideas' – they are essential if professional practice is to be informed, up-to-date, and effective. In setting defined professional standards, however, there is a psychological as well as a professional imperative 'to perform' and this must be taken into consideration when planning, designing and supporting the professional learning opportunities that will enable them to be met. This is particularly significant when considered in a school leadership context. Each professional will be able to undertake his or her responsibilities in a professional way only insofar as they are able to work in a culture of professionalism. Leadership that facilitates professionalism (and the principle of criticality) is central to this. However, in a culture of performativity (Ball 2003; Day 2010; MacBeath 2011; Wilkins 2011) and in a context in which national, local or institutional policy requires 'performance management' and inspection, this may produce professional and personal tensions, especially where leaders are not sensitive to individual needs. If, as Sackney and Mitchell argue (2008; cited in Cranston 2013), school leaders themselves tend to be 'more concerned with accounting than with learning, with control than with teaching, with compliance than with risk taking, and with public relations than with student experiences' the opportunities for teachers to embody the professional values above may be limited.

The use of the term 'critical professional learning' is now more common. Arguably the term 'professional' should encompass the element of criticality, but there are potentially significant tensions between being compliant as a professional and taking a moral stance in accordance with professional values. This in itself may have implications for well-being, so we should ask:

— How critical can we allow critical professional learning to be?

The existence of leadership standards alongside standards for teachers should make explicit the need to encourage critical professional learning and to display what Bottery (2004) refers to as a 'moral compass'. Among the standards in Wales are indications that teachers must:

... be actively involved in professional networks and learning communities which share and test beliefs. (Welsh Government 2012)

And in England, to:

... demonstrate a critical understanding of developments in the subject and curriculum areas. (Department for Education 2013)

These are interesting and potentially ironic requirements, that challenge effective professional learning communities to test beliefs, including those relating to policies of practice set down by national government. In this context, professional learning becomes extremely important, but it may also be extremely unsettling. Professional learning that truly tests beliefs must contain a degree of criticality in its application; but this may expose education policy to a level of scrutiny that is unacceptable to government or school leaders. And so the tension between what *must* be done and what *should* be done re-emerges. Perhaps, cynics might argue, this is why the term 'training' continues to be used in a professional context rather than the 'education' of teachers. The psychological balance that may result in tensions between what professionals must do and what they should do is addressed by Cranston (2013) who distinguishes between professional responsibility and accountability. He argues that:

... the constraints of accountability on school leaders need to be replaced by a new liberating professionalism for school leaders framed around notions of professional responsibility. Simply stated, leadership is a journey of learning. This locates the school leader as a learner, and as a proactive rather than a reactive professional.

Indeed, the mantra of all leadership development programmes is that '*Good leaders are always learning*'. This is reinforced in both academic and professional literature by the language used.

Journal articles often contain what may be called 'victory narratives' in which the success of an initiative or example of excellent practice (often introduced as part of a funded research project) is reported. Alternatively, examples of 'sector leading practice' are highlighted and disseminated to provide aspirational situations for others. The need for effective professional leadership at middle and senior levels is articulated and the language used is commonly inspirational, urging school leaders to be 'transformational', 'strategic', 'visionary' and 'challenging'. School leaders should 'set high expectations' and should be continually raising these; they should have high 'body and soul resilience', be able to 'meet targets' and be 'critically reflective'. The language may also be competitive in tone – such as the Race To The Top programme in the USA (US Department for Education 2009) – or suggest determined performance, like School Turnaround (2013), an organisation 'designed to bring about urgency and time-compressed change in one year' that has the motto *'Everyone achieves. No exceptions. No excuses.'* The emphasis is on a 'moral obligation' to perform, because underperforming schools and teachers are doing a disservice to young people and their parents. When the language of policy is used in a deficit way, therefore, the psychological balance facing both teachers and school leaders may make critical professional learning more difficult. An example of this is when the Chief Inspector of Schools in England in 1999, Chris Woodhead, stated that there were about 15,000 unsatisfactory teachers in England's schools (Barker 2010); this caused an outcry from the teaching profession at the time, and it is questionable whether any constructive benefits to teaching accrued from this aggressive stance.

Results of the Programme for International Student Assessment (PISA) are published every three years; they focus attention on the performance of education systems at a national level (Meyer and Benavot 2013). In Wales in 2010, the minister responsible for education, Leighton Andrews, responded to poor national PISA:

> *PISA is a wake-up call to a complacent system. There are no alibis and no excuses.*
> *It is evidence of systemic failure. (Andrews 2011)*

The reaction from education professionals in Wales at the time was more compliant, possibly because the comments were delivered as part of a clear twenty-point strategic statement from the minister that set out an agenda for action. Possibly the low performance of Wales relative to the other UK countries in the PISA rankings provided an unarguable position. In this case, the call to action was prompted by the need to address a deficit situation, but the intent to raise the achievement of pupils in Wales (measured by PISA test results) was seen as necessary. At an institutional level, however, there is a danger that motivation in a performance management context may arise more from fear of failure than from the desire to engage in professional citizenship behaviour. The use of test scores to measure the performance of teachers and schools has the tendency to generate what might be referred to as pyramidal accountability. Relative underperformance in PISA, for example, may create a chain of blame whereby the government minister responsible for education at the time feels the necessity to respond. Fuelled by the media, this usually results in blame being shifted elsewhere, often to middle-tier organisations such as local authorities.

It is the role of the middle tier to ensure the highest standards from schools in their regions, so headteachers in these schools will be held to account for any underperformance.

Headteachers often look to subject leaders to explain any relative underperformance of pupils in core subject areas, and subject leaders expect individual classroom teachers to account for poor results. Thus the pyramidal blame culture focuses in professional terms on the individual leader of learning who may, of course, move blame either back up to the school leaders (for lack of support or resources) or along to the pupils and parents (and highlight a poor quality of intake). In a culture of blame such as this, the classroom teacher may feel under particular pressure when their results are lower than expected. They can feel, in a school, local or national context, that they are 'letting the side down'.

On the other hand—theories of hope and optimism

For many professionals, the use of inspirational language does what it is intended to do and the setting of challenging targets and the avoidance of platitudes – telling it like it is – will stimulate change. For others, however, placing continued emphasis on the need to improve communicated through deficit language may be demotivating and stressful. The use of negatively critical – rather than constructive – language may not serve to motivate. School leaders with direct-line management responsibility for other professionals should be sensitive to the language used. They should endeavour to generate positive professional learning situations. Where this involves the setting of goals, either by the teacher themselves or the line manager, targets may be expressed in positive challenging terms or they may be expressed in terms of punitive requirements. Snyder's (1995) work on nurturing 'hope' in professional contexts provides some useful principles for engaging in the former. He argued that people are 'intrinsically goal oriented when we think about our futures' and that two necessary components exist to these goal-directed cognitions:

- The cognitive will power or energy to get moving toward one's goal – the 'agency' component.
- The perceived ability to generate routes to get somewhere – the 'pathways' component.

In street language, he suggested, this was akin to people having both the will and the way to reach their goals; however he argued that the phrase 'Where there's a will, there's a way' does not apply without the existence of both the agency and the pathway for the person to succeed. The involvement of a third party (a line manager or peer mentor) may enhance the formulation of agency and pathways in relation to specific goals, consequently facilitating an increased likelihood of achieving goals. Snyder proposed that the nature of emotions in the goal-setting process affects the likelihood of achievement of outcomes.

Higher-hope persons, with their elevated sense of agency and pathways for situations in general, approach a given goal with a positive emotional state, a sense of challenge, and a focus on success rather than failure. Low-hope persons, on the other hand, with their enduring perceptions of deficient agency and pathways in general, probably approach a given goal with a negative emotional state, a sense of ambivalence, and a focus on failure rather than success. (Snyder 1995)

Aligned with Hope Theory are theories of optimism that address the propensity of a person to take a positive or negative approach to challenges and targets – a personal disposition that can influence professional attitudes and performance. A particularly relevant construct within this theoretical grouping is that of Academic Optimism, whereby Hoy *et al.* (2008) observe:

... if teachers believe they are able to affect student learning, then they set higher expectations, exert greater effort, and persist in the face of difficulties.

Academic optimism, therefore, is the belief of a teacher (or a line manager or mentor) that the teacher can make a difference to the performance of pupils in schools. Hoy and colleagues (2008) point out that personally:

... being predisposed to optimism does not guarantee high academic optimism ... academic optimism describes teachers who are engaged, committed, energetic, resilient, and conscientious in the pursuit of student achievement. They do so through cooperation and connections rather than with pressures and punishments.

They argue further that 'optimism begets optimism, and that teacher academic optimism begets student academic optimism'. It is important to note that the Academic Optimism referred to here is not an amorphous emotional state, but is underpinned by three key concepts:

- The teacher's sense of efficacy (defined as a teacher's judgement of his or her capability to bring about desired changes to learning).
- The teacher's trust in students and parents (the ability to form trusting relationships to support effective learning).
- The creation of positive and challenging academic environments for pupils.

Following this, if the achievement of pupils is closely related to the academic optimism of teachers and school leaders, it is important that the professional learning process nurtures academic optimism through positive language and the support of professional learning opportunities, rather than continuing negative and deficit approaches to teacher performance.

Optimistic cultures of professional learning

Bubb and Earley (2004) draw attention to the importance of managing teacher workload in achieving work–life balance and well-being. They provide a variety of practical approaches through which teachers and their school leaders can ensure that the stress generated through excessive demands on professional time can be managed effectively. They cite government reports based on research and data from England to spotlight the potential for professional tensions to emerge as negative experiences for teachers. The use of the term 'stress' is qualified.

Pressure in itself is not necessarily bad and many people thrive on it, but stress is complex – there is good stress (eustress) and bad stress (distress) as well as too much (hyperstress) and not enough (hypostress). It is when pressure is experienced as excessive by an individual that poor health and stress-related illness could result (Bubb and Earley 2004)

Edworthy (2005) suggests that if we are to improve resilience to stress in general, then 'humans need to go regularly beyond their capabilities'. She explains that:

... increases in our stress levels are caused by the way we perceive situations and not by how threatening they are in reality.

The use of the term 'well-being' is sometimes seen as a euphemistic alternative to the focus on stress. Salter-Jones (2012) explains:

Emotional Well-Being (EWB) is seen as one strand of the concept Well-Being and EWB is viewed as part of a continuum, with positive and negative at either end.

She argues that in England:

... there has been a move away from the focus on pupils' EWB and their SEB [social, emotional and behavioural] competencies [and] instead, high-quality teaching and disciplining misbehaviour are viewed as imperative in managing pupils' behaviour within the classroom.

Paradoxically, the requirement for schools to ensure appropriate provision for the well-being of pupils is built into many inspection regimens, but this is less so for the well-being of teaching and non-teaching staff. There is also a danger that school leaders pay lip service to the principle of ensuring the well-being of their staff while, in their own professional dilemmas, they steer a line between measurable performance and supportive cultures. Ironically, 'inspirational' school leaders may be the cause of 'professional' anxiety. They may be 'workaholics' who have an expectation that staff will behave likewise; they may be 'driven leaders' who motivate their staff by emphasising that all professionals in education have a responsibility for the futures of young people and promote a strong ethic of care, social justice and accountability for others, especially the most vulnerable. The psychological gap between what can be achieved and what should be achieved may, in these cases, be accentuated when another person with energy and ability shows what can be done. It is in these cases that the pragmatic alternative emerges, whereby teachers find ways of interpreting or ignoring policy in order to retain their own professional or personal well-being.

The ways in which professional learning is supported in schools is fundamental to both the effectiveness and the well-being of the teacher and, therefore, to that teacher's performance. Kennedy (2005) identifies the deficit model as one approach to professional development which is 'designed specifically to address a perceived deficit in teacher performance' but argues that:

... to attribute blame to individual teachers, and to view CPD as a means of remedying individual weaknesses, suggests a model whereby collective responsibility is not considered, i.e. that the system itself is not considered as a possible reason for the perceived failure of a teacher to demonstrate the desired competence. It also assumes the need for a baseline measure of competence, and once this has been committed to paper, it begins to adopt an authority of its own.

There is a strong temptation for a performance management system to promote a deficit approach to identifying professional learning opportunities. The existence of professional standards, as indicated above, provides a checklist against which performance can be judged. Such checklists provide easily available, nationally and professionally validated criteria against which someone's professional practice can be measured. In the language of staff development management or professional development, this is often referred to as 'the identification of needs', which itself assumes a deficit approach. The use of passive terminology ('Our teachers are being developed') as opposed to active language ('We are supporting our teachers in their professional learning') is also significant. The use of the term 'professional learning' does not, therefore, have to be managerially 'soft'. Teachers should set themselves relevant, challenging but achievable goals, and any identified change in professional performance should be addressed in a spirit of academic optimism rather than as part of a demotivating deficit agenda. The involvement of a significant other (for example, a line manager or peer mentor) is important at this point (Bryan and Carpenter 2008). It is also important for the professional 'foil' or stimulus to be sensitive to the need for an optimistic approach to professional learning. The principle of strength-based mentoring to the professional learning of pre-service teachers may be effectively applied to the learning of professionals at any stage of their careers (He 2009), whereby strength-based mentoring is:

> ... *different from the traditional apprenticeship model – in which the mentor is the guide, supporter or advice giver and the mentee is the advice taker ... [It] starts from the development of the strength-based, appreciative mindset [rather than] the traditional deficit-based approach to mentoring when problems or weaknesses are identified by mentors and a change of behavior is expected from mentees – the strength-based approach calls for both the mentors and mentees to be involved actively in learning and change while emphasizing both parties' strengths, interests and passions.*

A second aspect of the strength-based approach is that it builds on a process of social construction, which:

> ... *centers on an alternative way of thinking that enhances the mentors' and mentees' confidence, resilience and creativity in everyday life. Mentors and mentees are motivated to not only be aware of their own strengths but to also maximize each other's strengths and enhance their appreciation of past experiences, hopes for the future and satisfaction with the present.*

For strength-based mentoring to be effective, therefore, the mentor needs to be sensitive to the personal–professional factors that influence a person's practice. Similarly, that person should have reflected on and gained a critical awareness of their own mental and professional limitations and potential. The ways in which teachers generate or respond to professional learning opportunities often depends on the ways in which they define their own professional identities. Swennen *et al.* (2010) looked at the professional identities of teacher educators, and noted both personal and professional elements to the role, and how professional learning priorities are contextual in relation to the subidentities of each person concerned. Pattie (2009) also highlights this, and indicates that change is not neutral to those involved in the process; in a study of a professional development in Hong Kong, he noted that:

> ... *much of the teachers' stress actually comes from the troubled school environment and not necessarily from teachers' deficits.*

To take a single approach to remedy deficit through professional learning is too simplistic, except in the case of capability and inability to perform to minimum standards (which requires a situation to be addressed in a more functional way), so the need to consider the 'person in context' is essential if effective professional change is to occur. In particular, the involvement of teachers in professional learning communities (Harris and Jones 2010; Stoll and Louis 2007) or co-learning opportunities such as lesson study (Lewis 2009; Saito 2012) would be essential to move away from the individual in context to the individual within the professional community. These are rarely achieved through deficit approaches to professional learning and development. The importance of school leaders in setting a culture of academic optimism (for themselves and for others) therefore becomes more relevant. It is possible to dismiss the use of terms such as 'optimism' and 'hope' as belonging to a pre-performative age, with no 'hard-edge' influence outcomes. However, He (2009) adapts Snyder's research (Snyder 1995) on high-hope versus low-hope participants by establishing concrete and operational suggestions for effective mentoring practice. These include:

- The setting of 'we' goals (in addition to 'me' goals).
- Mentors' supportive pathways thinking to help teachers identify strategies to achieve their goals.
- 'Enhancing agency thinking' to sustain the motivation to achieve the goals.

In addition, Hoy *et al.* (2008) spotlight the role of professional learning communities in either supporting or undermining the development of academic optimism and they argue that we should look more closely at the effects of accountability requirements on collective and individual optimism.

Concluding comments

The processes referred to in these theories are not 'carrot and stick' approaches because there is usually no carrot (the interactions are transformational rather than transactional) – and there may be no stick other than the need to avoid the gap of guilt that emerges when professional levels of performance fall below what, in relative terms, could or should be achieved. Strategies to support one's own professional learning or that of others should therefore be constructive and should nurture academic optimism. The model used may be individual or collaborative, school-focused or addressing a nationally defined priority, funded or not funded, but the process should always be rooted in what can be achieved and should take into account what must be achieved.

KEY MESSAGES FROM THIS CHAPTER

- Continuing improvement requires everyone to look critically at their own learning environments.

- Critical practice works best in professional learning cultures where there is a balance of challenge and support.

- Use of deficit language may demotivate rather than stimulate.

- Staff well-being is as important as pupil well-being.

- Optimistic professional learning in teachers is essential for stimulating the 'can do' mentality needed to challenge and support pupil learning.

Supporting evidence and further reading

Andrews L (2011) *Teaching makes a difference. Address to an invited audience.* Cardiff. 2 February 2011. Available at: wales.gov.uk/topics/educationandskills/allsectorpolicies/ourevents/teachingmakesadifference/ (accessed July 2015).

Ball S (2003) The teacher's soul and the terrors of performativity. *Journal of Education Policy* 18(2), 228.

Barker I (2010) *Fifteen years after Woodhead called 15000 teachers incompetent, the claim is back on Panorama tes connect 9 July 2010.* Available at: www.tes.co.uk/article.aspx?storycode=6049751 (accessed May 2015).

Bottery M (2004) *The Challenges of Educational Leadership.* London: Paul Chapman (cited in Cranston 2013).

Bryan H, Carpenter C (2008) Mentoring: a practice developed in community? *Journal of In-Service Education* 34(1), 47–59.

Bubb S, Earley P (2004) *Managing Teacher Workload: Work–Life Balance and Well-Being.* London: Paul Chapman Publishing.

Cranston N (2013) School leaders leading: Professional responsibility not accountability as the key focus. *Educational Management Administration and Leadership* 41(2), 129–42.

Day C (1999) *Developing Teachers: The Challenges of Lifelong Learning.* London: Falmer Press.

Day C (2010) The challenge to be the best: reckless curiosity and mischievous motivation. *Teachers and Teaching: Theory and Practice* 8(3), 421–34.

Department for Education (2013) *Teachers' Standards.* London: Department for Education.

DiPaola M, Hoy, WK (2005) Organizational properties that foster organizational citizenship. *Journal of* School *Leadership* 15, 391–410.

Edworthy A (2005) *Stress Management for Carers.* Carmarthen: Cerebra.

General Teaching Council for Scotland (2012) *The standard for career-long professional learning: supporting the development of teacher professional learning.* Available at: www.gtcs.org.uk/web/FILES/the-standards/standard-for-career-long-professional-learning-1212.pdf (accessed May 2015).

Harris A, Jones M (2010) *Professional Learning Communities in Action.* London: Leannta Press.

He Y (2009) Strength-based mentoring in pre-service education: a literature review. *Mentoring and Tutoring*: *Partnership in Learning* 17:3, 263–75.

Hoy AW. Hoy,WK, Kurz NM (2008) Teacher's academic optimism: The development and test of a new construct. *Teaching and Teacher Education* 24, 821–35.

Jones K (2010) Central, local and individual continuing professional development (CPD) priorities: changing policies of CPD in Wales. *Professional Development in Education* 37(5), 759–76.

Kennedy A (2005) Models of Continuing Professional Development: a framework for analysis. *Journal of In-service Education* 31(2), 249.

Lewis C (2009) What is the nature of knowledge development in lesson study. *Educational Action Research* 17(1), 95–110.

MacBeath J (2011) Close encounters of a congenial kind. *Cambridge Journal of Education* 41(3), 369–81.

Meyer HD, Benavot A (2013) *PISA, Power, and Policy: The Emergence of Global Educational Governance.* Oxford: Symposium Books.

Pattie L-FYY (2009) Teachers' stress and a teachers' development course in Hong Kong: turning 'deficits' into 'opportunities'. *Professional Development in Education* 35(4), 634.

Sackney L, Mitchell C (2008) Leadership for Learning: a Canadian Perspective. In: J MacBeath., YC Cheng (eds) *Leadership for Learning: International Perspectives.* Rotterdam: Sense.

Saito E (2012) Key issues of lesson study in Japan and the United States: a literature review. *Professional Development in Education* 38(5), 777–89.

Salter-Jones E (2012) Promoting the emotional well-being of teaching staff in secondary schools. *Educational and Child Psychology* 29(4), 18.

School Turnaround. Available at: www.schoolturnaround.org/index.php (accessed July 2015).

Snyder CR (1995) Conceptualizing, measuring and nurturing hope. *Journal of Counselling and Development* 73(3), 355–60.

Stoll L, Louis KS (eds) (2007) *Professional Learning Communities: Divergence, Depth and Dilemmas*. London: Open University Press.

Swennen A, Jones K, Volman M (2010) Teacher educators: their identities, subidentities and implications for professional development. *Professional Development in Education* 36(1–2), 131–48.

Timperley HS (2011) *Realizing the Power of Professional Learning*. Maidenhead: Open University Press.

US Department FOR Education (2009) *Race to the Top Fund*. Available at: www2.ed.gov/programs/racetothetop/index.htm (accessed July 2015).

Wells M (2013) Elements of effective and sustainable professional learning. *Professional Development in Education* 40(3), 488–504.

Welsh Government (2011) *Practising Teacher Standards*. Available at: learning.wales.gov.uk/yourcareer/professionalstandards/?lang=en (accessed July 2015) .

Welsh Government (2012) *Performance management for teachers: Revised performance management arrangements. 2012 Guidance Document 073/2012*. Cardiff: Welsh Government.

Wilkins C (2011) Professionalism and the post-performative teacher: new teachers reflect on autonomy and accountability in the English school system. *Professional Development in Education* 37(3), 409.

Other online resources

- **General Teaching Council for Scotland**
  Supporting the development of teacher professional learning:
  www.gtcs.org.uk/webFiles/the-standards/standard-for-career-long-professional-learning-1212.pdf/

CHAPTER 6

The classroom dynamic as a complex adaptive system

Stephen P. Day and Lynne Grant-McMahon

The classroom can be viewed, from the teacher's perspective, as a complex and dynamic environment, which reflects the cognitive load placed on the teacher, as well as the nature of the sociocultural interactions that emerge over time during the teaching and learning process. This complexity is, in many respects, the main reason why teaching as a profession is so demanding, with high levels of so-called burnout. This chapter attempts to describe some of the complex factors that influence the teaching and learning process and highlights areas that are within the control of the leader of learning and those that influence learning but are beyond the control of the leader of learning.

Teaching is a highly complex process with many different issues and concerns arising on a daily basis, whereby certain cognitive and sociocultural interactions influence the everyday learning process within the classroom. Teachers can be described as multilayered professionals; that is to say they possess a wealth of different experiences and influences that shape their day-to-day interactions and decision-making processes. These experiences and influences emerge from both their professional and their personal lives and can be defined as cognitive and sociocultural influences. Sociocultural and cognitive perspectives are only one way to examine the complexity of the classroom dynamic and the learning and teaching process that occurs within its confines. There are many other methods of doing so, including – but not limited to – the narratives that teachers employ to describe themselves and their teaching (Sfard and Prusak 2005) and the discourses teachers engage in to form a teaching identity (Alsup 2006). We have deliberately chosen to apply these perspectives in this overview of the complex classroom dynamic within the classroom environment throughout the world.

Throughout this chapter a series of 'influence maps' have been constructed to illustrate the many areas that influence the decision-making processes of teachers. Some are conscious decisions, and some are subconscious and automatic, based on both professional and personal experience. Note that these maps are only intended as starting points; other areas can be included in each map.

Teacher identity

Teacher identity is a complex, multifaceted construct. It is influenced by temporal and transient events in the person's life, and can fluctuate over time, under the influence of a range of factors that are internal (emotions, mood or attitude) and external (job and life experiences) to that person (Beauchamp and Thomas 2009). This complex situation is further compounded by teachers' collective conceptualisations of professionalism, as well as their individual views of themselves. The complex nature of the interactions between their professional and personal identities has a heavy influence on the decisions they make when planning lessons (in pedagogical terms) or how they organise the learning environment, which is central to how the emergent classroom dynamic evolves. This suggests that teacher identity is a fluid concept, characterised by a complex series of interactions within an interrelated network of internal and external factors that are emergent from, and influenced by, immediate context, previous conceptualisations of the self, social positioning, ontology (the nature of reality) and/or epistemology (the nature of knowledge) and awareness of the conceptualisation of professionalism of the individual (see FIGURE 6.1). Each of these are also fluid and dynamic constructs (Olsen 2008). From a sociocultural perspective, teacher identity is both a *product* – a result of internal and external influence on the teacher, and a *process* – an ongoing series of interactions within teacher development.

Focusing specifically on the dynamic interaction between professional and personal identity, Kelchtermans and Vandenberghe (1994) suggest that knowledge of self is critical in the way that teachers construe and construct the nature of their work. Events and experiences in their personal lives are inextricably linked to the performance of their professional role (Acker 1999; Goodson and Hargreaves 1994). Their identities are not only construed from the technical (i.e. pedagogical content knowledge, subject knowledge or understanding of classroom management) and emotional aspects of teaching and their personal lives, but also:

> *... as the result of an interaction between the personal experiences of teachers and the social, cultural and institutional environment in which they function on a daily basis.*
> *(Sleeger and Kelchtermans 1999)*

This is highlighted by the fact that collegiality (cooperation between colleagues) plays a key role in influencing (positively and negatively) the culture within educational establishments and also functions as either a support network for teachers or as a stressor (Hargreaves 1994). This point is explored further in CHAPTER 16 on culture and the health and well-being of leaders of learning. We argue that teaching demands a significant personal investment and commitment, and that there is undoubtedly a significant relationship between the personal and professional identities of teachers. Geert Kelchtermans (1993) suggests that the professional self – like the personal self – evolves over time and consists of five interrelated components. These are:

- **Self-image**: how teachers describe themselves through their career stories.
- **Self-esteem**: the evolution of 'self as teacher', how good or otherwise one is as defined by self or others.
- **Job motivation**: what makes teachers choose their profession, remain committed to it or leave it.
- **Task perception**: the way teachers view their role.
- **Future perspective**: teachers' expectations for the development of their career.

A positive sense of identity with subject, relationships and roles is important for maintaining self-esteem or self-efficacy, and commitment to and passion for teaching (Day 2004).

AGENCY

The concept of agency, we suggest, is also critical for developing a full understanding of teacher identity. Teacher agency is a sense of empowerment to be able to move ideas forward, to reach

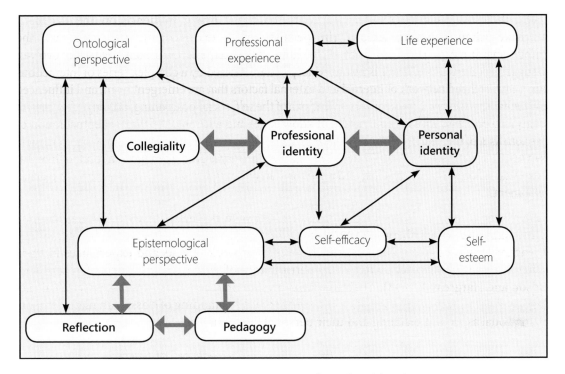

Figure 6.1: The dynamic nature of teacher identity.

goals or to transform their professional context. It is a product of the teacher's realisation of his or her identity; a heightened awareness of one's own identity may lead to a stronger sense of agency because humans are active agents who play decisive roles in determining the dynamics of their social life and in shaping individual activities (Sfard and Prusak 2005).

REFLECTION

This is a broad topic but it influences teacher identity in a number of important ways. Reflection is recognised as a key process by which teachers develop a greater sense of self and an understanding of how that self fits into the larger context that involves interactions with others; therefore reflection plays a role in shaping identity. It requires teachers to look back at thoughts or actions within their practice and to consider their value or effectiveness. It also allows them to look ahead and ways of thinking that can inform their future practice (Conway 2001).

The lesson-planning process

Effective lesson planning lies at the heart of effective teaching. Lesson planning can be described as the systematic development of instructional requirements, arrangement, conditions, resources and activities, as well as the assessment and evaluation of teaching and learning. It involves analysis of the learning needs of the pupils and the development of a delivery structure to meet those needs (Clark and Dunn 1991; Panasuk and Todd 2005). Schon (1983) described lesson planning as proactive decision-making that takes place before instruction. Clark and Dunn (1991) suggest that, consciously and unconsciously, teachers make decisions that affect their behaviour and that of their pupils. Lesson planning involves teachers' purposeful efforts in facilitating the evolution of the cognitive structures of their pupils. The quality of their decisions and efforts depends on their creativity and ability to apply learning and instructional theories, including how the teacher organises support mechanisms such as using learning assistants and differentiation to take forward pupil learning in a focused and meaningful way. This suggests that lesson planning is an intricate, complex and dynamic cognitive process, which requires the teacher to be able to balance and make professional judgements about:

- The *content* of lessons (knowledge, skills and values).
- The *context* of lessons (pedagogy, theories of learning, prior learning, progression and support needs of learners).

The complexity of the task is highlighted by Peter John (2006) when he asked: 'Why is developing and constructing lesson plans so difficult to learn as well as teach?' FIGURE 6.2 outlines the complex nature of the lesson planning process.

Classroom culture and ethos

The development of a positive classroom culture and ethos is highly dependent on the teacher's ability to foster and nurture good working relationships within their classroom. Good communication between the leader of learning and the learners is central to this process. In addition, effective communication between the teacher and his or her colleagues towards meeting the needs of the learner is essential. An important facet of building a working relationship in which a positive culture and ethos can flourish, is the development of a working consensus within the classroom (Hargreaves 1972). The teacher achieves this by:

- Establishing ground rules and routines.
- Being able to identify routines and tacit understandings.
- Being inclusive and fair in their dealing with the learners.
- Recognising the need for the professional and personal identity of the teacher (see FIGURE 6.1 and FIGURE 6.3).

A working consensus is based on the recognition of the legitimate interests of others, and a mutual exchange of dignity and respect between teachers and learners. A tacit, reciprocal recognition of the needs of others allows coping within the classroom environment on a day-to-day basis. It is possible for learners and teachers (if they each chose to) to make life difficult for one another, thus the teacher must be pragmatic when negotiating the basis for the working consensus. It will not just appear – it must be actively developed through conscious effort by the teacher. The onus is on the teacher to initiate, continually monitor and maintain all areas of setting ground rules, classroom routines, active listening and observation that will help structure the expected behaviour of the children in their classes. Most experienced teachers agree that learners of all ages expect these initiatives to come from the teacher and are unlikely to challenge their authority, as long as the teacher acts consistently and in a manner that the learners regard as fair within the framework of the working consensus of the class. The wider school climate and ethos impacts heavily on classroom culture and ethos, but teachers are able to make a difference to their own classroom culture and ethos in a positive manner.

Culture of the classroom: rules and routines

Learners expect their leaders of learning to set expectations and boundaries that are usually expressed as overtly formal rules, generally tailored to the age and stage of the learners. These may be overarching rules, such as treating others with respect, commitment to learning and behavioural expectations, in line with school policies. Teachers use classroom routines to operationalise these overarching rules and apply their principles to concrete activities. They may have subtly different expectations and rules within their classroom settings, leading to a subtle difference in cultures and ethos for each teacher. Teachers often have preferred routines, that vary according to the class context – how the children enter or leave the classroom, how they draw their attention or deal with interruptions, or the way they keep learners on task. All of these vary with the teacher and the age and stage of the learners' development. Routines are multipurpose procedures that operationalise rules in practice. They rapidly become internalised classroom norms and lead to expected levels of behaviour and engagement.

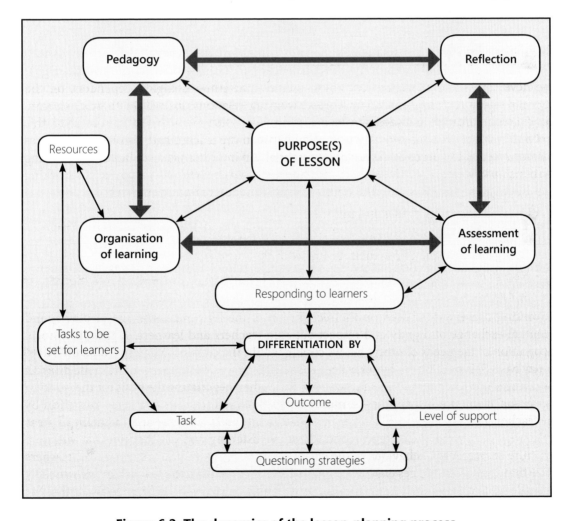

Figure 6.2: The dynamics of the lesson-planning process.

Teachers need to pay close attention to them in order to maintain them, which is why classroom routines are an important part of the negotiating process for the working consensus. As a positive classroom ethos develops, the good working relationship is in a state of flux because a key element of ethos is the sense of fairness and respect perceived by the learners and the teacher of each other. Learners feel vulnerable to the teacher's power and must be reassured that the he or she will interact reasonably with them. If the teacher acts without consideration for an existing rule, routine or tacit understanding that forms part of the working consensus, or performs actions the learners regard as unfair or outwith the working consensus, then the learners will tend to respond negatively.

Classrooms and the physical environment

The classroom and physical environment is a space for learning. Not just the bricks and mortar of the room itself, but the playground and wider community space. These environments must be structurally and physically secure for both learners and teachers. Tragic events at a few British schools clearly demonstrate how important it is for the learning environment to be structurally safe for all; the impact of failing to ensure this can have an enormous influence the pupils and the wider school community. The construction of the classroom environment can be examined in many different ways – their physical aspects, such as the dimensions, natural light sources and position of fixed resources. These have been the focus of studies into new school building projects throughout Europe, but some researchers believe it is hard to form conclusive views on the impact of classroom environments on teaching and learning because the process is multifaceted and so are classrooms (Higgins *et al.* 2005). Other aspects of the classroom environment are linked with the teacher's identity, pedagogy, beliefs and values, with a direct influence on the classroom culture and ethos. The classroom environment has been studied by many over the decades (Buckley *et al.* 2004; Duckin and Biddle 1974; Fraser 1984; Rosenshine and Furst 1973; Tanner 1999); Horne's (2004) suggestion was to 'tear down the school walls' and allow pupils to learn in various locations and environments without boundaries.

Classrooms with identical dimensions within a single school may have a vastly different physical appearances. Some of these depend on the age and stage of pupils being taught, but most relate directly to the way in which the class teacher organises the room and the resources, and how accessible the resources are to pupils, as well as the rules and routines they set. Class teachers take other issues into account when developing the classroom environment, such as the impact that busy classroom displays have on certain pupils, or there may be external influences such as open-plan schools. Open-plan classrooms have been around for over 60 years with research showing that they became fashionable during the progressive school movement in the 1950s and '60s. These are schools where normal classroom walls do not exist, McDonald (1997) uses the analogy of a 747 airplane to describe such a learning environment as being 'akin to positioning a newly-designed open cockpit of a 747 jet in the passenger compartment surrounded by 250 exuberant, noisy customers and ordering the pilot to fly the plane with patience, empathy and skill.' The personal and professional identity of the teacher is often on display within the classroom – from the ways in which they organise resources, manage pupil behaviour and movement about the classroom to the way in which they organise their teaching space and personal resources. Darmody and Smyth (2011) report on a link between school

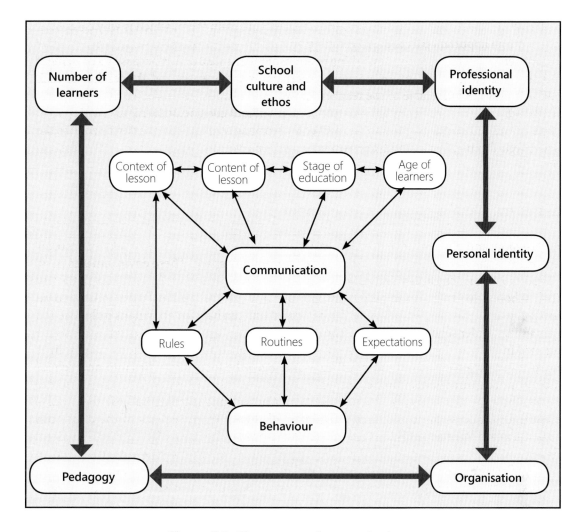

Figure 6.3: Classroom culture and ethos.

environment and pupil achievement. Teachers should be aware of such research and ensure that that the environment they can control is appropriate to the needs of everyone – staff and pupils.

The school and wider community

The wider community also influences the classroom dynamic. Many of the areas within the influence map in FIGURE 6.4 have already been discussed in depth within this chapter, or elsewhere in this book, therefore here we will focus on the impact of the local area on the school and school leadership. The wider community can impact in many ways on schools in the area, that there is evidence of a link between school improvement and community 'capacity building' and organising (Mediratta *et al.* 2008). Capacity building involves enhancing skills, competencies and abilities at an individual or organisational level to overcome obstacles and achieve measurable, sustainable outcomes.

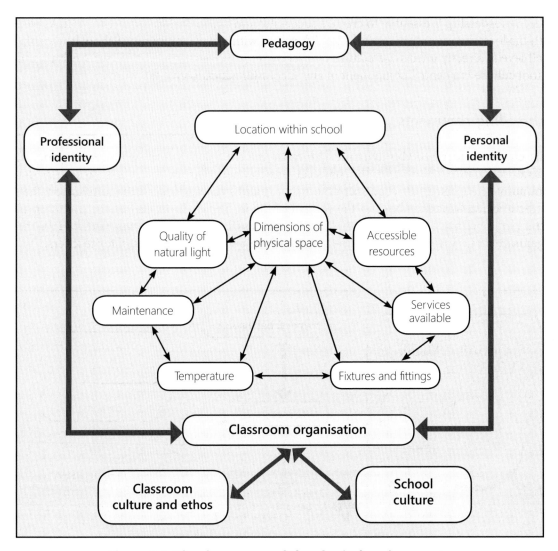

Figure 6.4: The classroom and the physical environment.

The geographical position of schools in relation to the local community and the availability of transportation links mean that schools are not immune to existing and historical issues based on socioeconomic factors and the demographic profile of the local population. For example, if a major employer within the community moves elsewhere, the loss of local employment has a detrimental effect on the community, which ripples into the confines of the school. Falling school rolls are a direct consequence of the age range of the local population and may lead to closure of the school or a merger with another school, according to the politics of the local authority and the proximity of other schools. A sudden influx of families into a community may mean a school building is no longer fit for purpose, so that new buildings or schools are needed to accommodate the increased demand.

Howley *et al.* (2000) suggests that in communities with lower socioeconomic ratings, schools should be smaller because this helps minimise the effect that background has on student achievement and attainment. As for perception of the school by the community, strong and effective leadership is essential to create a successful and dynamic establishment that links well with the local community and is held in high regard within that community. School leadership, at all levels, directly affects the culture of a school (see CHAPTER 16 on culture and health), and school culture is a central component of any successful educational establishment.

Concluding comments

This chapter addressed the dynamic nature of teacher identity and the learning process, classroom culture, ethos and the physical environment within it, as well as the wider community. The complex dynamics of the teaching and learning process are multifaceted; they can be affected by factors beyond the control of the teacher. Sometimes teachers can control factors in the classroom that affect the learning process, but many of the factors that make the organisation and management of the learning process are ultimately stressful for teachers.

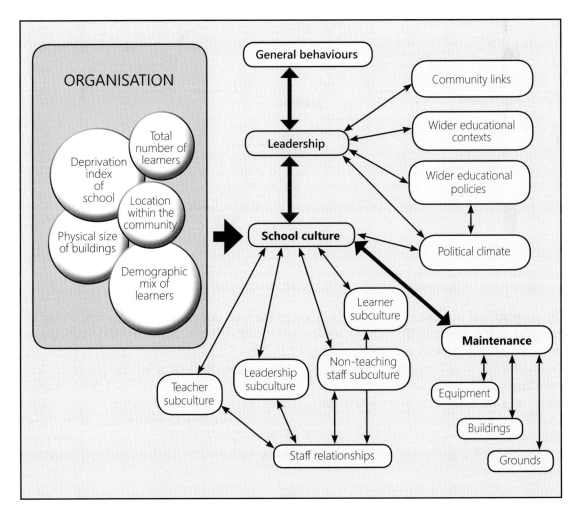

Figure 6.5: The dynamic of the school and the wider community.

KEY MESSAGES FROM THIS CHAPTER

- The teaching and learning process is complex and dynamic and can place a high level of psychological stress on all those involved in classroom interactions.

- Personal identity and life experiences significantly influence professional identity and experiences of leaders of learning.

- Personal and professional identity play a significant role in how learning is structured and enacted within the classroom, as well as influencing the classroom ethos.

- Many factors affecting the classroom dynamic are within the teacher's control, but some are beyond their power to influence.

- The willingness of learners to be cooperative with a teacher in the negotiation of a working consensus in the classroom is a major factor for developing a positive classroom culture for all involved in the learning and teaching process.

- The wider community exerts an additional influence on the culture of a school, and the way in which they interact in a mutually supportive role that benefit the learners.

Supporting evidence and further reading

Acker S (1999) *The Realities of Teachers' Work: Never a Dull Moment*. London: Cassell.

Alsup J (2006) *Teacher Identity Discourses: Negotiating Personal and Professional Spaces*. Mahwah, NJ: Lawrence Erlbaum.

Beauchamp C, Thomas L (2009) Understanding teacher identity: an overview of issues in the literature for teacher education. *Cambridge Journal of Education* 39(2), 189.

Buckley J Schneider M, Shang Y (2004) *LAUSD School Facilities and Academic Performance*. Washington, DC: National Clearinghouse for Educational Facilities.

Clark CM, Dunn S (1991) Second-generation research on teachers'' planning, intentions and routines. In: HC Warren, HJ Walberg (eds) *Effective Teaching: Current Research*. Berkeley, CA: McCatchum.

Conway, PF (2001) Anticipatory reflection while learning to teach: From a temporally truncated to temporally distributed model of reflection in teacher education. *Teaching and Teacher Education* 17(1), 89–106.

Darmody M, Smyth E (2011) *Job Satisfaction and Occupational Stress among Primary Schoolteachers and Principals*. Dublin: ESRI/TC.

Day C (2004) *A Passion for Teaching*. London: Routledge Falmer.

Dunkin M, Biddle B (1974) *The Study of Teaching*. New York: Holt, Rinehart &Winston.

Fraser BJ (1984) Differences between preferred and actual classroom environment as perceived by primary students and teachers. *British Journal of Educational Psychology* 54, 336–39.

Goodson IF, Hargreaves A (eds) (1996) *Teachers' Professional Lives*. London: Falmer Press.

Hargreaves A (1994) *Changing Teachers, Changing Times*. London: Cassell.

Hargreaves DH (1972) *Interpersonal Relationships and Education*. London: Routledge.

Higgins S Hall E Wall K Woolner P, McCaughey C (2005) *The impact of school environments: A literature review*. Available at: www.cfbt.com/PDF/91085.pdf (accessed July 2015).

Horne M (2004) Breaking down the school walls. *Forum* 46(1), 6.

Howley C, Strange M, Bickel R (2000) *Research about school size and school performance in impoverished communities*. EDO-RC-00–10. ERIC Clearinghouse on Rural Education and Small Schools.

John D (2006) Lesson planning and the student teacher: re-thinking the dominant model. *Journal of Curriculum Studies* 38, 483–98.

Kelchtermans G (1993) Getting the story: understanding its moral and political roots. *Cambridge Journal of Education* 26(3), 307–24.

Kelchtermans G, Vandenberghe R (1994) Teachers' professional development: a biographical perspective. *Journal of Curriculum Studies* 26(1), 62.

McDonald J (1997) *Lurching from Fad to Fad: The Open Plan Schools Were But One Costly Craze in a Long List*. Ontario: Organization for Quality Education.

Mediratta K, Seema S, McAlister S (2008) *Organized Communities, Stronger Schools*. Providence, RI: Annenberg Institute, Brown University.

Olsen B (2008) *Teaching What They Learn. Learning What They Live*. Boulder, CO: Paradigm.

Panasuk RM, Todd J (2005) Effectiveness of lesson planning: factor analysis. *Journal of Instructional Psychology* 32(3), 215–32.

Rosenshine B, Furst N (1973) The use of direct observations to study teaching. In: RMW Travers (ed.) *Second Handbook of Research on Teaching*. Chicago: Rand McNally.

Schon D (1983) *The Reflective Practitioner*. New York: NY: Basic Books.

Sfard A, Prusak A (2005) Telling identities: in search of an analytic tool for investigating learning as a culturally shaped activity. *Educational Researcher* 34(4), 22.

Sleegers and Kelchtermans G (1999) Inleiding op het themanummer: professionele identiteit van leraren **(**Professional identity of teachers**)**. *Pedagogisch Tijdschrift* 24, 374.

Tanner CK (1999) *The School Design Assessment Scale*. Baltimore: Council of Educational Facility Planners International.

CHAPTER 7

The education system
as a complex adaptive system

Stephen P. Day and Lynne Grant-McMahon

A body of research that embraces complexity has emerged over the last thirty years. Many of the studies examine how complex systems function, how they respond to internal and external influences and manage change. The application of complexity theory and 'systems thinking' to social systems, such as the education system, is receiving increased attention and research in the area is beginning to blossom. However, there is very little research that empirically tests and models how these systems behave in reality in response to structural, environmental and political change. This chapter summarises recent developments in the fields of complex adaptive systems theory and systems thinking,

The prevailing paradigm dominating academic thought (particularly within the sciences) over the last 300 years has been 'reductionism', but there has been a growing awareness (particularly within the scientific community) that the reductionist approach to research is limited in terms of the impact of advances in new knowledge on society. As a result, there has been a reaction against reductionism; it is appropriate for exploring and understanding largely 'simple' systems, but appears inappropriate for dealing with more complex systems. This growing awareness among the academic community has led to more holistic or systems approaches, as pioneered by Ludwig van Bertalanffy's in the 'general systems theory' (Bertalanffy 1968).

The study of complex systems such as education is multidisciplinary, focused on determining how these systems behave in complex, diverse and nonlinear ways. Studies examine the nature of interactions between interconnected components or agents and processes (within these systems) and change due to internal and external forces. Complex adaptive systems are comprised of many interacting components (agents or subsystems) with the capacity to self-organise, adapt and learn from different experiences over time. Most biological, social, economic and political systems are complex adaptive systems (Paina and Peters 2012), with interactions between components that are typically complex, nonlinear, and not easily controlled or predicted; they may also lead to unintended effects or paradoxical behaviours (Helbring *et al.* 2000).

This chapter discusses education as a social complex adaptive system, whereby the learning and teaching process lies at the heart of education, and primarily (but not exclusively) takes place within classrooms. The complex environments of classrooms are designed to stimulate and nurture the learning process through a network of rich interactions between learners and leaders of learning at physical, psychological and social levels. The chapter also outlines the underlying principles of systems theory and the components and characteristics of complex adaptive systems, with respect to education as a complex adaptive system in terms of its behaviour and nonlinear dynamics defined by its product or output. CHAPTER 6 on the dynamics of the classroom as a complex adaptive system will elaborate on these themes explored and apply them to the classroom to illustrate the dynamic interactions within the teaching and learning process.

What is systems theory?

Systems theory – and by extension systems thinking – relates to increasingly complex systems across a continuum that encompasses the person-in-environment (Anderson *et al.* 1999), and enhances understanding of the complex and dynamic interactions of the components of the system. The word 'system' is difficult to define precisely in this context, but von Bertalanffy (1901–1972) defined it as a complex of components in mutual interaction (Bertalanffy 1968), and saw systems theory as a holistic view of a system and its relations and interactions with other systems as a mechanism of growth and change. Central to system theory is the notion that a 'system' is an ensemble of interactive parts, the sum of which exhibits behaviour not localised in its constituents. In other words: the whole is more than the sum of the parts (Goodwin 1994). A system can be physical, biological, social or symbolic or a combination of these. Change relates to transformation of a system over time without altering the identity of the system as a whole (Chen and Stroup 1993). A system is actively organised in terms of goals, and exhibits goal-oriented behaviours that are seen in the character of change in the state of the system. Feedback mediates between the goal and behaviour of the system, where time is a key variable that provides a referent for the idea of dynamics. The boundary of a system delineates it from the environment and any subsystem from the system as a whole; such boundaries can be open, closed or semipermeable. System–environment interaction are defined as the input and output of information, matter or energy.

Systems thinking as an intellectual endeavour

Systems thinking emerged in the 1950s and led to the development of a wide range of theoretical positions and approaches to practice. Systems thinking can be conceptually difficult because it is an intellectual discipline that is not defined by the subjects or issues to which its ideas are applied; it is an intellectual approach to issues that apply to a wide range of human experience (although such application may not have universal appeal). Systems thinking can be useful for tackling issues that are embedded in complexity – particularly human activity. One way to illustrate systems thinking as an intellectual approach is to contrast it with the reductionist approach to tackling complexity. The success of reductionist thinking is remarkable, particularly for developing successful theories and models of the inanimate world when combined with scientific procedures. The key element to the reductionist approach – to deal with complexity by simplifying it – is achieved by dividing a problem into smaller and smaller subproblems, or lesser components, until they are simple enough to be analysed and understood. The operation of the original complex entity is then reconstructed from the operation of the components. However, this is a weakness of the approach if the essential characteristics of the complex entity being investigated are embedded in the interconnectedness of the components rather than being features of the components themselves, or if the complexity arises from the nature of the interaction between the components or the way they relate to one another. Thus simplifying by subdivision loses the interconnections and fails to truly account for or relate to the system holistically, rendering it incapable of resolving this aspect of a systems complexity.

Systems thinking, in contrast, deals with complexity by going increasing the level of abstraction, so losing detail, whereby the loss of detail provides the simplification. Discussions on the behaviour of organisations eliminates the rich details of how individual people or groups within the organisation function; the organisation is at a higher level of abstraction than the departments and individuals within it. Yet the interconnection of the components is maintained in the process of abstraction. A core systems idea is feedback – both positive (self-reinforcing) and negative (self-correcting) – whereby complexity often seems mysterious because of a series of feedback loops between components. By retaining the connections and avoiding the tendency to break things down, systems thinking provides a holistic approach to understanding and managing complexity.

Complex adaptive systems theory therefore provides a rich metaphor for discussing social complex adaptive systems. The essential aspect of the approach is that the social complex adaptive systems needs to be understood in terms that are quite different from normal linear, mechanical frameworks. Complex adaptive systems theory is essentially a theoretical framework that can be used to view real-world phenomena, and it provides a framework for understanding both natural and human-constructed environments.

TYPES OF SYSTEMS

Systems can be categorised into four main types – simple, complicated, complex and chaotic – based on the degree of complexity and the degree to which cause-and-effect relationships can be predicted (Kurtz and Snowden 2003). Simple, complicated and complex systems are usually founded on a set of connected components and a set of rules that more or less govern the behaviour of the system. A complex adaptive system is not merely a complicated system that changes over time. Complicated systems have greater predictability than complex ones. A car is a complicated system with many component parts that work together to produce the outcome of forward movement; changing the engine oil has no measurable effect on tyre pressure or the electrics or level of screen wash in the reservoir. But in a complex system, any change in one component can affect the balance of the whole system because of the interconnectedness of individual components, thus the system behaves in a nonlinear manner (responding to the change, or perhaps not). The ability to accurately predict cause and effect in a complex system is lower, and a complicated system has a fewer interconnected components. Complex adaptive systems can themselves be broadly categorised into three types (Axelrod and Cohen 2000; Holland 1996; Zimmerman, Lindberg, and Plsek 1998):

- Artificial (e.g. computer systems).
- Natural (e.g. the human immune system or an ecosystem).
- Social (e.g. the health or education system).

Our current understanding of complex adaptive systems is mainly derived from research into artificial and natural systems (Chapman 2004; Keshavarz, Nutbeam *et al.* 2010). However, the literature on complex adaptive systems theory has not always acknowledged the fundamental differences between artificial, natural and social systems, leading to oversimplification (in some cases confusion) and the over-enthusiastic use of the theory particularly in healthcare and other social systems (Rickles *et al.* 2007). Stacey (2000) and Strand *et al.* (2005) warn against the uncritical use of a complex adaptive systems construct derived from the study of artificial or natural systems for studying social systems. They emphasise the differences in the structural components of natural and social systems; behaviours in social systems and interactions in natural systems can be defined through rules in those systems when compared with those of the component parts of an artificial system such as a computer-modelling program. We recognise and accept these limitations, while acknowledging that complex adaptive systems theory is a well-regarded (if incomplete) construct for unifying the concept of complexity within various fields of research, but it is still only one of several theories of complexity (Chu *et al.* 2003). Wallis (2008) suggests there is a lack of consensus on the definition of CASs, but the characteristic structural components and defining properties of diverse CASs resemble a system with common features that help us understand them as a conceptual framework. The common features of complex adaptive systems are shown in FIGURE 7.1. Each is linked and interdependent, and each is seen as both a cause and an effect of the other properties (Axelrod and Cohen 2000; Casti 1997; Holland 1996; Zimmerman *et al.* 1998). These features are highly context specific and do not respond in a predictable way to the same stimulus at different times or under similar circumstances (Anderson 1999; Zimmerman *et al.* 1998). This is especially true for social systems (Holland 1998).

KEY FEATURES OF A COMPLEX ADAPTIVE SYSTEM (adapted from Keshavarz *et al.* 2010)

(i) Nested: Made up of diverse agents that are often considered to be CASs in their own right. Each system is a part of something bigger, thus, depending on the starting point, each system can be a subsystem for a bigger system, and a suprasystem for a smaller system. For example, a school is a system made up of diverse agents (teachers, technicians, pupils) nested in a network structure that includes larger systems (local education authority, local community); and a school is a also macrosystem within which agents are located in speciality disciplines or in specific departments as subsystems within.

(ii) Adaptive: Continuous and (perhaps) the only predictable phenomenon in CASs. Essential for system survival, but not always followed by positive results. There may be negative impacts on other components of the system due to its interconnectedness, leading to further change and adaptation in the system as a whole. Key drivers of adaption and change are interactions between agents, flow of information, effective feedback loops, attribution of credit and blame (reward and punishment), and time.

(iii) Distributed control: Distributed control gives speed to adaptation, unlike central control which is difficult, costly and intrusive because it slows down the system's capacity to react and adapt. Outcomes of CASs emerge from a process of self-organisation rather than by design or external control by a centralised body. Factors and resources contributing to decentralised control and self-organisation include individual autonomous action and rules. The ability to fully control CASs is limited by lack of central control, nonlinearity, its dynamic nature, and its unpredictability.

(iv) Emergence: At the scale of the system, the interplay between agents shape a hidden but recognisable regularity in the behaviour of the whole system. An example of this is consciousness; it is an emergent property of networks of neurons in the brain – no single neuron has consciousness. Most changes in complex systems are emergent.

(v) Unpredictability: It is difficult to predict the overall behaviour of complex adaptive systems by looking at the behaviour of a single element. There are strategies to assist in reducing uncertainty such as identifying recurring patterns, studying the whole system in its context, considering its history, and developing continuous feedback loops.

Keshavarz *et al.* (2010) suggest that complex adaptive systems comprise a population of diverse rules-based agents, located in multilevel and interconnected systems in a network shape. The systems are characterised by the behaviour of individual agents. In turn, components or agents in complex adaptive systems are often numerous, dynamic, autonomous, highly interactive, adaptive and capable of learning. These components or agents act in ways based on a combination of their knowledge, experience, and feedback from the environment, local values and formal system rules. These change over time, leading to continuously changing interactions and adaptations that are often novel and difficult to predict, especially in social systems. Components or agents within complex adaptive systems interact with and adapt to each other and the wider system within a network. The systems are open, with fuzzy boundaries, and they are highly context-dependent in terms of time, history and space, including location and proximity. They also have distributed control. As a result, complexity that is not necessarily a characteristic of individual components or agents emerges at system level.

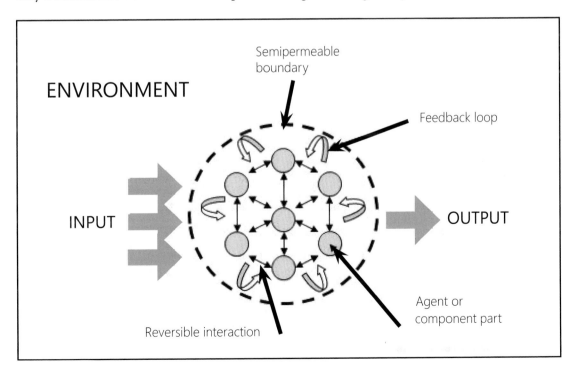

Figure 7.1: Diagram of a complex adaptive system (CAS).

How we understand the system depends on the way we construe and interpret the relationships and interactions between its components and agents, and the nature of these relationships with the entire system and its environment. Plsek (2003) suggests that behaviour in a complex adaptive system grows out of interactions between its components or agents and that they contain a network or group of related diverse agents that respond in a positive way to the environment. The components are independent but interconnected to other components. They may be a person, a class, or an organisation. The reactions of each component can have wide-ranging influence because of the many relationships within the system, and may have different or changing roles as the system itself evolves and interacts with its everchanging environment. The interconnections are important because they allow a diverse and adaptive system response; they make learning and co-evolution possible. A system does not evolve independently from its environment and the larger systems it exists within.

In a complex adaptive system, one single action does not cause a single expected result (as in a complicated mechanical system), but the effect can spread in unpredictable ways. This is nonlinearity, whereby one action can result in various actions – a small change can have an extensive effect and a large change can have a small effect. Complex adaptive systems are embedded within other complex adaptive systems. A schoolchild is a complex adaptive system, and is also an agent within the complex adaptive system of the classroom, which is an agent within the complex adaptive system of a department, which is an agent within the school, which is an agent within the local authority, which is an agent within the national education system. Each agent and system is nested within other systems, that all evolve and interact, thus a single entity cannot be understood without considering the others (for an example of this in the healthcare system, see Plsek and Greenhalgh 2001). The nested nature of complex adaptive systems is illustrated in FIGURE 7.2. Within a democratic society, systems such as education are managed by bureaucrats at the local authority level and by teachers at the school level, and all levels are accountable to the government who are ultimately accountable to the electorate. It could be argued that under the prevailing neo-liberal political culture that these systems are by definition hierarchical, because of the way in which they are managed and held accountable by those in political power.

Education as a complex adaptive system

The education system exhibits all the characteristics of a social complex adaptive system: it is complex, dynamic, adaptive and nested, has distributed control, and displays emergent properties and unpredictability (FIGURE 7.2). It is able to cope with adapting to external forces, as well as internal factors that exert influence on the system from the sociopolitical context (the environment) of the time, which in turn fluctuates over time. Establishments within a system experience frequent changes in agents. For example, teachers leave the profession through retirement, ill health and death, even disillusionment or stress burnout. The agents include teachers, heads of establishments and services, administrative staff and counsellors, as well as pupils, parents and families. Further, schools exhibit diversity in terms of their size, resources, and context. Change can be internally or externally introduced, and happens in almost all school functions over time. This dynamic character of the education system allows it to take advantage of the talent and capabilities of all agents within the system, and provides the system with the capacity to adapt – or more specifically to 'learn' – from experience. The education system has a nested and hierarchical character; all establishments within the system have observable subsystems (such as classes, departments, disciplines and year groups), but they also form part of 'suprasystems' (such as local community school clusters within the local authority) and parallel systems (such as families, community, friends and the media). Further, educational establishments have management structures through which there is a clear chain of command and control; they also have structures that are designed to hold the different areas of the system to account, even in establishments with a culture and ethos of devolved or distributed leadership.

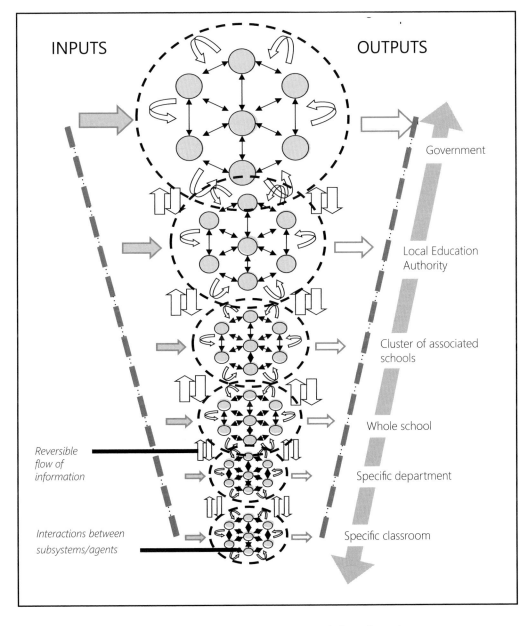

Figure 7.2: The nested hierarchical nature of the education system, showing the subsystem levels within.

All establishments within the system have well-organised systems that support the flow of information on educational issues, but not on health issues because this information is only shared on a need-to-know basis for reasons of confidentiality. Hence there is a limited flow of information about health-related information within establishments. However, all establishments within the system have processes for feedback, including both internal and external performance reporting, which is mostly about educational issues and performance. They also have policies, published rules and goals in the form of school improvement plans and so on. Most have reviewable curriculum structures that include health and personal development. Diverse interactions are observable within and between establishments within the system, as well as with families and the local community. Establishments within the system have freedom to act within a relatively fixed set of possibilities. Decision-making depends on the organisational 'culture', formal policies, expressed local community needs, available resources, and time. Provision of external interventions within the system does not always lead to predictable and intended changes. Establishments within the systems undergo changes in education sector policies and in agents (such as senior management, teachers and pupils) and respond to change in the wider community.

Concluding comments

The way in which education is organised and controlled takes slightly different forms depending on the political system of the host country. However, it is interesting that education systems – regardless of nationality – exhibit common characteristics that mark them out as complex adaptive systems. Namely, they are dynamic, nested, hierarchical and adaptive, exhibit distributed control, have emergent properties and are inherently unpredictable.

KEY MESSAGES FROM THIS CHAPTER

The control and management of education is difficult due to the complex dynamics of the system as a whole and its subsystems.

The complexity of the education system is culturally bound and is influenced by the political climate of its country and the extent to which neo-liberal accountability systems are incorporated into the management of the system as a whole.

Input into the system in the form of subject content, pedagogy, resources and student engagement (the stimulus) does not always guarantee successful learning (the response or output) because there are many variables that influence successful learning.

Hierarchically imposed structural changes to variables such as curriculum content and policy, assessment regimens and school structures invariably lead to unintended outcomes because of the complex interactions between and within different levels of the system.

Information flow between and within different levels of the system is influenced by the manner in which the information is presented, interpreted and implemented by different agents within the system, and this leads to further complexity, highlighting the nonlinear nature of the system.

 Different establishments (e.g. primary and secondary schools) within the system carry out different functions with different purposes at any one time. Further, similar establishments (e.g. secondary schools may engage with similar functions with very different approaches.

Supporting evidence and further reading

Anderson P (1999) Complexity and organisation science. *Organization Science* 10(3), 216–32.

Anderson RE, Carter I, Lowe GR (1999) *Human Behaviour in the Social Environment* (5th edn). New York: Aldine de Gruyter.

Axelrod R, Cohen MD (2000) *Harnessing Complexity: Organisational Implications of a Scientific Frontier*. New York: Free Press.

Bertalanffy LV (1968) *General Systems Theory: Foundations Developments and Applications*. New York: George Braziller.

Casti JL (1997) *Would-be Worlds: How Simulation is Changing the Frontiers of Science*. New York: John Wiley.

Chapman J (2004) System Failure: *Why Governments Must Learn to Think Differently* (2nd edn). London: Demos. Available at: www.demos.co.uk/files/systemfailure2.pdf (accessed July 2015).

Chen D and Stroup W (1993) General system theory: toward a conceptual framework for science and technology education for all. *Journal of Science Education and Technology* 2(3), 447–59.

Chu D, Strand R, Fjelland R (2003) Theories of complexity. *Complexity* 8, (19–30).

Goodwin B (1994) *How the Leopard Changed its Spots*. London: Weidenfeld & Nicolson.

Helbring D, Farkas I, Vicsek T (2000) Stimulating dynamical features of escape panic. *Nature* 407, 487–90.

Holland JH (1992) *Adaptation in Natural and Artificial Systems: An Introductory Analysis with Applications to Biology Control and Artificial Intelligence*. Cambridge, MA: MIT Press.

Holland JH (1996) *Hidden Order: How Adaptation Builds Complexity*. Reading, MA: Addison Wesley.

Holland JH (1998) *Emergence: From Chaos to Order*. Reading, MA: Perseus Books.

Keshavarz N, Nutbeam D, Rowling L, Khavarpour F (2010) Schools as social complex adaptive systems: A new way to understand the challenges of introducing the health promoting schools concept. *Social Science and Medicine* 70, 1467–74.

Kurtz CF, Snowden DJ (2003) The new dynamics of strategy: sense-making in a complex-complicated world. *IBM System Journal* 42(3), 462–83.

Paina L, Peters DH (2012) Understanding pathways for scaling up health services through the lens of complex adaptive systems. *Health Policy and Planning* 27, 365–73.

Plsek PE (2003) *Complexity and the adoption of innovation in healthcare. Accelerating quality improvement in health care – Strategies to speed the diffusion of evidence-based innovations*. Presented at the National Institute for Health Care Management Foundation and National Committee for Quality Health Care Conference Washington, DC, 27–28 January 2003.

Plsek PE, Greenhalgh T (2001) Complexity science: The challenge of complexity in health care. *British Medical Journal* 323, 625–28.

Rickles D, Hawe P, Shiell A (2007) A simple guide to chaos and complexity. *Journal of Epidemiology and Community Health* 61, 933–37.

Stacey RD (2000) *Strategic Management and Organisational Dynamics*. Harlow: Financial Times/Prentice Hall.

Strand R, Rotveit G, Schei E (2005) Complex systems and human complexity in medicine. *ComPlexUs* 2, 2–6.

Wallis SE (2008) Emerging order in CAS theory: mapping some perspectives. *Keybernetes* 37(7), 1016–29.

Zimmerman B, Lindberg C, Plsek PE (1998) *Edgeware: Lessons from Complexity Science for Health Care Leaders*. Dallas, TX: VHA.

PART II
The well-being of learners

CHAPTER 8

UK Government guidance on mental health disorders in school-children

Bethany R. Hampshire

The UK government acknowledged that more can be done by British schools to 'enrich the whole child' and increase personal wellness, rather than focus on their academic standing (Hyland 2009). Guidance with a more therapeutic slant has been drawn up by the Department for Education, based on the input from multiple informed sources, to advise schools on teaching pupils about mental health, to banish the stigma attached to mental health problems, and to make sure young learners receive the support they need, when they need it. Their 'fresh focus' also involves Child and Adolescent Mental Health Services (CAMHS), offering real hope for sustained investment and commitment, and long-term solutions. This chapter summarises the content of the guidance entitled *Mental Health and Behaviour in Schools: Departmental Advice for School Staff** published in March 2015. It addresses positive mental health in schools, early identification of at-risk learners, and how to make referrals, commission services, and manage young people in the school system with problems.

The scope of the guidance

The Department for Education guidance is designed for members of school staff who have daily contact with the same group of students and are therefore in a position to observe behaviours or risk factors indicative of an underlying problem (e.g. withdrawn learners). Some of the disruptive behaviour taking place in classrooms may be related to children with unmet mental health needs, and staff in these roles can be advised on how to identify so-called 'trouble-makers'. The importance of an early response by staff is highlighted throughout, to acknowledge that problems exist and develop an intervention plan, thus preventing issues becoming serious or long-term problems, and improving outcomes for the child (Green *et al.* 2005). The information is augmented by a series of case studies that describe interventions used at classroom and whole-school levels, details about common conditions and cites evidence of effective treatments. The guidance is based on inputs from a broad range of official sources, including the National Institute for Health and Care Excellence (NICE) , Child and Adolescent Mental Health Services (CAMHS), the Department of Health's Children and Mental Health team, and NHS England. Original research is cited where relevant, together with other sources of support and advice that can be accessed by headteachers, class teachers, youth counsellors and supervisors (FIGURE 8.1).

---

* *Available online at www.gov.uk/government/uploads/system/uploads/attachment_data/file/416786/Mental_Health_and_Behaviour_-_Information_and_Tools_for_Schools_240515.pdf.*

FOR CHILDREN AND YOUNG PEOPLE	
Childline www.childline.org.uk	Support for anyone up to the age of 19
Relate www.relate.org.uk	Advice, counselling, workshops and mediation for all ages
Parents and Youth Info A–Z www.rcpsych.ac.uk/expertadvice/youthinfo.aspx	Tailored mental health information from the Royal College of Psychiatrists
The HideOut www.thehideout.org.uk	Support for abused children and young people
Women's Aid www.womensaid.org.uk	Support for abused children and young people
FOR PROFESSIONALS WHO WORK WITH CHILDREN AND YOUNG PEOPLE	
Anti-bullying Alliance www.anti-bullyingalliance.org.uk/send-resources/mental-health	Guidance on child mental health and bullying
Counselling in Schools www.gov.uk/government/publications/counselling-in-schools	Guidance on setting up and improving school counselling services
Counselling MindEd www.counsellingminded.com	Evidence-based training for schools, youth counsellors and supervisors
Counselling in schools: advice for school leaders and counsellors www.gov.uk/government/publications/counselling-in-schools	Non-statutory, evidence-based advice on school counselling services
School nursing public health services www.gov.uk/government/publications/school-nursing-public-health-services	Guidance on effective commissioning of school nursing services
Education Endowment Foundation www.educationendowmentfoundation.org.uk	Guidance on using resources especially for disadvantaged pupils
HeadMeds www.headmeds.org.uk	Information about prescription medications
MindEd www.minded.org.uk	Guidance and training for adults supporting children and young people
NICE (National Institute for Health and Clinical Excellence) www.nice.org.uk	Evidence-based guidance on social, emotional and mental health conditions
Place2Be www.place2be.org.uk	Early interventional support for anyone aged 4-14
Play Therapy UK www.playtherapy.org.uk	Support primary school staff to alleviate social, emotional, behaviour and mental health problems
PSHE Association www.pshe-association.org.uk	Guidance on teaching about mental health and emotional well-being
Education Endowment Foundation www.educationendowmentfoundation.org.uk/toolkit/	Summary of research on use of school resources to improve pupil attainment
Young Minds www.youngminds.org.uk	Resources for dealing with children and commissioning support services
Parents and Youth Info A–Z www.rcpsych.ac.uk/expertadvice/youthinfo.aspx	Tailored information from the Royal College of Psychiatrists

Figure 8.1: National sources of information and support for child mental health issues.

The guidance outlines what constitutes a state of mental well-being by reference to the Mental Health Foundation (2002). It states that young learners should be able to:

- Develop psychologically, emotionally, intellectually and spiritually.
- Experience solitude usefully and enjoy it.
- Enjoy mutually satisfying relationships.
- Deal with problems and learn from them.
- Be aware of other people and develop empathy.
- Have a sense of right and wrong.

The scale of the problem

According to the guidance, one in seven children aged 5–16 in the UK has a mental health problem that may worsen over time, and one in ten has a clinically diagnosed disorder. Kessler *et al.* (2007) report that half of all diagnosable mental illness begins in children aged 14 or less. The percentage spread of diagnoses of the most common disorders is shown in FIGURE 8.2 (Green *et al.* 2005), but note that these figures are likely to have changed given a recent survey of teachers who report unprecedented levels of anxiety, stress and mental health problems among school pupils (Association of Teachers and Lecturers 2015). According to Hutchings (2015), these figures are even higher around exam times, and all the more so in children and young people with pre-existing disadvantages, disabilities and special needs.

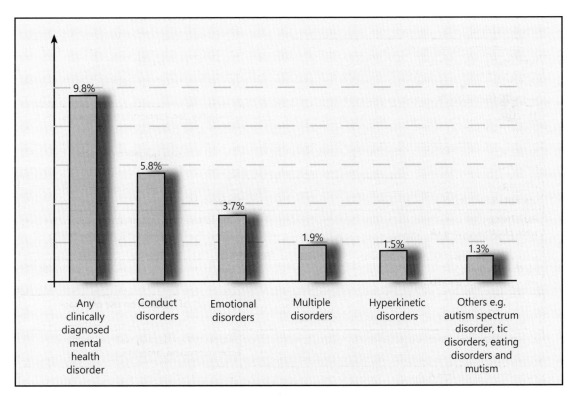

Figure 8.2: Mental health problems diagnosed in learners aged 5–16 in the UK (adapted from Green *et al.* 2005).

Risk factors and protective factors

The guidance discusses risk factors for poor mental health among young people, at individual, family and community levels, and emphasises the fact that they are cumulative – more risk factors mean greater problems (Brown *et al.* 2012). One study cited by the guidance found a nineteen-fold increase in the number of children with conduct disorder who had five or more risk factors (Murray 2010). However, there are also protective factors, and the more of these a person has, the more they can withstand the risk factors, helping them to remain mentally well when faced with challenges. This 'resilience' relates to a range of inner resources such as self-esteem, self-confidence, self-belief, self-efficacy and adaptability in addition to problem-solving skills (Rutter 1985), and results in a sense of connectedness and emotional intelligence (Catalano *et al.* 2003; Weare 2011). The role of schools in promoting resilience is firmly addressed by the guidance, particularly with respect to children and young people from unsupportive home environments. FIGURE 8.3 lists some of the risk factors affecting this age group as well as factors that afford protection.

DISRUPTION OF THE RESILIENT BALANCE

Unfortunately, the delicate balance between protective and risk factors can be disrupted by a single difficult event, such as the loss of a loved one, regardless of cause (e.g. through death, hospitalisation, being taken into care, deployment in the armed forces), or a significant life-change such as a birth in the family, moving house or a new school. Sudden trauma can also have a profound effect, whether it arises by accident or from abuse, violent crime, bullying, or a natural disaster.

Recommended practice in schools

A particular focus of the guidance is on supportive whole-school approaches, involving an effective pastoral system in which each learner is known by at least one member of staff who is in a position to spot any unusual behaviours or risk factors that arise.

SCHOOL-LEVEL RECOMMENDATIONS

The school premises should be a safe and trustworthy environment in which young learners have an overall sense of belonging and feel valued and supported. The whole-school approach suggested by Public Health England (April/May 2014) and previous Department for Education guidance (2011, 2013) involves safeguarding the health and well-being of all learners. School climate and culture were discussed in the last section, but the guidance cites the following desirable aims:

- Provide learners with clear policies about acceptable and unacceptable behaviours.
- Make sure good behaviour is rewarded and disruptive behaviour sanctioned (and attended to if it relates to an unmet health need).
- Encourage pupils to talk openly with staff and staff with parents, and encourage them to share information held by healthcare practitioners. All problems should be voiced and listened to in a non-stigmatising way.
- Provide effective support for learners at risk of developing mental health problems.

RISK FACTORS	PREVENTIVE FACTORS
INDIVIDUAL	**INDIVIDUAL**
Genetic influences	Genetic and congenital factors
Learning/communication disorder	Secure attachment as infant
Development delay	Outgoing temperament as infant
Temperament disorder	Positive personality traits
Physical illness	Sociable nature and sense of humour
Academic failure	Good communication problem-solving skills
Low self-esteem	Ability to plan and reflect
Loss of parents or friends	Success and achievement
Adopted or fostered	Spiritual nature
Bullied or discriminated against	Absence of severe discord
PARENTAL	**PARENTAL**
Overt conflict between parents	Positive factors
Hostile, abusive or rejecting	Supportive relationships
Unable to provide consistent discipline	Affectionate with clear, consistent discipline
Unable to adapt to changing needs	Supportive educationally
Psychiatrically ill	
Personality disorder	**SCHOOL**
Criminal behaviour	Strong sense of belonging and morale
Alcoholism	Positive peer group and classroom environment
	Fosters discussion of problems
SCHOOL	Clear policies on behaviour, attitudes and bullying
Peer pressure	Whole-school promotion of mental health
Deviant peer group	
Poor relationship with teacher	**COMMUNITY**
Discrimination	Good housing conditions
	Good standard of living
COMMUNITY	Sport and leisure facilities available
Low socioeconomic status	Supportive network
Poor housing conditions	Social roles valued

Figure 8.3: Common risk factors and preventive factors for mental health disorders in children and young people (adapted from Department for Education 2015).

- Build positive relationships with other schools in the area and share good practice

- Ensure all staff understand their responsibilities towards learners, and know how to identify problems, when to inform colleagues, and what referral and accountability systems are in place.

- Maintain awareness of and seek information from local NHS, health professionals, voluntary sector services and organisations that aim to improve mental well-being.

- Establish links with health services commissioned locally through the local Health and Wellbeing Board (Department of Health 2012; Local Government Association 2015).

- Maintain awareness of and seek information from relevant national organisations.

CLASSROOM-LEVEL RECOMMENDATIONS

School staff have a role in the lives of their pupils, even if it simply involves teaching their pupils that mental health is as important as physical health, and that they have the ability to foster positive mental health to better manage their own emotional lives, face social pressures and obstacles, and achieve their goals. The following list describes some practical approaches that can be used in the classroom setting.

- Use a positive classroom management approach.
- Maintain a well-ordered environment.
- Arrange seats in rows rather than groups.
- Use small group or one-to-one sessions to promote positive behaviour, social development and self-esteem.
- Use PSHE (personal, social, health and economic) sessions for discussing relevant issues or those suggested by the PSHE Association.

LEARNER-LEVEL RECOMMENDATIONS

The guidance is partly intended to help class teachers or classroom assistants to recognise changes in a child's behaviour or emerging risk factors. As well as listening to any concerns raised by parents or the learners themselves, the guidance bases its recommendations on those of the charity MindEd, which require paying attention to children who display:

- Consistently disruptive or withdrawn behaviours.
- Signs of self-harm, substance abuse or eating disorders.
- Unexplained physical symptoms or mood changes.
- Changed levels of attainment or attendance.

FIGURE 8.6 at the end of the chapter contains a list of common disorders encountered in the classroom, as recognised by the guidance, together with useful information on their relative occurrence, specific 'red flag' signs to look out, and what might be done for pupils in whom they are present. It is known that exam times are associated with greater levels of self-harm, suicide attempts, self-starvation, depression and diagnoses of ADHD in 14–16-year olds (Hutchings 2015; Meikle 2015). Recognising a problem is only part of the solution, however; clear referral and accountability systems should be in place at all schools, so that staff members are able to inform the relevant colleagues of their suspicions, and any undiagnosed learning difficulties or underlying health issues can be assessed promptly.

In-school assessments towards diagnosis

Accurate diagnosis depends on many factors and should involve a variety of methods and information sources from as many settings as possible. There may be specialist testing, interviews, observations and review of developmental and social and emotional status, but a clinical diagnoses can only be made by a professional healthcare practitioner – usually via a GP. This limits what can be done within the school, but the guidance cites some simple, evidence-based tools that can be used by school staff to assess pupils with suspected mental health issues. Two of them are described here.

STRENGTHS AND DIFFICULTIES QUESTIONNAIRE (SDQ)

This reliable test has similar efficacy to Rutter's Children's Behaviour Questionnaire (Goodman 1997; Rutter 1985) but it focuses more on strengths than weaknesses, and evidence continues to grow with respect to its effectiveness among children of different ages. It contains twenty-five questions that address emotionality, peer relationships, conduct, hyperactivity/ inattention and pro-social problems (Goodman *et al.* 2010). It can be downloaded free of charge from *www.sdqinfo.com* and it is available in eighty languages.

Different versions are available for different age groups, so it can be completed by the parents or teachers of children as young as 2, or self-completed by those over the age of 11. There are also versions that contain additional information for clinicians to assess young people with chronic problems, distress or social impairment (Goodman, 1999) and to follow-up the effect of any intervention.

COMMON ASSESSMENT FRAMEWORK (CAF)

This instrument was introduced in the Green Paper entitled *Every Child Matters* and is freely available from www.education.gov.uk via the reference for *Working Together to Safeguard Children* (Department for Education 2004, 2010). It is designed to assess the health, development, welfare and behaviour and learning progress of learners, as well their family environment, providing standardised information that can be shared by support services to help coordinate planning and care of the child and facilitate early intervention. It is part of a four-step assessment for the Common Assessment Framework (CAF), as shown in FIGURE 8.4, and comprises a consent statement for voluntary assessment, a pre-assessment checklist, a standard form for recording assessments, and a delivery plan and review form.

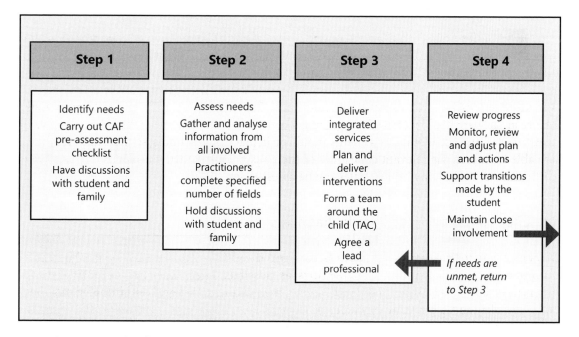

Figure 8.4: The four-step process for the Common Assessment Framework (CAF).

Examples of successful strategies cited in the guidance

In-school health and emotional well-being services (e.g. in collaboration with local CAMHS) involving regular group meetings with students during term-time.

Counselling services for students at risk of becoming NEET (Not in Education, Employment, or Training).

Trained pastoral staff support before, during and after involvement with CAMHS, for students who are not making sufficient progress or whose behaviours have recognised triggers, achieved through collaboration with other local schools.

Ventures such as The White Horse Federation and the Multi-Academy Trust for supporting vulnerable families and learners with challenging behaviours, in collaboration with other local schools and children's centres.

Peer-support schemes.

Anonymous 'bullying' or 'praise' boxes.

Relaxation and mindfulness programmes (e.g. 'thought for the day' and 'circle time') for raising worries and concerns.

Lunchtime 'nurture clubs'.

Cross-curricular 'well-being days' for raising awareness of mental health.

PSHE classes to raise health issues and promote self-esteem, independence and personal responsibility, healthy relationships, healthy work–life balance and stress management and topics like rape and self-harm.

'Concern sheets' for individual children to identify and monitor problems, that are available to all staff and can be updated as they move up the school.

Behaviour policies based on Friendship, Respect, Excellence and Equality (FREE), with sessions on friendship, conflict resolution, anger management and family break-up.

Safe places or rooms for use by vulnerable children to get ready for the school day or visit during the day if upset, angry or overwhelmed, to calm down or explore issues about their behaviour with a trained supporter.

School-based support

The kind of support provided within schools includes special educational needs (SEN) provision, counselling, peer mentoring and parental involvement (Department for Education 2015). These are all valid and recommended options for dealing with emerging or diagnosed problems. While stigmatisation remains a significant issue, it is clear that many young learners benefit overall when their particular learning difficulty, disability or disorder is acknowledged, especially when they find it much more difficult to learn than children of the same age, or are unable to use educational facilities used by others of the same age. The school will contribute to the care plan for children with a diagnosis, but a wide range of professionals may also be involved. The box above summarises some tried and tested strategies used by schools around the UK, which are cited in the current guidance. They are testament to the commitment and creativity of the headteachers and staff involved.

SPECIAL EDUCATIONAL NEEDS PROVISION

The SEN Code of Practice gives information on teaching approach, support at schools and specialist staff and services (Department for Education 2014a). SENCos (special educational needs coordinators, or inclusion coordinators) are named members of the school staff who have responsibility for learners with special needs. They should be supported by the headteacher and other colleagues. Their role is to arrange assessment of pupils' needs and coordinate additional support, liaising with their parents, teachers and healthcare professionals to draw up a treatment plan; they may be included in the team around the child (TAC), attending planning and review meetings as required, and be responsible for requesting external service involvement. Much of the work of SENCos revolves around students with Down syndrome, autism-spectrum disorders (ASD) and fetal alcohol spectrum disorders (FASD), attentional problems, cerebral palsy, and acquired brain injury, to help them in the classroom setting because of learning disabilities. The SENCo seeks effective ways to overcome barriers to learning so that the child receives effective teaching, and may collaborate with curriculum coordinators in the school and set targets for improvement. Many children with learning disabilities see, hear and process information differently, resulting in difficulties (not related to intelligence) in one or more academic areas such as reading, mathematics, physical activity and communication. Some of the common learning disorders are listed in FIGURE 8.5.

Learning disorder	Difficulty experienced	Skills affected
Aphasia/ dysphasia	Difficulty understanding or producing spoken language	Fluency of speech, receiving directions, or telling/retelling a story
Auditory processing disorder	Difficulty distinguishing between subtle differences in sounds or may hear sounds at the wrong speed	Reading, writing and spelling
Dyscalculia	Difficulty sequencing or organizing numbers, memorizing signs and number 'facts', counting principles and telling time	Mathematical skills
Dysgraphia	Difficulty forming words and letters, organising thoughts on paper and expressive writing, spelling, comprehension and synthesis of information	Written and spoken communication
Dyslexia	Difficulty understanding the relationship between sounds, letters and words, recognising letter and word forms, grasping the meaning of words, phrases, paragraphs	Reading
Dyspraxia	Difficulty with sensory integration, fine and gross motor coordination, manual dexterity, balance and hand–eye coordination	Physical activities, sports, dressing, writing, handling and cutting
Visual processing disorder	Difficulty with depth perception, interpreting visual information, recognising different shapes and printed information	Reading, writing, maths, motor skills, comprehension of visual materials

Figure 8.5: Typical learning disorders encountered in the learning environment.

COUNSELLING SERVICES

The guidance cites the effectiveness of specific psychological therapies for young people and how they improve engagement of learners with studying (Cooper 2013; Department for Education 2015). In the UK, around 80,000 children per year undergo counselling with school-based counsellors (Cooper 2013; Hanley 2012). Counselling is aimed at children with wide-ranging issues, from those experiencing grief, abuse or psychotic symptoms, to those who are self-harming or harbouring suicidal thoughts; from those with eating disorders, underlying depression or misuse of alcohol and drugs to those with hyperkinetic, developmental or autism-spectrum disorders (Cooper 2013). Counselling sessions usually last for up to an hour and offer an opportunity to talk in confidentiality. They are usually carried out on a one-to-one basis, but may involve small groups, and often rely on talking therapy or play therapy; the latter is especially valuable for children younger than 12 who do not readily discuss difficult issues. The approach is usually relational, focused on developing a supportive, trustworthy relationship, and collaborating to find ways to address problems and improve mental health and wellbeing (Hill 2011). Person-centred counsellors allow space for the client to find their own way forward; those who take a more integrative therapeutic stance challenge the client or ask questions, and use solution-focused therapies such as psychodynamic and cognitive–behavioural therapy (Hill 2011). Good collaboration with CAMHS is desirable, because of the capacity to make referrals in both directions (Cooper 2013).

The guidance emphasises the role of the school in identifying good counselling services; to this end, it points to valuable sources of information such as the British Association of Counselling and Psychotherapists (BACP) and Counselling MindEd. While a teacher, chaplain or school nurse may undertake the role, schools typically employ one or two external counsellors, usually on a sessional basis for one or two days a week. They may be funded through the school budget, the local authority, an external agency or on teachers' conditions (Hanley 2012). Pupils may wait between one week and one month to be seen, but there is usually no limit to the number of sessions they can attend. Parental consent is not always necessary, which is useful because not all children wish their parents to know, and parents of at-risk children can be hard to engage by staff (Hanley 2012).

PEER MENTORING

Peer support initiatives in various forms have become increasingly popular among primary and secondary schools over the last 20 years, mostly as anti-bullying strategies and for easing transition from primary to secondary school (and increasingly from secondary to higher education) (Gulati and King 2009; Houlston *et al.* 2009; Nelson 2003). Peer mentoring involves training older learners, either within the school or from an external centre (usually college or university), to provide support to younger learners in groups or one-to-one. Schemes vary considerably, from simple befriending or buddying to provision of a wide range of tailored activities for both soft and hard skills, or even aimed at narrowing the attainment–achievement gap.

In all cases, the mentors represent a role model while providing informal support, reassurance and advice. Involving peers in mentoring schemes has greater impact than using adults as mentors (Frankham 1998; Mentoring and Befriending Programme 2010), not least because mentees hear positive messages from other students (rather than parents and teachers) to whom they can relate because of their generational closeness, similarity of experiences and culturally relevant wisdom. It has been shown that the mentors benefit too, in terms of personal development and social and interpersonal skills (ChildLine 2005). All mentoring schemes build on the child's inner resources to enhance their resilience and minimise the impact of psychosocial risk factors. The body of evidence – both qualitative and quantitative – continues to grow on the impact that mentoring has on pupils and schools as a whole (for example, Catalano *et al.* 2003; Powell 1997; Weare 2011). The areas in which peer-mentoring schemes have a positive impact are diverse.

Direct pupil improvements:

- Coping skills, adaptability and emotional intelligence.
- Motivation and outlook.
- Self-esteem, self-belief, self-confidence and self-efficacy.
- Social skills, team working, citizenship skills and attitudes toward school.
- Study and organisational skills, independent learning, and problem-solving ability.
- Life aspirations and academic achievement.
- Overall well-being.

School-level improvements:

- Non-attendance, truancy and drop-out rates.
- Pupil violence, incidents of concern and exclusions.
- School climate and relations between staff and pupils.
- Bullying and cyber-bullying.
- Exam results.

In its guidance, the Department for Education acknowledges that mentoring is an effective, inexpensive and sustainable strategy for use in schools that adds an extra level to a school's pastoral support. Furthermore, the active involvement of young people as mentors aligns well with current policy initiatives and the Big Society focus on 'active citizenship'.

PARENTAL INVOLVEMENT

Engaging parents in a child's school career is essential for keeping them on track and for addressing problems before they become serious. Class teachers are the first point of contact for parents when problems arise; this works best when a positive and proactive relationship exists between teacher and parents, and the best clinical improvements are seen when input from a teacher is reinforced by parents.

However, the parents of at-risk children can be difficult to engage with. Most schools provide other opportunities for parental engagement. In primary schools there may be nurture groups, play-based sessions and self-instruction programmes; the guidance cites the *Incredible Years Program*, *Family Skill Force* and the *Triple P Positive Parenting Program*. Secondary schools generally hold family induction days for new intakes, and some have clearly signposted open-door policies or parent advisors, or offer tailored courses for dealing with high-risk children. Some schools connect parents who have concerns with appropriate school personnel, such as heads of year, nurses and counsellors, or to external services such as the police or social workers.

Parental involvement is known to be of great benefit to young children with mild behavioural problems (Brosnan and Carr 2000). The parents can contribute by smoothing the child's routines outside the school day, ignoring certain negative behaviours, and employing reward and goal-setting systems. For children with chronic conditions, the treatment plan should ideally be drawn up in consultation with their family. The support services also work with parents, guiding them to manage their child's behaviour and improve their engagement with learning. Unfortunately older students do not always give consent for family involvement.

Making referrals and commissioning support services

The guidance recommends that every school should have a clear process for making referrals for social, mental and emotional problems. Learners with difficulties or behaviours that are immediately apparent or particularly disruptive, and those who are withdrawn or anxious should be referred. NICE (2013) advises referral for specialist CAMHS input for children assessed by the SDQ test for suspected depression, post-traumatic stress disorder, hyper-kinetic disorders, autism-spectrum disorder and substance misuse. Staff who notice any concerning signs should be able to speak to the school psychologist or other designated support staff, as well as the child's parents. Advice is available from Clinical Commissioning Groups (CCGs), local authorities and local voluntary and community sector (VCS) services.

Schools may also contact the Health and Wellbeing Board, access counselling or pastoral support, or engage the services of an educational psychologist either through the local authority or directly. The school is responsible for ensuring that the support organisation is accredited and that their interventions have been shown to improve outcomes for children. *Learning from Best Practice Review* is cited as a source of information on the role of lead commissioners, on transparency of offers from service providers, referral criteria, and working with CAMHS (Rees and Anderson 2012).

Interventions for learners with diagnosed disorders

As is clear from the section on school-based interventions, there are many options for accessing mental health specialists within the school or outside. For chronic or severe problems, several weekly sessions of targeted multisystemic, multi-agency therapy, involving at least one specialist clinician, are recommended in order to engage with several social systems of the child or young person, including their home and school. Input from the teacher is crucial, but it is best when reinforced by parental input.

For children with complex problems, teachers should be helped to manage their behaviour in the classroom, and receive specialist training if required. Some children are prescribed medication; for those that are, all school staff should be informed. There is no legal duty for the staff to administer medicines, but those that do must be trained to do so. The value of a making a 'safe haven' in the school cannot be overemphasised. This is a physical space within the school building where students can feel totally safe, whether it is a dedicated room or a corner of one, perhaps the library or school counsellor's room, and vulnerable children can seek refuge during the school day.

Additional in-school interventions for children with more complex problems include the following:

- Providing family support and family therapy.
- Guiding the class teacher in managing the pupil's behaviour in the context of the whole class.
- Arranging additional one-to-one therapeutic work with a mental health specialist.
- Providing additional one-to-one support to help the pupil cope better in the classroom.

Mental health disorders encountered in educational settings

One of the effects of this guidance is to make school staff more confident in identifying at-risk pupils or those with overt mental health issues. This underpins their role in helping to prevent deterioration and instigate intervention at a timely point. To be effective, staff must have increased mental health literacy (Whitley *et al.* 2013). Annex C of the guidance outlines some of the common problems seen in schools and colleges, which are summarised in FIGURE 8.6. For each disorder there is a list of the signs that may be apparent during the school day, together with the types of interventions for which there is some evidence of efficacy (Department for Children Schools and Families 2008; Murphy and Fonagy 2012, 2013).

The classification system used in FIGURE 8.1 is directly based on information in the guidance document, and is particularly useful for framing specific disorders within a wider context and providing a degree of insight into their root causes.

Concluding comments

The current government guidance offers a glimmer of hope towards improving mental and emotional well-being in British schools. It points concerned school staff to valuable tools and resources, such as pupil assessment questionnaires, teacher training toolkits and health fact sheets and may go some way to offsetting the findings of the Association of Teachers and Lecturers (ATL), whereby teachers in the UK report seeing more anxiety, depression, ADHD, hyperactivity, eating disorders, substance misuse and self-harm among pupils in recent years (Association of Teachers and Lecturers, 2015). Many of these teachers also report that they feel inadequately trained to confidently spot signs of mental illness among the children in their care. Some also express how difficult it is to gain access to services, and that their schools do not channel sufficient resources into the problem.

The initiatives described in the guidance all serve to raise awareness of the issues surrounding mental illness, with the aim of identifying potential issues rather than labelling such children as 'trouble-makers', instigating effective therapies and combating stigma. The guidance also says:

Systematic reviews of work [on activities that bolster mental health] show that the best of interventions, when well implemented, are effective in both promoting positive mental health for all, and targeting those with problems.

Figure 8.6: Key features of common disorders in school-children in the UK.

DISORDER	MAIN FEATURES	WHAT TO LOOK OUT FOR
ANXIETY DISORDERS *Covered in Mental Health and Behaviour in Schools (DfE 2015)*	Extreme or persistent feelings of worry and fear that affect the ability to develop, learn and carry out normal activities. Cause stress, emotional disorders, relationship problems and family conflict. Subtypes include: • *Generalised anxiety disorder (GAD):* excessive anxiety, fear and worry in many different situations. • **Separation anxiety disorder (SAD):** extreme distress when separated from primary caregiver; affects 2% of children; lasts for months; may lead to school refusal. • **Obsessive–compulsive disorder (OCD):** persistent intrusive thoughts linked to specific behaviours and actions that serve to reduce the anxiety caused by the thought (often relating to dirt or germs). • **Panic disorder (panic attacks):** regular occurrences of intense psychological symptoms (overwhelming fear and physical symptoms (nausea, sweating, trembling, palpitations); occur for no apparent reason; may be due to underlying physical illness. • **Phobias:** extreme, irrational fear of specific factor (place, object, situation, feeling, animal, school); may lead to school refusal.	Signs of unusual or unexpected fear or distress, such as breathlessness, trembling, fidgeting Irritability and tearfulness Inability to make or sustain friendships Repeated concerns that something bad is going to happen, or about dirt, mess or germs Frequent complaints about school Frequent requests to go to the nurse's office (e.g. with headache, stomach ache, sore throat), or to call (or go) home, and absences that coincide with specific events Presence of caregivers more often or for longer than normal
ATTACHMENT DISORDERS *Covered in Mental Health and Behaviour in Schools (DfE 2015)* See also *Chapter 9*	Rare behavioural, mood and social functioning, usually due to inconsistent or lack of care in early childhood (especially in first two years), e.g. neglect, abuse, frequent relocation, carer separation through death, illness, military deployment, adoption, illness or pain that cannot be alleviated by caregiver and neurological conditions that inhibit their perception of care. Some do not have the skills to 'act their age'. Most act from a 'place of fear' and believe they are worthless and unlovable (as reinforced when they drive people away with behaviours that evoke a range of emotions). They need to feel in total control to survive to avoid debilitating anxiety. Subtypes are: • **Reactive attachment disorder of childhood (RAD):** Persistent, pervasive patterns of behaviour such as social withdrawal and abnormal attachment behaviour. • **Disinhibited attachment disorder of childhood (DAD):** Persistent, pervasive patterns of behaviour with indiscriminate giving of affection, overfamiliarity with unfamiliar adults.	Odd behaviour when separated and reunited with caregiver (e.g. unusual levels of distress or indifference) Poor peer interaction and understanding of social boundaries Inappropriately demanding, 'clingy', attention-seeking; over-affectionate or over-familiar with adults; or difficulty showing or receiving affection, do not seek help from others as expected, irresponsive or averse to comfort, lack of trust in others Controlling behaviour, disobedience, defiant attitude; tells lies; 'tricks' people; may steal food Emotional disturbances, poor impulse control and anger management' hyper-vigilant; aggressive towards self/others Little interest in playing with peers or joining social games; acting younger than their age; poor work effort and a 'Why even try?' attitude
AUTISM SPECTRUM DISORDER (ASD) See also *Chapter 12*	Umbrella term for a range of neurodevelopmental! disorders. Affects more boys than girls. Characteristics include restricted, ritualistic and repetitive interests, activities and behaviours, with intense interests in a particular subject, toy or device. They react differently to sight, sound, smell, touch, taste (thus background sounds may be unbearably loud or distracting, and tend to play and behave ritualistically or repetitively. They desire routine and predictability.	May have several learning disabilities and delayed speech development Repetitive self-stimulatory behaviours (hand flapping, rocking, pinching, spinning, or putting inedible items in their mouth) Avoiding eye contact Concrete thinking, with only literal understanding of speech and difficulty understanding figurative language or sarcasm

CAMHS = Child and Adolescent Mental Health Services; IPE = individualised education plans; PSHE = personal, social, health and economic.

WHAT TO TRY IN THE CLASSROOM	SPECIALIST INTERVENTIONS
Provide a calm, supportive, organized, structured classroom; use a signal before giving directions (flashing lights, clapping hands) and warn of any major disruptions to routine (e.g. the day before) Practice group mindfulness or silent non-doing Assign a buddy; reinforce participation; allow group work with two or three children but vary members of the group For question and answer sessions, signal the child that their turn is coming and Allow 'yes or no' answers; encourage sharing of knowledge on known topics Consider allowing silent reading and presentations to be made to the teacher alone, or on audio- or videotapes made at home. Encourage use of a quiet area for calming and concentrating (e.g. taking tests); allow the child to leave the room with minimum of fuss using a time-out pass Consider the inclusion of caregivers in some school activities, and consider brief check-ins with someone who understands their worries and anxieties (e.g. a guidance counsellor) Build in time to catch-up with missed work; consider extending deadlines for homework and reducing homework load	Strongest evidence for early intervention through regular small-group work on problem-solving; reinforced through work with caregivers Cognitive behavioural therapies for OCD, GAD and phobias, with involvement of caregivers if child is below 11 years Medication for resistant cases Child-focused programmes such as Coping Cat Exposure and response prevention (ERP) Social skills training for social phobia Play therapy Psychoanalytic therapy Family psychotherapy
Welcome pupils on arrival; maintain a sense of predictability and safety in the classroom with consistent rules, routines and structure; provide a quiet safe space and incorporate group mindfulness or silent non-doing Acknowledge good and bad behaviour neutrally, highlighting cause-and-effect and giving logical consequences e.g. 'You've finished your work sheet, so now you can go and play'; too much praise as this leads to scepticism and mistrust Calmly address disobedient, hurtful or defiant behaviour and actions, by stopping the activity and addressing them discreetly; do not ask questions like 'Why did you do that?' but briefly explain how you feel about it with a mild show of disapproval, then use an assuring and accepting voice and give a logical consequence ('I see you've wiped paint across the desk. Here's a cloth to wipe it up') Give concrete feedback e.g. 'You did really well to answer all the questions' (vs 'Well done') or 'You took that away from Dean but he was still using it' (vs 'You weren't nice to Dean'); provide choices within set limits (e.g. ask whether they want to use a pen or a pencil to complete a task, or to work alone or with a friend) Develop good partnerships with carers, health professionals and colleagues to avoid the child's efforts to pit one adult against the other Treat according to emotional age; be empathic and nurturing; notice their response to you and respond accordingly (i.e. a hand on their shoulder might make them anxious); promote social interactions with peers who behave appropriately; for inappropriate actions (e.g. hugging adults) suggest shaking hands instead	Strong evidence for video feedback interventions for parental sensitivity to child's needs Carry out awareness and prevention programmes caregivers and carers of young children on maternal sensitivity and attachment Help caregivers of preschool children to face adversity and improve child–carer relations Multisystemic therapy Family therapy Play therapy Mentalisation-based programmes Psychotherapy Cognitive–behavioural therapy
Establish consistent rules, routines, timetables and structure; give warning of any disruptions to routine; provide consistent and focused guidance on the social aspects of school life, with a circle of friends, a buddy bench in the playground, and buddy to meet them at the school gate or accompany them between classes; consider allowing them to leave early to avoid noisy crowds; use role play to explore social interactions Use IEPs and ABC charts (for Antecedents, Behaviour and Consequences) and reward charts (e.g. for spontaneous communication or sharing well); use any strong interests to motivate them; listen to their feelings at the end of the day by asking them to score each activity (for low scores, ask why); consider using a traffic light system for feelings (e.g. green for 'I am calm' to red for 'I am angry')	Caregiver education and training programmes Occupational therapy Sensory integrative therapy Speech and language therapy Behavioural therapy (e.g. applied behaviour analysis (ABA), verbal behaviour approaches, discrete trial training)

Figure 8.6 *(cont.)*

DISORDER	MAIN FEATURES	WHAT TO LOOK OUT FOR
	They often do not communicate or react to other people normally. They are unable to understand and interpret other's thoughts, feelings and actions, and may be aggressive with other children and invade personal space. They often do not make direct eye contact and fail to draw attention to significant objects or events. They are intelligent but not academic, with a limited capacity to predict what might happen or sense danger. Poor balance and body awareness are common, leading to problems navigating rooms and avoiding obstructions.	Echolalia (repetition of words or phrases made by another person) Unresponsive to name being called and little engagement with others, with repetitive, unimaginative play with toys Distressed if routine disrupted Aversion to certain sounds, colours, patterns or textures Clumsiness and knocking into objects Standing too close to other people
BEREAVEMENT AND GRIEF *Covered in Mental Health and Behaviour in Schools (DfE 2015)*	Grief can have a profound negative impact on a child's ability to perform and engage in school activities, and interact with peers. Around 92% of children below 16 are affected by the death of at least one significant person, but grief may arise with any significant loss, such as divorce, military deployment, or relocation. A range of emotions and behaviours occur as they face grief, loss of stability or sense of safety, disruption of daily routines and the care they receive. The impact may be particularly severe if the loss: • Was sudden or traumatic. • Has a particularly adverse effect on close family members.	'On and off' anger, sadness, anxiety irritability, for a long time or at unexpected moments Over-boisterous play Acting and talking like a much younger child; becoming more demanding, needy and attention seeking Denying or forgetting the death of the person Reduced interest in activities and friends; drop in school performance; increase in absences Repeatedly imitate the dead person or want to join them
CONDUCT DISORDER *Covered in Mental Health and Behaviour in Schools (DfE 2015)*	Behavioural disorder that is characterised by repetitive and significant aggressive, oppositional, antisocial and defiant behaviours. Affects 4-14% of children, with higher incidence in boys. Subtypes include: • **Oppositional defiant disorder.** • **Socialised conduct disorder**: characterised by normal peer relations. • **Unsocialised conduct disorder**: characterised by poor peer relations. • **Conduct disorder within the family**: as reported by caregiver.	Persistent behaviour issues with frequent or severe tantrums; verbal and physical aggression; defiant attitude and actively opposing rules or requests Doing things with an apparent intent to irritate or hurt others; frequent fighting with peers Stealing and deliberate damage or destruction to the property of others (e.g. setting fires, breaking, vandalising) Frequent truancy/running away from school
DEPRESSION *Covered in Mental Health and Behaviour in Schools (DfE 2015)*	Emotional disorder with dominant feelings of hopelessness, sadness or feeling 'low' that interfere with life, with behaviour problems that impair social and personal function and limit the child's ability to develop and learn. Affects 2% of under-12s and 5–10% of 14–16 year olds (peaking during exam times). Subtypes include: • **Major depressive order**: Severe impact on work, social and personal functioning. • **Dysthymic disorder**: Depressed mood every day for more than two years.	Negative patterns of thought; indications of suicidal thoughts; restless and irritable; emotional hypersensitivity (easily hurt, crying, anger) Memory and concentration problems; slow, poor completion of work Profound sleepiness, sometimes due to medication (also nausea and sickness; cognitive dulling, visual blurring) Lack of participation, withdrawal from peers increased absences

CAMHS = Child and Adolescent Mental Health Services; IPE = individualised education plans; PSHE = personal, social, health and economic.

WHAT TO TRY IN THE CLASSROOM	SPECIALIST INTERVENTIONS
Say the child's name before addressing them but do not expect eye contact; use clear, simple, literal language, simple facial expressions, gestures and body language; leave up to thirty seconds before checking for understanding (repeat if necessary); use positive 'do' language where possible ('Speak quietly' vs 'Don't shout'); avoid irony, sarcasm, idioms and rhetorical questions and over-questioning Provide a quiet safe space and sensory calming environment or activities such as silent non-doing; deploy coping strategies such as stress scales and time-out passes so they can leave if they are anxious Address individual learning disabilities (see Developmental disabilities below); Have regular discussions with caregivers and colleagues according to school policy; support SENCos and classroom assistants	
Keep the classroom routine as normal as possible Encourage discussion of death and the grieving process for death and other losses, on expression of feelings; answer all questions and give reassurance that feelings of grief are normal and they are not to blame Allow them to keep a photograph of their loved one with them, or a comforting item (e.g. a piece of fabric, pebble or stone to help them remain grounded) Suggest the child fills out a secret diary with notes or drawings and leaves it in an agreed location for the teacher to review and respond to before replacing Encourage use of signs with drawings of faces (e.g. happy and sad) so they can show non-verbally how they are feeling Arrange a quiet safe space for taking time-out (with a time-out card) Practice silent being and mindfulness-based episodes Discuss with caregivers and colleagues according to school policy	Bereavement counselling CAMHS Trauma-focused School-based trauma and grief component therapy (e.g. Cognitive Behavioural Intervention for Trauma in Schools, CBITS)
Use a positive classroom management style; with consistent rules; display rules and timetables with pictures/photographs of the activities/lessons for the day Use ABC charts (Antecedent, Behaviour and Consequences; use reward and sanction systems; reinforcement even short periods of flexibility, cooperation, effort and achievement; For unacceptable behaviour, remain calm and low-key; say 'You broke this rule so you have to...'. Change seating from groups to rows and provide a quiet safe space (and time-out opportunities) and minimise distractions and transitions Give additional responsibilities (e.g. helping others in an area of strength); make good use of circle time, drama, role play, peer mentoring, mindfulness or silent non-doing Agree a signal for getting attention (e.g. a song, sound, gesture or object); be approachable and interact with empathy; break tasks into manageable chunks	Self-instruction programmes for self-management Parent training programmes (e.g. Triple P Positive Parenting) Multisystemic therapy Cognitive–behavioural therapy Nurture groups and play therapy Multi-component prevention programmes Family therapy if also depression Psychosocial therapy if also have ADHD
Raise issues in PSHE and small-group work on thinking patterns and problem-solving; encourage practice of mindfulness or silence; discuss (according to school policy) what should be done in cases of suicidal ideation (e.g. do not leave the child alone) Seat in a brightly (naturally) lit area to avoid tiredness; allow short periods of standing up and moving or give a physical task to overcome tiredness/tension; with a time-out card for leaving the classroom to go to a safe place (or toilet) Consider a later or gentler start to each school day, teaching less demanding subjects first; shortening the day; short periods of sleep in the day (with advice) Consider extending homework deadlines; arrange catch-up sessions and copies of notes of missed work; minimise the amount of reading (e.g. consider books on tape); give tests at optimum time of day, with multiple-choice or oral questions where possible; consider answering by tape-recorder or dictation	Strongest evidence for prevention, early intervention and small group work Non-directive supportive counselling for mild cases Cognitive–behavioural therapy Interpersonal and family therapy Medication for severe cases (often a three-month course) Psychoanalytic psychotherapy if also have comorbid anxiety

Figure 8.6 *(cont.)*

DISORDER	MAIN FEATURES	WHAT TO LOOK OUT FOR
DEVELOPMENTAL AND BEHAVIOURAL DISORDERS *Covered in Mental Health and Behaviour in Schools (DfE 2015)* See also *Figure 12.1*	Range of conditions covering genetic abnormalities (e.g. Down syndrome, William syndrome), behavioural deficits, learning disorders, language and speech disorders, motor/co-ordination disorders, and conditions acquired through environmental factors. May have profound and lifelong impact. Comorbidity is common, affecting functioning in several domains. Affects 6.6% children and young people (CAMHS). Types include: • **Fetal alcohol spectrums disorders** (FASD): see *below*. • **Autism spectrum disorder** (ASD): see *above*. • **Dyscalculia**: difficulty with mathematics and numeracy. • **Dysgraphia**: difficulty with writing coherently. • **Aphasia/dysphasia**: difficulty expressing or understanding speech. • **Speech apraxia**: difficulty coordinating mouth movements for speech. • **Dyslexia**: difficulty with reading, writing and spelling. • **Dyspraxia**: difficulty with physical coordination.	Problems with spatial awareness, navigating environment (clumsiness) and physical activities (e.g. PE and in the playground) and interpreting visual information (e.g. depth and shapes) Problems holding a pencil, writing, using scissors, fastening buttons, etc. Difficulty speaking fluently, unusual speech (stressing wrong syllable or syllables of a word), slow transition from one sound to another, misformed vowels or consonants Problems making eye contact, listening, understanding spoken words, answering open-ended questions, remembering instructions or tasks of several steps Problems with reading, spelling, sequences; skipping words and lines Difficulty recognising 'how many', telling time, distinguishing left/right, over/under), remembering numbers and sequences Poor bladder control
EATING DISORDERS *Covered in Mental Health and Behaviour in Schools (DfE 2015)*	Eating disorders are more common in older children and girls than in younger children and boys. There are serious changes in eating behaviour, associated with persistent thoughts about body weight, leading to significant risk of ill-health, hospitalisation and death. Early intervention significantly improves chances of recovery. Subtypes include: • **Anorexia nervosa**: intense fear of 'fatness', restriction of food and deliberate weight loss induced and/or maintained by the child. • **Bulimia nervosa**: typically involves binging (excessively eating) and purging (e.g. vomiting or use of laxatives). • **Overeating**: binging without purging (with weight gain).	Any signs of eating very little, dieting behaviour and avoidance of 'fattening' foods or excessive eating Rapid and/or extreme weight loss or weight gain Mood changes, sadness, bouts of fainting, dizziness and tiredness Signs of vomiting or laxative use (e.g. frequent trips to the toilet, smell of vomit, calluses on fingers knuckles, damaged tooth enamel) Eating in secret or unusual eating habits, or unusual interest or disinterest in food Changes in clothing (e.g. baggy clothes)
FETAL ALCOHOL SPECTRUM DISORDER (FASD) See also *Chapter 13*	Umbrella term covering a range of behavioural–cognitive deficits and physical abnormalities that arise from exposure to alcohol during development in the womb. Affects roughly 1% of babies born in the UK. Fetal alcohol syndrome (FAS) is characterised by a cluster of distinctive facial features, growth deficiencies and central nervous system issues, sometimes with behavioural and social issues, movement and coordination problems, developmental delays, learning disorders, sensory hyposensitivity and hypersensitivity, impaired memory and attentional deficits. Comorbid ADHD is common. Other types on the spectrum are partial fetal alcohol syndrome (pFAS) and fetal alcohol effects (FAE).	Underdeveloped jaw and chin, small eyes, undefined groove running beneath the nose to the upper lip, and thin upper lip; small-for-age Difficulty with physical activities Impulsive, disruptive behaviour; little sense of danger; erratic and unfocused; disengage quickly from learning; poor organisational skills and memory (e.g. fail to complete work and forget materials) Learning disabilities (see Developmental Disorders) including difficulty with problem-solving, especially numeracy, mathematical computation and abstract thought

CAMHS = Child and Adolescent Mental Health Services; IPE = individualised education plans; PSHE = personal, social, health and economic.

WHAT TO TRY IN THE CLASSROOM	SPECIALIST INTERVENTIONS
Apply a positive classroom management style, clear and consistent routines, structure and rules; consider alternating between easy and academic lessons and vary their pace and duration; seat close for discreet assistance Encourage good personal organisation and goal-setting; reward effort and have realistic expectations; use IEPs; reinforce participation in group work; suggest appropriate speech in helping roles (e.g. 'Would you like a new pencil?') Train peers to model appropriate social interactions, e.g. asking 'What's that?' or 'Can I join your game?'; assign buddies for study and playing outside Gain attention before speaking; use clear, simple language and visual aids; check for listening and understanding and repeat if necessary after allowing time for processing of information Marking out areas for play, for concentration and for calming with floor tape, screens and rugs; organise resources on accessible shelves in see-through/labelled containers and establish a procedure for accessing them (e.g. raise hand and ask first); consider providing pencil grips and print-outs on lightly-coloured paper and talking calculators Tell them how much work is there is, how to do it, when to do it and when it is complete, using prompts to guide them through sequence of activities, verbally and visually (e.g using models, objects, pictures, song, hands-on activities); allow them to master one key skill at a time Support work of SENCOs and classroom assistants, meet regularly with caregivers and SENCOs to review progress, and discuss according to school policy	Occupational therapy Speech and language therapy Support to learn and use alternative communication methods such as sign language, electronic devices, Picture Exchange Communication System (PECS)
Use PSHE curriculum and small-group work to discuss expression of emotions, body types, weight control, fasting, body building, critical viewing of the media, good nutrition, acceptance of imperfection with the emphasis on functionality, health and positive role models Provide a quiet safe space for calming and concentration, and opportunities for group mindfulness or silent non-doing Do not comment on the appearance of class members Notice eating habits and classroom absences Speak to the student privately about concerning behaviours; listen actively and be non-judgmental, compassionate; make no promises about confidentiality; discuss what will happen next, about support and sharing information with school and family Give realistic goals for project completion Encourage positive social interaction such as team activities, goal-oriented tasks, peer support, extracurricular sport and drama	Peer-support groups for self-esteem and body image Structural systemic or behavioural family therapy for anorexia Cognition and behavioural therapy for bulimia Hospitalisation for restoring weight
Use a positive classroom style, with clear, predictable structure, and give warning before disrupting routines; set up specific areas of room for e.g. relaxation, independent work (consider erecting screens); incorporate IEPs Use clear, simple and consistent language, rules and routines, breaking down information into smaller chunks; check for understanding; if a rule is broken, tell them without scolding and encourage them to try again Use concrete and positive (do) language instead of negative (do not) language (e.g. 'Speak quietly' vs 'Don't shout'; 'Walk' vs 'Don't run'); use written words, symbols, gestures and pictorial cues (particularly for abstract concepts); all staff use the same words Provide a quiet space, for short regular breaks for reflection and stress relief; encourage small-group work, group mindfulness and silent non-doing	Caregiver education and training programmes Drug therapy for comorbid ADHD Occupational therapy Speech and language therapy

Figure 8.6 *(cont.)*

DISORDER	MAIN FEATURES	WHAT TO LOOK OUT FOR
	• Alcohol-related neurodevelopmental disorder (ARND). • Alcohol-related birth defects (ARBD).	Problems making and maintaining friendships, and with team activities
HABIT AND TIC DISORDERS *Covered in Mental Health and Behaviour in Schools (DfE 2015)*	Repetitive, uncontrollable, compulsive bursts of movement or speech, usually in boys aged 2–15. Can suppress tics temporarily with conscious effort, but discomfort builds and they cannot engage with what is going on around them. Worsened by stress, tiredness, boredom and excitement. May be learning disorders, low self-esteem, poor relationships and social isolation, depression, fatigue, anger and rage. Tic disorders include: • **Transient tic disorder:** frequent vocal and/or motor tics lasting more than 4 weeks but less than a year. • **Chronic motor or vocal tic disorder:** frequent tic (either motor or vocal) lasting at least a year. • **Tourette syndrome:** frequent multiple motor and vocal tics (not necessarily simultaneously) lasting at least 12 months; affects 4–24% of children under 11.	Short repetitive actions usually of under a second (e.g. knee bends, eye blinking, grimacing, head jerking) Long actions that appear purposeful (e.g. kicking one leg and then the other, facial gestures, touching an item or person, obscene gestures or actions, rearranging hair or clothing) Imitating words or actions of other people; self-injury; sexual touching; smelling or sniffing things Repetitive phrases and noises (e.g. coughing, barking, hissing, throat clearing, grunting, swearing, animal sounds, whistling, spitting, shrieking); unusual speech rhythms, tones or intensities
HYPERKINETIC DISORDERS OF ACTIVITY AND ATTENTION *Covered in Mental Health and Behaviour in Schools (DfE 2015)* See also *Chapter 11*	Situationally pervasive and persistent inattention and restlessness that is developmentally inappropriate and lasts at least 6 months. Struggle with impulse control, inappropriate behaviour and inability to sustain attention. Highly distractible and highly disruptive in the classroom. Agitated by pressure and competition. Profound effects on emotional and social skills. Affects about 1.5% of under 18s with diagnosed mental health disorders, mostly boys. Subtypes include: • **Attention deficit disorder (ADD).** • **Hyperkinetic disorder.** • **Attention deficit hyperactivity disorder (ADHD):** affects 2–5% of all children and young people; diagnosis depends on symptoms occurring before the age of 7 and in at least two environments.	Problems sitting still and playing quietly; excessive fidgeting and squirming; leaving activities unfinished and moving onto something else; lose focus on task; daydreaming Inappropriate attention seeking and clowning around; interrupt others, answering questions before they are finished; unable to wait or take turns; unconcerned about dangers; negative comments about self and others Difficulty following instructions; unable to draw important points out of written material; slow and laborious writing Unorganised, with homework and materials regularly unfinished or lost; difficulty noticing and correcting errors; poor personal care
MUTISM *Covered in Mental Health and Behaviour in Schools (DfE 2015)*	This is rare, usually occurring before the age of 5. Associated with extreme anxiety, mood disorders, trauma and ASD. Can have a considerable negative impact on social communication, school work and school activities. Characterised by consistent lack of speech in specific situations (e.g. in the classroom) for at least one month, despite the ability to converse age-appropriately in other situations (e.g. at home).	Excessive 'shyness' May communicate verbally with very brief utterances or very quietly, or non-verbally with gestures, facial expressions and head movements Contrary descriptions of child's speech (e.g. caregivers describe as 'chatterbox') May be unable to answer direct questions, or may show fear of social embarrassment May not socialise with peers or only a select few May 'freeze' in certain situations (becoming expressionless and/or motionless)

CAMHS = Child and Adolescent Mental Health Services; IPE = individualised education plans; PSHE = personal, social, health and economic.

WHAT TO TRY IN THE CLASSROOM	SPECIALIST INTERVENTIONS
Discuss with colleagues according to school policy and support work of SENCOs and classroom assistants and maintain regular communication with the family	
Refrain from drawing attention to tic, even if they are humorous Seat in an area likely to minimise disruption (not in the front or middle of the room or near something breakable) and consider a separate room for tests Use positive (do) language rather than 'not do' language Teach stress management strategies and practice group mindfulness or silent non-doing; raise issues in PSHE sessions Provide a quiet safe space and consider issuing a 'time out' pass If reluctant to read aloud or ask or answer questions, permit silent reading, avoid asking open questions and agree a way of asking for help Pair up with supportive and understanding buddy Maintain effective and clear communication between the school and home	Psychosocial therapy for Tourette's with ADHD Behaviour therapy (contingency management, massed negative practice) Habit reversal Multidisciplinary holistic approach Family education Medication (in rare cases) Self-monitoring by child (tic record) Relaxation exercises and awareness training
Ensure consistent rules, routine and structure and give warning when a change or transition will take place; make a quiet, safe, low-stimulus area for working and permit use of earphones; allow guided daydreaming or practice silent non-doing Seat near the front to monitor behavior and maintain attention, next to non-disruptive peers and away from distractions (e.g. windows, switches) Call out name to gain attention; ask direct questions and give simple step-wise instructions in a soft voice, backed up with written or visual cues (e.g. a checklist); ask the child to repeat and/or wait 10–15 seconds for answers Maintain interest using films, flash cards, listening games; alternate between physical/mental and fun/academic activities, with short breaks to get up and move around; regain attention by asking a simple question, touching their shoulder gently, or tapping the page of their book Encourage group activities and give responsibility (e.g. team captain, passing out equipment, keeping score); reward desired behaviours, effort, cooperation, paying attention, timely accomplishment and good organization (assign a buddy to help with notebooks, a pencil pouch, a book bag, lists, calendars, mnemonics, etc.)	Best evidence is for drug therapy and small-group sessions with a focus on cognitive skills and social behaviour Caregiver education and training programmes School-based behaviour therapy, contingency management) and cognitive–behavioural therapy Self-monitoring of behaviour by child Social skills training Psychosocial therapy for comorbid conduct disorder or Tourette's syndrome
Seat to the side of the classroom (not front or centre where can be seen by all) preferably next to an outgoing buddy or child he or she interacts with Assure the child that you do not expect talking; suggest using gestures (e.g. nodding the head), symbol cards and electronic devices to communicate; allow silent reading; do not pursue eye contact; if the child speaks, remain low key or give brief gentle praise Use techniques to reduce stress levels with quiet calm areas and routines; consider a time-out pass to leave discreetly and go to a designated safe place In the child's absence, promote acceptance of non-speaking without referring to the child; tell them to include the child in all activities, not to try to make him or her talk, or say 'He doesn't talk', and how to react if he or she does talk Encourage carers to arrange peers from the non-speaking environment to visit the family home (if the child speaks there); consider including someone the child speaks with in school activities	Behaviour therapy (e.g. controlled exposure) Antianxiety drugs or antidepressants Speech and language therapy (SALT)

Figure 8.6 *(cont.)*

DISORDER	MAIN FEATURES	WHAT TO LOOK OUT FOR
POST-TRAUMATIC STRESS DISORDER (PTSD) *Covered in Mental Health and Behaviour in Schools (DfE 2015)*	Follows direct or threatened physical or emotional harm, or witnessing it in other. Characterised by long-term thoughts, feelings and behaviours related to a shock or traumatic experience. Younger children are likely to show signs of separation anxiety or 'clinginess' while adolescents tend to withdraw socially. Psychological and physical symptoms include: • Re-experiencing: involuntarily re-experiencing of the traumatic incident, through flashbacks, nightmares, repetitive and intrusive thoughts and images, and physical sensations such as pain, shaking or nausea. • Emotional numbing and avoidance: attempts to avoid reminders of the incident, including discussing it, and reduced ability or readiness to 'feel'. • Hyperarousal: hypervigilant threat-detecting and responding behaviour, and feeling 'on edge.	Experience of traumatic incident (as witness or direct involvement) may be known Detectable changes in thinking, feeling or behaviour; loss of concentration; daytime tiredness detachment from normal activities and peers Becoming distracted by thoughts of the incident or repetitive playing out, or avoiding reminders of it (including people, places, activities and talking) Becoming more irritable, agitated, tearful, angry or easily startled by noises, sights or smells Childlike regression (e.g. thumb-sucking or loss of bladder control)
PSYCHOTIC DISORDERS See also *Chapter 10*	Psychotic disorders or episodes refer to a loss of contact with reality. Can be a single episode or a 'breakdown' following a stressful event (e.g. bereavement, severe infection, use of drugs like cannabis). May be caused by underlying illness or chemical imbalance in the brain. Early recognition and treatment improves recovery and reduces long-term harm. Positive symptoms include delusions (a belief that is contradicted by reality), disordered (jumbled) thinking, and hallucinations (sounds, voices, images, sensations). Negative symptoms include depressed (flattened) mood and cognitive deficits in thinking and speech. Affect approximately 0.4% of children aged 5 to 18. Disorders include: • Schizophrenia/schizophreniform disorder. • Affective (mood) disorders (e.g. severe depression, bipolar disorder). • Schizoaffective disorder. • Brief psychotic disorder. • Delusional disorder.	Signs of firm, bizarre beliefs that are often suspicious or paranoid (e.g. that someone or something aims to harm or 'get' them, that they possess special powers or skills, or that they are someone else); jumbled ideas that are hard to understand or keep up with Anxiety and unpredictable emotional changes (mood swings, lack of emotion); impulsive, erratic behaviour (e.g. shouting at people unexpectedly or talking or laughing to themselves); distractable and fidgety Loss of motivation, concentration, energy; disengagement from normal activities; problems with attention, problem solving, listening, organisation; poor attendance Use of drugs or alcohol and self-harming Decline in physical health and personal hygiene and 'disorganised' clothing
SELF-HARM *Covered in Mental Health and Behaviour in Schools (DfE 2015)*	Deliberate actions to cause harm to the self. Around 5% of young people self harm, and about 1% experience suicidal thoughts. Self-harming behaviour, attempted suicide and self-starvation are most common in 14–16 year olds, peaking during exam time. May be a coping mechanism, or be used to punish, validate or manipulate others. There are significant risks to health, long-term well-being, and personal relationships.	Evidence of cutting or burning self (e.g. cuts and scars on wrists, keeping skin hidden from sight by wearing long sleeves even when hot) or unusual or repeated lesions and bruises Signs of pulling hair (e.g. bald patches), self-strangulation (e.g. red marks around neck) or fresh injury (e.g. blood on clothing) Frequent or long trips to the toilets Avoidance of PE or swimming lessons Giving excuses for an injury that do not seem to fit Signs of substance abuse or overdose Low self-esteem and self-blaming thought patterns; withdrawal from peers and/or problems with friends

CAMHS = Child and Adolescent Mental Health Services; IPE = individualised education plans; PSHE = personal, social, health and economic.

WHAT TO TRY IN THE CLASSROOM	SPECIALIST INTERVENTIONS
Reinforce participation with simple socialising-related tasks and encourage re-engagement with normal activities Raise relevant issues in PSHE, including normal reactions to trauma Give the child assurance that it is okay to talk about the incident when they want to; provide opportunities for talking and listening (remain calm and non-judgemental); encourage talking with family, friends and the school counsellor Incorporate relaxation techniques, mindfulness or silent non-doing into the day; provide access to a quiet safe space with a time-out card Discuss with caregivers and colleagues according to school policy Consider extending time allowances for completing class work and homework	Psychoanalytic family psychotherapy Trauma and grief component therapy (e.g. Cognitive Behavioural Intervention for Trauma in Schools, CBITS) Trauma-focused cognitive–behavioural therapy (CBT) NB: there is little evidence for 'debriefing' or drug therapy
Use a positive management style and reinforce participation; encourage social skills training and peer-mentoring schemes Do not dismiss delusions or paranoia; be sympathetic and considerate and reassure them that they are safe; answer any questions calmly Learn to recognise psychotic thoughts and utterances Have discussions with caregivers and colleagues according to school policy, and consider support and safety measures in case of an acute episode of psychosis (e.g. removing the child to safety) Raise issues in PSHE; teach stress management strategies and mindfulness approaches; provide a quiet safe space and time-out options Consider allowing extended deadlines for homework Frequent communication with the caregiver for consistency	Attend to underlying physical or drug problems Talking treatments with whole family Antipsychotic medication Cognitive–behavioural therapy (CBT) for hallucinations Psychiatric care via CAMHS or local Early Intervention Team or Service Hospitalisation for severe episodes
Reinforce participation and social interaction through group work, structured play Use class work and PSHE to emphasise effective coping skills, relaxation and mindfulness-based practises, and dealing with emotional distress Keep track of visits to the toilet (and duration); consider implementing a time-limit on bathroom visits for all pupils and a 'no injuring at school' rule; consider a time-out pass (with parental permission) to go to a safe place Allow child to wear long sleeves (especially in PE) to cover bandages/wounds Be aware of health and safety issues and first-aid Listen with curiosity and empathy; be calm, low-key and non-judgemental; do not express strong emotions, punish, over-question or tell them to stop; do not promise confidentiality; refer the child to a school nurse, counsellor or nominated teacher, or Childline Discuss with colleagues and carers, especially suicidal ideation (according to school policy) and consider mediating between them and parents	Psychodynamic therapy Mentalisation-based programmes Behaviour therapy, e.g. dialectic behaviour therapy and cognitive–behavioural therapy (CBT) Family therapy for suicidal ideation with depression Brief interventions with child and family after suicide attempts and hospitalisation

Figure 8.6 *(cont.)*

DISORDER	MAIN FEATURES	WHAT TO LOOK OUT FOR
SOMATIC DISORDERS *Covered in Mental Health and Behaviour in Schools (DfE 2015)*	Around 4% of young people have somatic disorders, commonly in those with a history of physical or sexual abuse. Characterised by long-term physical symptoms with no known physical cause. Symptoms are genuine – not fabricated – and look real. They include digestive, nervous and reproductive complaints, chronic pain, sickness and soreness. They affect relationships, school work and social, interpersonal and family behaviour. Often accompanied by mood disorders, anxiety disorders and personality disorders.	Frequent, persistent complaints about ill health or requests to go to the nurse's office or home, discussion about health and consequences of illness, and a belief that they have a defect or disease Frequent, persistent symptoms such as joint and abdominal pain, dizziness, headaches, nausea, palpitations, shortness of breath, limb weakness, numb patches, seizures (with or without epilepsy), tremors, movement and vision disorders, drooping eyelids, loss of sound production (but normal cough and whisper) Signs of mood and anxiety disorders
SUBSTANCE MISUSE *Covered in Mental Health and Behaviour in Schools (DfE 2015)*	Around 1.5% of schoolchildren misuse substances such as alcohol, marijuana, opiates, solvents (e.g. glue and aerosols), stimulants (e.g. amphetamines, cocaine, crystal meth) and hallucinogens (e.g. LSD and PCP). They cause physical and emotional harm and there is a risk of addiction. • **Misuse** increases during times of transition, such as changing schools, moving home or divorce, but experimental use does not automatically lead to addiction. • **Addiction** involves compulsive use of a substance despite its negative consequences, with drug-seeking and drug-using behaviours that interfere with normal life.	Distinctive odours on the breath or from the body or clothing; needle marks on arms Glassy bloodshot eyes (marijuana), contracted pupils (depressants and heroin) or dilated pupils (hallucinogens and stimulants); persistent nasal secretions and rashes around mouth and nose Slurred speech, giddiness, clumsiness, doziness, hyperactive, euphoric behaviour, excessive loud talking or laughter, tremors Mood swings, angry outbursts, agitation and increased involvement in fights and accidents Skipping classes, late to classes or frequently asking to leave classes (e.g. to go to the toilet); drop in performance, concentration and participation in after-school activities; decline in personal grooming; weight loss

CAMHS = Child and Adolescent Mental Health Services; IPE = individualised education plans; PSHE = personal, social, health and economic.

BASIS OF THE SUGGESTED CLASSROOM STRATEGIES:

Autistic spectrum disorder: www.autism.org.uk/professionals/teachers/in-your-school/pack.aspxfile:/C:/Users/Owner/Pictures/1960s%20to%201980s%20young%20us/Autism-a%20resource%20pack%20for%20school%20staff.pdf

Attachment disorder: studentsfirstproject.org/wp-content/uploads/Quick-Fact-Sheet-attachment-Strategies-2.24.14.pdf

Bereavement: www.childbereavement.uk.org/support/schools/supporting-bereaved-pupil/support-ideas/

Conduct disorder: www.sess.ie/categories/emotional-disturbance-andor-behavioural-problems/conduct-disorder tips-learning-and-teach

Depression: www.ascd.org/publications/educational-leadership/oct10/vol68/num02/Responding-to-a-Student's-Depression.aspxwww.schoolbehavior.com/Files/tips_mood.pdf

Developmental disabilities: www.interventioncentral.org/behavioral-interventions/special-needs/teaching-children-developmental-disabilities-classroom-ideas

WHAT TO TRY IN THE CLASSROOM	SPECIALIST INTERVENTIONS
Help pupils get organised for the day and promote participation in tasks and social interactions, but do not force engagement in normal activities Be sympathetic and considerate of the symptoms that are situationally relevant Practice group mindfulness or silent non-doing and allow access to a quiet safe space and time-out if required Discuss with caregivers and colleagues according to school policy	School nurse or GP check for underlying physical problems Psychotherapy Cognitive–behavioural therapy (CBT) for triggers of symptoms and coping Counseling for stress
Use PSHE sessions and group work on resilience, communication, problem solving and coping skills; have groups of different sizes and genders (mixed and single) and always respond to difficult questions Devise interactive and participatory drug education programmes, using film, music, invited speakers, workshops, role play, drama, discussions, quizzes, games, videos Encourage participation in non-drug-related extracurricular and after-school activities, and provide opportunities for social interaction Have a designated area in the classroom for personal items to be stored so access to them can be observed Keep track of requests to visit the bathroom (and when and how often) Practice group mindfulness or silent non-doing Discuss issues with caregivers and colleagues according to school policy and follow the school's child protection policy Consider thought showers, mind-mapping, circle time, creative writing	Brief recovery-oriented cognitive–behavioural therapy (CBT) and family programmes for experimental users Ongoing support and treatment for underlying mental health issues for dependent users Systemic therapy Multidimensional family therapy Adolescent community reinforcement approach

Eating disorders: studentsfirstproject.org/wp-content/uploads/ED-Quick-Fact-Sheet-Strategies.pdf

Fetal alcohol syndrome disorder: complexld.ssatrust.org.uk/uploads/1c%20fasd-info.pdf

Mutism: www.selectivemutism.org/resources/library/School%20Issues/Classroom%20Strategies%20for%20Teachers%20of%20SM%20Children.pdf

Psychosis: www.sess.ie/categories/emotional-disturbance-andor-behavioural-problems/childhood-psychosis/tips-/

Post-traumatic stress disorder: kidshealth.org/en/parents/ptsd-factsheet.html

Self-harm: www.scar-tissue.net/schoolsipolicy.pdf

Somatic disorder: www.minddisorders.com/Br-Del/Conversion-disorder.html

Substance abuse: www.mentoruk.org.uk/wp-content/uploads/2012/12/2004-schools-guidance.pdf

Tics: www.tourettes-action.org.uk/storage/downloads/1410791447_KFFT-leaflet-2.pdf

---

KEY MESSAGES FROM THIS CHAPTER

📄 In the UK, as many as one in seven children aged 5–16 has a mental health problem that may worsen over time, and one in ten has a clinically diagnosed disorder.

📄 Schools play an important part in promoting 'resilience' against mental health risk factors.

📄 Various valuable school-based options exist to support pupils, including special education needs provision, peer mentoring, counselling and parental involvement.

📄 It is important that members of school staff are advised on how to identify behaviours indicative of, and emerging risk factors for, mental health issues in pupils.

📄 Evidence-based tools such as the Strengths and Difficulties Questionnaire (SDQ) and Common Assessment Framework (CAF) are valuable for school staff for assessing pupils with suspected mental health needs.

📄 Schools should be equipped with a clear process for accessing relevant mental health services and resources outside or within the school and making referrals for pupils' emotional, social and mental health problems.

Supporting evidence and further reading

Association of Teachers and Lecturers (2015) *Press Release: Schoolchildren's mental health at serious risk*. London: ATL. Available at: www.atl.org.uk/Images/March%2026%20for%2028%202015%20-%20ATL%20Mental%20 Health%20Survey.pdf (accessed October 2015).

Autti-Ramo I (2002) Foetal alcohol syndrome–a multifaceted condition. *Developmental Medicine Child Neurology* 44(2), 141-44.

Birrell J, Corden A, Macduff C *et al.* (2013) *Socio-economic costs of bereavement in Scotland literature scoping report. Scottish government health directorates.* At www.york.ac.uk/inst/spru/pubs/pdf/secobLit.pdf (accessed December 2015).

Brosnan R, Carr A (2000) Adolescent conduct problems In: A Carr P (ed.) *What Works with Children and Adolescents*. London: Routledge.

Brown E, Khan L, Parsonage M (2012) *A chance to change: Delivering effective parenting programmes to transform lives*. Available at: www.centreformentalhealth.org.uk/pdfs/chance_to_change.pdf (accessed October 2015).

Catalano RF, Mazza JJ, Harachi TW, Abbott RD, Haggerty KP, Fleming CB (2003) Raising healthy children through enhancing social development in elementary school: Results after 15 years. *Journal of School Psychology* 41(2), 143–64.

ChildLine (2005) *Every School Should Have One – How Peer Support Schemes Make Schools Better*. London: National Society for the Protection of Cruelty to Children.

Cooper M (2013) *School-Based Counselling in UK Secondary Schools: A Review and Critical Evaluatio*n. Lutterworth: BACP/Counselling MindEd.

Department for Children Schools and Families (2008) *Targeted Mental Health in Schools Project: Using Evidence to Inform Your Approach. A Practical Guide for Headteachers and Commissioners*. London: DCSF.

Department for Education (2004) *Every Child Matters: Change for Children*. London: DfE.

Department for Education (2010) *Working Together to Safeguard Children: A Guide to Inter-Agency Working to Safeguard and Promote the Welfare of Children*. London: DfE.

Department for Education (2011) *Healthy Schools*. London: DfE.

Department for Education (2013) *Working Together to Safeguard Children*. Safeguarding Guidance. London: DfE.

Department for Education (2015) *SEN Code of Practice: 0 to 25 years*. London: DfE. Available at: www.gov.uk/government/publications/send-code-of-practice-0-to-25 (accessed December 2015).

Department for Education (2015) *Counselling in Schools: A Blueprint for the Future Departmental Advice for School Leaders and Counsellors*. London: DfE.

Department for Education (2015) *Mental health and behaviour in schools' guidance*. Available at: www.gov.uk/government/uploads/system/uploads/attachment_data/file/416786/Mental_Health_and_Behaviour_–_Information_and_Tools_for_Schools_240515pdf (accessed December 2015).

Department of Health (accessed December 2015) *Children and Young People's Mental Health and Well-Being Taskforce*. Available at: www.gov.uk/government/groups/children-and-young-peoples-mental-health-and-well-beingtaskforce/.

Frankham J (1998) Peer education: the unauthorised version. *British Educational Research Journal* 24(2), 179–93.

Fraser M, Blishen S (2002) \\. *Supporting Young People's Mental Health: Eight Points for Action: A Policy Briefing from the Mental Health Foundation* London: Mental Health Foundation. Available at: www.mentalhealth.org.uk/sites/default/files/supporting_young_people_0.pdf (accessed December 2012).

Goodman A, Lamping DL, Ploubidis GB (2010) When to use broader internalising and externalising subscales instead of the hypothesised five subscales on the Strengths and Difficulties Questionnaire (SDQ): data from British parents, teachers and children. *Journal of Abnormal Child Psychology* 38,1179–91.

Goodman R (1997) The Strengths and Difficulties questionnaire: a research note. *Journal of Child Psychology and Psychiatry* 38, 581–86.

Goodman R (1999) The extended version of the Strengths and Difficulties Questionnaire as a guide to child psychiatric caseness and consequent burden. *Journal of Child Psychology and Psychiatry* 40, 791–801.

Green H, McGinnity A, Meltzer H, Ford A, Goodman R (2005) *Mental Health of Pupils in Great Britain*. Basingstoke: Palgrave.

Gulati A, King A (2009) *Supporting Vulnerable Young People in Transition. Addressing Poverty of Wellbeing*. Bristol: InPerspective UK.

Hanley T (2012) *A scoping review of the access to secondary school counselling* (internal document). Lutterworth: BACP.

Heegard M (1991) *When Someone Very Special Dies–-Children can Learn to Cope with Grief.* Minneapolis, MN, Woodland Press.

Hill A (2011) *Evaluation of the Welsh School–based Counselling Strategy*. Cardiff: Welsh Government Social Research.

Houlston C, Smith PK, Jessel J (2009) Investigating the extent and use of peer support initiatives in English schools. *Educational Psychology* 29(3), 37.

Hutchings M (2015) *Exam Factories? The Impact of Accountability Measures on Children and Young People*. London: National Union of Teachers.

Hyland T (2009) Mindfulness and the therapeutic function of education. *Journal of the Philosophy of Education* 43(1), 119–31.

Isherwood T, Burns M, Naylor M and Read S (2007) 'Getting into trouble': A qualitative analysis of the onset of offending in the accounts of men with learning disabilities. *Journal of Forensic Psychiatry and Psychology* 18(2), 221-34.

Job N, Francis G (2004) *Childhood Bereavement: Developing the Curriculum and Pastoral Support.* London: National Children's Bureau.

Kearney CA (2001) *School Refusal Behavior in Youth: A Functional Approach to Assessment and Treatment.* Washington DC: American Psychological Association.

Kessler RC, Amminger GP, Aguilar-Gaxiola S (2007) Age of onset of mental disorders: a review of recent literature. *Current Opinion in Psychiatry* 20, 359–64.

Lowton K, Higginson IJ (2003) Managing bereavement in the classroom: A conspiracy of silence? *Death Studies* 27, 8(10), 717-41.

May PA, Gossage JP (2001) Estimating the prevalence of fetal alcohol syndrome. A summary. *Alcohol Research Health* 2001, 25(3), 159-67.

Meikle J (2015) Children 'in complete meltdown' over exams. *The Guardian* Saturday 4 July.

Meltzer H, Gatward R, Corbin T, Goodman R, Ford T (2005) *The Mental Health of Young People Looked After by Local Authorities in England. The Report of a Survey carried out in 2002 by Social Survey Division of the Office for National Statistics on Behalf of the Department of Health.* London: The Stationery Office.

Melvin D, Lukeman D (2000): Bereavement: a framework for those working with children. *Clinical Child Psychology and Psychiatry* 5, 521–39.

Mentoring and Befriending Foundation (2011) *MBF Outcomes Measurement Programme.* Available at: www.mandbf. org/wp–content/uploads/2011/02/Peer_Mentoring_in_Schools.pdf (accessed October 2015).

Mentoring and Befriending Programme (2010) *Peer Mentoring in Schools. A Review of the Evidence Base of the Benefits of Peer Mentoring in Schools Including Findings from the MBF Outcomes Measurement Programme.* Available at: www.mandbf.org/wp-content/uploads/2011/02/Peer_Mentoring_in_Schools.pdf (accessed October 2015).

Murphy M, Fonagy P (2012) Mental health problems in children and young people. In: *Annual Report of the Chief Medical Officer, Our Children Deserve Better: Prevention Pays.* London: Department of Health.

Murphy M, Fonagy P (2013) Mental health problems in children and young people. In: *The Chief Medical Officer's Report.* Available at: www.gov.uk/government/uploads/system/uploads/attachment_data/ (accessed October 2015).

Murray JJ (2010) Very early predictors of conduct problems and crime: results from a national cohort study. *Journal of Child Psychology and Psychiatry* 51(11), 1198–1207.

National Autistic Society (2013) *Befriending and Mentoring.* Available at www.autism.org.uk/befriending (accessed December 2015).

National Institute for Health and Clinical Excellence (2013) *NICE Guidance CG158. Antisocial Behaviour and Conduct Disorders In Pupils: Recognition Intervention and Management.* London: NICE.

NHS Choices (accessed October 2015) *Consent to Treatment: Children and Young People.* Available at: www.nhs.uk/ conditions/consent–to–treatment/pages/children–under–16.aspx.

NICE (2015) *Children's Attachment. NICE Guidelines.* www.nice.org.uk/guidance/NG26/history.

National Institute for Health and Clinical Excellence (2013) *NICE Guidance CG158. Antisocial Behaviour and Conduct Disorders in Pupils: Recognition, Intervention and Management.* London: NICE.

Powell MA (1997) Peer tutoring and mentoring services for disadvantaged secondary school students. *California Research Bureau Note* 4(2), 1–10.

Rees D, Anderson Y (2012) *BOND Consortium. Learning from Practice Review.* London: Department of Education.

Ribbens McCarthy J (2007) They all look as if they're coping but I'm not: the relational power/lessness of 'youth' in responding to experiences of bereavement. *Journal of Youth Studies* 10(3), 285–303.

Royal College of Psychologists (accessed December 2015) *Mental Health and Growing-Up Factsheet.* Available at: http:// www.rcpsych.ac.uk/healthadvice/parentsandyouthinfo.aspx.

Rutter M (1985) Resilience in the face of adversity. Protective factors and resistance to psychiatric disorder. *British Journal of Psychiatry* 147, 598–611.

Rutter M, Taylor E (2008) *Rutter's Child and Adolescent Psychiatry* (5th edn). London, Blackwell Publishing.

Schultz K (1999) Bereaved children. *Canadian Family Physician* 45, 2914-2921.

Shepherd J (2010) Truancy rate at record high. *The Guardian* 25 March.

Skovgaard AM (2010) Mental health problems and psychopathology in infancy and early childhood. An epidemiological study. *Dan Medical Bulletin* 57, B4193.

Weare K (2011) Improving mental health and wellbeing in schools In: *Thinking Ahead: Why We Need to Improve Children's Mental Health and Wellbeing*. London: Faculty of Public Health.

Whitley J, Smith DJ, Vallancourt T (2013) Promoting mental health literacy among educators: Critical in school-based prevention and intervention. *Canadian Journal of School Psychology* 28(1), 56–70.

Volmer L (1995) Best practices in working with students with autism. In: A Thomas and J Grimes (eds) *Best Practices in School Psychology* (3rd edn). New York: Wiley & Sons.

CHAPTER 9

Attachment theory and forming relationships

Suzanne Thomson

Contemporary explanations of child development are based on a range of theoretical perspectives. One of these is 'attachment theory' – a theory of relationships in which the child's formative experiences with his or her primary caregiver are emphasised for future social and emotional development and capacity for interpersonal relationships. Although related concepts have been the subject of some debate, attachment theory is increasingly represented in the commissioning, planning and delivery of children's services, including education. An awareness of how early attachments with the primary caregiver are formed and influence social and emotional development and future relationships is fundamental to the effective translation of the theory into policy and practice. It is the aim of this chapter to outline the key principles underpinning attachment theory and consider them in the context of the learning environment. Key messages of encouragement will be highlighted from the literature for educators seeking to make a difference with respect to child development and academic outcomes using attachment-based approaches.

Attachment theory has its origins in the work of British psychiatrist and psychoanalyst, John Bowlby, who carried out an ethological study of children living within institutions following the Second World War. Intrigued by observations of child behaviour after separation from their parents, he set out to investigate the nature of the child–parent bond; how quickly it develops, how it is maintained, how long it persists for, and what functions it fulfils. The resulting theoretical framework is still valid to child development.

According to attachment theory, early interactions between children and their main caregivers determine the development of their emotional and social capacities, with outcomes extending throughout childhood into adolescence and adulthood. The concepts developed by Bowlby (1969) were supported and extended by empirical evidence, most notably by Ainsworth and her colleagues (Ainsworth *et al.* 1978). More recently, sophisticated brain imaging techniques have revealed the flexibility of the infant brain and how soon it becomes hard-wired in adapting to a caring environment, providing further support for Bowlby's theoretical stance. For example, the effect of a secure attachment has been shown on the development of the infant's rapidly maturing right brain, which is associated with regulation of emotion and the ability to manage stress (Schore 2001). Emotional and social development encompass the ability to experience, regulate and express emotions, form close interpersonal relationships and explore and learn from the environment (Zeanah 2009); they also form the foundation for effective learning (Kennedy and Kennedy 2004), thus attachment theory is an increasingly important part of the educator's toolkit.

What is attachment?

The term attachment describes a deep and enduring affectionate bond that develops between a child and the parent or main caregiver (Bowlby 1969). Very young children are completely dependent on others for nurturing and protection from harm and are predisposed from birth to seek proximity to a caregiver – by crying, searching and clinging – for the things that close relationships should provide during times of danger, stress or novelty, including protection from external threats such as predators and regulation of internal threats such as overwhelming emotions (Harris 2004). Attachment can therefore be described as a system of child behaviours and caregiver responses with the biological aim of survival and the psychological aim of felt security. Zeanah and Fox (2004) define attachment as:

> ... the organisation of behaviours in the young child that are designed to achieve physical proximity to a preferred attachment figure at times when the child seeks comfort, support, nurturance or protection. In response the caregiver provides comfort for distress, emotional availability for support, warmth and care for nurturance and protection from danger.

Who is the attachment figure?

With societal change and an increasing tendency for parents to share childcare, often with help from the extended family, attachment theory has attracted some criticism for focusing on the mother as the attachment figure; children are able to form attachments with more than one person. However, a hierarchy of attachment figures can be proposed because attachment behaviours tend to be directed towards a preferred caregiver, with other caregivers identified as 'subsidiary' or secondary (Bowlby 1969). The preferred caregiver is normally the primary provider of care which is a role most likely to be adopted by the mother (Bowlby 1969), but this depends on family circumstances. In this chapter, the term 'primary caregiver' is used.

Key principles of attachment theory

Two key concepts underpinning attachment theory are the 'internal working model' and the 'secure base'.

'INTERNAL WORKING MODEL' OF SELF AND OTHERS

Children are born without the capacity to interpret meanings and emotions within their interactions and rely on their attachment figure to learn how to navigate the social world (Cassidy and Shaver 1999). According to attachment theory (Bowlby 1969), repeated early interactions with the attachment figure are internalised by the child, forming a conceptual 'internal working model' (IWM) or mental representation of self, others and self-relating to others. Consequently, the model acts as a filter for information received from the child's environment, directing feelings, behaviour and thoughts about relationships (Weinfield, Ogawa and Sroufe 1997). Each child's specific attachment style is formed this way, with an established pattern of thinking, feeling and behaving apparent in social interactions and relationships with people other than the attachment figure (Al-Yagon and Mikulincer 2004).

In other words, the way in which a child's need for nurturing support, comfort and protection is negotiated within their early relationship with a primary caregiver is taken forward in the child's attitudes, beliefs and expectations about new relationships and favoured strategies for managing emotions, thus the relationship with the primary carer acts like a prototype for future relationships.

ATTACHMENT FIGURE AS A 'SECURE BASE'

When the primary caregiver is emotionally available and can be relied on to decipher and respond promptly and sensitively to a child's attachment behaviours (at least most of the time because perfection is not realistic or indeed required), the child forms a mental representation of themselves as being held in mind by the attachment figure (Perry 2009; Sroufe 2000). This promotes confidence in the attachment figure as a secure base, from which the child can explore the world, and a safe haven for accessing support, comfort and protection when needed. Exploration in this context includes learning about relationships as well as the physical surroundings (Levy *et al.* 2011). As indicated by Malekpour (2007):

> *Through this exploration of the environment, the child gains greater competence, acquiring greater independence in future experiences.*

Attachment is not about dependency; rather it is about security that liberates the child to explore the world and gain self-mastery (Bergin and Bergin 2009).

The formation of attachment

Although attachments are 'enduring', the critical period for their formation is infancy – specifically between birth and two years. During this time, attachment is constructed from repeated child–caregiver interactions (Bowlby 1969), through a series of phases as the child begins to predict responses of the caregiver and organises his or her attachment behaviours accordingly (FIGURE 9.1). This is adaptive because the child is finding ways to manage threat within the context of a particular caregiving environment. Attachments are therefore not all the same, because the principal determinant of attachment security is caregiver response (Ainsworth *et al.* 1978). A secure attachment depends on a reciprocated system of attachment behaviours and attuned responses, which are often likened to synchronised dance. It is a complex process, and over-simplifying it by focusing exclusively on caregiver sensitivity, for example, can contribute to a culture of blame (Sroufe 2005). It is therefore important to be mindful of the contextual factors of every child, caregiver and caregiving environment that can exert pressure on the attachment relationship, with the potential to compromise attachment security. Examples of such factors are:

- **Child factors**: prematurity, complex medical needs, difficult temperament (Cassibba *et al.* 2011; Zeanah and Fox 2004).

- **Caregiver factors:** own negative childhood attachment experiences, mental ill health (Ming *et al.* 2007).

- **Environmental factors:** limited access to supportive social networks (Green *et al.* 2011).

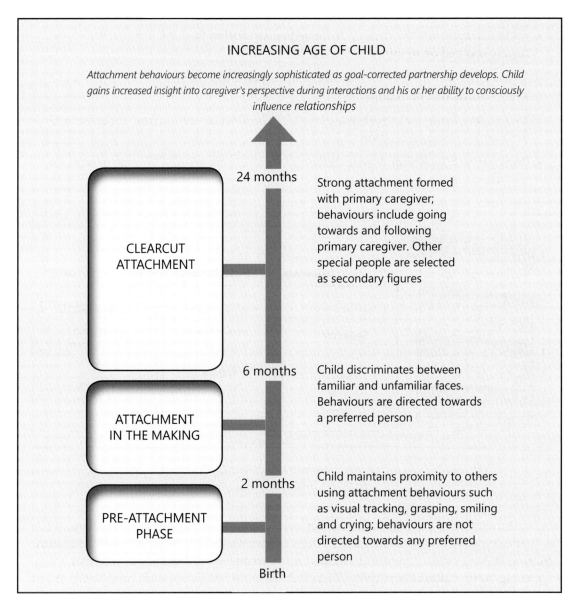

Figure 9.1: Phases of attachment formation (adapted from Bowlby 1969).

Types of attachment

Ainsworth worked closely with Bowlby to investigate differences in the quality of attachment by measuring child attachment behaviours. One method was the 'strange situation' (Ainsworth *et al.* 1978), in which infants aged 12–18 months and their primary caregiver are observed for three minutes in different situations to trigger attachment behaviours, such as the caregiver leaving the infant alone with a stranger. Of particular significance is the infant's behaviour at the points of separation and reunion. Several distinct patterns of child–caregiver interaction were observed, classified as shown in FIGURE 9.2.

- **Secure attachment**: the child is distressed on separation from primary caregiver but readily soothed on reunion.

- **Avoidant (insecure) attachment**: little or no response to separation from caregiver and avoids interaction on reunion.

- **Ambivalent (insecure) attachment**: very distressed on separation from caregiver and difficult to soothe on reunion.

- **Disorganised (insecure) attachment**: no consistent response on separation or reunion with the caregiver.

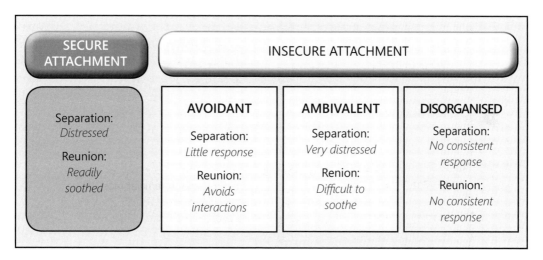

Figure 9.2: Types of attachment identified by Ainsworth in the Strange Situation study.

The study has similar findings in different cultures (Van Ijzendoorn and Kroonenberg 1988); the predisposition to form attachments is universal, with secure attachment being the most common style. There are subtle variations in the frequency of insecure attachment styles, suggesting some cultural sensitivity. The findings from the Strange Situation were (Scott 2011):

- Secure attachment: 62–66%.
- Insecure avoidant: 15–22%.
- Insecure ambivalent: 9–12%.
- Insecure disorganised: 15%.

SECURE ATTACHMENT

A secure attachment is formed when reliable and sensitive caregiver responses are attuned with the child's attachment behaviours. The caregiver comes to represent a secure base from which the child can explore the social world, while developing skills, confidence and independence, and is a safe haven to whom the child returns if he or she is anxious or distressed. Children learn effective strategies for regulating their own emotions (self-regulation) from their experience of being comforted by their caregiver (co-regulation) (Perry 2009). The attuned responses are internalised by the child in terms of being worthy of care, thus promoting positive feelings about themselves and self-esteem (Clark and Symons 2009). Children carry these experiences into future relationships with an internal working model of themselves as lovable and autonomous and others as available and co-operative (FIGURE 9.3).

INSECURE ATTACHMENTS

(i) Avoidant

This occurs when caregivers are unable to tolerate distress and therefore find the child's emotional needs too demanding (Golding 2007). They respond to attachment behaviours with annoyance or rejection and any outward expressions of upset by the child are discouraged (Howe 2011). The avoidant strategy develops whereby displays of negative emotions are suppressed and attachment behaviours minimised in order to maintain proximity to the caregiver. Any feelings of anger towards the attachment figure will be expressed in relationships with other people (Perry 2009). These caregivers do not represent a safe haven or a secure base. When these early interactions are carried forward, the internal working model is of self-reliance with other people viewed as rejecting and unreliable (FIGURE 9.3).

(ii) Ambivalent

This attachment style develops from inconsistent caregiver responses, related to difficulties in interpreting and responding sensitively to the child's signals of anxiety and distress (Golding 2007). Attachment behaviours are rapidly escalated in order to increase the likelihood of obtaining proximity and emotional availability (Sroufe 2005). This child experiences a rapid rise of emotions and an inability to confidently predict whether the caregiver will be there for them; the resulting strategy is hypervigilance about threat and availability of the caregiver, producing excessively clingy and demanding behaviour, even when the threat appears minimal. When comfort is forthcoming, the child is difficult to soothe and may be angry and resistant (Muris *et al.* 2000). This level of hypervigilance and near-continuous activation of attachment behaviours leads to a child for whom exploration is inhibited, and the caregiver is not a secure base (Malekpour 2007). The future internal working model of self is of ineffectiveness and dependence, and others are viewed as insensitive and unpredictable (FIGURE 9.3).

(ii) Disorganised

The disorganised style is associated with the least favourable social and emotional outcomes. It is derived from caregiving that takes place in a high-risk environment, with factors such as abuse, stress or poverty (Kennedy and Kennedy 2004).The attachment figure often has psychological difficulties; there may be little emotional capacity left for the child and difficulty in prioritising the child's needs over their own. Threats may be overt – in the form of neglect or abuse directed at the child (Malekpour 2007). The child is biologically compelled to seek proximity during times of danger, stress or novelty, but the caregiver is frightened or frightening, thus the source of comfort is also a source of fear, and the child does not know what to do and cannot develop an organised attachment strategy (Sroufe 2005). These children's attachment behaviours appear erratic, contradictory or bizarre and are easily activated, even without an obvious threat, and they cannot use the attachment figure as a secure base. They develop internal working models of themselves as frightened, ignored or 'bad' and others as unavailable, confusing and frightening (FIGURE 9.3).

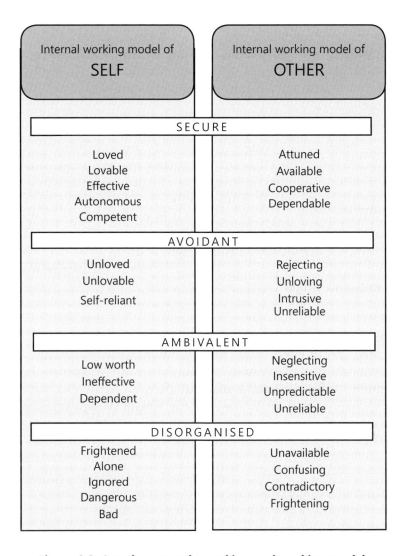

**Figure 9.3: Attachment styles and internal working models
(adapted from Howe 2011).**

Influence of attachment style in the learning environment

Drawing on Bowlby's position (1969) in which attachment behaviour is increasingly directed toward others outside the family, Mackay *et al.* (2010) note that attachment to the primary caregiver broadens to peer and teacher relationships. There is ample support within the literature linking child–caregiver attachment with social, emotional and academic outcomes for children from pre-school to secondary school. This includes findings from the so-called Minnesota study, a large longitudinal investigation of child development conducted by Sroufe *et al.* (2005).

When children enter the learning environment, the value of their social competence and capacity for emotional regulation are significant in terms of their ability to benefit from learning opportunities (Myers and Pianta 2008). The learning environment is a complex social situation involving multiple interactions and relationships, and the process of learning is demanding, presenting unfamiliar tasks; the experience of 'not knowing' can elicit fear of failure and trigger insecure attachment behaviours (Greig *et al.* 2008). In this situation, secure attachment does not guarantee a positive outcome, and insecure attachment does not guarantee negative outcomes (Granot and Mayseless 2001). Understanding attachment issues provides critical insights for educators, and there has been renewed interest over the past decade in attachment in the context of the learning environment. The key themes relating to each attachment style within the classroom environment are summarised from the work of Bergin and Bergin (2009), Geddes (2006), Golding *et al.* (2013), Kennedy and Kennedy (2004) and Sroufe *et al.* (2005).

Secure attachment in the classroom

Children with a secure attachment style are more likely than those with insecure attachments to engage successfully in school, maintaining a balance between exploration and proximity-seeking behaviours, and generally being less dependent on the teacher. They have the confidence to tackle new and challenging activities and to persist in the task of learning while feeling able to approach the teacher for help – but only when needed. Having positive expectations of other people means these children can develop close, trusting relationships and cultivate supportive social networks, on which they can rely when challenged. They are more likely than insecure peers to develop effective emotional regulation, which enhances their capacity for coping when confronted by novelty or stress in the learning environment; they also display an increased ability for mutuality in relationships. Contributing factors include their capacity to consider the perspective of others and to empathise with them, as well as an ability to cope with shared communication of feelings. Being better equipped to manage conflict positively, they can successfully combine maintenance of close personal friendships with participation in activities with a wider peer group.

Insecure attachment in the classroom

INSECURE AVOIDANT

The over-regulation of emotions and need to keep people at a distance characteristic of these children can be misinterpreted as independence. Teachers are more likely to report them as overly dependent compared to securely attached children. Contact with teachers is made obliquely, in an unobtrusive manner during quiet times. They are sensitive to teacher proximity but do not directly approach them when upset or uncertain, maintaining focus instead on the task. When uncertain about a task or finding it difficult, avoidant attachment children are indifferent to the teacher and reject support. They use less effective strategies instead, such as defiance and refusal to engage in the activity; they may have protective denial of caring about learning. This attachment style elicits intervention by adults, including teachers, but this tends to be instructive and controlling rather than nurturing. Expressions of anger or hostility toward the teacher are unlikely, but they may be directed toward peers. These children are uniquely challenged by activities that require interpersonal closeness and they have difficulty developing trusting relationships. They are less likely than securely attached children to be able to interpret the feelings of other children or to empathise with them. Angry behaviours and emotional disconnection can make these children unpopular with their peers, and there is little sense of belonging to their peer group, which increases their risk of social withdrawal and exclusion.

INSECURE AMBIVALENT

In contrast to children with avoidant styles, those with an ambivalent attachment style are characterised by under-regulation of their emotions; they are also preoccupied with holding the attention of adults at the expense of directing attention towards their environment. They cannot believe they will be 'held in mind' and are unable to take attention away from teachers long enough to concentrate on learning tasks. Thus they can take a long time to get started on tasks and they persist less than their avoidant peers. They can be easily frustrated and may 'walk away' as a coping strategy. Displays of what appear to be exaggerated emotional and behavioural reactions to stress are typical, even for threats that seem minimal. Often they need excessive reassurance, and find novel, highly stimulating or cognitively challenging situations particularly demanding. These children can present as helpless, immature, easily frustrated and attention-seeking and are more likely than avoidant children to elicit nurturing interventions by adults, including teachers. Their over-dependence on teachers means they tend to share their problems and exchange personal information; they are sensitive to feeling ignored and may become abusive if they perceive this. Anxiety about the availability of the teacher and fear of losing their attention may present in externalised behaviours such as over-activity, impulsiveness and aggression. While they are orientated towards their peer group, they will probably be ineffective in their relationships, thus they tend to loiter on the periphery of the group, almost as onlookers. They also find it difficult to combine peer group membership with personal friendships; other children may be irritated by their behaviour and their need for constant adult attention. Ultimately, this may lead to social withdrawal and exclusion.

INSECURE DISORGANISED

Children with a disorganised attachment style often display the most unpredictable and challenging behaviours in the learning environment. Behaviours include features associated with both avoidant and ambivalent styles and can change from week to week. It is difficult for these children to derive benefit from their relationships with teachers or to maintain focus on learning tasks. Other features are poor emotional regulation and a marked sensitivity to change. Without an organised strategy to rely on in stressful or novel situations, they have a limited capacity for coping with feelings of uncertainty, frustration, fear or distress. They act out their experience in behaviours that appear exaggerated for the situation and immature, with explosive, angry outbursts of aggression and restless movements, perhaps pacing around the classroom. Their propensity for destructive behaviours is high, which may be directed towards themselves or others. Children with this style of attachment sometimes protect themselves by switching off from difficult feelings and becoming unresponsive. They generally do not have the requisite emotional and social competencies for mutuality in relationships, tending to develop a profound mistrust of other people. In relationships, they are likely to want to exert control, sometimes in a coercive way. Their behaviours are often misinterpreted as confidence rather than a manifestation of vulnerability.

Opportunities to make a difference

Children with insecure attachment styles might account for as many as a third of pupils in the average classroom. Teachers often believe challenging behaviours that originate at home cannot be addressed in school. However, the positive impact of the educational environment, especially the leader of learning, cannot be underestimated. For some children, the teacher is the only consistent adult in their lives who is positive and supportive, and the quality of their relationship can have a positive influence on children at increased risk of poor social, emotional and academic outcomes (Sabol and Pianta 2012). Assessment of attachment disorders is complex, requiring specialist training (Scott 2011). Interventions on a one-to-one basis are reserved for children who are referred for specialist services, including Educational Psychology or Child and Adolescent Mental Health Services (CAMHS). Family-based interventions may be used to enhance interactions between the child and primary caregiver. Class teachers are unlikely to engage in formal assessment or delivery of interventions on a one-to-one basis, not least because of time constraints. According to Sabol and Pianta (2012), the preferred option is to broadly apply strategies based on the principles of attachment at classroom, school and curriculum levels, which ultimately has a positive impact at the level of individual child–teacher relationships within the classroom (Hughes 2012).

THE TEACHER AS A SECONDARY ATTACHMENT FIGURE AND SECURE BASE

There is some debate within the literature about the role of the class teacher as a secondary attachment figure. Verscheuren and Koomen (2012) conclude that class teachers are likely to fulfil an 'ad hoc' if not 'fully fledged' attachment role, but they suggest this debate is an unnecessary distraction from the real issue of how attachment theory and research can be used to the benefit of children's social, emotional and academic outcomes. According to Hughes (2012), while research is ongoing, our current knowledge is sufficient for helping teachers create a positive emotional and learning environment. Kesner (2000) supports the view that children with insecure attachments may develop secure relationships with teachers that compensate for insecure attachments with their primary caregivers. This is based on the knowledge that child–teacher relationships are not only determined by the child's attachment history, but also the current behaviour of the teacher, especially their level of sensitivity (Buyse *et al.* 2011). The concept of 'closeness' is one possible factor that determines how much a child's relationship with his or her teacher can facilitate exploration from a secure base and provide a safe haven (Verscheuren and Koomen 2012). Closeness refers to the extent to which the teacher's communication is open, warm and attuned, and it encompasses how comfortable children are in approaching the teacher, talking about their feelings and experiences, and using him or her as a source of support.

CHILD–TEACHER RELATIONSHIPS AND INTERNAL WORKING MODELS

A child's internal working model is only useful if it is updated through a process of subtle but continual modification (Bowlby 1969). Attachment status and internal working models are established within the early 'critical period' of child development, but opportunities arise throughout childhood for these to be reshaped by new experiences (Grossman and Grossman 1991). The links between experiences of life events and changes in attachment status are complex. Nevertheless, when adults (including teachers) increase their sensitivity and responsiveness to children, the security level and associated outcomes can alter (Bergin and Bergin 2009). Based on a 'prototype' relationship with a primary caregiver and resulting internal working model, children are pre-programmed to behave in ways that elicit predictable responses. Their interactions with teachers can therefore become similar to those with their primary caregiver, with reinforcement of patterns of behaviour (O'Connor *et al.* 2012). Using attachment theory as a conceptual framework, the teacher is equipped to understand classroom behaviour in terms of relationship histories and strategies for coping with stress. They can decipher social and emotional cues from the children, and respond accordingly, offering emotional support or establishing limits as required (Sabol and Pianta 2012). In this way, teachers can avoid reinforcing certain established patterns of behaviour by responding in a different way from the primary caregiver, thus 'disconfirming' the child's internal working model and their expectations of relationships (Kennedy and Kennedy 2004).

ATTACHMENT AND SCHOOL BONDING

A supportive school ethos and increased levels of school satisfaction foster resilience and provide a buffer against the negative effects of insecure attachment (Elmore and Heubner 2010). This is supported by Oelsner *et al.* (2011) who conceptualise children's inherent need to form attachments in terms of 'bonding' with their school; this relates to their experiences in school, the degree to which they feel cared for and respected by teachers, their level of participation and involvement in the school, and their commitment to the values and beliefs of the school. Not surprisingly, attachment theory has informed a range of initiatives in nursery, primary and secondary schools. For example:

- The Key Person Approach (Elfer *et al.* 2003) aims to provide continuity in terms of developing relationships between individual children and named members of staff within nursery schools.

- Nurture Groups (Boxall 2002) have been widely adopted in primary and secondary schools to help children experiencing social and behavioural difficulties to overcome barriers to learning in a supportive and inclusive way.

Awareness of attachment issues may also support the argument for moving away from centralised secondary education within large institutions to smaller secondary schools or small-scale learning communities within larger schools. These will provide nurturing learning environments with the priority on active school community membership and healthy relationships (Pemberton 2010).

Concluding comments

This chapter outlines the increased understanding of attachment with respect to the learning environment. This is accompanied by a growing interest in research into relevant training and professional development opportunities for teachers. The early results from new strands of attachment-related research are encouraging. One study shows that teachers who routinely have the opportunity to reflect on their behaviours, intentions and feelings about individual children, have a greater capacity for responsiveness and sensitivity (Split *et al.* 2012). Further research is needed on long-term outcomes for children, but according to Sabol and Pianta (2012) the current knowledge base already provides a compelling argument for relationship-focused professional development opportunities to be supported at policy level.

KEY MESSAGES FROM THIS CHAPTER

According to attachment theory, a child's formative experiences with his or her primary caregiver play a role in their social and emotional development and capacity for interpersonal relationships.

Emotional and social development forms the foundation for effective learning, thus attachment theory is gaining recognition as an important part of the educator's toolkit.

Attachments are not all the same; it is the responses of the primary caregiver that is the main determinant of attachment security.

Insecure attachments are not deterministic, but increase vulnerability of the child to poor social, emotional and academic outcomes.

Children with insecure attachment histories are capable of developing secure relationships with teachers and these relationships can compensate for insecure attachments made with the primary caregiver.

Child–teacher relationships are not only determined by the child's attachment history but also the current behaviour of the teacher, and especially their level of sensitivity.

The opportunity to reflect on behaviours, intentions and feelings toward each child in the classroom can enhance the teacher's capacity for responsiveness and sensitivity.

Supporting evidence and further reading

Two particularly valuable resource materials on this subject are Attachment in the Classroom by Heather Geddes (2006) and a journal article with the same name written by Christi Bergin and David Bergin in 2009.

Ainsworth M, Blehar M, Waters E, Wall S (1978) *Patterns of attachment: A Psychological Study of the Strange Situation.* Hillsdale, NJ: Erlbaum.

Al-Yagon M, Mikulincer M (2004) Socioemotional and academic adjustment among children with learning disorder: The mediational role of attachment-based factors. *Journal of Special Education* 38(2), 111–23.

Bergin C, Bergin D (2009) Attachment in the classroom. *Educational Psychology Review* 21, 141–70.

Bowlby J (1969) *Attachment and Loss: Volume 1. Loss.* New York: Basic Books.

Boxall M (2002) *Nurture Groups in Schools: Principles in Practice.* London: Sage.

Buyse E, Verschueren K, Doumen S (2011) Preschoolers' attachment to mother and risk for adjustment problems in kindergarten: can teachers make a difference? *Social Development* 20(1), 33–50.

Cassibba R, van Ijzendoorn MH, Coppola G (2011) Emotional availability and attachment across generations: variations in patterns associated with infant health risk status. *Child Care, Health and Development* 38(4), 538–44.

Cassidy J, Shaver PR (1999) *Handbook of Attachment: Theory, Research and Clinical Applications.* New York: Guilford Press.

Clark SE, Symons DK (2009) Representations of attachment relationships, the self and significant others in middle childhood. *Journal of Canadian Academy of Child and Adolescent Psychiatry* 18(4), 316–21.

Elfer P, Goldschmied E, Selleck D. (2003) K*ey persons in the nursery.* London: David Fulton.

Elmore G, Heubner ES (2010) Adolescents' satisfaction with school experiences: relationships with demographics, attachment relationships and school engagement behaviour. *Psychology in the Schools* 47(6) 525–37.

Geddes H (2006) *Attachment in the Classroom. The Links Between Children's Early Experience, Emotional Well-Being and Performance in School.* London: Worth Publishing.

Golding K (2007) *Attachment Theory into Practice. Division of Clinical Psychology Briefing Paper 26.* London: British Psychological Society.

Golding KS, Fain J, Frost A *et al.* (2013) *Observing Children with Attachment Difficulties in School: A Tool for Identifying and Supporting Emotional and Social Difficulties in Children Aged 5–11.* London: Jessica Kingsley Publishers.

Granot D, Mayseless O (2001) Attachment security and adjustment to school in middle childhood. *International. Journal of Behavioural Development* 25(6), 530–41.

Green BL, Furrer CJ, McAllister CL (2011) Does attachment style influence social support, or the other way around? A longitudinal study of Early Head Start mothers. *Attachment and Human Development* 13(1), 27–47.

Greig A, Minnis H, Millward R *et al.* (2008) Relationships and learning: a review and investigation of narrative coherence in looked after children in primary school. *Educational Psychology in Practice* 24(1), 13–27.

Grossman KE, Grossman K (1991) Attachment quality as an organiser of emotional and behavioural responses in a longitudinal perspective. In: Parkes CM, Stevenson-Hinde J, Marris P (eds) *Attachment Across the Life Cycle.* London/ New York: Tavistock/Routledge.

Harris, T (2004) Implications of attachment theory for working in psychoanalytic psychotherapy. *International Forum Psychoanalysis* 13, 147–56.

Howe D (2011) A*ttachment Across the Lifespan: An Introduction.* Basingstoke: Palgrave Macmillan.

Hughes JN (2012) Teacher-student relationships and school adjustment: progress and remaining challenges. *Attachment and Human Development* 14(3), 319–27.

Kennedy JH, Kennedy CE (2004) Attachment theory: Implications for school psychology. *Psychology in Schools* 41(2), 247–59.

Kesner JE (2000) Teacher characteristics and the quality characteristics and the quality of child–teacher relationships. *Journal of School Psychology* 38(2), 133–49.

Levy K, Ellison E, Scott L, Bernecker S (2011) Attachment style. *Journal of Clinical Psychology: In Session* 67(2), 194–203.

Mackay T, Reynolds S, Kearney M (2010) From attachment to attainment: the impact of nurture groups on academic achievement. *Educational and Child Psychology* 27(3), 100–08.

Malekpour M (2007) Effects of attachment on early and later development. *British Journal of Developmental Disabilities* 53(2), 81–95.

Ming WW, Salmon MP, Riordan DM, Appleby L, Webb R, Abel K (2007) What predicts poor mother–infant interaction in schizophrenia? *Psychological Medicine* 37, 537–46.

Muris P, Mayer B, Meesters C (2000) Self-reported attachment style, anxiety, and depression in children. *Social Behaviour and Personality* 28(2), 157–62.

Myers SS, Pianta RC (2008) Developmental commentary: individual and contextual influences on student–teacher relationships and children's early problem behaviours. *Journal of Clinical Child and Adolescent Psychology* 37(3), 600–08.

O'Connor EE, Collins BA, Supplee L (2012) Behaviour problems in late childhood: the roles of early maternal attachment and child–teacher relationship trajectories. *Attachment and Human Development* 14(3), 265–88.

Oelsner J, Lippold MA, Greenberg MT (2011) Factors influencing the development of school bonding among middle school students. *Journal of Early Adolescence* 31(3), 463–87.

Pemberton C (2010) Schools need a nurturing culture. *Community Care* 1819: 26.

Perry A (2009) Insecure attachment and its consequences. *Healthcare Counselling and Psychotherapy Journal* 9(3), 1–5.

Sabol TJ, Pianta RC (2012) Recent trends in research on child–teacher relationships. *Attachment and Human Development* 14(3), 213–31.

Schore AN (2001) Effects of a secure attachment relationship on right brain development, affect regulation and infant mental health. *Infant Mental Health Journal* 22(1–2), 7–66.

Scott E (2011) *Briefing on Attachment*. Edinburgh: NHS Health Scotland.

Split JL, Helma HMY, Thijs JT, Van der Leij A (2012) Supporting teachers' relationships with disruptive children: the potential of relationship-focused reflection. *Attachment and Human Development* 14(3), 305–18.

Sroufe LA (2000) Early relationships and the development of children. *Infant Mental Health Journal* 21(1–2), 67–74.

Sroufe LA (2005) Attachment and development: A prospective, longitudinal study from birth to adulthood. *Attachment and Human Development* 7(4) 349–67.

Sroufe LA, Egeland B, Carleson E, Collins WA (2005) *The Development of the Person: The Minnesota Study of Risk and Adaptation from Birth to Adulthood*. New York: Guilford.

Van Ijzendoorn MH, Kroonenberg PM (1988) Cross-cultural patterns of attachment: a meta-analysis of the strange situation. *Child Development* 59(1), 147–56.

Van Ijzendoorn MH, Schuengel C, Bakermans-Kranenburg MJ (1999) Disorganized attachment in early childhood: Meta-analysis of precursors, concomitants, and sequelae. *Development and Psychopathology* 11, 225–49.

Verschueren K, Koomen HMY (2012) Child–teacher relationships from an attachment perspective. *Attachment and Human Development* 14(3), 205–11.

Weinfield NS, Ogawa JR, Sroufe LA (1997) Early attachment as a pathway to adolescent peer competence. *Journal of Research on Adolescence* 7(3), 241–65.

Zeanah C (2009) *Handbook of Infant Mental Health* (3rd edn) New York: Guilford Press.

Zeanah C, Fox N (2004) Temperament and attachment disorders. *Journal of Clinical Child and Adolescent Psychology* 33(1), 32–41.

CHAPTER 10

Early signs of psychosis

Hilary Mairs and Tim Bradshaw

In this chapter, we present an overview of the key features of psychosis and the early signs that might indicate a young person is at an increased risk of developing psychosis. We discuss the importance of early recognition and signposting to appropriate services where access to optimal evidence-based treatments is likely to promote recovery or minimise the impact of the problem. It outlines signs and symptoms of those who might benefit from specialist assessment and possible intervention, and discusses the evidence-based treatments and guidance available for accessing appropriate treatments and services. We also address some of the common myths and stigma about psychosis; these cause those with symptoms, and their families, to delay seeking help and even to keep their problems a secret (Schizophrenia Commission 2012).

The term psychosis covers a range of mental health problems where there is some loss of contact with reality. The onset is usually gradual and typically occurs in late adolescence or early adulthood (Perkins and Lieberman 2012). Many people make a full recovery from an episode of psychosis, however, some develop a more severe form of illness with significant personal, family and societal costs (Barbato 1998). Most people develop symptoms of psychosis between the ages of 14 and 30 (Yung *et al.* 1998). Early recognition of the symptoms and prompt treatment are vitally important for improving long-term outcomes (French and Morrison 2004), but this can be complex because many of the behaviours associated with developing psychotic symptoms, such as frequent mood changes, are common in young people who are not developing psychosis (Perkins and Lieberman 2012). There are several key features and early signs that suggest a heightened risk of psychosis in a young person; if spotted, these facilitate early recognition of the problem and signposting to the appropriate services. Early access to optimal evidence-based treatments may facilitate recovery or minimise the impact of the problem. Much of the stigma surrounding psychosis is associated with the traditional diagnostic term used for those with severe psychosis, that is schizophrenia, a term that has become linked with assumptions about violence and danger, and the need for long-term input from mental health services (Schizophrenia Commission 2012). For this reason, the term psychosis is used throughout this chapter.

Key symptoms of psychosis

All people with psychosis have a particular combination of symptoms that affect their thoughts, feelings and behaviour in different ways. However, they share typical symptoms such as disorganised speech and behaviour, delusions and hallucinations and negative symptoms (Lindenmayer and Khan 2012). We provide a brief overview of each of these below.

DISORGANISED SPEECH AND BEHAVIOUR

The patterns of disorganised language reflect disordered thinking. One example of disordered thinking is 'tangentiality' whereby the person responds to a question in an oblique or irrelevant manner; 'derailment' occurs when talks about one idea slips off track to another idea that is only obliquely related or totally unrelated (Andreasen 1979). Sometimes people with psychosis make up and use new words, called 'neologisms'. For these reasons, conversations with people with disorganised speech can be difficult to follow (Lindenmayer and Khan 2012). Disorganised behaviour manifests in a number of ways including aimless wandering or unpredictable agitation. The behaviour may be judged to be socially inappropriate, for example, muttering loudly in public or shouting or swearing. Some people with psychosis adopt an odd or bizarre physical appearance.

POSITIVE SYMPTOMS

Both delusions and hallucinations are described as positive symptoms because they were traditionally held to be 'in addition' to usual experience (Crow 1980).

(i) Delusions

Delusions were once defined as false, fixed beliefs, held with absolute conviction and not amenable to reason. The distinction between a delusion and a strongly held belief is not as clearcut now; they usually involve misinterpretation rather than a completely false and fixed belief (Rathod *et al.* 2008). Common delusions among people with psychosis are (Morrison *et al.* 2004a):

- **Persecution**: a belief that others are plotting to harm them.
- **Reference:** a belief that special or personal messages are being communicated to them from, for example, the television or radio.
- **Grandeur**: a belief that they are famous, infamous, or important, or have special powers.
- **Control**: a belief that their thoughts and actions are influenced by an external force.

(ii) Hallucinations

Hallucinations are sensory perceptions with a compelling sense of the reality of a true perception, but they occur in the absence of an external source (Lindenmayer and Khan 2012). They can occur in any sense (e.g. sight, vision or touch) but most commonly involve hearing voices or verbal auditory information (Morrison *et al.* 2004a). The voices they hear can be male or female, be known to the person or not known, and be critical or complimentary, although they tend to be unpleasant and negative. Sometimes a voice provides a running commentary on what the person is doing, or there are two voices talking to each other about the person, usually in a derogatory way (Lindenmayer and Khan 2012).

NEGATIVE SYMPTOMS

Negative symptoms are labelled as those that are judged to be reduced or absent in people with psychosis (Strauss *et al.* 1989). They include loss of motivation, reduced activity levels, limited expression of feelings, and decreased conversation (Foussias and Remington 2010).

Causes of psychosis

The specific causes of psychosis are not well understood. Evidence does not point to any one single cause, rather there is an interaction between multiple factors as conceptualised by early stress–vulnerability models (Zubin and Spring 1977). These models propose that we all have a degree of vulnerability which, under suitable circumstances, expresses itself as episodes of psychosis (Zubin and Spring 1977). Personal vulnerability factors can be:

- **Biological**: such as genetic predisposition and prenatal and perinatal injury.

- **Psychological**: early experience and triggers including acute stressful life events, such as bereavement or leaving home, or chronic (ambient) long-term personal circumstances (e.g. poor housing and bullying).

- **Environmental**: these include migration (McGrath *et al.* 2008), urban living (McGrath *et al.* 2008) and cannabis use (Moore *et al.* 2007).

According to the model, someone with low vulnerability may tolerate a high level of environmental stress before psychosis is triggered, but someone with high vulnerability may experience psychosis even with low levels of environmental stress.

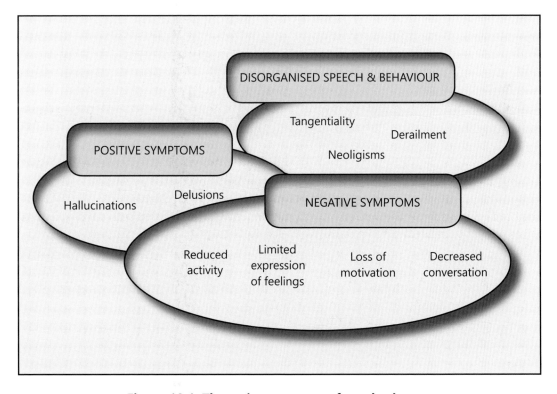

Figure 10.1: The main symptoms of psychosis.

In the classroom

French and Morrison (2004) point out that many of the fears people have about psychosis are due to the stigma, myths and assumptions related to schizophrenia. Traditionally it was seen as a biological disorder that always followed a deteriorating course, and media portrayals of people with schizophrenia are rarely positive, often involving violent crime (Schizophrenia Commission 2012).

There is widespread dissatisfaction with the term schizophrenia. It is highly stigmatising and is not a useful clinical diagnosis, lacking both reliability and validity (Bentall 2009), which is why there is a shift to the word psychosis. This is important because more young people will seek help if they are not judged as being 'mad' when they experience unusual, distressing or strange mental events. Much-needed guidance may be available for school and college staff in the form of a checklist that is already is available for use by doctors and nurses in primary care (French and Morrison 2004) for making decisions about whether to refer a child to services or prompt them or their family to seek help.

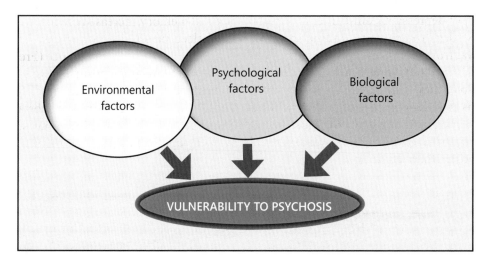

Figure 10.2: Personal vulnerability factors as causes of psychosis symptoms and episodes.

The checklist (FIGURE 10.3) covers several indicators of an increased risk of developing psychosis, where referral for assessment might be advisable:

- Deterioration in function or an increase in stress in a child with a close family member who has been treated for psychosis.
- The expression of odd beliefs or ideas of reference.
- Thoughts of being watched by other people.
- Hearing and seeing things that other people cannot hear or see.

Certain other changes may cumulatively suggest the onset of psychosis, including family factors, such as (French and Morrison 2004):

- Increased use of drugs or alcohol.
- Increased number and intensity of arguments.
- Spending more time away from others (e.g. in his or her own room).
- Changes in mood, and odd expressions of mood.
- Altered sleep patterns and appetite.
- Changed behaviour and appearance.

The onset and course of psychosis

It is rare for the onset of psychosis to be sudden or 'come out of the blue'. Usually it is preceded by a gradual change in functioning over an extended period of time, whereby the person and their friends and family may notice subtle changes – mood variations (increased anxiety, irritability or depression), difficulties in concentration and memory, increased preoccupation with new ideas (often of an unusual nature), altered sleep patterns, lower energy levels, withdrawal from social settings and a deterioration in school or work performance (French and Morrison 2004). Some also begin to experience transient low-grade positive symptoms, for example, they may have ideas of reference or become suspicious or paranoid. Such symptoms are brief and intermittent initially but intensify during times of stress or substance misuse (Parker and Lewis 2006). Most people recover from their first episode but some go onto experience severe mental health problems, with significant individual, family and societal costs (Tarrier and Wykes 2004).

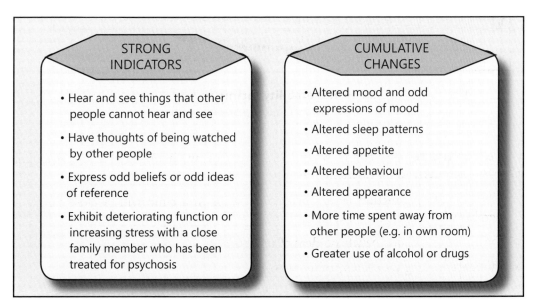

Figure 10.3: Checklist of warning signs for the development or presence of psychosis (based on French and Morrison 2004).

Symptoms such as hearing derogatory voices can be very distressing, but severe enduring psychosis can also elicit anxiety and depression and be highly traumatising, often leading to social exclusion not least because of the associated stigma (Schizophrenia Commission 2012). There is also an increased risk of potentially life-threatening health problems such as diabetes and coronary heart disease (Tiihonen *et al.* 2009). Suicide occurs in 5–10% of cases, more than half of which occur in the first five years of the illness (Verdoux *et al.* 2001). Recent estimates suggest that 0.2% of 16–24 year olds experience a psychotic episode (McManus *et al.* 2009). There are many reasons why young people may exhibit features of psychosis. They can be associated with physical health problems such as migraine, with side-effects of prescribed medication or illegal drugs, and with mental health problems such as depression (Perera *et al.* 2011). Consequently it can be difficult to distinguish between normal human development and experience and the onset of a psychotic mental health problem, but there has been significant progress in developing screening tools to identify who may be at an increased risk of developing psychosis.

Referral to specialist services

The referral is usually made by a GP, and more rarely by school-teachers, college lecturers and family members. Assessment of young people of 18 or more is often performed by the Increasing Access to Psychological Therapies (IAPT) service. They are unlikely to accept someone on the basis of suspicion of developing psychosis, but do provide signposting to relevant services. The IAPT also includes a Children and Young People's project, to improve collaborative practice in Child and Adolescent Mental Health Services and embed evidence-based practices within such services. Further detail of all IAPT developments can be found at the NHS IAPT websites.

Early detection and screening

Most people develop symptoms of psychosis between the ages of 14 and 30 (Yung *et al.* 1998). Early detection involves identifying children who are at risk of developing the illness, with the idea of preventing or delaying the transition to psychosis, but this is highly controversial (French and Morrison 2004; Lloyd-Evans *et al.* 2011). The value of preventing an episode and its negative consequences at a crucial stage of development must be offset against the high rates of false-positive diagnoses, whereby significant numbers of children are identified who do not have psychotic episodes.

THE AT-RISK MENTAL STATE

The so-called 'at-risk mental state' is marked by a various factors, with a combination of state (temporary) and trait (more permanent) factors (Yung *et al.* 2004). Other factors include:

- **Age:** children and young people aged over 14.
- **Family history:** a first-degree relative with psychosis and a change in mental state that lasted at least one month accompanied by a decline in psychosocial functioning.

Stress vulnerability models (e.g. Zubin and Spring 1977) account for the aetiology of psychosis, and the role of biological and genetic factors. The state factors, as mentioned above, are often present as low-grade positive symptoms and brief limited intermittent psychotic symptoms (or BLIPS). Low-grade positive symptoms may manifest as a 'sense' of being stared at, or talked about, or seeing shadows and hearing noises when there is nothing to see or hear (Perkins and Lieberman, 2102). BLIPS are short, intense, frank psychotic experiences that tend to last less than a week and resolve without intervention.

PREVENTION STRATEGIES

Detecting an at-risk mental state is only useful if preventive strategies are in place. Given concerns about antipsychotic medication, the most useful developments are those that focus on non-pharmacological treatments, such as cognitive–behavioural therapy (CBT). Research in this area is relatively new, but a meta-analysis of the combined data from a series of previous studies found that CBT-informed treatments were associated with a reduced risk of transition to psychosis after 6, 12 and 18–24 months (Taylor 2013). More research on optimal treatment strategies will be of great value given the costs of severe, long-term psychosis. Specialist mental health teams, referred to as Early Intervention Services (EIS), target children from the age of 14 with a first episode of psychosis. Their primary aim is to reduce delays in treatment and the duration of untreated psychosis (DUP) (Lloyd-Evans *et al.* 2011). A long DUP – the time between onset of symptoms of a first episode of psychosis and initiation of treatment – is associated with poorer outcomes (Marshall *et al.* 2005). In the UK, a three-year programme is usually offered, comprising a combination of pharmacological and psychosocial treatments, using a non-stigmatising approach and a philosophy for recovery model based on hope for the future. Treatment is delivered in the community whenever possible, to avoid admission to hospital, and young people are encouraged to maintain their social networks and re-establish attendance at school or college as soon as they are well enough. The ultimate aim is to *prevent* transition to a severe and enduring mental health problem. EISs also offer support and interventions for families, friends and carers (Care Services Improvement Partnership 2005), as well as providing community-wide education programmes to increase awareness of the signs and symptoms, reduce stigma, and overcome obstacles to early engagement with the services (Lloyd-Evans *et al.* 2011).

Treatment options

Caution is needed to avoid unnecessary 'illness labelling' and unnecessary treatment with antipsychotic drugs that can have serious side effects (Hutton and Taylor 2013; Warner 2005); this is why talking therapy such as CBT is often the preferred strategy (Morrison *et al.* 2004b). In some cases, people with psychosis are admitted to hospital and treated against their will under the Mental Health Act (Department of Health 2007). The treatment itself can be traumatic (Larkin and Morrison 2007). In the UK, treatment is usually multidisciplinary, involving psychiatrists, psychologists, psychological therapists, nurses, social workers or occupational therapists. NICE (2009) suggest that people with psychosis are offered medication and a range of psychological and psychosocial interventions, such as CBT, and family intervention that aims to support friends and families.

ANTIPSYCHOTIC DRUGS

Neuroleptic antipsychotic drugs are usually prescribed. They can be beneficial for reducing positive symptoms (Boter *et al.* 2009), but there is less evidence for reducing negative symptoms (Murphy *et al.* 2006). For many people they have no effect, and they also have unpleasant and potentially serious side-effects. An increase in appetite, for example, leads to weight gain – an average of one kilogram per week during the first weeks of treatment and nearly twenty kilos over the first year (Foley and Morley 2011; Strassnig *et al.* 2007). Such rapid weight gain is of concern because of the poor physical health of people with psychosis (Tiihonen *et al.* 2009) and it is associated with unhealthy cardiometabolic changes that increase the risk of type II diabetes and heart disease (Tiihonen *et al.* 2009). When a young person is prescribed antipsychotic medication, they must be advised to eat healthily, within their calorie allowance (Bradshaw and Pedley 2012), and to get plenty of exercise, which is also beneficial for their stress levels (Wynaden *et al.* 2012).

COGNITIVE–BEHAVIOURAL THERAPY (CBT)

CBT was originally devised to treat depression, but there is evidence that it can be an effective treatment for a number of other mental health problems including psychosis (NICE 2009). It is based on the idea that our thoughts, feelings and behaviour are interrelated and that the way we feel is often determined by the way we think about what is happening to us and what we do, based on the fact that our thinking can be distorted (Beck *et al.* 1979). Thus someone with psychosis who hears tapping on their phone may believe it is bugged and decide they are under surveillance; they may feel frightened, end their phone conversation, and throw away the phone. A CBT therapist might offer alternative explanations for the tapping noise that are grounded in reality, such as having a poor connection. Therapy may last for weeks, and NICE recommends a minimum of sixteen sessions (NICE 2009). The aim is not to remove symptoms, but to reduce the distress and disability frequently associated with them (Birchwood and Trower 2006). Research suggests that people who do not want or need mental health services, or other forms of help, also hear voices, hold unusual beliefs (ghosts, telepathy, etc.) and experience negative symptoms (Lovatt *et al.* 2010; Wright *et al.* 2009). Children often see or hear things that may be distressing or have imaginary friends they talk to or play with (Majors 2013); withdrawal and inactivity are common among young adults during adolescence or during periods of unemployment (Wright *et al.* 2009). Psychotic experiences are part of normal human experience and do not require treatment, but these occurrences may suggest the development of a first episode of psychosis. A key aspect of CBT involves normalising psychotic experiences by viewing them on a continuum with normal human experiences (Strauss *et al.* 1989), by explaining that hearing voices is relatively common in the general population (Tien 1991), or naming famous people who had psychotic experiences. CBT practitioners do not minimise any associated distress felt by the child, or negate their need for professional assessment and possible intervention; rather, they convey the message that anyone can have strange, unusual, even odd experiences, particularly when they are under stress.

FAMILY INTERVENTION

The onset and progression of psychosis also has an influence on the family, but supporting the family can improve the risk of further relapse for the person with established psychosis. The intervention usually involves family meetings with two mental health workers on a regular basis, to provide accurate information about psychosis and help them develop coping strategies to minimise stress (Barrowclough and Tarrier 1997). NICE (2009) recommend that all families of people with psychosis should be offered this support for three months to a year.

Concluding comments

This chapter reviewed the concept of psychosis and charted the development of early intervention and detection strategies designed to prevent transition to psychosis and minimise delays to treatment. It describes opportunities for early detection in the school environment, with insights into specific observable changes that may indicate the need for a referral to a specialist, with an emphasis on support using non-drug-based therapies such as CBT, and support systems that encourage rehabilitation rather than stigmatising the condition.

KEY MESSAGES FROM THIS CHAPTER

- The onset of psychosis is common in late adolescence and preceded by a gradual decline in function.

- Many people recover completely from an episode of psychosis but a few develop severe and long-term mental health problems.

- Severe mental health problems carry significant costs the person affected, their family, the local community and society as a whole.

- Researchers have developed tools that can identify people with an increased risk of developing psychosis (an at-risk mental state).

- Specialist teams have been introduced in many countries with the responsibility or providing prompt assessment and treatment, in order to facilitate recovery and prevent long-term disability.

- Early detection aims to postpone or prevent transition to full psychosis, to reduce the duration of untreated psychosis in those who develop psychotic symptoms, and to increase access to appropriate mental health services including evidence-based psychological therapies.

Supporting evidence and further reading

Andreasen NC (1979) Thought, language and communication disorders. II. Diagnostic significance. *Archives of General Psychiatry* 36(12), 1325–30.

Barbato A (1998) *Schizophrenia and Public Health*. Geneva: World Health Organisation

Barrowclough C, Tarrier N (1997) *Families of Schizophrenic Patients: Cognitive Behavioural Intervention*. Cheltenham: Stanley Thornes.

Beck AT, Rush AJ, Shaw BF (1979) *Cognitive Therapy for Depression*. New York: Guildford Press.

Bentall RP (2009) *Doctoring the Mind: Why Psychiatric Treatments Fail*. London: Penguin Books.

Birchwood M, Trower P (2006) The future of cognitive–behavioural therapy for psychosis: not a quasi-neuroleptic. *British Journal of Psychiatry* 188, 107–08.

Boter H, Peuskens J, Libiger J *et al.* (2009) Effectiveness of antipsychotics in first-episode schizophrenia and schizophreniform disorder on response and remission: an open randomised controlled trial (EUFEST). *Schizophrenia Research* 115(2–3), 97–103.

Bradshaw T, Pedley R (2012) The evolving role of mental health nurses in the physical health care of people with serious mental health problems. International. *Journal of Mental Health Nursing* 21, 266–73.

Care Services Improvement Partnership (2005) *Report of Early Detection and Intervention for Young People at Risk of Developing Psychosis.* London: CSIP.

Crow TJ (1980) Molecular pathology of schizophrenia: more than one disease process? *British Journal of Medicine* 280, 66–68.

Department of Health (2007) *Mental Health Act.* Available at: www.legislation.gov.uk/ukpga/2007/12/pdfs/ ukpga_20070012_en.pdf/ (accessed December 2015).

Foley D, Morley KI (2011) Systematic review of early cardio-metabolic outcomes of the first treated episode of psychosis. *Archives of General Psychiatry* 68(6), 609–16.

Foussias G, Remington G (2010) Negative symptoms in schizophrenia: Avolition and Occam's Razor. *Schizophrenia Bulletin* 36(2), 359–69.

French P, Morrsion A (2004) *Early Detection and Cognitive Therapy for People at high Risk of Developing Psychosis: A Treatment Approach.* Chichester: John Wiley.

Hutton P, Taylor PJ (2013) Cognitive behavioural therapy for psychosis prevention: A systematic review and meta-analysis. *Psychological Medicine* 44(3), 449-468.

Larkin W, Morrison AP (2007) *Trauma and Psychosis: New Directions for Theory and Therapy.* London: Routledge.

Lindenmayer J, Khan A (2102) Psychopathology. In: J Lieberman, T Stroup and D Perkins (eds) *Essentials of Schizophrenia.* Washington DC: American Psychiatric Publishing.

Lloyd-Evans B, Crosby M, Stockton S (2011) Initiatives to shorten duration of untreated psychosis. *British Journal of Psychiatry* 198(4)256–63.

Lovatt A, Mason O, Brett C *et al.* (2010) Psychotic-like experiences, appraisals and trauma. *Journal of Nervous and Mental Disease* 198, 813–19.

Majors KA (2013) Childhood perceptions of their imaginary companions and the purposes they serve: An exploratory study in the United Kingdom. *Childhood.* Doi: 10.1177/0907568213476899.

Marshall M, Lewis S, Lockwood A *et al.* (2005) Association between duration of untreated psychosis and outcome in first episode patients: A systematic review. *Archives of General Psychiatry* 62, 975–83.

McGrath J, Saha S, Chant D *et al.* (2008) Schizophrenia: A concise overview of incidence, prevalence and mortality. *Epidemiologic Reviews* 30, 67–76.

McManus S, Meltzer H, Brugha T (2009) Adult Psychiatric Morbidity in England 2007; Results of a Household Survey. London: NHS.

Moore TH, Zammit S, Lingford-Hughes A (2007) Cannabis use and use of psychotic or affective mental health outcomes: A systematic review. *Lancet* 370(9584) 319–28.

Morrison A, French P, Lewis S *et al.* (2004b) Cognitive therapy for prevention of psychosis for people at ultra-high risk: A randomised controlled trial. *British Journal of Psychiatry* 185, 291–97.

Morrison A, Renton J, Dunn H *et al.* (2004a) *Cognitive Behavioural Therapy for Psychosis: A Formulation-Based Approach.* Hove: Brunner Routledge.

Murphy BP, Chung YC, Part TW *et al.* (2006) Pharmacological treatment of primary negative symptoms in schizophrenia: a systematic review. *Schizophrenia Research* 88 (1–3) 5–25.

National Institute for Health and Clinical Excellence (2009) *Guidelines for the treatment of schizophrenia. Clinical Guideline No. 82.* London: NICE.

Parker S, Lewis S (2006) Identification of young people at risk of psychosis. *Advances in Psychiatric Treatment* 12, 249–55.

Perera H, Attygalle U, Jeewandara C *et al.* (2011) Non-psychotic auditory hallucinations in children and adolescents. *Sri Lankan Journal of Psychiatry* 2(1), 9–12.

Perkins D, Lieberman JA (2102) Prodrome and first episode. In: Lieberman J, Stroup T, Perkins D (eds) *Essentials of Schizophrenia*. Washington DC: American Psychiatric Publishing.

Rathod S, Kingdon D, Weiden P *et al.* (2008) Cognitive–behavioral therapy for medication-resistant schizophrenia: A review. *Journal of Psychiatric Practice 14*(1), 22–33.

Strassnig M, Miewald J, Keshavan M *et al.* (2007) Weight gain in newly diagnosed first-episode psychosis patients and healthy comparisons: one-year analysis. *Schizophrenia Research* 93, 90–98.

Strauss JS, Rakfeldt J, Harding CM *et al.* (1989) Psychological and social aspects of negative symptoms. *British Journal of Psychiatry* 155(Suppl.7), 128–32.

Tarrier N, Wykes T (2004) Is there evidence that cognitive behavioural therapy is an effective treatment for schizophrenia? A cautious or cautionary tale? *Behaviour Research and Therapy* 42(12), 1377–1401.

Schizophrenia Commission (2012) *The Abandoned Illness: A Report of the Schizophrenia Commission*. London: Rethink Mental Illness.

Tien AY (1991) Distribution of hallucinations in the population. *Social Psychiatry and Psychiatric Epidemiology.* 26(6), 287–92.

Tiihonen J, Lönnqvist J, Wahlbeck K *et al.* (2009) 11-year follow-up of mortality in patients with schizophrenia: a population-based cohort study (FIN11 study). *Lancet* 374, 620–27.

Verdoux H, Liraud F, Gonzales B *et al.* (2001) Predictors and outcome characteristics associated with suicidal behaviour in early psychosis: a two-year follow-up of first-admitted subjects. *Acta Psychiatrica Scandinavica* 103(5), 347–54.

Warner R (2005) Problems in early and very early intervention in psychosis. *British Journal of Psychiatry* 187(Suppl.48), 104–07.

Wright JH, Turkington D, Kingdon D *et al.* (2009) *Cognitive Behavior Therapy for Severe Mental Illness:* An Illustrated Guide. Washington DC: American Psychiatric Publishing.

Wynaden D, Barr L, Omari O *et al.* (2012) Evaluation of service users' experiences of participating in an exercise programme at the Western Australian State Forensic Mental Health Services. *International Journal of Mental Health Nursing* 21, 229–35.

Yung A, Phillips LJ, McGorry PD *et al.* (1998) A step towards indicated preventions of schizophrenia. *British Journal of Psychiatry* 172(Suppl.33), 14–20.

Yung A, Phillips LJ, Yuen HP *et al.* (2004) Risk factors for psychosis in an ultra high-risk group: psychopathology and clinical features. *Schizophrenia Research* 67, 131–42.

Zubin J, Spring B (1977) A new view of schizophrenia. *Journal of Abnormal Psychology* 86(2), 103–26.

CHAPTER 11

Attention–deficit hyperactivity disorder (ADHD)

Bill Colley

Attention deficit hyperactivity disorder (ADHD) is a major presentation that influences the educational well-being and development of a significant number of children in schools worldwide. Surprisingly, the condition and the pattern of its impact on educational attainment, is often poorly understood – not only by parents, but also by those in educational authority and those responsible for provision and delivery of education. This chapter addresses the issue of ADHD within the classroom and examines approaches and strategies to maximise engagement and learning. In children and young people of school age, it is strongly associated with exclusion, early disengagement, academic under-achievement, behavioural difficulties and social isolation (Barbaresi 2007; Beeri and Lev-Wiesel 2012). It is also implicated in developmental trajectories that lead to juvenile offending, substance misuse and poor mental health outcomes, as well as occupational under-employment and low socioeconomic status.

The impact of ADHD on school attainment has been the subject of extensive research over the last three decades but convincing evidence has yet to emerge to support specific interventions that reduce academic under-attainment and improve the experience of school for children and young people who have the disorder. This is attributed in part to the heterogeneity of ADHD expression per se, as well as the contribution of common comorbidities and the complex interplay between genetic and environmental factors; these lead to generic approaches that are imprecise and of limited value. Caution should also be exercised when developing programmes based on the efficacy of interventions used in North America and elsewhere, where school systems, teacher perceptions of ADHD and the ADHD population itself, are very different from those currently found in the UK. There is, however, a growing consensus that multimodal methodologies (those combining ADHD treatment with academic and behavioural support), are more likely to succeed than either medical or psychosocial programmes delivered in isolation (Richters *et al.* 1995), but research is often compromised because of difficulties in consistent reporting and intervention (Owens *et al.* 2005).

Is ADHD a learning difficulty?

It is not in itself considered to be a learning difficulty, which can be defined as a 'significantly reduced ability to understand new or complex information, to learn new skills, or a reduced ability to cope independently which starts before adulthood with lasting effects on development' (Department of Health 2001). However, it does cause disruption to the learning process and the capacity of children to use their own cognitive resources to address academic tasks (Sheridan *et al.* 2007). The most obvious examples of this are in the symptomatic behaviours (impulsivity, hyperactivity and inattention) that often interfere with their ability to engage in classroom activities and derive benefit from tuition. Weaknesses that are common in ADHD include working memory, executive control and temporal management (Martell 2007).

ADHD and the school setting

The current clinical guidelines offer only generalised support for managing ADHD in the school setting. The National Institute for Health and Care Excellence (NICE 2008, 2013) recommends that:

> *Teachers who have received training about ADHD and its management should provide behavioural interventions in the classroom to help children and young people with ADHD.*

They do not specify what form this should take, its duration or what training they have undertaken. The Scottish Intercollegiate Guidelines Network (SIGN 2009) guideline suggests that:

> *Contingency management strategies and academic interventions are more effective for behaviour change than cognitive behavioural strategies ... [the] short term effects of behavioural interventions are typically limited to the periods when the programmes are actually in effect. When treatment is withdrawn, children often lose the gains made during treatment.*

Given the importance of 'attending to task' as part of the learning process, and the frequency and severity of this core deficit in children with ADHD, SIGN recommend the following to address high levels of distractibility (FIGURE 11.1):

- Smaller class sizes.
- Resource rooms rather than regular classrooms.
- Giving direct versus indirect instructions.
- Whole-class engagements.

The success of support programmes is likely to depend on three key elements (FIGURE 11.2):

- Accurate and comprehensive assessment of all learning and developmental needs.
- Provision of appropriate support to further the development of the 'whole child'.
- Specific interventions to target specific deficits, such as poor working memory and weak executive function.

The support programmes should be continually assessed, review and captured, if appropriate, in the form of an individualised educational programme (IEP), and based on strong collaborative relationships between home and school (Pfiffner *et al.* 2007). The diagnostic label is essential for understanding the needs of each child and to secure services; it may be insufficient for guiding planning at school level unless further assessment of need is undertaken by staff trained in ADHD and learning difficulties. Schools are environments for social development as well as academic learning, therefore it is important to assess social functioning, especially because the deficits typical of ADHD can affect their capacity to learn in the peer-setting and to respond to instructions from the teacher. The route to successful support may be indirect; to improve attainment, children should first be helped in their interactions with their peers and their whole-school experience – not just their academic performance (DuPaul and Power 2008). For all that we know about the impact of ADHD on the functioning of children – both in terms of the disparities that arise between their performance and potential, and the contrasts that exist between them and their peers (Andrade *et al.* 2005) – research has yet to clarify the effects of the disorder on early development and the subtle but significant processes that shape personality and enhance skills. Recent studies have highlighted the often undiagnosed language and communication deficits of school-age children with ADHD, and the impact that this has on their ability to access the curriculum, as well as their ability to understand the social world around them and the demands it makes on their day-to-day functioning.

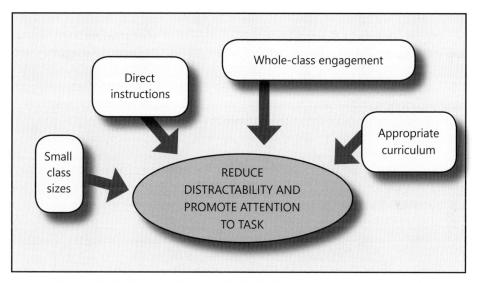

Figure 11.1: Factors that can help limit distractibility and optimise 'attending to task'.

Neurocognitive factors

The weaknesses in executive control function (ECF) may account for many of the difficulties these children face at school level and beyond. Executive control relates to higher cognitive functions that manage processes associated with memory, planning and executing tasks, reasoning and problem-solving. Inefficiencies in the signalling mechanisms in the pre-frontal cortex are related to the difficulties children with ADHD have in achieving age-appropriate ECF. They can, in part, be moderated by enhancing the availability of neurotransmitters such as dopamine and norepinephrine using stimulant and non-stimulant medications (Barbaresi *et al.* 2007). Executive demands on children increase gradually through the primary education, as class-based play is replaced by more formal learning, so that patients are expected to sit still, remain on task and regulate their own behaviour (Waschbusch *et al.* 2007). This is when behavioural problems begin to emerge and become conspicuous among their peers (Mrug *et al.* 2001); they have problems starting tasks and seeing them through to completion, spotting and correcting errors, following instructions and avoiding class distractions. Cognitive studies show that these children find it difficult to recall key information from stories and 'lose the thread' (Flake *et al.* 2007); this makes it difficult to complete associated tasks, to fully understand the topic or assignment, or alleviate boredom (Leonard and Lorch 2009). Mundane teaching can lead to 'under-stimulation', but the lack of engagement by the child can render an interesting task too demanding. Broader health and well-being issues, such as sleep disturbance, are also significant for day-to-day functioning; similarly, side-effects of medication can exacerbate pre-existing problems. Learning in school may also be compromised by adversity at home, in relationships with siblings and peers, chaotic lifestyles, or exposure to alcohol and other substances (Lunde *et al.* 2008). In all children, a 'default mode network' operates when the brain is not focused, but this intrudes inappropriately and undermines executive functions associated with attention and goal-oriented tasks (Metin *et al.* 2014) in children with ADHD. The appearance is of an absent-minded or day-dreaming pupil who struggles to meet the demands of the classroom; these children miss vital opportunities to learn from social experiences and interactions with their peers (Hinshaw *et al.* 1982).

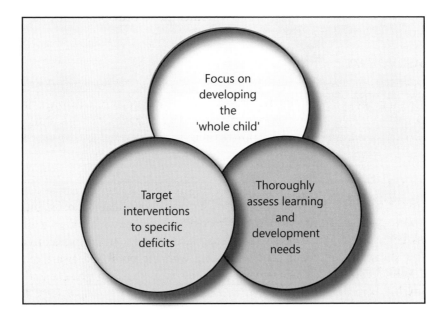

Figure 11.2: The components of a successful support programme.

In the classroom

INATTENTION

Inattention in class can be supported by careful observation by the class teacher and periodic intervention if the pupil appears to be 'off-task'. Calling his or her name, asking direct questions and encroaching on their personal space, rather than remaining at the front of class, are basic classroom techniques that work for most children, but they can be reinforced by note-taking and visual representation of oral instructions using bullet points or numbered task lists on the blackboard or screen. Working memory deficits explain why multistage tasks are challenging to children with the cognitive ability to complete them; they also explain why error counts are high and task completion is low. For example, when making a percentage calculation, the first step is held in the memory before the second or thirds steps are performed. Similarly, long lesson introductions and complex instructions lose impact unless they are supported by visual representations or aide-memoires of what is expected. Understanding this helps teachers to appreciate the importance of breaking tasks into chunks and regularly reviewing the work that has been covered. When reading a story or watching a movie, children with attention difficulties have only partial and fragmented information, and thus may find it difficult to follow the narrative or recall the names of key characters unless reminded periodically of what has gone before.

LANGUAGE AND COMMUNICATION DEFICITS

These often go undetected if their presentation is attributed to low levels of attention or problem behaviour. Failing to 'follow instructions' may be more accurately described as a 'difficulty in understanding' written and oral commands; this is associated not only with academic underperformance but issues in interacting with peers. It is not yet clear whether language deficits are a core feature of ADHD or whether the disorder interferes with the subtle processes of language acquisition through childhood.

BREAKING TASKS DOWN

The most obvious way of supporting pupils through extended tasks is to break them into manageable 'chunks' and review information that may have been lost through inattention. Short written tasks and discussion points during the course of a film or story book, for example, are likely to increase rather than decrease learning, despite interrupting the flow of the narrative.

GIVING FEEDBACK

There is evidence that attention is also reinforced by using continual feedback, rather than a summary at the end, and reward systems that recognise progress rather than sanctions that punish off-task behaviours. The feedback can include eye contact, facial expressions and bodily movements that show the teacher is communicating with the pupil and aware of his or her contributions. Sound classroom management promotes sustained engagement and minimise class disruption. Measures include seating the pupil near the teacher or supplying fidget toys to satisfy the need for movement and sensory input. It is also preferable to create an environment with few distractions, with reduced likelihood of noise and changes to routines, resulting in improved academic performance and social interactions.

SUSTAINING EFFORT

Tasks that require sustained effort can be particularly challenging, especially if they involve extended writing. Children with ADHD commonly have problems communicating their understanding on paper. Slow writing speeds and poor presentation are often the result of weak fine motor control and can lead to frustration and boredom; the academic challenge being less onerous than the physical task of writing. Assessment based on written tests must take into account the fact that consistent under-performance results in reduced motivation and self-esteem and thus disengagement from the learning process. Computers and assistive technology are useful, but they can be difficult to access and they require careful management to avoid becoming a distraction in themselves.

Transition to secondary school

The transition from primary to secondary school puts significant pressure on executive functioning occurs because expectations of children are higher – they are expected to organise their time and priorities around multiple teachers, subjects, and classrooms. Secondary school also involves a more complex and demanding social and academic challenges (Mrug *et al.* 2007). Children with relatively high levels of cognitive ability may appear disorganised with a drop in academic attainment, and this may be incorrectly attributed to a lack of effort or the onset of puberty when the real struggle is with the extra demand on executive function both at home and at school.

The move also presents challenges to the clinician who must source reliable broad-based information about the child's performance to inform treatment and assess progress. Many transitions are made during the school day, making good quality reporting difficult during class time because of the involvement of multiple teachers. Furthermore, low staff levels during break and lunch times mean that pupils are often unobserved at times when their social choices and interactions are at their most challenging – and revealing (Pelham *et al.* 2005). Thus assessment and adjustment of medications – sometimes a key part of the therapy – are more problematic, and it is harder to evaluate the success of the education strategies that have been used. The better the child adapts to a planned intervention, the less they stand out from their peers, which makes it hard to positively reinforce success.

Secondary schooling also tends to place a higher demand on the child in terms of estimating and evaluating time, whether getting to a class, completing assignments, or planning their work schedule. Inefficiencies in this area lead to lower academic performance and more disciplinary events; anxiety and stress may increase in line with academic demands and procrastination leads to bottlenecks in personal plans and a sense of being overwhelmed. Such children may benefit from visual representations of tasks, schedules and lists, and individualised support may help them meet deadlines and submit work on time (Gureasko-Moore *et al.* 2007). There may be a reluctance to provide this level of support to students with good cognitive ability, but evidence suggests that the impact is high and helps reduce the gap between performance and potential.

Gender differences

The common perception is that girls do not 'act out' their ADHD as much as boys, and they tend to internalise their difficulties, but there is conflicting evidence on this (Biederman *et al.* 2007; Lahey *et al.* 2007). Academic and social problems usually occur, but tend to become more obvious in the early stages of secondary school, when other factors, such as the onset of puberty, may be considered to be the cause. Boys with ADHD usually become conspicuous because of rule violations, disruptive behaviour and oppositional responses to authority figures, while girls are characterised by withdrawal, social isolation and anxious or phobic difficulties leading to a similar disengagement from learning and high-risk behaviours. Many children also choose to cease involvement with treatment programmes during their later teenage years, and lose the associated benefits at a time of increased risk.

Behavioural issues

ADHD is closely associated with behavioural difficulties and a tendency to 'act out' and disrupt lessons; this is worse if the curriculum is inappropriate or delivered in an uninspiring manner. These children are more likely to receive multiple fixed-term exclusions than their 'neurotypical' peers. Any child who has been excluded more than once should undergo a simple screening process to identify whether they have undiagnosed ADHD or any other developmental disorder, learning difficulty or mental health problem. Good tools for this are the Goodman's Strengths and Difficulties questionnaires. They are easy to access and process and helpful for pastoral teams for investigating the cause of disruptive behaviour in particularly vulnerable pupils (Goodman 1997) and can be accessed easily online.

There is insufficient evidence on the effectiveness of specific psychosocial or educational approaches for improving performance and attainment, or in arresting decline, but gains have been reported for (Pelham *et al.* 2005):

- Learning opportunities delivered in outdoor settings.

- Use of daily report cards.

- Classes with teachers who are trained to recognise the symptoms and impact of ADHD on learning and behaviour.

Transition to college or university

The behaviours established at secondary level tend to extend beyond the school years, even in young people with higher levels of cognitive ability (Rasmussen and Levander 2009). Additional risk factors in higher education environments, such as alcohol and recreational drugs, contribute to high rates of course non-completion and academic under-performance (Robin *et al.* 2008). Social isolation is also significant, as well as poor financial and time management skills, but significant improvements occur when study support is provided and help given with note-taking and structuring of assignments.

Concluding comments

DuPaul and Power (2008) state 'it is time for researchers to shift their focus to relationships and to develop an integrated approach that promotes the right strategies with the right relationships'. They suggest a high level of responsibility on all educators in terms of forging strong working relationships with learners who are difficult to teach, and they make clear the need for high-quality professional development and critical self-reflection to this end.

KEY MESSAGES FROM THIS CHAPTER

- ADHD is not a 'learning difficulty'.

- ADHD presents a number of behavioural challenges in the traditional classroom environment.

- Most children with ADHD have a general and specific profile that includes neurocognitive deficits, particularly in terms of executive function, but also in memory.

- ADHD is accompanied by a significant emotional and social burden to the child.

- Learning can be maximised by recognising elements of both the deficits and strengths of the child.

- Strategies that accommodate and recognise the neurocognitive profile of children with ADHD may allow optimisation of learning, behavioural control and self-mastery.

Supporting evidence and further reading

Adams JW, Snowling MJ (2001) Executive functioning and reading impairment in children reported by their teachers as 'hyperactive'. *British Journal of Developmental Psychology* 19, 293–306.

Andrade BF, Brodeur DA (2009) Selective and sustained attention as predictors of social problems in children with typical and disordered attention difficulties. *Journal of* Attention Disorders 12(4), 341–52.

Barbaresi WJ, Katusic SD, Colligan RC (2007) Long-term school outcomes for children with ADHD: a population based perspective. *Journal of Developmental and Behavioural Pediatrics* 28, 265–73.

Barbaresi WJ, Katusic SD, Colligan RC (2007) Modifiers of long-term outcomes for children with ADHD: does treatment with stimulant medication make a difference? *Journal of Developmental and Behavioural Pediatrics* 28, 274–87.

Beeri A, Lev-Wiesel R (2012) Social rejection by peers: a risk factor for psychological distress. *Child and Adolescent Mental Health* 17(4), 6.

Biederman J, Ball SW, Monuteaux MC (2007) Are girls with ADHD at risk for eating disorders? Results from a controlled 5-year perspective study. *Journal of Behavioural Pediatrics* 28, 302–07.

Biederman J, Petty CR, Wilens TC (2008) Familial risk of attention deficit hyperactivity disorder and substance use disorders. American. *Journal of Psychiatry* 165, 107–15.

Department of Health (2001) *Valuing People: A New Strategy for Learning Disability for the 21st Century.* London: DH.

DuPaul GJ, Power TJ (2008) Improving School Outcomes for Students with ADHD. *Journal of Attention Disorders* 11(5),

519–21.

Erhardt D, Hinshaw S (1994) Initial sociometric impression of attention deficit hyperactivity disorder and comparison boys; predictions from social behaviours and non-behavioural variables. *Journal of Consulting and Clinical Psychology* 62, 8.

Evans SW, Langberg J, Raggi V, Buvinger EC (2005) Development of a School-Based Treatment Programme for Middle School Youth with ADHD. *Journal of Attention Disorders* 9(1), 343–53.

Flake RA, Lorch EP, Milich R (2007) The effects of thematic importance on story recall among children with ADHD and comparison children. *Journal of Abnormal Child Psychology* 35, 43–53.

Goodman R (1997) The Strengths and Difficulties questionnaire: a research note. *Journal of Child Psychology and Psychiatry* 38, 581–86.

Gureasko-Moore S, DuPaul GJ, White GP (2007) Self-management of classroom preparedness and homework: Effects on school functioning of adolescents with ADHD. *School Psychology Review* 36, 647–64.

Hinshaw S, Melnick S (1995) Peer relationships in boys with ADHD with and without comorbid aggression. *Development and Psychopathology* 7, 622–47.

Hoza B, Mrug S, Gerdes A, Hinshaw S (2005) What aspects of peer relationships are impaired in children with ADHD?. *Journal of Consulting and Clinical Psychology* 73, 411–23.

Kaiser N, Hoza B, Pelham W (2008) ADHD status and degree of positive illusions. *Journal of Attention Disorders* 12(3), 227–38.

Lahey BB, Hartung CM, Loney J (2007) Are there sex differences in the predictive validity of DSM IV ADHD among younger children? *Journal of Clinical Child and Adolescent Psychology* 36, 113–26.

Lavigne JV, LeBailly SA, Hopkins J, Gouze KR, Binns HJ (2009) The prevalence of ADHD, ODD, depression, and anxiety in a community sample of 4-year-olds. *Journal of Clinical Child and Adolescent Psychology* 38(3), 315–28.

Leonard M, Lorch EP (2009) Parent–child joint picture book reading among children with ADHD. *Journal of Attention Disorders* 12(4), 361–71.

Lunde LL, Zevenbergen AA, Petros TV (2008) Psychological symptomatology in siblings of children with ADHD. *Journal of Attention Disorders* 12(3), 239–27.

Martell M, Molly N, Nigg JT (2007) Executive functions in adolescents with ADHD. *Journal of the American Academy of Child and Adolescent Psychiatry* 46, 1437–44.

Metin B, Krebs RM, Wiersema JR *et al.* (2014) Dysfunctional modulation of default mode network activity in attention-deficit/hyperactivity disorder. *Journal of Abnormal Psychology* 124, 1.

Mrug S, Hoza B (2009) Discriminating between children with ADHD and classmates using peer variables. *Journal of Attention Disorders* 12(4), 372–80.

Mrug S, Hoza B, Geddes AC (2001) Children with attention-deficit/hyperactivity disorder: peer relationships and peer-oriented interventions. *New Directions for Child and Adolescent Development* 91, 51–77.

Mrug S, Hoza B, Pelham W, Gnagy E, Greiner A (2007) Behaviour and peer status in children with ADHD. *Journal of Attention Disorders* 10(4), 12.

National Institute for Health Care and Clinical Excellence (2013) *Attention deficit hyperactivity disorder: Diagnosis and management of ADHD in children, young people and adults.* London: NICE.

Owens SO, Richerson L, Beilstein EA, Crane A, Murphy CE, Vancouver JB (2005) School-based mental health programming for children with inattentive and disruptive behaviour problems: first-year treatment outcome. *Journal of Attention Disorders* 9(1), 261–74.

Pelham W, Bender M (1982) Peer relationships in hyperactive children: description and treatment. *Advances In Learning and Behaviour Difficulties* 1, 365–436.

Pelham WE, Massetti GM, Wilson T *et al.* (2005) Implementation of a comprehensive schoolwide behavioral intervention: the ABC program. *Journal of Attention Disorders* 9(1), 248–60.

Pfiffner LJ, Mikami AY, Huang-Pollock C (2007) A randomized controlled trial of integrated home-school behavioural treatment for ADHD – predominantly inattentive type. *Journal of the American Academy of Child and Adolescent*

Psychiatry 46, 1041–50.

Rasmussen K, Levander S (2009) Untreated ADHD in adults: are there sex differences in symptoms, comorbidity and impairment? *Journal of Attention Disorders* 12(4), 353–60.

Richters JE, Arnold LE, Jensen S, Abikoff H, Conners CK, Greenhill LL (1995) The NIMH collaborative multimodal treatment study of children with attention-deficit/hyperactivity disorder (MTA). *Journal of the American Academy of Child and Adolescent Psychiatry* 34, 987–1000.

Robin AL, Tzelepis A, Bedway M (2008) A cluster analysis of personality style in adults with ADHD. *Journal of Attention Disorders* 12(3), 254–63.

Sheridan M, Hinshaw S, D'Esposito M (2007) Efficacy of the pre-frontal cortex during working memory in ADHD. *Journal of the American Academy of Child and Adolescent Psychiatry* 46, 1357–66.

Scottish Intercollegiate Guidelines Network (2009) *Management of attention deficit and hyperkinetic disorders in children and young people* (No. 112). Edinburgh: SIGN.

Waschbusch DA, King S, Gregus A (2007) Age of onset of ADHD in a sample of elementary school students. *Journal of Psychopathology and Behavioural Assessment* 29, 9–16.

CHAPTER 12

Autism spectrum disorder (ASD)

David Rawcliffe

ASD is a group of long-term disorders that last for a lifetime, affecting both the person with autism and their family. In the UK, it affects between one and two people in every 100 people (Isherwood et al. 2011; National Autistic Society 2013a). According to the National Audit Office (2009), it affects half a million people in England alone – 100,000 children and 400,000 adults. There is a gender difference too; 1.8% of men in England were estimated to have ASD compared to 0.2% of women (Brugha 2009). Boys are diagnosed more frequently, partly because girls are more able to express themselves – especially emotionally – and are therefore less likely to be diagnosed (Attwood 2000). Diagnosis is also lower in certain ethnic groups (Strand and Lindsay 2012). This chapter covers the concept of a fulfilling and rewarding life for people on the spectrum, as well as models of care, comorbid conditions, the role of CAMHS (Child and Adolescent Mental Health Service) and specialist autism teams. It also addresses different options for schooling and how to make schools 'ASD friendly'. Therapy is discussed in the context of health, social care, education and self-help, and how different options contribute to skills in specific areas in order to increase personal fulfilment. Everyone involved in the care of children and young people with autism – including their teachers – need to fully understand the specific issues involved so that they are 'able to live fulfilling and rewarding lives within a society that accepts and understands them' (Department of Health 2010).

My first experience of autism was during agency work. Charlie, who was thirteen, was a twiddler, twiddling a stick, and a rocker, going backwards and forwards. His mother asked me to take him for a walk. During the walk, there was noise that was distressing for him. He reacted by running up to and hitting a small boy, hurting him badly. Grabbing Charlie's hand, I pulled him away and embarrassedly shouted 'Sorry' as we retreated. Telling his mother what had happened later that day, it struck me that Charlie needed a regular routine and anyone involved in his care should be informed about it. Since then, I have cared for people with autism in day-care settings, psychiatric wards, specialist community placements and supported living environments, and have supported groups of families with autism and specialist hospitals.

Models of care and legal frameworks

There is continuing debate between the medical and social models of care about terminology – should we say 'autistic people' or 'people with autism'? It is really about who holds the power to make decisions for the person with autism. The term 'autistic person' implies the autism is the person and that their signs and symptoms are essentially predictable; whereas the term 'person with autism' implies he or she is more than just the disorder. Theorists argue over which is correct (Harris and Roulstone 2010; Shakespeare 2013). The biopsychosocial model of disability contains elements of both, and is especially relevant because health and social care is delivered in partnership with educational care, working with both the expert patient (the person with ASD) and the expert carer (initially his or her parents). This requires collaborative care, involving all professionals from first contact through to discharge (Barnes and Mercer 2010; Goodman and Clemow 2010; Herbert 2005; Quinney 2006).

Children and young people with ASD must be treated fairly and as partners in their care, in line with the Equality Act 2010. For those at the mild end of the spectrum this is easy, but for those with more severe impairments, with a comorbid condition, it is far more difficult to achieve partnership, and the Mental Capacity Act 2005 is more relevant, with professionals and guardians often making the decisions. ASD is the only condition in the UK about which all health and social care providers are duty bound (under the Autism Act 2009) to educate all their staff, with a focus on understanding and communicating with children with autism. Other legal frameworks that can be applied to people with ASD are the Educational Act 2011, Special Educational Needs: Code of Practice 2002, Mental Health Act 2007 and the Human Rights Act 1998.

Diagnosis

The diagnostic criteria are in the DSM V (American Psychiatric Association 2013) and relate to social communication and restricted, repetitive behaviours. Diagnosis requires symptoms to be seen in the first couple of years of life (American Psychiatric Association 2013). For diagnosis, there must be persistent deficits in:

- Social communication and social interaction across multiple contexts (currently or by history).
- Social–emotional reciprocity.
- Non-verbal communicative behaviour used for social interaction.
- Developing, maintaining and understanding relationships.

There should also be restricted, repetitive patterns of behaviour, interests or activities (currently or previously) in at least two of the following areas:

- Repetitive motor movement, use of objects (e.g. twiddling) or activities (e.g. rocking).
- Insistence on sameness, inflexible adherence to routines, or ritualised patterns of verbal or non-verbal behaviour.
- Highly restricted, fixated interests that are abnormal in intensity or focus.
- Hyper- or hyposensitivity to sensory input or unusual interest in sensory aspects of the environment.

Additional criteria include the age at first concern, the presence or loss of established skills, and the level of severity. Some children also have a comorbid medical or genetic condition, or a neurodevelopmental, mental or behavioural disorder. Symptoms are typically present in the early developmental period, but may not become fully apparent until social demands exceed the child's limited capacities; or they may be masked by learned strategies in later life. There are significant impairment in social, occupational, or other important areas of current functioning.

RESTRICTIVE, REPETITIVE BEHAVIOURS

Repetitive symptoms might involve hand-flapping, head-rolling or body-rocking. These movements are compulsive, and they are restrictive because they cannot be stopped. Children often play the same game again and again and ignore everything else around them; they may arrange row upon row of toy cars or pencils in perfectly straight lines – a classic symptom. If these 'rigid and restrictive play patterns' are interrupted, they start again (Lask *et al.* 2003).

Routines and rituals are a constant focus and the child has set ways of completing tasks. Some set their own routines, while others follow those set by their primary carers. Grandin and Barron (2005) suggest that such rituals may be used by clinicians to help with therapy or by the person with ASD to find suitable employment.

SOCIAL COMMUNICATION

The theory of mind is based on 'the ability to figure out what the other person does or does not already know – or might not be interested in hearing about' (Kutscher 2005), and this is the key to normal conversation. Both parents and professionals should be aware of the normal pattern of developing communication skills (Buckley 2008) and how this deviates in children with ASD, as shown in FIGURE 12.1. Diagnosis before the child is two is challenging because many parents do not know which communication issues are significant (Rutter 2011). Moreover, communication may seem normal during the first eighteen months, but at the age of two a child may completely regress (Grandin and Barron 2005). Wetherby and Prizant (2002) developed a useful observational checklist for toddlers that looks for 'emotion and eye gaze, communication, gestures, sounds, words, understanding and object use'.

SEVERITY OF ASD

The severity is graded from Level 1 to Level 3, and the clinical picture of people at these levels is very different, and the severity reflects the child's level of need.

- **Level 1:** Children at the high-end of this level appear to function well. There is no accompanying intellectual impairment or language impairment. They talk and make eye contact, although every child may have some limitations in these areas. They often miss metaphor, irony and sarcasm because they tend to think in concrete terms and their pragmatic responses can be interpreted as flippant (Kutscher 2005; Lask *et al.* 2003). These children require some support.

- **Level 2:** These children use simple sentences, but listening carefully and conversations fail. They make inappropriate interruptions and do not allow others into the conversation, talking so much on one subject they are perceived as boring. When first meeting someone, they may give the impression of communicating orally if they use a few key remembered phrases, such as 'Hello' and 'How are you?' as well as the common replies. This permits a five-minute conversation, with the appearance that they are communicating appropriately. For those whose speech varies little in tone or rhythm, it is often perceived as an absence of expression, which frustrates the person talking to them who feels frustrated at their inability to get through to them (Lask *et al.* 2003). These children require substantial support.

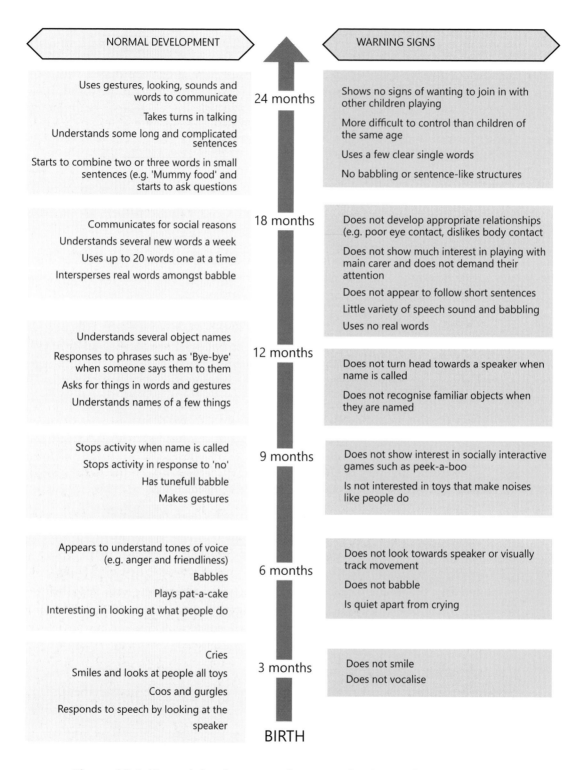

Figure 12.1: Normal development of communication and warning signs in infants (adapted from Buckley 2008).

- **Level 3:** At this level, there is an accompanying intellectual and language impairment, thus very substantial support is needed. The child may be unable to speak or have only a few words; others may repeat sentences with no meaning. Herbert (2005) believes that up to half will never learn to talk, or will only speak in a very rudimentary manner. Words may be limited to 'Mum', 'Dad', 'Yes' and 'No', and some other people may understand these specific words, but not necessarily their sentences.

> ### Personal reflection
>
> *Second-year student nurse, Zohra Butt, started working with Gabriel, who did not speak, and did not respond when she said hello. After watching how others interacted with him, she first gaining his attention by holding his hand and, using literal language, said 'Hello'. He responded by smiling and he used his visual cards to help him communicate with her. It is vital to remember that everyone is unique and everyone communicates in different ways.*

Children at Level 2 and 3 have abnormal language patterns, such as neologisms (made-up words that they attribute meaning to) and ritualistic use of words, that can make them seem rude, odd or socially unwelcoming (Kutscher 2005; Rutter 2011). This can negatively affect their self-esteem and can contribute to depressive feelings. Some behave appropriately at school, but are a 'nightmare' when they get home (National Autistic Society 2013b), often because they are unable to express anxiety or other feelings while at school (Lask *et al.* 2003), so that feelings are released uncontrollably with their families. Until everyone understands what is happening, this can cause feelings of conflict and rejection, ending in outbursts or sulking. People with ASD do not understand about relationships, and their communication issues make it even more difficult. For instance, they may avoid eye contact or hold contact for an inappropriately long time; they may invade other people's personal space, touch them inappropriately, or over-react to being touched by them (Anderson 2003; Mesibov *et al.* 2005). Some are very sociable and overly affectionate (Brown and Harris 2005).

Sensory sensitivity (integration)

Around 95% of children with ASD have sensory processing problems. They can affect all five senses, as well as the vestibular system (balance) and proprioception (sense of body position). Difficulties commonly start at a young age (Lask *et al.* 2003), with hyposensitivity (under-sensitivity) or hypersensitivity (oversensitivity). Some have fluctuating levels of sensitivity on a daily basis (Dodd 2005; Grandin and Barron 2005); and some have rituals using different parts of the eye to view things (Wing *et al.* 2011). DSM-V considers such sensory integration to be a restricted and repetitive behaviour (APA 2013). The senses might be affected in the following ways.

- **Touch**: delayed or inappropriate responses to pain; holding things tightly to themselves; self-harming (and not knowing they are hurting); reaction to materials in clothes so that clothing may be removed; dislike of being touched; eating issues (e.g. preferences for different textures) (Dodd 2005; Grandin and Scariano 2005; Isherwood *et al.* 2011; Lask *et al.* 2003; Stillman 2003).

- **Sight**: fascinated by contrasting light; peering at objects in unusual ways (e.g. using peripheral vision); difficulties catching things thrown to them; clumsy walking (e.g. knocking into things or people); unable to tolerate bright or fluorescent lights, or certain patterns or colours (Lask *et al.* 2003; Stillman 2003; Williams 1996; 2008).

- **Hearing**: enjoy noisy places, high base tones or rhythmic drumming; or becoming anxious, in busy, noisy social situations.

- **Smell**: no sense of smell or heightened sense of smell; sniffing things to explore them; detect low-level smells and become pre-occupied with them (Wing 1996).

- **Taste**: food fads; over-awareness of certain flavours (Isherwood *et al.* 2011; Lask *et al.* 2003).

- **Balance**: enjoy swings, roundabouts, twirling around; susceptible to travel sickness; walk on tiptoes (Dodd 2005).

- **Proprioception**: clumsiness, bumping into things, standing in other people's personal space.

- **Temperature**: oversensitive or insensitive to temperature; prefer wearing summer clothes during winter months, or have domestic heating turned down low (Wing 1996).

Personal reflection

Second-year student nurse, Bella Stratton, was working with Randall, a nine-year-old boy who had ASD, learning disabilities and challenging behaviours. He could not talk, but communicated using the Picture Exchange Communication system, Makaton, and pointing. He enjoyed eating smooth leaves, so at break times he had to be escorted outside. One day he quickly went over to a tree, pulled some leaves off and began to eat them, enjoying the smooth sensation on his tongue. Bella said 'No' verbally and in Makaton, then took the leaves off of him. His response was to bite her hand hard. This behaviour may have been managed better if he had been guided into another garden in which there were no plants with smooth leaves, or by offering him something else with a smooth surface that was edible.

Information from all the senses comes together to form a whole sensory stimulus, thus specific behaviours are stimulated by combinations of different stimuli working together. Someone who smears faeces may have no sense of smell but love the feel of smooth things; thus smearing certain substances feels good. In response to angry sounds, anxiety may increase, especially if they are hypersensitive to sound, and they are unlikely to hear what is being said. A calm voice is required, giving clear and literal instructions, preferably one at a time.

COMORBID CONDITIONS

Comorbidity is common with ASD which influences the severity of ASD and the type of therapy provided. Children with level 3 ASD are 70% more likely to have a comorbid mental health condition (NICE 2011; Wooff and O'Driscoll 2011). Around 40% have two or more mental health problems alongside ASD, most commonly depression, anxiety and obsessive compulsive disorder (OCD). There is a significant overlap between learning disabilities and a mental health in about 38% of people with ASD (FIGURE 12.2), and it is also associated with many other conditions (Anderson 2003; Attwood 2000; Irlen 2005, 2010; Isherwoord *et al.* 2011; National Collaborating Centre for Mental Health 2012; NICE 2011; Rutter 2011):

- Epilepsy that usually begins in the teenage years.
- Eating disorders with underlying sensory issues.
- Attention deficit hyperactivity disorder (ADHD).
- Irlen syndrome (Irlen 2010).

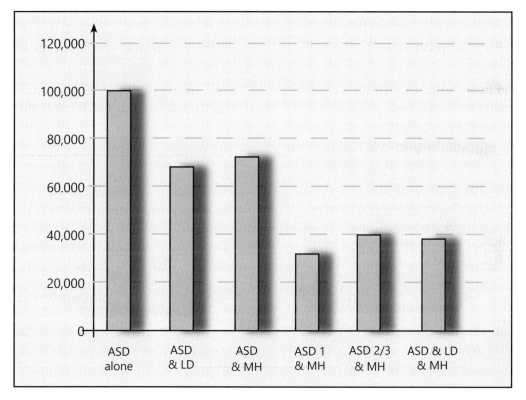

Figure 12.2: Rates of comorbid learning disabilities (LD) and mental health (MH) conditions among children and adolescents with ASD (Anderson 2003; NICE 2013; Wooff and O'Driscoll 2011).

The role of CAMHS in diagnosis and care

CAMHS are multiprofessional teams who care for the mental and physical health needs of children and young people up to the age of eighteen, in collaboration with families. Approximately 10% of children who are under the umbrella of CAMHS are on the ASD spectrum (National Autistic Society 2010), mostly with high-end autism and comorbid mental health issues, but accessing the services and obtaining ongoing support can be difficult, so that most people with ASD do not receive targeted support (National Autistic Society 2010). The organisation monitors their mental well-being and comorbidity and provides ongoing support to both the child and the family. Teams consist of a paediatrician or a child and adolescent psychiatrist, educational or clinical psychologist and a speech and language therapist (SALT), with occupational therapists, specialists teachers and social workers available as needed.

REFERRAL TO CAMHS AND ASSESSMENT

Most referrals to CAMHS are made by GPs although they can be made by teachers, school nurses and health visitors; they are based on the child's behaviour, routines, self-esteem and interactions with others. They are not accepted from parents. At the first meeting, a report is prepared on the whole family, to inform decisions about further referral to specialists. The autism team does not rely on one single diagnostic tool or checklist (NICE 2011), and they recognise parents as a reliable source of information on the child (Mesibov *et al.* 2005). They obtain details on many relevant issues on the child's strengths, skills and impairments and needs in the home, social and school environments. The NICE (2011) require observation of the child in the classroom, and this is compared with the parents' perspectives for similarities.

> ### Personal reflection
>
> *Georgina and Steven knew there was something wrong with Shane; they wondered why he wasn't talking or making friends, and rocked back and forth most of the time. They raised the issue of his temper tantrums with the GP who came to no conclusion. After exploring the internet, they decided it was probably autism. They went back to their GP and he agreed to make a referral to CAMHS. The assessment involved watching eight-year-old Shane at play and interviewing his parents. A family history was taken. Another meeting was held with an autism specialist who had reports from both the school and the parents. These were compared and further symptoms were investigated, resulting in a diagnosis of high-end (level 1) ASD.*

After the diagnosis is confirmed, an annual needs assessment should be carried out by a professional with a good knowledge of autism, preferably someone who knows the child personally (Department of Health 2010). A plan of how each need will be met is developed with the child and family; if appropriate; it involves a consideration of capacity (Children's Act 2004 and Mental Capacity Act 2005. However, the teams and carers must act on the behalf of the individual to ensure their best interests are met.

Family life

Parents of children with ASD often have issues of loss within the first two years of the child's life. The common stages of grief apply because of the loss of dreams or hopes for both the child and the parents (Kubler-Ross and Kessler 2005). People go through the various stages of grief in different ways and may even go through more than one stage at the same time

(Britton 2013; Kubler-Ross 1969). There is often disruption of family routines and rituals and the impact on siblings can be profound (Larson 2006; Wolpert *et al.* 2006). Parents often feel isolated and judged by people around them (Wallace *et al.* 2013). Some parents label themselves 'autism parents' and 'autism warriors' because the term has a tremendous influence on how they organise their lives, so they own it, use it and manipulate it (DeWolfe 2013). DeWolfe says: 'Autism may disorder the family, but it also orders it, and re-orders it.'

Parenting programmes such as the Stepping Stones Triple P Group (Triple P 2013) give parents new ways of coping, especially if their child has challenging behaviours (Department for Education 2013); its tailored sessions aim to enhance the experience of the whole family, and to unite parents with others facing similar issues. Emotional support is increasingly provided by local and online support groups.

Autistica – the UK's leading charity for autistic research – conducted a large survey and found a lack of early interventions or information for diagnosed children, as reported by three-quarters of adults and half of all parents (Wallace *et al.* 2013). In Wooff and O'Driscoll's study (2011) it was suggested that an information pack should be made available, covering:

- What happens during and after assessment.
- Local and national support networks for both child and family.
- Training and therapy packages.
- Autism teams.
- Carer assessment.
- Respite care.
- Benefits.
- Organisations dealing with comorbid conditions (e.g. MIND).
- 'Statementing' a child and what it means for their education (*see below*).
- Managing challenging behaviours.

Recently there has been a movement towards personalised budgets and direct care payments (Department of Health 2010) so the parents of children with ASD can make their own decisions about what health, social and educational care they receive. A child on the autistic spectrum will have a number of professionals involved in his or her care (DfES 2001; National Audit Office 2009) such as (and see FIGURE 12.3):

- **Educational and clinical psychologists**: offer behavioural support programmes, such as positive parenting techniques and anger management sessions.

- **Family therapists**: help family members to communicate and relate to each another, especially to minimise conflict, and help the child with ASD to understand the needs of other family members.

- **GPs**: monitor the child's health and that of other family members, who may be referred to counselling and/or prescribe antidepressants.

- **Health visitors**: provide early checks over an agreed time period, on language development, playing behaviour and routines.

- **Learning disability nurses**: work with children with low-functioning autism or concurrent learning disability, provide behaviour management programmes and help to find appropriate placements.

- **Parents**: note any issues in development and discuss them with various professionals; Enderby *et al.* (2009) call for professionals to empower parents as therapists.

- **Occupational therapists**: help develop skills for life, such as cooking and transferable (e.g. work-based) skills, and work with the family to minimise conflict.

- **Psychiatrists**: monitor the child's mood and behaviour and discuss with parents the need for antipsychotic medication or behavioural approaches.

- **School nurses**: oversee immunisations, monitor hearing and vision and provide information to the school staff, the child and the parents.

- **Special educational needs coordinators (SENCOs)**: a teacher appointed responsibility for the day-to-day operation of the school's SEN policy. They have regular meetings with the child to facilitate a peaceful and positive way forward; advise teachers on effective interactions; and develop educational plans in collaboration with the child, parents and teacher.

- **Speech and language therapists (SALTs)**: support non-verbal communicators or those with minimal communication skills, and teach Makaton and how to use communication boards (e.g. the Picture Exchange Communication System, PECS; or the Pyramid Approach 2013).

- **Teachers**: observe social interactions, how emotional needs are expressed, and confirm relevant issues to specialist autism services.

Educational options

There are several different types of school, each with its own advantages and disadvantages:

- **Mainstream schools (with or without a specialist unit)**: For most children with ASD level 1, this is most appropriate, especially if the school has a good SENCO and a team of specialist teachers. The child is less likely to be perceived as being different beyond the school, but the school may not be able to address his or her specific needs.

- **Specialist schools (day or residential)**: The staff are already interested in working with children with ASD, and often have multidisciplinary teams made up of teachers, teacher assistants, educational psychologists, occupational therapists, speech and language therapists, and family therapists. Some specialist schools use the SPELL system that hinges on the principals of structure, positive expectations and approaches, empathy, low arousal and links; others used TEACCH, which focuses on collaboration between the children, parents and the school (Hearsay and Williams 2013; Mesibov *et al.* 2005), with individualised class work based on the cognitive ability and learning style of the pupil, and structures related to the routine needs of the child.

- **Home schooling**: Permission from the local authority is needed as well as proof that the child will be educated to a reasonable level. Routines are maintained and the child has an individualised plan, but there are few opportunities for social interactions, and finding good teachers can be a problem (Hajidiacos 2011).

- **Day school or boarding**: The choice between day and residential schooling should be based on the best interests of the child. Children who come home at the end of the day can be closely monitored by their parents; but they may be frustrated by that point and be difficult at home, but residential care staff have a deep understanding of ASD.

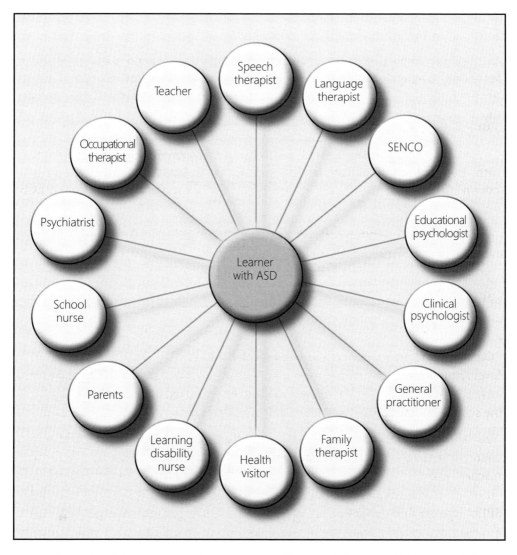

Figure 12.3: The range of professionals involved in care of children with ASD and their responsibilities and roles.

The school environment

Nearly 54,000 children in British schools have autism as their primary need; for nearly 10,000 it is a secondary need (Strand and Lindsay 2012). This represents over 1% of all school-children, with an overall prevalence of nearly 2% (Isherwood *et al.* 2011). Three-quarters of these children are in mainstream schools, and just over a quarter in special schools. This partly reflects the government's drive for inclusive education (Department for Education 2011). The average school of 1000 pupils will have between 10 and 17 pupils with autism. School staff need to fully understand the specific issues involved, so that social communication can be promoted and repetitive patterns of behaviour can be addressed. There are several pertinent issues for pupils with ASD.

(i) The issue of disclosure

Certain decisions must be made with the school, for example, on the level of disclosure in terms of whether the headmaster, SENCO and form teacher are the only people who should know, or whether other pupils and their parents should be told. Fuller disclosure allows open discussions to take place, so promoting a better understanding of the needs of the child, while introducing him or her 'as a whole person complete with likes, dislikes, strengths and weaknesses' (Ochs *et al.* 2001).

(ii) The issue of exclusion

Around 20% of children on the spectrum are excluded from school because of disruptive behaviour – that is nine times more than other pupils (Department for Education 2012). This highlights the importance of providing educational support, one-to-one sessions and vocational training when the child is not at school (Professional Association of Teachers of Students with Specific Learning Disabilities 2010).

(iii) The issue of statementing

Additional support is provided by school action plans, in a third of cases, and statementing in two-thirds. The school action plan states when a student needs additional support, and is realised through current student provision. Statementing involves negotiating additional support through the local authority by gaining funding. Nearly 2% of school-children with ASD receive neither (Strand and Lindsay 2012). Replacement of these systems with a new single SEN category, covering people aged from birth to adults aged 25, has been recommended (National Autistic Society 2013d; Timpson 2013).

(iv) The issue of bullying

Although it occurs less often than in the general population, children with ASD do get bullied, which affects their self-esteem (Attwood 2000; Chamberlain *et al.* 2010; Enderby *et al.* 2009). This is unacceptable, so schools address the problem by raising specific issues with the pupils and their parents, perhaps using disclosure and a 'circle of friends' system (Fredrickson and Cline 2009).

In the classroom

A new child moving into a new area and school might be asked by the new class teacher 'Where do you come from?', to which a child with ASD might reply 'The hall.' The teacher might interpret this pragmatic response as flippancy (Kutscher 2005), but other warning signs should spur on discussions when he or she notices the child is not making friends, or reacts strongly to changes in routine, or escalates issues when being disciplined. Such warning signs may compel them to speak with the child's parents. Some families work with teachers, explaining their child's likes and dislikes, and giving tips on how to communicate with him or her and handle specific behaviours.

> ## Personal reflection
>
> *When Shane started school he had not been diagnosed with ASD. His school reports were good, but as the level of study increased issues began to emerge. He began to look bored in the classroom; he did not make eye contact with other students or teachers; he spoke infrequently, and when he did he used a minimum of words.*

It is imperative that teachers are given help to understand the disorder and the challenges faced by the family. These issues might be raised with a health visitor or GP, and reviewed by a school nurse who might notice poor patterns of communication, but may interpret them as shyness. Teachers may also be asked to confirm a particular child's issues to the specialist autism services, with involvement of the SENCO, an educational psychologist and referral to CAMHS. For children with a learning disability, the Community Learning Disability team will probably already have considered the possibility of ASD.

WORKING WITH THE CHILD

Trying to get all the children to work together can make the classroom seem particularly chaotic for children with ASD (Dunsmuir and Fredrickson 2005). Some feel anxious or isolated and express their frustration in unacceptable ways, by swearing or being disruptive (Department for Education 2011). This may lead the school to consider exclusion, but appropriate planning is beneficial, including providing a mechanism for the child to go to a quieter place to work. If they cannot communicate their level of distress, it becomes unbearable and can lead to temper tantrums and unacceptable behaviour like screaming or breaking things (Shields and Hare 2001). If the triggers are identified, then these issues can be prevented. Teachers are recommended to find routines that distract the child from negative behaviours, and promote positive ones. Practical information is provided by the Challenging Behaviour Foundation (2013).

INDIVIDUALISED PLANNING SYSTEMS

Individualised planning systems, such as TEACCH, are particularly useful in the classroom. The key principals relate to having a few clear rules, working within set routines, and using literal (not abstract) language. Directions should be given one at a time whenever possible. Escape plans can be prepared to account for 'glitches' in behaviour, such as a safe, quiet place for the child to go to. Positive behaviours should be encouraged, using a positivity diary, for example, in which good things can be recorded and messages sent from the teacher to the parents. Regular meetings between the parents, teacher and SENCOs are helpful for reviewing progress.

Another system is SCERTS (SC for social communication, ER for emotional regulation and TS for transactional support). There is building evidence of its effectiveness; in one school, a child who had been unable to sit in a classroom all day was able to remain all day and have an active role, with greatly improved behaviour (Pappanikou 2007; Prizant *et al.* 2010). For children with more severe communication impairments, two important tools are Makaton and the Picture Exchange Communication System (PECS). Makaton uses a combination of signs and symbols, and can be taught to parents who teach it to their child. The PECS system uses 3,160 pictures to express need, make comments, and ask and answer questions (Dodd 2005; Ferris-Taylor 2003; Howlin 2010; Pyramid Approach 2013; Ryan and Pryjmachuk 2011).

Personal reflection

Angela was diagnosed with Down syndrome and autism. She was non-verbal, and used a combination of Makaton and the PECS. Student nurse, Richard Peacock, worked with her using these tools to maintain her routines and to confirm her needs. Angela used them to ask for things, such as food, and to help develop a care passport to inform new staff of her needs and how to interact with her.

PLAY AND DRAMA

Play greatly helps social skills development (Batten *et al.* 2006), but for people with ASD it is can be repetitive, and they find it difficult to function in the fictional (Dodd 2005; Kangas *et al.* 2012). They are, however, attracted to the repetitive nature of computer games, and through them can be trained to recognise elements of social behaviour (Barakova *et al.* 2009). Play in different settings and with different people is important and should include child-led and adult-led elements (Theodorou and Nind 2010; Wing 1996; Wolpert *et al.* 2006). Drama helps to improve their ability to express themselves in social situations, and certain techniques can be used to improve emotional understanding and regulation of emotional responses (Baron-Cohen *et al.* 2013; Britton 2013; Gray 2013; Hajidiacos 2011). Drama also helps them to express affection, but developing this skill often takes intensive training (Britton 2013; Gray 2013: Kangas *et al.* 2012).

Personal reflection

One student nurse working in day services found building a relationship with Justin to be frustrating. One day, Meskerem Ferde decided to sit next to the boy as he played and to copy the way he was playing with the bricks. When Justin smiled at Meskerem, it proved that there are more ways of communicating than words.

CIRCLE OF FRIENDS

This scheme offers peer support to children with ASD, who must consent to taking part and permit disclosure to the other pupils in the circle. It improves levels of social integration and anxiety (Barratt (*no date*); Fredrickson and Cline 2009), and the friends report pride and pleasure from the experience.

Interventions

LOVAAS TRAINING

Lovaas training is recommended for improving IQ, language, social skills and aggression level (Ryan and Pryjmachuk 2011; Wolpert *et al.* 2006). Intensive one-to-one sessions with the child aim to establish rapport and the concept of positive reinforcement (Dodd 2005; Lovaas Institute 2013) using an ABC system for rewarding what is deemed good behaviour: A – give a clear instruction; B – get a correct response; C – give positive feedback. The level of challenge increases so that the child takes on more positive patterns of behaviour (Dodd 2005).

SENSORY INTERVENTION THERAPY

This is a commonly used form of therapy for people with autism, and while it is not consistently effective, it is highly beneficial (Atlantic Partnership in Autism in Education (APSEA) 2013; Attwood 2000; Law 2006). It aims to help children and young people with ASD to manage sensory input in practical ways, such as allowing the child to leave the classroom slightly ahead of the others if they tend to get upset at the end of the school day because of noise in the classroom. If light sensitivity is a particular problem, Irlen filters (coloured or tinted spectacles) can be used (Attwood 2000; Irlen 2005 2010; Stone 2002; Williams 1996), resulting in fewer symptoms, like headaches, lower anxiety, reduced clumsiness, and improvements in academic skills (Irlen 2005, 2010).

MEDICATION

Medication may be indicated for hyperactivity or comorbid conditions such as depression and anxiety (Dodd 2005; Rutter 2011; Ryan and Pryjmachuk 2011; Wolpert *et al.* 2006). CAMHS staff tend to prescribe medication for symptomatic relief (National Autistic Society 2010; Wooff and O'Driscoll 2011) but this can harm the early therapeutic relationship.

Transition from secondary school

This can be problematic and isolating, so a clear transition plan should be in place near the end of schooling. Connexions offers this kind of transition support into further education, or work, by appointing the child with a personal adviser when they are thirteen or fourteen, who remains committed to them until they are 25. The planning process begins immediately and advises on local services and entering further education or employment (Department of Health 2010; National Audit Office 2009).

Children who leave school at 16 and go to college often find little support; expulsions are common, highlighting the need for support from college staff and to address disclosure issues and adjustment plans (Baird *et al.* 2006; Reid 2007). Students often have to speak directly to their tutors about their condition and what they need, but for those who struggle with developing relationships, this is very challenging. Despite the success of innovative schemes, such as internships offering on-the-job training and coaching (Timpson 2013), there is a pressing need to educate colleges and universities in this area, as well as employers given that employment for young people with ASD is disproportionately low and does not reflect their qualifications (Howlin *et al.* 2005).

Concluding comments

ASD is a spectrum of conditions that have slightly different presentation of signs and symptoms. These symptoms start in the early part of life, and diagnosis may follow many years later. Getting a diagnosis can be difficult, but teachers do have a role in this process, and support is multiprofessional – spanning education, health and social care. In order to help people with ASD to grow, the correct combination of therapies is needed, but this is complicated, not least because of the spectrum of conditions. Tailored support of the child and his or her family always maximises the potential for a fulfilling and rewarding life.

KEY MESSAGES FROM THIS CHAPTER

Children with ASD can have fulfilling and rewarding lives, but many have a comorbid condition that increases the problems and challenges they and their families face.

It is hard to get a diagnosis of autism, but observations from schools can help, from either nurses or teachers.

Once a diagnosis is confirmed, then education, health and social services will be informed. A specific care package is negotiated between professionals and the child and family and may involve a variety of professionals who have specific roles to play.

In the classroom, the teacher may be challenged by communication difficulties, abnormal emotional responses, oversensitivity to noise or light, tantrums, and a range of unacceptable behaviours.

Supporting evidence and further reading

American Psychiatric Association (2013) Diagnostic and Statistical Manual of Mental Disorders (DSM-VTM). London: APA.

Atlantic Partnership in Autism in Education (2013) Information Paper: Research to inform practice: Sensory differences and autism spectrum disorder. Atlanta: APSEA. Available at: studentservices.ednet.ns.ca/sites/default/files/Sensory%20Issue%20Paper%20-%20Final%20for%20post.pdf (accessed July 2015).

Anderson M (2003) Autistic spectrum disorder. In: *Gates B (ed.) Learning Disabilities: Towards inclusion.* London: Churchill Livingstone/Elsevier.

Attwood T (2000) *Asperger syndrome: some common questions.* Do girls have a different expression of the syndrome? Available from: www.connect.networkofcare.org/mh/library/article_aspx?id=959&cat=126 (accessed August 2015).

Baird G, Simnoff E, Pickles A, Chandler S, Loucas T, Meldrum D (2006) Prevalence of disorders of autism spectrum in a population cohort of children in South Thames: The Special Needs and Autism Project (SNAP). *Lancet* 368, 9531, 210–15.

Barakova E, Gillessen J, Fellis L (2009) Social training of autistic children with interactive intelligent agents. *Journal of Integrative Neuroscience* 8(1), 23–24.

Barnard J, Harvey V, Potter D, Prior A (2001) *Ignored or Ineligible: The Reality for Adults with Autism Spectrum Disorders.* London: National Autistic Society.

Barnes C, Mercer G (2010) *Exploring Disability.* Cambridge: Polity Press.

Baron-Cohen S, Golan O, Ashwin E (2013) The relationship between emotion recognition ability and social skills in young children with autism. *Autism* 17(6), 762–68.

Barratt Joy H, Potter M, Thomas G, Whitaker I (2013) *Circle of Friends.* Autism Outreach Team Leicestershire County Council. Available at: www.leics.gov.uk/autism_circle_of_friends.pdf (accessed July 2015).

Batten A, Corbett C, Rosenblatt M, Withers I, Yulle R (2006) *Make School Make Sense. Autism and Education.* The Reality for Families Today. London: National Autistic Society.

Beresford B, Moran N, Sloper T *et al. (2013) Transition to adult services and adulthood for young people with autistic spectrum conditions: Final report.* Working paper No. 2525. Department of Health. York: Social Policy Research Unit, University of York.

Britton V (2013) *Appreciating autism: stories of my son.* Autoethnography for her degree of doctor of philosophy. Simon Fraser University. Available at: summit.sfu.ca/system/files/iritems1/12915/etd7721_VBritton.pdf (accessed July 2015).

Brown J, Harris E (2005) Autism spectrum disorder. In: Cooper M, Hooper M, Thompson CM (eds) *Child and Adolescent Mental Health*: Theory and Practice. Bocaraton, FL, CRC Press.

Brugha T (2009) *Autism spectrum disorders in adults living in households throughout England: report from the Adult Psychiatric Morbidity Survey 2007.* London: NHS Information Centre for Health and Social Care.

Buckley B (2008) *Children's Communication Skills: From Birth to Five Years.* London: Routledge Taylor and Francis.

Challenging Behaviour Foundation (2013) *What is challenging behaviour?* Available at: www.thecbf.org.uk/ (accessed July 2015).

Chamberlain T, George N, Golden S, Walker F, Benton T (2010) *Tellus 4 National Report.* National Foundation for *Educational Research* on behalf of the Department for Children, Schools and Families.

College of Occupational Therapists (2015) *Occupational therapy evidence: Occupational therapists can help children and young people with autistic spectrum disorder to participate in everyday tasks and cope with busy environments.* London: College of Occupational Therapists.

Department for Education (2011) School exclusion statistics for the academic year 2009 to 2010. London: Department for Education.

Department for Education (2012) *Statistical First Release: SFR 17/2012.* London: Department for Education.

Department for Education (2013) *Stepping Stones Triple P: Standards and Group.* Available at: www.education.gov.uk/commissioning-toolkit/Content/PDF/Stepping%20Stones%20TripleP.pdf (accessed July 2015).

Department for Education and Schools (2001) *Special Educational Needs Code of Practice (DfES/581/2001).* London: DfES.

Department of Health (2010) *Implementing 'Fulfilling and Rewarding Lives'.* London: DH.

Department of Health/Department for Children's Schools and Families (2009) *Healthy Child Programme: From 5–19 Years Old.* London: DH/DCSF.

DeWolfe J (2013) *Parents speak: an ethnographic study of autism parents.* PhD Thesis, Graduate School of Arts and Science, Columbia University.

Dodd S (2005) *Understanding Autism.* London: Elsevier.

Dunsmuir S, Fredrickson N (2005) *Autistic Spectrum Disorder.* London: Educational Psychology Publishing/University College London.

Enderby Pickstone C, John A, Fryer K, Cantrell A, Papaioannou D (2009) *RCSLT Resources Manual for Commissioning and Planning Services for SLCN: Autistic Spectrum Disorder.* London: Royal College of Speech and Language Therapists.

Ferris-Taylor R (2003) Communication. In: *Gates B (ed.) Learning Disability: Toward Inclusion.* London: Churchill Livingstone/Elsevier.

Fredrickson N, Cline T (2009) *Special Educational Needs, Inclusion and Diversity.* Maidenhead: Open University Press.

Goodman B, Clemow R (2010) *Nursing and Collaborative Practice: A Guide to Interprofessional and Interpersonal Working.* Exeter: Learning Mattes.

Grandin T (2013) *Why is it important to consider sensory therapy?* Available at: templegrandin.com.faq.html (accessed July 2015).

Grandin T, Barron S (2005) *The Unwritten Rules of Social Relationships: Decoding Social Mysteries Through the Unique Perspectives of Autism.* Arlington: Future Horizon.

Grandin T, Scariano, MM (2005) *Emergence: Labelled Autistic.* New York: Grand Central Publishing.

Gray C (2013) *What are social stories?* Available at: www.thegraycenter.org/social-stories/what-are-social-stories (accessed July 2015).

Hajidiacos D (2011) *The imagination room: teaching drama to children on the autism spectrum.* One mother's journey to receiving a treasured education. An auto-ethnographic study. MEd Graduate Studies of the University of Manitoba, Winnipeg.

Harris JL, Roulstone AC (2010) *Disability, Policy and Professional Practice.* London: Sage Publications.

Hearsay KA, Williams GA (2013) T*EACCH On-Line Course: Structured TEACCHing Individualized Schedules.* North Carolina: University of North Carolina.

Herbert M (2005) *Developmental Problems of Children and Adolescence: Prevention, Treatment and Training.* Oxford; British Psychological Society/Blackwell.

Howlin P (2010) Evaluating psychological treatments for children with autism-spectrum disorders. *Advances in Psychiatric Treatment* 16, 133–40.

Howlin P, Alcock J, Burkin C (2005) An 8-year follow up of a specialist supported employment service for high-ability adults with autism and Asperger syndrome. Autism 9(5), 533–49.

Irlen H (2005) *Overcoming dyslexia and other reading difficulties through the Irlen Method.* Reading by the colours. New York: Berkley Publishing Group/Penguin.

Irlen H (2010) *The Irlen Revolution.* New York: Square One Publishers.

Isherwood E, Thomas K, Spicer B (2011) *Dietary Management of Autism Spectrum Disorder.* London: British Dietetic Association.

Kangas S, Maatta K, Uusitutti S (2012) Alone and in a group: ethnographic research on autistic children's play. *International Journal of Play* 1(1), 37–50.

Kubler-Ross E (1969) *On Death and Dying.* New York: MacMillan.

Kubler-Ross E (2001) *Living with Death and Dying.* New York: Touchstone Books/Simon & Schuster.

Kubler-Ross E, Kessler D (2005) *On Grief and Grieving: Finding the Meaning of Grief through the Five Stages of Loss.* London: Simon & Schuster.

Kutscher ML (2005) *Kids in the Syndrome Mix of ADHD, LD, Asperger's, Tourette's, Bipolar and More. The One-Stop Guide for Parents, Teachers and Other Professionals.* London: Jessica Kingsley.

Larson E (2006) Caregiving in autism. How does children's propensity for routinization influence participation in family activities? Occupational Therapy. *Journal of Research: Occupation, Participation, and Health* 26(2), 69–79.

Lask B, Taylor S, Nunn K (2003) *Practical Child Psychiatry: The Clinician's Guide.* London: British Medical Journal.

Law M (2006) A*utistic Spectrum Disorders and Occupational Therapy.* Available at: www.caot.ca/pdfs/Autism%20Brief%20 Nov%2006.pdf (accessed July 2015).

Lovaas Institute (2013) The Lovaas Approach. California Department for Developmental Services. Available at: www.lovaas. com/about.php (accessed July 2015).

Makaton (2013) *Makaton: The Makaton Charity.* Available at: www.makaton.org/ (accessed July 2015).

Mesibov GB, Shea V, Schopler E (2005) *The TEACHH Approach to Autism Spectrum Disorders (Issues in Clinical Child Psychology).* New York: Springer.

Mills R, Francis J (2010) Research Briefing: Access to Social Care and Support for Adults with Autism Spectrum Condition. London: Social Care Institute for Excellence.

National Audit Office (2009) Supporting people with autism through adulthood. Available at: www.nao.org.uk/wp-content/uploads/2009/06/0809556es.pdf (accessed July 2015).

National Autistic Society (2010) You Need to Know Campaign. London: NAS.

National Autistic Society (2013a) About autism. Available at: www.autism.org.uk/about-autism/autism-introduction/what-is-autism.aspx (accessed July 2015).

National Autistic Society (2013b) Autistic Spectrum Disorder: A Resource Pack for School Staff. London: NAS.

National Autistic Society (2013c) *Learning approach SPELL.* Available at: www.autism.org.uk/our-services/education-and-schools/about-our-schools/learning-approach-spell.aspx (accessed July 2015).

National Autistic Society (2013d) *End the battle for support: take action on SEN reform.* Available at: www.autism.org.uk/news-and-events/news-from-the-nas/end-the-battle-for-support.aspx (accessed July 2015).

National Collaborating Centre for Mental Health (2012) *Autism: The NICE Guidelines for Recognition, Referral, Diagnosis and Management of Adults on the Autism Spectrum.* London: Royal College of Psychiatrists/British Psychological Society.

NICE (2011) *Autism Spectrum Disorders in Children and Young People: Recognition, Referral and Diagnosis of Children and Young People on the Autism Spectrum.* 128. London: National Institute for Health and Care Excellence.

National Sleep Foundation (2013) *Sleep hygiene.* Available at: www.sleepfoundation.org/article/ask-the-expert/sleep-hygiene (accessed July 2015).

Ochs E, Kraemer-Sadler L, Solomon O, Sirota, KG (2001) *Inclusion as social development.* Practice: Views of Children with Autism 10(3) 299–19.

Office of National Statistics (2013) *Living arrangements of young adults 2011.* Available at: www.ons.gov.uk/ons/rel/family-demography/young-adults-living-with-parents/2011/young-adults-rpt.html (accessed July 2015).

Pappanikou AJ (2007) *A tale of two students. The Inclusion Notebook: Problem Solving in the Classroom and Community,* I(1), 3–4.

Privett D (2013) Autism spectrum disorder: research suggests good nutrition may manage symptoms. *Today's Dietitian* 15(1), 46.

Prizant BM, Wetherby AM, Rubin E, Laurent AC (2010) *The SCERTS Model and Evidence-Based Practice.* Available at: www.scerts.com/docs/SCERTS.RM.pdf (accessed July 2015).

Professional Association of Teachers of Students with Specific Learning Disabilities (PATOSS) (2010) *Specific Learning Difficulties.* Evesham: SPLD Resources.

Pyramid Approach (2013) *Pyramid Exchange Communication System (PECS).* Available at: www.pecs-unitedkingdom.com/aboutus.php (accessed July 2015).

Quinney A (2006) *Collaborative Social Work Practice.* London: Learning Matters.

Reid B (2007) *Moving On Up? Negotiating the Transition to Adulthood for Young People with Autism,* London: National Autistic Society.

Rodgers S, Umaibbalan V (2011) The routine and rituals of families a typical developing children compared with families of children with autistic spectrum disorder: An exploratory study. *British Journal of Occupational Therapy* 74(11), 20–26.

Royal College of Psychiatrists (2013) *Is work good for your mental health?.* Available at: www.rcpsych.ac.uk/usefulresources/workandmentalhealth/worker/1isworkgoodforyourmh.aspx (accessed July 2015).

Rutter, ML (2011) Progress in understanding autism: 2007–2010. *Journal of Autism Development Disorder* 41, 395–404.

Ryan N, Pryjmachuk S (2011) Helping children with mental health problems. In: *Prymachuk S (ed.) Mental Health Nursing: An Evidenced Based Introduction.* London: Sage.

Shakespeare T (2013) D*isability, Rights and Wrongs.* Abingdon: Routledge.

Shields J, Hare D (2001) Communication and mental health in people with autism and Asperger's syndrome. In: *France J, Kramer S (eds) Communication and Mental Illness: Theoretical and Practical Approach.* London: Jessica Kingsley.

Stedman's (2005) *Stedman's Medical Dictionary for the Health Professions and Nursing.* London: Lippincott, Williams & Wilkins.

Stillman W (2003) *Demystifying the Autistic Experience: A Humanistic Introduction for Parents, Caregivers And Educators.* London: Jessica Kingsley.

Stone R (2002) *The Light Barrier: A Color Solution to your Child's Light-Based Reading Difficulties.* New York: St Martin's Press.

Strand S, Lindsay G (2012) *Ethnic Disproportionality in the Identification of Speech, Language and Communication Needs (SLCN) and Autistic Spectrum Disorder (ASD) 2005–2011 (DFE-RR247-BCRP15).* London: Department for Education.

Theodorou F, Nind M (2010) *Inclusion in play: a case study of a child with autism in an inclusive nursery.* Available at: eprints.soton.ac.uk/153075/1/JORSEN_special_issue_for_eprints.doc, (accessed July 2015).

Timpson E (2013) *Conference Report: Edward Timpson speaks about special education needs policy reform.* London: Ambitious About Autism.

UK Government (2013) *Access to work.* London: UK Government, Available from: www.gov.uk/access-to-work/print (accessed July 2015).

Wallace S, Parr J, Hardy A (2013) *One in a Hundred: Putting Families at the Heart of Autism Research.* London: Autistica.

Wetherby M, Prizant BM (2002) *Communication and Symbolic Behaviour Scales Development Profile.* Baltimore, MD: Paul H Brookes.

Williams D (1996) *Autism: An Inside-Out Approach: An Innovative Look at the 'Mechanics' of 'Autism' and its Developmental 'Cousins'.* London: Jessica Kingsley.

Williams D (2008) *The Jumbled Jigsaw: An Insider's Approach to the Treatment of Autistic Spectrum `Fruit Salads'.* London: Jessica Kingsley.

Wing L (1996) *The Autistic Spectrum: AQ Guide for Parents and Professionals.* London: Constable.

Wing L, Gould J, Gillberg C (2011) Autism spectrum disorder in the DSM-V. Better or worse than the DSM-IV. *Research in Developmental Disabilities* 32, 768–73.

Wolpert M, Fuggle EP, Cottrell D *et al.* (2006) *Drawing on the Evidence: Advice for Mental Health Professionals Working with Children and Adolescents.* London: CAMHS Evidenced-Based Unit, University College London.

Wooff M, O'Driscoll H (2011) *The experience of parents of children with autistic spectrum disorder when using CAMHS.* Wokingham Local Involvement NetworK (LINK). Available at: www.makesachange.org.uk/cms/site/docs/CAMHS%20Report.pdf (accessed July 2015).

CHAPTER 13

Fetal alcohol spectrum disorder (FASD)

Susan J. Young, Ben Greer, Colin R. Martin and Maria Carter

When a woman drinks alcohol during pregnancy it crosses the placenta and reaches the developing fetus. In sufficient quantities, this leads to irreversible brain damage in the fetus and causes permanent physical, developmental and functional problems. The UK's binge-drinking culture is getting worse, which means that the number of children suffering the effects of alcohol will continue to rise (Donaldson 2009). When they enter mainstream schooling, the leaders of learning will need to know how to respond to them and their specific learning needs (Department for Education and Skills 2004; HM Government 2004). The purpose of this chapter is to inform those within the educational setting of the relevance and importance of the condition. The earlier the diagnosis, the greater the chance to optimise schooling and avoid mental health issues, alcohol and drug problems, criminal behaviour and inappropriate sexual behaviour.

Fetal alcohol spectrum disorders (FASD) are a range of abnormalities in children who were exposed to alcohol in the womb (British Medical Association 2007); the severity depends on the stage of pregnancy at which they were exposed. In general, the earlier the exposure, the worse the defects. Fetal exposure to alcohol is a major cause of intellectual disability, affecting about 1% of babies born in the UK – between 6000 and 7000 per year (Autti-Ramo 2002; British Medical Association 2007; May and Gossage 2001). The spectrum includes:

- Full fetal alcohol syndrome (FAS).
- Partial fetal alcohol syndrome (pFAS).
- Fetal alcohol effects (FAE).
- Alcohol-related neurodevelopmental disorder (ARND).
- Alcohol-related birth defects (ARBD).

Symptoms of FASD

AT BIRTH AND IN INFANCY

Birth weight may be low, and some infants fail to thrive, often having a weak sucking reflex, disrupted sleep patterns and proneness to infections. In addition to brain damage, there may be functional defects of the kidney, heart, joints and bones, with poor motor skills, tremors, seizures, and hypersensitivity to light and sound.

IN YOUNG CHILDREN

In children, the symptoms can be wide ranging.

- **Physical characteristics:** They tend to be of small stature and have characteristic facial abnormalities (dysmorphia) with features such as a small head circumference, small eye openings or drooping eyelids, a thin upper lip with undefined groove between the lips and the nose (philtrum), a short or upturned nose with a flat nasal bridge, underdeveloped ears, and a receding chin (see FIGURE 13.1). These anomalies tend to reduce with age and when present they do not accurately reflect the level of impairment (Stratton *et al.* 1996).

- **Physical function:** The child may have poor motor skills and muscle control, and impaired coordination and balance.

- **Development:** This is usually delayed, and educational progress is slow, although intelligence is usually normal or above average.

- **Senses:** Speech defects may be present due to structural anomalies of the face, and the voice may be distinctively hoarse. Hearing impairment is common due to glue ear. Many children have either hypersensitivity or deficient sensitivity to stimuli such as light, touch and sound.

- **Behavioural issues:** Common traits are a lack of self-discipline, organisation skills, spatial awareness and ability to recognise consequences, even of dangerous situations. Behaviours can be erratic, impulsive and unfocused and they tend to be easily distracted. Heightened emotions and low self-esteem occur in many.

- **Cognitive issues:** The range of impairments includes attention and memory deficits with difficulty in both storing and retrieving information, difficulty with numeracy, maths and time concepts (Goswami 2004; Kopera-Frye *et al.* 1996), and following normal speech.

- **Social issues:** These occur as a result of poor social skills, poor teamwork and problems with establishing and maintaining relationships.

- **Comorbidity:** They may also have epilepsy and attention-deficit hyperactivity disorder (ADHD). Mental health issues are prevalent in these children – attempted suicide rates in children aged 6–11 is 3% and in 12–20-year-olds 12%. These rates are far greater than children of the same age in the general population (Streissguth *et al.* 1996).

IN SENIOR SCHOOL-CHILDREN AND YOUNG ADULTS

Memory problems, attention deficits and difficulties with abstract concepts and problem-solving can extend into adulthood, as can poor emotional control and impulsiveness. Feelings of negativity and poor self-esteem are common. Poor social skills lead to poor relationships. Consequently mental health issues are common, manifesting as alcoholism and drug addiction, criminal activities and inappropriate sexual behaviour (Baer *et al.* 2003). Around 60% of teenagers get into trouble with the law, and rates of depression, self-harm and suicide are high (Streissguth *et al.* 1996).

Diagnosis of FASD

Early diagnosis is protective, especially it if is made before the age of 6 years. However, the symptoms described above are not specific to FASD, and children with the disorder are often undiagnosed. Diagnosis depends on the presence of all the following:

- Confirmed alcohol exposure during pregnancy.
- Growth deficiency.
- Facial dysmorphia.
- Signs of central nervous system damage.

COMMON PHYSICAL ANOMOLIES SEEN IN YOUNG CHILDREN WITH FULL FASD

Facial anomolies

- Flat mid-face with low nasal bridge and short, upturned nose.
- Thin upper lip and long, smooth philtrum (vertical groove above upper lip).
- Small head circumference (microcephaly).
- Small eye openings with epicanthal skin folds in the inside corners.
- Underdeveloped upper ears so that creases have a 'railroad track' appearance.
- Underdeveloped chin (micrognathia).

Hand anomolies

- Curved fifth finger (clinodactyly).
- Upper palm crease widens as it approaches end point between the index finger and third finger ('hockey stick' crease).

In the classroom

These children have sustained brain damage that causes them to feel disorientated in classroom settings. They tend to disengage quickly from learning, and are limited in their ability to absorb new information and link it with previous knowledge. Academic ability is below their IQ level. Some need constant supervision because they have poor understanding of danger, or they get lost. Some have difficulties that become more obvious as they progress through school.

Teachers and support staff should treat children with FASD in the context of the English National Curriculum and National Education Strategies (Carpenter 2009, 2011; Department for Education and Skills 2004). There is little guidance from the government on this, but the Training and Development Agency for Schools (TDA; now Department for Education) are supporting relevant research programmes (Blackburn 2010). The emphasis is on the role of leaders of learning in building on the child's positive personality characteristics, strengths and talents (usually in practical and artistic areas), in order to develop a personalised learning plan that builds on those strengths and promotes self-esteem. Collaboration with parents is essential for addressing behaviour and ensuring a consistent approach across school and home settings. The class teacher can also inform other staff members of the child's specific difficulties. The overarching aim is to prevent disrupted school experiences as suffered by 60% of children aged 11 years and adverse mental health problems of an even greater proportion (O'Connor *et al.* 2002; Riley 2003). Brain-based teaching techniques might be used to address several issues.

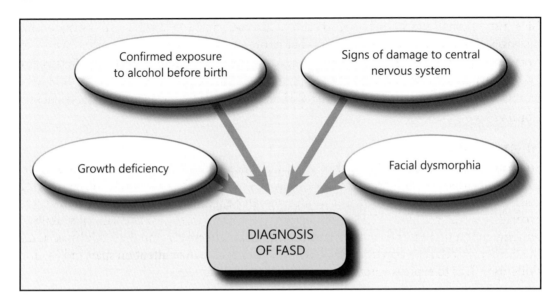

Figure 13.1: Criteria required for diagnosis of FASD.

(i) Bad and antisocial behaviour

Chronic frustration on behalf of the child leads to defensive behaviours, fatigue, tantrums, anger, aggression, anxiety, fear, withdrawal, stealing, lying, running away, and failed attention. The key is to keep the classroom setting predictable and simple, with consistent routine, rules and rewards. It is imperative to give warnings before instigating any major changes in routine, or before changing activities, with explanations for the change. Bad behaviour should be corrected immediately, without scolding, and the rule tried again. If the child has a tantrum, he or she should be allowed to calm down before talking. In the longer term, specific triggers of distress may be identified and avoided.

(ii) Environmental factors

To help maintain orientation, keep the classroom organised and provide specific areas for specific activities, for relaxing, working independently, or being safe if the child gets angry. The child's personal space can be arranged to minimise distractions; there also are benefits of seating the child at the front to promote eye contact and ensure delivery of auditory and visual input. Incorporate frequent short breaks to relieve stress, perhaps allowing a few minutes of physical activity.

(iii) Sensory experience

Lessons should be multisensory experiences, stimulating sound, touch and hearing. Use visual prompts, signs, symbols and pictures whenever possible. An occupational therapist might conduct a sensory assessment for pupils who 'zone out' frequently, or become overwhelmed by the many classroom stimuli such as ticking clocks, the movements of classmates, build-up of heat, background chatter, florescent lighting, scraping of chairs, strong sunlight or chemical smells.

(iv) Communication

Give instructions both verbally and visually. Language should be simple and convey positive messages about what to do rather than what not to do, for example: 'Walk' rather than 'Don't run'. Avoid jargon, idioms and abstract concepts such as 'Be careful'. Break long instructions into smaller chunks, reinforce them with pictures and symbols, and repeat until the child shows understanding of what is required Other staff members should be encouraged to use the same wording for the same rules.

(v) Teaching tools

Structured teaching approaches such as TEACCH (Mesibov and Shea 2011) are recommended. Computer-based learning programmes are successful, too, if they are repetitive, highly visual and give rapid feedback. The learning plan should be tailored to the child's specific profile according to their level of sensory perception, their motor and visuospatial skills, ability to remember and process information and communicate effectively, and their academic ability. Music therapy offers an opportunity for the child to improve their attention span and listening skills, as well as to express emotions, and reduce levels of anxiety.

Transition to secondary school

Families usually need additional support at this worrying time, especially as the child's impairments are compounded by the normal issues of adolescence, such as puberty, making new friends, sexual activity, seeking independence and extra academic pressure (Connor and Huggins 2005). Support services are often disrupted and communication can break down between the various professionals involved in the care of the child (Ward *et al.* 2003), thus it is especially important to maintain effective communication with the parents to minimise anxiety and develop an ethos of partnership.

FASD in combination with ADHD

FASD often exists hand-in-hand with other disabilities, including autism spectrum disorder (ASD) and attention-deficit hyperactivity disorder (ADHD) (O'Malley 2007). Comorbidity is high, with overlapping symptoms, and for children with comorbid FAS/ADHD the impact on their education can be enormous (Bolea-Alamanac *et al.* 2014; Elgen *et al.* 2007, 2007a; Nanson and Hiscock 1990). Children with prenatal exposure to alcohol are at more than twice the risk of having comorbid ADHD (Gronimus *et al.* 2009). It was the most prevalent comorbid diagnosis among 2000 children and young people with prenatal exposure, affecting over 40% of them, more so at higher levels of exposure (Bhatara *et al.* 2006).

The occurrence of ADHD in children with FASD has been reported at 91% (Elgen *et al.* 2007) and 92% (Lane *et al.* 2014). Another study followed 375 children with FASD (aged 11 or less) for over ten years and found ADHD in nearly half of them (Mela, McFarlane, Sajobi and

Rajani 2013). There is little awareness currently about the relationship between FAS and ADHD, but it is important because educators at all levels will be coming into contact with more children and young people with the conditions.

BRAIN PATHOLOGY

The comorbid condition is associated with neurological differences that can be seen on brain scans using magnetic resonance imaging (MRI) and computerised tomography (CT). Two small studies on children aged 3 to 16 who had ADHD plus either FAS or FAE, showed low levels of the neurotransmitter serotonin in the medial frontal cortex of the brain. Binding of another neurotransmitter, dopamine, was increased in the striatum and other abnormalities were observed in the cortex and subcortex (Riikonen *et al.* 1999, 2005). Normal left–right dominance seemed to be lacking in the frontal lobe and there was lower perfusion of blood in the left hemisphere.

NEUROPSYCHOLOGICAL STUDIES

A growing number of studies have been carried out on children and young people with comorbid ADHD and FASD, and reveal various psychological impairments.

- In the *Test of Everyday Attention for Children (TEA-CH),* they were outperformed by unaffected children in attentional switching but not selective attention (Lane *et al.* 2014).

- The *NEPSY-II (NEuroPSYchological Assessment)* revealed no significant differences between children with FASD/ADHD and those with FASD alone, but they were superior at basic attention, visuospatial processing and social perception (Rasmussen *et al.* 2013).

- The *Wechsler Intelligence Scale for Children (WISC-IV),* the *Delis–Kaplan Executive Function System (D-KEFS)* and the *Cantab* tests found complex psychological and behavioural impairments among 344 children with ADHD without alcohol exposure and FASD/ADHD, but no significant difference between the two groups (Glass *et al.* 2013).

- The *Vineland Adaptive Behaviour Scales* were used with 317 children, with the 82 children with comorbid ADHD and prenatal alcohol exposure performing worse in communication, socialisation and daily living skills compared to controls (Ware *et al.* 2014).

- The *Disruptive Behaviour Disorder (DBD)* rating scale, *Continuous Performance Task (CPT)* and *Actigraphy (ACT)* tests were used in one small study of 34 children and young people. Those with FASD/ADHD and ADHD alone scored significantly higher for hyperactivity and inattention, and were significantly more inattentive than controls, but the differences between groups were not significant. Activity levels in the comorbid group were also not significantly different from controls, suggesting that hyperactivity is less prominent in comorbid groups (Glass *et al.* 2014).

- The *Wisconsin Card Sorting Task (WCST), Trail-Making Task B* and *Controlled Oral Word Association Test (COWAT)* were used to test children with ADHD alone and those with FASD/ADHD; only those with the comorbid condition had overall deficits in letter fluency and performance on the Trail-Making Task B (Vaurio *et al.* 2008).

Drug therapy

Children with FASD/ADHD are treated with central nervous system stimulant drugs such as methylphenidate (Ritalin™ and Concerta™), and dextroamphetamine, either alone or in combination. Both drugs increase brain levels of dopamine, and the amphetamine-based drugs affect levels of another neurotransmitter, norepinephrine. These drugs have side effects, but are widely and successfully used worldwide. In one small study, nearly half of 132 children with FASD/ADHD responded to treatment with methylphenidate (O'Malley and Hagerman 1998); this finding is partly supported by Oesterheld *et al.* (1998). In a randomised, blinded crossover study, it led to significant improvements in hyperactivity as assessed by the Conners Parent Rating Scale (CPRS-48) and Conners Teacher Rating Scale (CTRS-39). In another study, 79% of children responded positively to dextroamphetamine alone and 22% to methylphenidate alone (O'Malley *et al.* 2000); however their definition of a positive response was questioned by Chandrasena *et al.* (2009). Other studies in children aged 5 to 14 showed that nine medications improved scores for hyperactivity/impulsivity and opposition/defiance more than scores for inattention (Doig *et al.* 2008).

Concluding comments

A child with FASD needs support throughout each stage of their lives. Their lifelong disabilities will benefit from integrated efforts of the school, the family and the community that foster an approach that supports his or her long-term future. Neuropsychological assessments may be needed at various times to capture their evolving strengths and weaknesses accurately, and to plan appropriate interventions. Those involved in the care of children with FASD also need to be aware of the coexistence of ADHD and the implications of this comorbidity for their progress, educationally and socially, and their need for high-quality, tailored support, including mental health provision if required. The comorbid condition is a growing area of interest and, as our knowledge matures, more evidence-based interventions are likely to be identified.

KEY MESSAGES FROM THIS CHAPTER

- FASD is a lifelong condition which will require long-term support and repeated assessment to optimise the learning experience and mental well-being of the child.

- ADHD may coexist with FASD, with wider implications for the educational progress of the child.

- Comorbid FASD/ADHD may require significant mental health intervention to ensure consistent, continued and effective educational provision.

- The learning and teaching environment may require modification and additional resources to ensure appropriate support for learners with FASD.

- The development of evidence-based interventions to support learners with FASD and coexisting FASD/ADHD depends on obtaining a more comprehensive understanding of both disorders, to foster a 'therapeutic line to the evidence'.

Supporting evidence and further reading

Alberta Learning (2004) *Teaching Students with Fetal Alcohol Spectrum Disorder: Building Strengths, Creating Hope.* Edmonton, Canada: Alberta Learning.

Autti-Ramo I (2002) Fetal alcohol syndrome: a multifaceted condition. *Developmental Medicine and Child Neurology* 44, 141–144.

Baer JS, Sampson PD, Barr HM, Connor PD, Streissguth AP (2003) A twenty-one year longitudinal analysis of the effects of prenatal alcohol exposure on young adult drinking. *Archives of General Psychiatry* 60(4), 377–85.

Banerjee TD, Middleton F, Faraone SV (2007) Environmental risk factors for attention-deficit hyperactivity disorder. *International Journal of Paediatrics* 96(9), 1269–74.

Benton Gibbard W, Wass P, Clarke ME (2003) The neuropsychological implications of prenatal alcohol exposure. *Canadian Child and Adolescent Psychiatry Review* 12(3), 72–76.

Bhatara V, Loudenberg R, Ellis R (2006) Association of attention-deficit hyperactivity disorder and gestational alcohol exposure: an exploratory study. *Journal of Attention Disorders* 9(3), 515–22.

Blackburn C (2010) *Facing the challenge and shaping the future for primary and secondary aged students with fetal alcohol spectrum disorders (FAS-eD project).* Available at: www.nofas-uk.org/documents/FAS-eD%PRIMARY %20FRAMWORK.pdf (accessed July 2015).

Blackburn C, Carpenter B, Egerton J (2010) Shaping the future for children with fetal alcohol spectrum disorders. *Support for Learning* 25(3), 139–45.

Bolea-Alamañac B, Nutt DJ, Adamou M *et al.* (2014) Evidence-based guidelines for the pharmacological management of attention-deficit hyperactivity disorder: update on recommendations from the British association for psychopharmacology. *Journal of Psychopharmacology* 28(3), 179–203.

British Columbia Ministry of Education. *Handbook on teaching children with fetal alcohol syndrome.* Available at: complexld. ssatrust.org.uk/uploads/1c%20fasd-info.pdf (accessed July 2015).

British Medical Association (2007) *Fetal Alcohol Spectrum Disorders: A Guide for Healthcare Professionals.* London: BMA.

Brown RT, Coles CD, Smith IE *et al.* (1991) Effects of prenatal alcohol exposure at school age. II. Attention and behavior. *Neurotoxicology and Teratology* 13(4), 369–76.

Burger H, Goecke TW, Fasching A *et al.* (2011) How does maternal alcohol consumption during pregnancy affect the development of attention-deficit hyperactivity syndrome in the child? *Fortschritte Der Neurologie Psychiatrie* 79(9), 500–06.

Carpenter B (2005) Early childhood intervention: possibilities and prospects for professionals, families and children. *British Journal of Special Education* 32(4), 176–83.

Carpenter B (2011) Pedagogically bereft: improving learning outcomes for children with fetal alcohol spectrum disorder. *British Journal of Special Education* 32(4), 176–83.

Chandrasena AN, Mukherjee RA, Turk J (2009) Fetal alcohol spectrum disorders: an overview of interventions for affected individuals. *Child and Adolescent Mental Health* 14(4), 162–67.

Chen ML, Olson HC, Picciano JF, Starr JR, Owens J (2012) Sleep problems in children with fetal alcohol spectrum disorders. *Journal of Clinical Sleep Medicine* 8(4), 421–29.

Clarren S (2004) *Teaching Students with FASD.* Alberta, Canada: Alberta Learning.

Coles CD, Platzman KA, Raskind-Hood CL, Brown RT, Falek A, Smith IE (1997) A comparison of children affected by prenatal alcohol exposure and attention-deficit hyperactivity disorder. *Alcoholism: Clinical and Experimental Research* 21(1), 150–61.

Connor PD, Huggins J (2005) Prenatal development: fetal alcohol spectrum disorders. In: K. Thies (ed.) *Handbook of Human Development for Healthcare Professionals.* Sudbury, MA: Jones & Bartlett.

Crocker N, Vaurio L, Riley EP, Mattson SN (2011) Comparison of verbal learning and memory in children with heavy prenatal alcohol exposure or attention-deficit hyperactivity disorder. *Alcoholism: Clinical and Experimental Research* 35(6), 1114–21.

De Zeeuw, Zwart F, Schrama R, Van Engeland H, Durston S (2012) Prenatal exposure to cigarette smoke or alcohol and cerebellum volume in attention-deficit hyperactivity disorder and typical development. *Translational Psychiatry* 2(3), 84–93.

Department for Children, Schools and Families (2008) *The Children's Plan: One Year On.* Annesley, Notts: DCSF.

Department for Education and Skills (2004) *Removing Barriers to Achievement: The Government's Strategy for SEN.* Annesley, Notts: DfES.

Doig J, McLennan JD, Gibbard WB (2008) Medication effects on symptoms of attention-deficit hyperactivity disorder in children with fetal alcohol spectrum disorder. *Journal of Child and Adolescent Psychopharmacology* 18(4), 365–71.

Donaldson L (2009) *Annual Report of the Chief Medical Officer.* London: Department of Health.

Elgen I, Bruaroy S, Laegreid LM (2007a) Lack of recognition and complexity of fetal alcohol neuroimpairments. *International Journal of Paediatrics* 96(2), 237–41.

Elgen I, Bruaroy S, Laegreid LM (2007b) Complexity of fetal alcohol or drug neuroimpairments. *International Journal of Paediatrics* 96(12), 1730–33.

Ellison AT, Semrud-Clikeman M (2007) *Child Neuropsychology: Assessment and Interventions for Neurodevelopmental Disorders.* New York: Springer.

Florida Department FOR Education (2005) *Teaching Students with Fetal Alcohol Spectrum Disorders.* Florida: Florida State University Center.

Glass L, Graham DM, Deweese BN, Jones KL, Riley EP, Mattson SN (2014) Correspondence of parent report and laboratory measures of inattention and hyperactivity in children with heavy prenatal alcohol exposure. *Neurotoxicology and Teratology* 42, 43–50.

Glass L, Ware AL, Crocker N *et al.* (2013) Neuropsychological deficits associated with heavy prenatal alcohol exposure are not exacerbated by ADHD. *Neuropsychology* 27(6), 713–24.

Goswami U (2004) Neuroscience, education and special education. *British Journal of Special Education* 31(4), 175–83.

Graham DM, Crocker N, Deweese BN *et al.* (2013) Prenatal alcohol exposure, attention-deficit hyperactivity disorder and sluggish cognitive tempo. *Alcoholism: Clinical and Experimental Research* 37(1), 338–46.

Green CR, Mihic AM, Brien DC *et al.* (2009) Oculomotor control in children with fetal alcohol spectrum disorders assessed using a mobile eye-tracking laboratory. *European Journal of Neuroscience* 29(6), 1302–09.

Gronimus R, Ridout D, Sandberg S, Santosh P (2009) Maternal alcohol consumption. *London Journal of Primary Care* 2, 28–35.

Hagerman RJ (1999) *Neurodevelopmental Disorders: Diagnosis and Treatment.* New York: Oxford University Press.

Hagerman RJ (1999) Psychopharmacological interventions in fragile X syndrome, fetal alcohol syndrome, Prader–Willi syndrome, Angelman syndrome, Smith Magenis syndrome and velocardiofacial syndrome. *Mental Retardation and Developmental Disabilities Research Reviews* 5(4), 305–13.

Hammond DC (2012) Lens neurofeedback treatment with fetal alcohol spectrum disorder and neglect. *Journal of Neurotherapy* 16(1), 47–52.

Herman LE, Acosta MC, Chang (2008) Gender and attention deficits in children diagnosed with a fetal alcohol spectrum disorder. *Canadian Journal of Clinical Pharmacology* 15(3), 411–19.

HM Government (2004) *Every Child Matters: Change for Children.* London: HMSO.

Huggins JE, Grant T, O'Malley K, Streissguth AP (2008) Suicide attempts among adults with fetal alcohol spectrum disorders: clinical considerations. *Mental Health Aspects of Developmental Disabilities* 11(2), 33-41.

Ipsiroglu OS, McKellin WH, Carey N, Loock C (2013) 'They silently live in terror.' Why sleep problems and night-time related quality of life are missed in children with a fetal alcohol spectrum disorder. *Social Science and Medicine* 79(1), 76–83.

Jones KL, Smith DW (1973) Recognition of the fetal alcohol syndrome in early infancy. *Lancet* 2 (7836), 999–1001.

Kemmis S, Wilkinson M (1998) Participatory action research and the study of practice. In: B Atweh, S Kemmis and P

Weeks (eds) *Action Research in Practice: Partnership for Social Justice in Education*. London: Routledge.

Kodituwakku P, Coriale G, Fiorentino D *et al.* (2006) Neurobehavioral characteristics of children with fetal alcohol spectrum disorders in communities from Italy: preliminary results. *Alcoholism: Clinical Experimental Research* 30(9), 1551–61.

Kopera-Frye K, Dehaene S, Streissguth AP (1996) Impairments of number probably induced by prenatal alcohol exposure. *Neuropsychologia* 34, 1187–96.

Lane KA, Stewart J, Fernandes T, Russo N, Enns JT, Burack JA (2014) Complexities in understanding attentional functioning among children with fetal alcohol spectrum disorder. *Frontiers in Human Neuroscience* 8(119), 1–8.

Lemoine P, Lemoine P (1992) Avenir des enfants des mères alcooliques (études des 105 cases retrouvés à l'age adulte) et quelque constatons d'intérets prophylactiques. *Annales de Pédiatrie* 39, 226–35.

Lemoine, P, Harouusseau, H, Borteyru JP *et al.* (1968) Les enfants de parents alcooliques: anomalies observées à propos de 127 cas. *Ouest Médical* 21, 476–82.

Lovell RW, Reiss AL (1993) Dual diagnoses: psychiatric disorders in developmental disabilities. *Pediatric Clinics of North America* 40(3), 579–92.

Mattson SN, Roesch SC, Glass L *et al.* (2013) Further development of a neurobehavioral profile of fetal alcohol spectrum disorders. *Alcoholism: Clinical and Experimental Research* 37(3), 517–28.

May PA, Gossage JP (2001) Estimating the prevalence of fetal alcohol syndrome: a summary. *Alcohol Research and Health* 25(3), 159–67.

Mela M, McFarlane A, Sajobi TT, Rajani H (2013) Clinical correlates of fetal alcohol spectrum disorder among diagnosed individuals in a rural diagnostic clinic. *Journal of Population Therapeutics and Clinical Pharmacology* 20(3), 250–58.

Mesibov GB, Shea V (2011). TEACCH. In: *Encyclopaedia of Clinical Neuropsychology*. New York: Springer.

Mukherjee RAS, Hollins S and Turk J (2006) Fetal alcohol spectrum disorder: an overview. *Journal of the Royal Society of Medicine* 99, 298–302.

Nanson J, Hiscock M (1990) Attention-deficit in children exposed to alcohol prenatally. *Alcoholism: Clinical Experimental Research* 14(5), 656–61.

National Children's Bureau (2003) *Guidelines for Research*. London: National Children's Bureau.

Nguyen TT, Glass L, Coles CD *et al.* (2014). The clinical utility and specificity of parent report of executive function among children with prenatal alcohol exposure. *Journal of the International Neuropsychological Society* 20(7), 704–16.

O'Connor MJ, Shah B, Whaley S, Cronin P, Gunderson B, Graham J (2002) Psychiatric illness in a clinical sample of children with prenatal alcohol exposure, American. *Journal of Drug and Alcohol Abuse* 28, 743–54.

Oesterheld JR, Kofoed L, Tervo R, Fogas B, Wilson A, Fiechtner H (1998) Effectiveness of methylphenidate in native American children with fetal alcohol syndrome and attention-deficit hyperactivity disorder: a controlled pilot study. *Journal of Child and Adolescent Psychopharmacology* 8(1), 39–48.

Oldani MJ (2009) Uncanny scripts: understanding pharmaceutical employment in the aboriginal context. *Transcultural Psychiatry* 46(1), 131–56.

O'Malley KD (2007) *ADHD and Fetal Alcohol Spectrum Disorders*. New York: Nova Publishers.

O'Malley KD (1994) Fetal alcohol effect and ADHD. *Journal of the American Academy of Child and Adolescent Psychiatry* 33(7), 1059–60.

O'Malley KD, Nanson J (2002) Clinical implications of a link between fetal alcohol spectrum disorder and attention-deficit hyperactivity disorder. *Canadian Journal of Psychiatry* 47(4), 349–54.

O'Malley KD, Hagerman RJ (1998) *Developing clinical practice guidelines for pharmacological interventions with alcohol-affected children. Proceedings of a special focus session of the Interagency Coordinating Committee on fetal alcohol syndrome*. Chevy Chase, MA, USA. September 10–11.

O'Malley KD, Koplin B, Dohner VA (2000) Psychostimulant response in fetal alcohol syndrome. *Canadian Journal of Psychiatry* 45(1), 90–91.

Ortega García JA, Ferrís I, Tortajada J *et al.* (2006) Environmental neurotoxins. IV. Tobacco, alcohol, solvents, fluoride, food additives: Adverse effects on the fetal and postnatal nervous system. Preventive measures. *Acta Pediatrica Espanola* 64(10), 493–502.

Plant ML (1985) *Women, Drinking and Pregnancy.* London: Tavistock.

Plant ML, Abel E, Guerri C (1999) Alcohol and pregnancy. In: Macdonald I (ed.) *Health Issues Related to Alcohol Consumption* (2nd edn). Oxford: Blackwell.

Rasmussen C, Benz J, Pei J *et al.* (2010) The impact of an ADHD comorbidity on the diagnosis of FASD. *Journal of Population Therapeutics and Clinical Pharmacology* 17(1), 165–76.

Rasmussen C, Tamana S, Baugh L, Andrew G, Tough S, Zwaigenbaum L (2013) Neuropsychological impairments on the NEPSY-II among children with FASD. *Child Neuropsychology* 19(4), 337–49.

Riikonen R, Salonen I, Partanen K, Verho S (1999) Brain perfusion SPECT and MRI in fetal alcohol syndrome. *Developmental Medicine and Child Neurology* 41(10), 652–59.

Riikonen RS, Nokelainen P, Valkonen K *et al.* (2005) Deep serotonergic and dopaminergic structures in fetal alcoholic syndrome: A study with nor-beta-CIT single photon emission computed tomography and magnetic resonance imaging volumetry. *Biological Psychiatry* 57(12), 1565–72.

Rowles BM, Findling RL (2010) Review of pharmacotherapy options for the treatment of attention-deficit hyperactivity disorder (ADHD) and ADHD-like symptoms in children and adolescents with developmental disorders. *Developmental Disabilities Research Reviews* 16(3), 273–82.

Sampson PD, Streissguth AP, Bookstein FL *et al.* (1997) Incidence of fetal alcohol syndrome and prevalence of alcohol-related neurodevelopmental disorder, *Teratology* 56(5), 317–26.

Snyder J, Nanson J, Snyder RE, Block GW (1977) Stimulant efficacy in children with FAS. In: Streissguth. A, Kanter J (eds) *The Challenge of Fetal Alcohol Syndrome: Overcoming Secondary Disabilities*. Seattle, WA: University of Washington Press.

Stratton K, Howe C, Battaglia F (1996) *Fetal Alcohol Syndrome: Diagnosis, Epidemiology, Prevention and Treatment*. Washington, DC: National Academy Press.

Streissguth A, Kanter J (1997) *The Challenge of Fetal Alcohol Syndrome: Overcoming Secondary Disabilities*. Washington, DC: University of Washington Press.

Streissguth AP, O'Malley K (2000) Neuropsychiatric implications and long-term consequences of fetal alcohol spectrum disorders. *Seminars in Clinical Neuropsychiatry* 5(3), 177–90.

Streissguth AP, Barr HM, Kogan J, Bookstein FL (1996) *Understanding the occurrence of secondary disabilities in clients with fetal alcohol syndrome (FAS) and fetal alcohol effects (FAE)*. Final Report to the Centers for Disease Control and Prevention (CDC) 96-06.

Vaurio L, Riley EP, Mattson SN (2008) Differences in executive functioning in children with heavy prenatal alcohol exposure or attention-deficit hyperactivity disorder. *Journal of the International Neuropsychological Society* 14(1), 119–29.

Visser J (2009) *Diversity and Personalised Learning*. London: Routledge.

Ward, L, Mallett, R, Heslop P, Simons K (2003) Transition planning: how well does it work for young people with learning disabilities and their families? *British Journal of Special Education* 30(3), 132–137.

Ware AL, Glass L, Crocker N *et al.* (2014) Effects of prenatal alcohol exposure and attention-deficit hyperactivity disorder on adaptive functioning. *Alcoholism: Clinical and Experimental Research* 38(5), 1439–1447.

Ware AL, O'Brien JW, Crocker N *et al.* (2013) The effects of prenatal alcohol exposure and attention-deficit hyperactivity disorder on psychopathology and behavior. *Alcoholism: Clinical and Experimental Research* 37(3), 507–516.

Way EL, Rojahn J (2012) Psychosocial characteristics of children with prenatal alcohol exposure, compared to children with Down syndrome and typical children. *Journal of Developmental and Physical Disabilities* 24(3), 247–268.

CHAPTER 14

Teaching life skills and coping strategies to learners

Alison Toner and Mark Gillespie

Life skills are an essential component of development and learning. To maximise learning, the dual contribution of life skills and coping are pivotal. The ability to problem solve could be considered as the foundation of coping, and if the skill is deficient it may influence a person's mental health. Thus the leader of learning has an influential role in the development of effective problem-solving skills, resulting in more positive outcomes for learners.

> *Life skills can facilitate the development of the psychological skills that are required with the demands and challenges of everyday life. (Papacharisis et al. 2005)*

> *A man will be imprisoned in a room with a door that's unlocked and opens inwards; as long as it does not occur to him to pull rather than push. (Wittgenstein; cited by Steibauer 2015)*

Within the UK, formal education at most levels requires learners to show they have reached a defined level of development in their skills and knowledge, and possibly behaviour. Such summative assessment provides evidence that they have attained sufficiently to be awarded whatever qualification the programme bestows. Students often require formal qualifications for academic or occupational advancement, so the assessments, and the programme itself, are likely to become a source of stress; while a certain level of stress is considered motivational (Gibbons *et al.* 2008), some students manage the demands and stresses less well than others. The ability of learners to manage stressors can influence their academic performance (Anderson-Darling *et al.* 2007), thus it is worth identifying precisely what generates stress among those undertaking formal education, and finding ways to mediate the impact of stress by reviewing the attributes and coping strategies associated with academic success. These attributes can be explored with a view to enhancing them or adapting the study programme to accommodate the different abilities. To do this, we must first define what constitutes 'stress' and the sources of stress, and then identify what attributes predict good academic performance.

What is stress?

Meichenbaum (1985) identifies stress as a complex interaction that occurs between the environment and a person, whereby he or she perceives that their well-being is threatened by demands that may stretch (or exceed) their capacity to cope. The same author considers coping as a series of cognitive and behavioural techniques that are used to meet the demands of environmental pressures. It is useful to identify the causes of stress commonly experienced within academic settings, and to explore the most effective strategies and resources to manage them.

ACADEMIC STRESSORS

Academic study does not take place in a vacuum. The people undertaking studies are subject to the same environmental pressures as everybody else, however engagement with academic endeavours brings its own set of challenges that often complicate existing life demands. While some of these challenges are generic, such as exam stress, some are associated with the stage of education of the learner.

- **For primary school-children** education-related concerns include bullying – the most persistent and underestimated difficulty in schools (MacDonald and Swart 2009) – and adjustment to school life, which is influenced by stressors external to the school setting (Murray-Harvey and Slee 2006).

- **For secondary school-children** the transition engenders similar anxieties, as there are changed expectations as well as exposure to new authority figures (Slater and McKeown 2004); this is further complicated by puberty and the minefield of adolescence.

- **For young people moving on to further or higher education** factors such as changes to daily routine, changed eating and sleep patterns, new home environment and travel arrangements, increased academic demands, changes in social activities and exposure to new challenges such as IT problems, may all contribute towards increasing stress levels (Steinhardt and Dolbier 2008).

ACADEMIC COMPLICATIONS

It is useful to appreciate the interaction between the learner's educational demands with their wider life experiences, because separating them prevents a holistic understanding of their position. For example, undertaking tertiary education is often associated with significant financial costs, both directly through payment for the programme of study, and indirectly by limiting opportunities for paid employment. The time required for attendance and private study can also have a considerable influence on the other roles, as a parent, partner or carer, by requiring their focus elsewhere and detracting from the time and energy needed for such obligations.

Meichenbaum's conceptualisation model allows us to see that it is not only identifiable challenges like these that constitute the phenomena we understand as stress, but also that stress can be considered as an interaction between internal physical, intellectual and emotional make-up, and the stressors and protectors surrounding us mediate their relative impact. Ross, Niebling and Heckert (1999) provide useful categories for exploration, namely intrapersonal, interpersonal and environmental domains.

This chapter uses these domains to frame the attributes and coping responses identified as being influential to academic performance.

Intrapersonal factors

Intrapersonal variables are the characteristics that comprise every person. Factors such as intelligence (reasoning) and the personality traits of conscientiousness (being diligent and actively working towards educational attainment) and low extraversion (being active, sociable, positive and open to new experiences) are strongly associated with academic success (Smrtnik-Vitulic and Zupancic 2011). Variables such as working memory, analytic style, gender and present knowledge are also influential (Riding 2007). Two other cited factors are resilience and emotional intelligence.

EMOTIONAL INTELLIGENCE (EI)

Studies on the role of personal characteristics and their influence on performance within the fields of education and occupation have received growing attention over the past twenty years, particularly the concept of emotional intelligence. This relates to the ability of a person to perceive and manage their own emotional state and their adeptness in engaging with others (Goleman 1998). Skipper and Brandenberg (2013) advocate these attributes enable the person to interpret and interrelate with their environment in a way that facilitates intrapersonal adaptation and enhances their ability to develop and maintain interpersonal relationships. To have good skills in this area should promote success in managing the demands of academic life (e.g. self-awareness about which the person is most receptive to study; good impulse control to recognise when an assignment takes precedence over watching a favourite leisure pursuit) and successfully engaging in support sessions with their peers or academic staff. Unlike IQ (the intelligence quotient), these skills can be developed, and understanding the factors that mediate the effects of stress are as important as understanding the causes of stress. Resilience is another concept for which this is relevant.

RESILIENCE

Resilience can be regarded as being at the *opposite* end of the continuum from risk (McElwee 2007). Traditionally the emphasis when managing perceived threats to human development was to identify the risks involved. While there are many possible risk factors (several of which have been identified above) and many combinations of such factors, the number of people who experience such challenges and who go on to thrive, suggests there is value in shifting focus to allow identification of the characteristics that enable people to negotiate such trials effectively.

There are many definitions of resilience. The word derives from the Latin term meaning to bounce or jump back, providing a strong clue to its meaning within this context. It relates to inner strength that enables someone to successfully respond to life's adversities (Poulou 2007), and the development of resilience can be linked with spirituality, caring relationships, high-quality external supports, such as a nurturing educational environment and the presence of intrapersonal factors such as good self-efficacy, resoluteness and higher levels of self-esteem.
(Wilks 2008)

Resilience can be considered as a set of malleable abilities and characteristics, thus managing educational programmes may enhance these protective factors (Poulou 2007).

Environmental factors

Intrapersonal characteristics emerge through complex interactions with the person's interpersonal and environmental influences, among which the family plays a prominent role.

FAMILY AND HOME FACTORS

Moon and Lee (2009) found that family income, psychological health of parents and their education levels were all associated with school achievement.

INSTITUTIONAL FACTORS

The setting for knowledge transfer at all levels is important, that is the educational institution, which itself sits within a broader education system. Factors that are likely to have an influence on learners and learning include the abilities of those designing and delivering the teaching, the philosophy guiding the institution, and the resources available (Riding 2007). Importantly the student's expectations and the (often unofficial) priorities transmitted by academic staff also have a significant effect on shaping their learning behaviours; such effects often conflict with the stated aims of the institution (Gillespie 2012).

WORK FACTORS

In further or higher education, financial concerns are prominent, often leading students to take part-time employment in order to manage. Exposure to the work environment is suggested to enhance emotional intelligence by placing them in situations in which they develop interpersonal skills, so developing better relationships with their peers and fellow students (Olan-Skipper and Brandenberg 2013). Watts (2001) surveyed students attending an English university and found mixed reports on the impact of the work on their studies – while some felt it was beneficial because it funded their learning, others saw it as a distraction from their ability to study. However, there was no noticeable difference in the end-of-year results between students who undertook part-time work and those who did not. The study suggested that the greater number of hours worked, the greater the influence learning, with a limit to the amount of time students can successfully allocate to work.

Interpersonal factors

One of the key factors in determining how well we manage stressors, including those occurring within the academic setting, is the quality of social support available. For children, the presence of a relationship that contains affection, support and warmth is considered to be protective, even for those in high-risk environments (McElwee 2007). While parental figures are often associated with the provision of such relationships, there is evidence that peer support also helps children successfully negotiate school-related stress (Slater and McKeown 2004). For university students, social support in the form of friends and strong social networks has been shown to reduce the impact of academic stressors and to aid the development of attributes considered protective against future stressors. Such protective traits are often categorised as part of their resilience (Wilks 2008).

Predictors of academic success

The discussion so far has addressed the intrapersonal, interpersonal and environmental factors that contribute towards a person's ability to successfully negotiate their education. There is significant value for educators to consider this information, and to use it to improve understanding of the needs of learners and to tailor study programmes accordingly. The factors that correlate with educational success should be identified, which can be achieved by determining the main predictors of academic achievement. Academic programmes provide developmental opportunities in a wide range of areas. Consequently, academic success has been measured through the concepts of grade point ratios (Skipper and Brandenberg 2013) and grade point averages (Houglum *et al.* 2005) in addition to diverse phenomena such as analytic ability and attainment of social and interpersonal skills (Smrtnik-Vitulic and Zupancic 2011). This diversity of outcome means it can be difficult to identify specific factors associated with a global definition of success, but some studies have attempted to do so by exploring the factors associated with a broader definition of achievement – this includes the attainment criteria set by the institution, and the personal goals identified by the student. Using grade point averages plus a measure of personal success, one study in Canadian university students (George *et al.* 2008) found that certain attributes strongly correlated with meeting personal targets and achieving academic success. These are:

- Having clearly defined goals.
- Good time management skills.
- Less time spent in passive leisure.
- A healthy diet.
- Waking up earlier.
- Owning a computer.
- Spending less time sleeping.

The intrapersonal attribute of conscientiousness fits well with these factors, manifesting as enhanced study behaviours and better engagement with study in general (Smrtnik-Vitulic and Zupanic 2011). Thus this characteristic seems well suited to equipping learners for the rigours of study. Background factors such as a stable and inspiring home environment and favourable genetics are important (Riding 2007). Awareness of the home environment is important because of its significant influence on educational performance, including the aspects of parent education and income whereby higher income often equates with higher academic performance (Moon and Lee 2009). Other features indicative of likely academic success include (unsurprisingly):

- Previous academic performance, both positive and negative (Houglum *et al.* 2005).
- The way in which the student identifies with the educational institution, whereby a sense of belongingness is thought to enhance academic achievement (Ruiz 2009).

Giving recognition to these factors means that support can be targeted to the learners' unique requirements, whereby phenomena such as stress can be incorporated. Perceived stress has a detrimental effect on performance because it impairs cognitive processes (Boals and Banks 2012), and prevents learners from thinking clearly. Strategies known to reduce the impact of stress allows learners to adapt more quickly to study (Sasaki and Yamasaki 2007), thus optimising cognitive performance and academic attainment. The promotion of academic success involves more than just educational underpinnings to enhance the attainment of knowledge; the alignment of several factors is essential, including the enhancement of learner's life skills.

Life skills and coping

In everyday life, competence in practical life skills are instrumental to success. Life skills may appear mundane, however they are vital for developing a child's ability to work towards independence and mastery. Early development of these skills makes it possible to provide learners with skills for success (Amato and Ochiltree 1986). Educators should lead students through the process of understanding one concept before moving onto the next, to enable them to understand and thus master the concept; the educator then moves onto the next concept and the student gains confidence.

If the student does not grasp the concept and the educator moves on, the student has no chance of being able to cope and this will affect their self-confidence (Mercer 1986). Confidence plays an important part in the development of knowledge and skills and building self-esteem, and all are essential elements of success and strategies for lifelong learning.

Life skills are an essential component of overall learning. Developing them effectively can have a positive influence on problem-solving skills and managing anxiety in challenging situations (Heppner and Lee 2002). If not well developed, the learner's ability to problem solve and cope with everyday situations will not be optimal, and may influence how the learner integrates in the education setting (and workplace). Learners who struggle to develop coping skills will have negative outcomes.

COPING STRATEGIES

Coping involves using diverse strategies to deal with perceived stressors, that may be social, environmental or personal. The role of motivation as a way of coping can be effective depending on the person and how they react to the adverse situation; successful people are generally more adept at responding to adversity than less successful people (Kovacs 2007). When a situation is dealt with effectively, positive emotions result, and when situation is not dealt with effectively, negative emotions result (Folkman and Mosokowitz 2004). To enable people to maximise their life opportunities and build their self-esteem through development of key life skills is a pivotal role for an educator. The time spent within the school system is the only time that children attend an educational establishment for a long period and is the best opportunity for influencing, nurturing, developing and enhancing their skills.

PROBLEM SOLVING

Cognitive appraisal of a situation is required to identify whether or not there is a problem with the situation. In a study of school-children, Spivak *et al.* (1976) identified four key elements of problem solving:

- Recognising the existence of a problem.

- Defining the problem.
- Considering possible solutions.
- Selecting the most appropriate solution after weighing up the evidence.

If this process is followed effectively there should be a positive outcome. However, when learners are unable to follow the stages, the problem is left unresolved, and can influence the strategies they use next time they encounter a problem. This can lead to a self-fulfilling situation whereby they cannot solve problems and therefore cannot cope.

MENTAL HEALTH ISSUES

In the context of mental health, poor coping and problem solving may incur significant distress; impacting on people's ability to cope with everyday stressors. A key transitional time when this has the most impact could be considered to be moving from primary to secondary school and the transition from school life into adulthood whether that is employment/ unemployment, university or college. Key times on this timeline also include the stress of exam success or failure and the impact this has on self-esteem. Who then manages this time when disappointment is a potential outcome?

Currently, with the lack of traditional apprenticeships that were normality over 30 years ago, more people are now being encouraged to carry on or return to education as there are limited alternatives. However, do educators feel they are skilled in dealing with the raw emotion of failure and the rebuilding of confidence and self-esteem?

Weare (2002) suggests that the view of mental health has moved from the medical model to a broader more inclusive concept. Thus it is now everyone's business – not just mental health practitioners, or those who are involved with target population, or those who come into contact with people where mental health issues may become problematic (e.g. in health, education and social work settings). Educators who entered teaching to teach, find they have a whole other broader role that has been passed back to them because society lacks responsibility.

LIFE SKILLS TRAINING

Life skills training for people who experience mental health problems incorporates the skills to enable ordinary social survival such as financial management, budgeting, personal self-care, domestic management, and allied consumer and civic skills (complaining and voting, respectively) (Barker 2009). Many of these skills could be, and are, reflected within the education system. Rui Gomes and Marques (2013) illustrate that this training benefits areas of development that relate to life satisfaction and tendencies to be optimistic. By enhancing these, life satisfaction can have a positive impact, promoting the learner's autonomy in decision making and confidence building.

TYPICAL LIFE SKILLS

According to Rui-Gomes and Marques (2013), these are:

- **Behavioural:** such as managing time effectively.
- **Cognitive:** such as managing negative thoughts.

- **Interpersonal:** such as managing conflict with other people.
- **Intrapersonal:** such as managing lack of motivation by setting personal goals.

Life skills can be viewed as a set of competencies that facilitate both academic progress and personal and social development and career. They are evident in everyday life and incorporate self-efficacy skills that facilitate academic progress, as well as essential attitudes or predispositions such as persistence, resilience, effort, work ethic, optimism, empathy, respect, responsibility, integrity and initiative (Yuen *et al.* 2010).

Responsibilities of educators

Children and young adults spend a considerable amount of time each week with an educator, thus the educator is in an ideal position to influence and guide them towards achieving success in life. However we must consider the position of the educators. Do they feel their responsibility lies within academic success only or if this extends onto other life skills? Is this what they signed up for? Most educators would assert that they signed up to teach and to share a passion for learning. However, modern teaching in schools, colleges and universities incorporates a hidden element of student support that relates to their personal lives and influences their education. These personal issues can at times be extremely complex and beyond the scope of the anticipated role. Educators are in an ideal position for having an influence on the development of self-esteem of the students they work with. Furthermore there are numerous stories about students who have overcome issues with self-esteem because of the help and encouragement they received from an educator (Hymel and McDougall 1998) and the positive impact this made on their life.

The influential and nurturing position that teachers are in should not be underestimated – it should be maximised. Teachers who facilitate effective learning bring qualities such as empathy and respect to create a powerful learning environment that brings about respect for the 'personhood' of the student (Rogers 1983). Personhood enables someone to be treated with deep respect for who they are and the unique interactions they have with others (Kitwood 1997; Penrod *et al.* 2007).

ENGAGING STUDENTS

A study by Singal and Swann (2011) investigating learning inside and outside school identified that pupils felt more confident in their learning outside school than in the classroom. The children reported that out-of-school learning was more active, collaborative and challenging, and this helped them connect to the learning opportunity. Teachers may consider it is their role to enrich the learning that takes place within schools to reduce the disparity between environments and engage pupils more effectively.

Bearing in mind the stressors experienced by communities of learners, the transition between adolescence and young adulthood can be highly pressured by studies, relationships, employment and the mental perplexity common at this stage. Males tend to problem solve by themselves, whereas as girls tend to seek out advice from those around them (Wang 2013). This is valuable knowledge for educators who can develop different strategies for the young people they are educating.

PROMOTION OF EFFECTIVE LIFE SKILLS

Education can have a dramatic effect on a person's life. Many students sail through formal education, but others will struggle. The focus of formal education is generally on academic attainment as a measure of success, and high attainment positively reflects on the institution, which is the fundamental purpose of the school, college or university. However, there is another aspect of education that provides a more holistic perspective. The value of life skills development cannot be underestimated in the overall development of a child; fundamental to these skills is the development of self-awareness which enables growth of personal and social awareness. Working together in a group can enable learners to learn, re-learn, practise and refine their skills and behaviours, and enrich their interactions with others (Watson 1987). For learners to feel they can positively contribute, regardless of their academic ability, helps motivate them to maximise their potential.

POINTING OUT WHEN STUDENTS ARE UNAWARE

Life skills training aims to enable development of a balanced, self-determined person who has the ability to effectively problem solve in their day-to-day living (Schmidt, Brown and Waycott 1988). When students are unaware of how to successfully achieve, the educator has a responsibility to enlighten them. The concept of insight is the process of thinking well and acting well; insight enables us to organise our behaviour rationally, based on what we have learnt in the past (Luntley 2005). In education, the key is to enable learners to learn what they need to know, but this is mainly focused on academic achievement.

What drives learning?

Active learning, in which participants are involved in the process, can be a very effective way for students to retain information. There is a high correlation between knowledge and performance when working together in small groups (Lamb *et al.* 2006). Therefore, when considering life skills programmes it is important to take into account how these skills are delivered and what methods are used to maximise the immediate acquisition of skills and longer-term retention of knowledge.

SELF-MOTIVATION AND SELF-REGULATION

How learners approach tasks relating to knowledge and skills acquisition can influence their success. Students who approach educational tasks confidently with perseverance and resourcefulness are considered to be self-regulated learners, where self-regulation is the action of a person transforming their mental abilities into the skills required for success in academic learning (Zimmerman 2000). Such learners have a heightened awareness when they know a fact, or possess a skill, and are more adept at problem-solving when they encounter obstacles (Zimmerman 1990). Self-regulated learners can also be recognised by their skills of self-motivation. Academic goals are influenced by learners, teachers and parents; however, learners tend to set lower goals for achievement than teachers and parents. It is essential therefore that academic experiences are organised to maximise the learner's sense of academic efficacy (Zimmerman, Bandura and Martinez-Pons 1992). The factors that influence a student's self-motivation are determined by others as well as their own personal determination (FIGURE 14.1). Learners come in all guises, some with a well-developed sense of self and an effective ability to articulate their knowledge within the bounds of the assessment criteria. Some still have to find the formula that enables them to unlock their own ability and demonstrate this to others. Often these learners are frustrated and appear disengaged and unable to meet the tasks set for them. This is when the educator needs to provide guidance and support so that they realise their full potential.

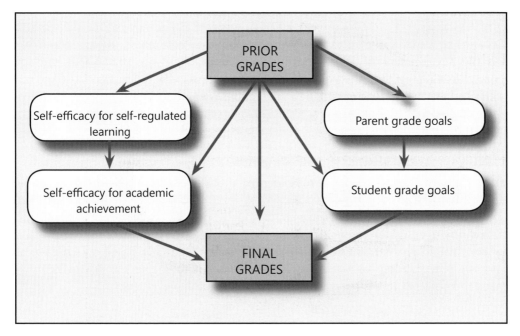

Figure 14.1: Causal model of student self-motivation (adapted from Zimmerman *et al.* 1992).

METACOGNITION

Having awareness about one's own thinking is defined as metacognition. Learners who have poorly developed or no metacognitive awareness have personal limitations and are unable to compensate for this (Zimmerman 2002). Developing self-regulation will enable them to apply these skills throughout lifelong learning, which encompasses a variety of skills that learners can positively acquire in order to deal with their life educationally, socially and psychologically. Capturing learners early – regardless of their social and parental backgrounds – and giving them encouragement will maximise the benefits to them and enhance their engagement in the process of lifelong learning. An example of this can be seen in Scotland, where recent changes in the education strategy led to a focus on learners flourishing, which is now a fundamental aspect of their approach.

DEMONSTRATING ACHIEVEMENT

The Scottish Government introduced a new framework for assessment that supports learning in pre-school and school from age 3 to 18. This focuses on four key capabilities that students will be expected, through their experiences, to demonstrate achievement as effective contributors, responsible citizens, confident individuals and successful learners (FIGURE 14.2).

Some aspects of these changes in education raise concerns, but it is easy to identify the overall contribution of education to the development of life skills. Maximising the ability of young people to flourish in lifelong learning and work – now and in the future – will enhance their lives and overall contribution to society (Education Scotland 2013).

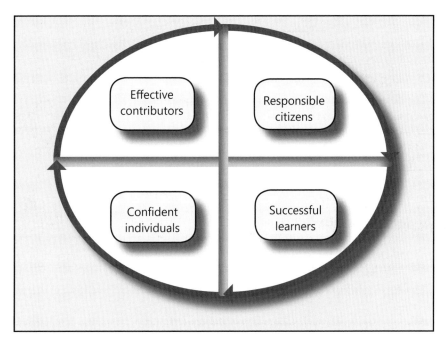

Figure 14.2: Criteria for assessing achievement in the Scottish framework for education of pupils from age 3 to 18.

Concluding comments

The broad range of skills required of educators, including a pastoral one, is essential for the success of many learners. Strategies are available to help educators maximise their roles and ensure they are supporting learners to meet their needs. The complexities of learning within (and outside) the education system are vast and attention must be given to each aspect to ensure that all learners entering the system are benefitted and advantaged by it.

Enhancing life skills in tandem with coping skills should produce learners in the future who will be able to deal with and survive all aspects of lifelong learning.

We need educators who go that 'extra mile', who notice when learners are troubled and support them professionally to help them achieve their hopes, dreams and aspirations.

KEY MESSAGES FROM THIS CHAPTER

 Academic programmes provide a source of stress that is detrimental to the way some students will perform.

 The way in which students respond to academic demands is determined by a complex interplay of intrapersonal, interpersonal and environmental factors.

 Education programmes should accommodate the specific needs of their students in both the design and delivery of their programme.

Supporting evidence and further reading

Amato R, Ochiltree G (1986) Children becoming independent: An investigation of children's performance of practical life-skills. Australian *Journal of Psychology.* 38(1), 59–68.

Anderson-Darling C, McMey LM, Howard SN, Olmstead SB (2007) College student stress: the influence of interpersonal relationships on sense of coherence. *Stress and Health* 23, 215–29.

Barker P (2009) *Psychiatric and Mental Health Nursing: The Craft of Caring* (2nd edn). London: Hodder Arnold.

Bergsteiner H, Avery G, Neumann R (2010) Kolb's experiential learning model: critique from a modelling perspective. *Studies in Continuing Education* 32(1), 29–46.

Boals A, Banks, JB (2012) Effects of traumatic stress and perceived stress on everyday cognitive function. *Cognition and Emotion* 26(7), 1335–43.

Education Scotland (2013) *Understanding the curriculum as a whole.* Available at: www.educationscotland.gov.uk/thecurriculum/whatiscurriculumforexcellence/understandingthecurriculumasawhole/index.asp (accessed July 2015).

Folkman S, Mosokowitz JT (2004) Coping: pitfalls and promise. *Annual Review of Psychology* 55, 745–74.

George D, Dixon S, Stansal E, Lund Gelb S, Pheri T (2008) Time diary and questionnaire assessment of factors associated with academic and personal success among university undergraduates. *Journal of American College Health* 56(6), 707–15.

Gibbons C, Dempster M, Moutray M (2008) Stress and eustress in nursing students. *Journal of Advanced Nursing* 61(3), 282–90.

Gibbons C, Dempster M, Moutray M (2011) Stress, coping and satisfaction in nursing students. *Journal of Advanced Nursing* 67(3), 621–32.

Gillespie M (2012) Do academic assessments deter compassion in student nurses? *Scottish Educational Research Association Bulletin* 2, 14–16.

Goleman D (1998) *Working with Emotional Intelligence.* London: Bloomsbury.

Heppner P, Lee D (2002)Problem-solving appraisal and psychological adjustment. In: Snyder CR, Lopez SJ (eds) *Handbook of Positive Psychology.* Oxford: Oxford University Press.

Houglum JE, Aparasu RJ, Delfinis TM (2005) Predictors of academic success and failure in a pharmacy professional programme. *American Journal of Pharmaceutical Education* 69(3), 283–89.

Hymel S, McDougall P (1998) Moving into middle school: Individual differences in the transition experience. *Canadian Journal of Behavioural Science* 30(2), 108–20.

Kitwood T (1997*) Dementia Reconsidered: The Person Comes First.* Buckingham: Open University Press.

Kovacs M (2007) Stress and coping in the workplace. *The Psychologist* 20(9), 48–60.

Lamb R, Joshi MS, Carter W, Cowan G, Matthews A (2006) Children's acquisition and retention of safety skills: the Life Skills program. *Injury Prevention* 12, 161–65.

Lazarus RS, Folkman S (1987) Transactional theory and research on emotions and coping. *European Journal of Personality* 1, 141–70.

Luntley M (2005) The character of learning. *Educational Philosophy and Theory* 37(5), 689–704.

MacDonald H, Swart E (2009) The culture of bullying at a primary school. *Education as Change* 8(2), 33–55.

McElwee N (2007) A focus on the personal and structural: resilience explored. *Child and Youth Services* 29(1/2), 57–69.

Meichenbaum D (1985) *Stress Inoculation Training*. Oxford. Pergamum Press.

Mercer D (1986) Mastery learning. *British Journal of In-Service Education* 12(2), 115–18.

Moon SS, Lee J (2009) Multiple predictors of Asian–American children's school achievement. *Early Education and Development* 20(1), 129–47.

Murray-Harvey R, Slee PT (2006) Family stress and school adjustment: predictors across the school years. *Early Child Development and Care* 145(91), 133–49.

Olan-Skipper C, Brandenburg S (2013) Emotional intelligence and academic performance of engineering students. *Engineering Project Organization Journal* 3(1), 13–21.

Papacharisis V, Goudas M, Danish SJ, Theodorakis Y (2005) The effectiveness of teaching a life skills programme in a schools-based sport context. *Journal of Applied Sport Psychology* 17(3), 247–54.

Penrod J, Yu F, Kolanowski A, Fick DM, Loeb SJ, Hupcey JE (2007) Reframing person-centred nursing care for persons with dementia. Research and Theory for Nursing Practice: *An International Journal* 21(1), 57–72.

Poulou M (2007) Social resilience within a social and emotional learning framework: the perceptions of teachers in Greece. *Emotional and Behavioural Difficulties* 12(2), 91–104.

Riding R (2007) Individual differences and Educational performance. Educational Psychology: *An International Journal of Experimental Educational Psychology* 25(6), 659–72.

Rogers C (1983) *Freedom to Learn for Eighties*. Ohio: Merrill.

Ross SE, Niebling BC, Heckert TM (1999) Sources of stress among college Students. *College Student Journal* 33(2), 312–18.

Rui-Gomes A, Marques B (2013) Life skills in educational contexts: testing the effects of an intervention programme. *Educational Studies* 39(2), 156–66.

Ruiz Y (2009) Predictors of academic achievement for Latino middle schoolers. *Journal of Human Behaviour in the Social Environment* 19(4), 419–33.

Sasaki M, Yamasaki K (2007) Stress, coping and the adjustment process among university freshmen. *Counselling Psychology Quarterly* 20(1), 51–67.

Schmidt JR, Brown T, Waycott AM (1988)Developing the individual: life skills and family therapy. *British Journal of Guidance and Counselling* 16(2), 113–28.

Singal N, Swann M (2011) Children's perceptions of themselves a learner inside and outside school. *Research Papers in Education* 26(4), 469–84.

Skipper CO, Brandenberg S (2013) Emotional intelligence and academic performance of engineering students. *Engineering Project Organization Journa*l 3(1), 13–21.

Slater P, McKeown M (2004) The role of peer counselling and support in helping to reduce anxieties around transition from primary to secondary school. *Counselling and Psychotherapy Research* 4(1), 72–79.

Smrtnik-Vutilic H, Zupancic M (2011) Personality traits as a predictor of academic achievement in adolescents. *Educational Studies* 37(2), 127–40.

Spivak G, Platt JJ, Shure MB (1976) *The Problem-Solving Approach to Adjustment.* San Francisco, CA: Jossey Bass.

Steinbauer A (2015) *All or nothing. Philosophy Now.* Available at: www.philosophynow.org (accessed May 2015)

Steinhardt M, Dolbier C (2008) Evaluation of a resilience intervention to enhance coping strategies and protective factors and decrease symptomatology. *Journal of American College Health* 56(4), 445–53.

Wang Z (2013) Coping style and mental health of high school students. *Health* 5(2), 170–74.

Watson B (1987) Teaching and learning life skills. Pastoral Care in Education: *An International Journal of Personal, Social and Emotional Development* 5(3), 178–82.

Watts C (2001) *Pay as you learn: the effects of part-time paid employment on academic performance.* Paper presented at the Higher Education Close-Up Conference 2, Lancaster University, 16–18 July 2001. Available at: www.leeds.ac.uk/educol/documents/00001749.htm (accessed July 2015).

Weare K (2002) Work with young people is leading the way in the new paradigm for mental health. *International Journal of Mental Health Promotion* 4(4), 55–58.

Wilks, SE (2008) Resilience amid academic stress: the moderating impact of social support among social work students. *Advances in Social Work* 9(2), 106–25.

Yuen M, Chan RMC, Gysbers NC *et al.* (2010) Enhancing life skills development: Chinese adolescents' perceptions. Pastoral Care in Education: *An International Journal of Personal, Social and Emotional Development* 28(4), 295–310.

Zimmerman BJ, Bandura A, Martinez-Pons M (1992) Self-motivation for academic attainment: the role of self-efficacy beliefs and personal goal-setting. *American Educational Research Journal* 29(3), 663–76.

Zimmerman BJ (1990) Self-regulated learning and academic achievement: an overview. *Educational Psychologist* 25(1), 3–17.

Zimmerman B (2000) Attainment of self-regulation: A social cognitive perspective. In: *Boekaarts M, Pintrich R, Zeidner M (eds) Handbook of Self-Regulation.* San Diego, CA: Academic Press.

Zimmerman B (2002)Becoming a self-regulated learner: an overview. *Theory Into Practice* 41(2), 64–70.

CHAPTER 15

Practising positive silence

Maria Carter

In most classrooms in the UK, more value is placed on talking and being busy than on silence and inaction. Silence is traditionally perceived in a negative light, often signifying oppression and punishment, but positive silence is different. In the learning environment, it involves taking a few moments to be quiet and still – to do nothing, thus creating space in the mind and a gap in activity. There is increasing evidence of its benefits for well-being, creative and personal thinking, and for learning by encouraging deep engagement with the material being learned (Alerby and Elidottir 2003; Caranfa 2004; Lees 2013). As well as a pedagogical tool, it can be viewed as an intervention, one that is simple, cheap and powerful, with the potential to 'revolutionise schooling' and 'elevate the entire platform of our society (Lees 2013; Rice 2015).

The leaders of today's young learners are required to incorporate personal wellness into the education setting as part of an increasingly therapeutic educational policy (Hyland 2009); this is partly in recognition of the fact that over half of adult mental health problems begin in children under the age of 14 (World Health Organization 2012). One promising strategy is the use of deliberate, collaborative episodes of 'doing and saying nothing', for its positive effects on the learning environment, for promoting group intimacy and enhancing democracy. Democracy is essential for achieving a state of 'non-doing' in the classroom (Fielding 2012, 2013; Fox Eades 2015; Harber 2009; Lees 2013; Trafford 2003).

What is 'doing nothing'?

Stillness is the basis of yoga, meditation and mindfulness, but the practice of doing nothing, or non-doing, is different. This was fundamental to the Alexander Technique, devised in the 1800s, which taught students to stop and quieten their minds and bodies to increase awareness of their self and their environment before making a change through movement, thinking or learning (Higgins 2010). In the current context, it relates to observing periods of silent stillness, involving need to speak or carry out any physical activity, but allowing thinking (unconscious or otherwise). This *positive* silence can be carried out in any position and in any setting.

Why is 'doing nothing' so important in school?

Modern life can be 'cacophonic' (Corrigan 2011). We are bombarded with information through all five senses in an overstimulating social, consumer-led, deadline-hitting, agenda-driven, quota-fulfilling climate. This is true for both adults and children, but children are also subject to pressure from their pressurised peers, their bodies' rapid hormonal and physical changes, and the stress of the adults in their lives. On top of this, communications technologies force them to continually consider how they exist in the minds of others and contribute to 'media-driven externalising tendencies of the self' (Lees 2012). The typical school environment can also be overwhelming, with non-stop listening, responding, reading, writing, performing tasks, collaborating, cramming in knowledge, remembering, revising, moving hastily from one room to another, incessant playground buzz and the drone of the dining hall. Students face a constant flow of noise, sights, facts, opinions and demands amid a fixed daily structure in which there is little space for calm, introspection or creative engagement (Cain 2011; Hyland 2009).

Much of this hyperactivity is driven by pressure on schools and staff to follow improvement agendas and meet rising attainment standards and educational outcomes (Delandshere 2001; Peim and Flint 2009). Teachers' voices and 'rigid teacher talk' tend to dominate the classroom – and their own welfare suffers in the process too (Haskins 2010; Hayes and Matusov 2005; Higgins 2010). As Cantor says (2009):

Without room for silence, the language in our classrooms risks being reduced to just so much noise in our students' already cacophonic lives.

All information that enters the conscious brain must be coded and processed – even if it is completely useless. Multiple inputs are difficult for anyone to assimilate, regardless of their age or level of cognition. According to cognitive psychologists and researchers in the field of 'decision science', which uses techniques such as MRI scanning to analyse brain function, the so-called working memory can become 'saturated' in overstimulating environments, causing impaired information processing, decision making and cognitive function (Begley 2011; Cowan 2005; Dimoka 2012), leading to dis-ease, dis-function and suboptimal performance. For people with disabilities, who often have weak working memories, the impact can significant (Numminen *et al.* 2002).

Attitudes to silence

The tendency in western societies is to encourage 'overt expression' and an 'excess of speech' (Zimmermann and Morgan 2015). Silence and stillness are not viewed as natural states. In fact, most people in these cultures are uncomfortable when they are given space to 'switch off', whether in formal situations, such as observing a two-minute silence, or in informal situations where 'awkward silences' are to be avoided (Steinbock 2012). Within centres of education, 'teacher-initiated activity' and 'overt teacher interventions' tend to dominate (Ollin 2008), and value is placed on talking and action. Slowness, stillness and silence, in contrast, are perceived as failure to achieve, unproductivity and non-participation – and even as threats to educational compliance (Haskins 2010; Ollin 2008; Schultz 2009; von Wright 2008; Zembylas and Michaelides 2004). Alerby (2012) recognises that silent students often have valid opinions and responses, but choose not to express them; this right should be respected on a wider scale, but doing so will require a significant change to the status quo.

The learning environment is also characterised by 'enforced' silence, imposed by leaders of learning to regain control over their pupils, or demonstrate a position of strength or superiority. This is 'negative' silence; it is not educational and it does not contribute to teaching or learning (Fox Eades 2015). Furthermore, it can be associated with punishment, and the negative feelings that arise in such cases can extend to the entire institution and lead to alienation.

The benefits of positive silence

FOR INDIVIDUALS

Silence allows a 'pulling back' from unnecessary input and freeing up of the unconscious mind, allowing it to absorb and process information, set-up connections with existing knowledge, determine patterns and unravel problems. Thoughts can take shape and new meanings and understandings emerge, producing original answers and ideas, turning experiences into learning and integrating emotion with reason (Alerby and Elidottir 2003; Buchholz 1998; Caranfa 2004; Higgins 2010; Ollin 2008; Zimmermann and Morgan 2015). Some of these processes may relate to neuroplasticity of the brain (Begley 2009).

People who regularly practise positive, silent stillness, or 'meta silence' as coined by Ollin (2008), learn how both internal and external factors affect their well-being. They learn to use their inner resources to adapt, heal and renew, bringing about positive effects on their emotional, social and physical functioning (Haskins 2010). Improvements have been observed in the behaviour of student towards each other, producing a calmer atmosphere, so that creativity, memory and the ability to learn can flourish (LeClaire 2009; Lees 2012; Semple *et al.* 2010; von Wright 2012). Leaders of learning who build silence and stillness into their day can be receptive once more to the 'joy of teaching' (Fox Eades 2015).

The research on positive silence to date is mostly qualitative in nature. More controlled studies and meta-analyses have been conducted in recent years, adding to a growing body of evidence of its benefits – in mental ill-health (such as addictive behaviours, psychiatric conditions and recurrent depression), physical conditions (such as hypertension), and conditions with both mental and physical aspects, such as chronic physical pain. Researchers in these areas include Burke (2010), Cain (2011), Caranfa (2004), Flook and colleagues (2013), Fox Eades (2015), Huppert and Johnson (2010), Lees (2012, 2013, 2014), Semple and colleagues (2010), von Wright (2012), and Zenner (2014) and Zoogman (2014) and coworkers. FIGURE 14.1 summarises some of the benefits of positive silence.

FOR GROUPS

Practising planned stillness in a group situation brings about several shared benefits. Among these are:

- An increased respect for and ability to get along with others in the group (e.g. classmates), while relieving group tension to produce a calmer classroom atmosphere (Lees 2012; Semple *et al.* 2010; von Wright 2012).

- The promotion of group intimacy and a sense of sharing and togetherness; visible signs of 'tuning in' to one another are evident through synchronised behaviours such as coughing, sniffling and scratching (Lees 2013; Steinbock 2012).

- Fewer episodes of bullying and school drop-outs (Fielding 2013; Stronach 2010; Walton 2005).

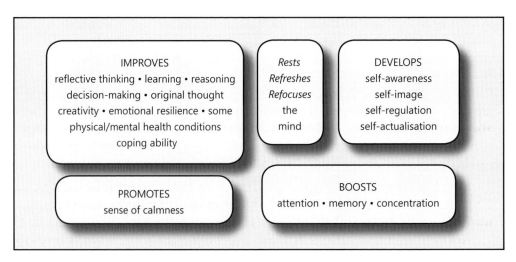

Figure 15.1: Benefits gained from regular practise of positive silence.

FOR WIDER SOCIETY

When group intimacy encourages respect, sharing, equality and democratisation, it not only enriches the immediate learning environment but also spreads to the entire institution (Fielding and Moss 2011; Lees 2013; Miller 2008). Furthermore, people who use planned silence from a young age are more inclined to participate in and contribute to their wider community, and thus society a whole (Flint and Peim 2012; Rowe 2003; Trafford 2003). It is a type of transformative learning that develops sustainable skills which can be used in other situations, including other centres of learning, in the workplace, in the family and in social settings; as such, they represent a form of citizenship education and help the development of 'wise global citizens' (Kelley 2008).

The practicalities of achieving positive silence

Teachers who practise silence in their personal life readily bring it into the classroom setting. But most do not and they require training or support at a whole-school level, which sometimes requires a change in school ethos and teaching approach (Bathmaker and Avis 2005; Ollin 2008; Schultz 2009). Observational assessments of trainee teachers still focus on student–teacher talk, and – as Ollin points out – a teacher is unlikely to impress the assessor if his or her students remain silent for the entire lesson, even if they are thinking deeply or assimilating their learning (Ollin 2007, 2008). Schools and educators must be guided to understand what silence offers and to realise that imposing an intensely social environment on all learners allows no space for individual learners; it even increases feelings of exclusion for some. So-called 'enstatic' schools teach pupils how to be comfortable within themselves and to enjoy *healthy solitude* in the communal context (Stern 2014, 2015).

NEGOTIATING MOMENTS OF DELIBERATE SILENCE

Making silence part of the daily routine is a democratic process, and does not follow easily in institutions that place learners at the bottom of the hierarchy, involving them little in matters relating to the learning environment or the content and pace of their learning. Such authoritarian structures lead to demotivation, resistance and alienation (Berg and Corpus 2013; Gutmann 2008; Harber 2009; Olson 2009). Achieving silence requires non-coercive negotiation with learners, to give them a sense that their thoughts matter and they have personal choice (Lees 2013). They may then view silence as an option rather than a required response to cries for 'Silence!' from an authority figure (Alerby 2012; Leander 2002; Lees 2012, 2013; Ollin 2008; von Wright 2012; Wingate 1996). Teachers should engage with students positively in order to establish how, where and when planned silence is introduced into the routine (Haskins 2010; Picard 2002). This involves four key elements (as illustrated in FIGURE 15.2):

- **First**, students should be made aware of the benefits of silent stillness, and the fact that it is a pleasurable experience because it offers time and space for themselves, to use however way they wish – to close their eyes or stare into space, to relax or daydream, to think actively about what they have learned or events outside the school, to meditate or let their thoughts float randomly, or to sketch or write poetry.

- **Second**, they should know they should agree to observe just one simple 'rule': that each of them must respect the choice of their fellow students to be silent and not spoil the silence for them.

- **Third**, discuss opportunities for practising silence, whether planned, unplanned, or a combination of both forms, as well as signals used for instigating periods of silence.

- **Fourth**, they should be asked whether they have any concerns, and these should be addressed before asking whether they want to 'give it a go'.

When Haskins (2010) negotiated silent time in this way, the students were immediately enthusiastic and loved it from the offset.

INSTIGATING MOMENTS OF DELIBERATE SILENCE

The easiest way to incorporate agreed episodes of planned silence is to link them with particular activities on the timetable. Reading, writing and computer work may be carried out in silence; for younger children, story-telling might be followed by a few moments of silence. These episodes can become part of the daily routine, before or after each learning period, for example, or at the start or end of the school day. Periods of unplanned silence may also be agreed. These need to be instigated by a signal that is understood by all students in the group. The signal should be pleasant, non-threatening and non-authoritarian (Haskins 2010; Wingate 1996). Suitable sounds include a bell, or humming, clapping and whistling, all of which have a different pitch from normal speech. Suitable visual cues include raising a hand, switching on a lamp or turning over a large hour-glass in a prominent place. Some teachers use silent 'positioning' (or 'anchoring' in neurolinguistic programming terms), whereby students stop talking when the teacher moves to a specific place in the room, first by agreement and ultimately by unconscious association (Ollin 2008; Wingate 1996). Picking the moment for unplanned silences depends on the skill and sensitivity of the teacher, and again may relate to situations identified during initial negotiations; for example, to reinstate a calm atmosphere when levels of tension are high. Whether the silence is planned or unplanned, some teachers ask the students to talk all at once for thirty seconds before stopping together; unusual though this sounds, it brings them closer to a 'natural energy level for silence' (Wingate 1996). A warning of a minute or two can be built in to allow pupils to finish what they are saying or doing before doing nothing.

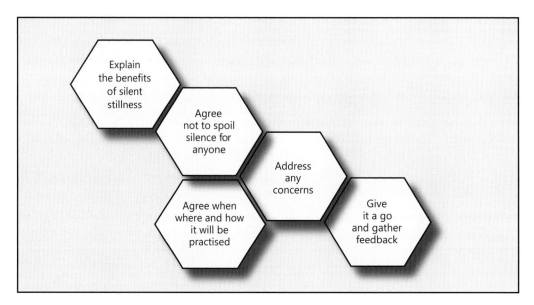

Figure 15.2: Negotiating silence in the classroom setting.

HOW LONG SHOULD SILENT EPISODES LAST FOR?

Young people need to practise the skill of doing nothing, so it is best to start short and lengthen episodes slowly, perhaps from half a minute or so in the first instance. A guiding rule is to aim for one minute of silence for each year of age. Older students are capable of long sessions of fifteen or twenty minutes.

OTHER OPPORTUNITIES FOR SILENCE

There are many ways in which teachers can incorporate more silence into their teaching routine.

- Introduce pauses at the end of all lessons or signal for two short pauses, of two or three minutes, in every two hours of teaching.
- Stop talking more often and abstain from 'initiating' and 'intervening'.
- Establish a 'community of enquiry' for collaborative tasks.

- Wait longer for responses after asking questions – for three seconds or so (most) teachers wait for less than one).
- Pause before and/or after speaking, when the students are attentive.
- Establish defined areas in the classroom for silent activity, perhaps a place where students go routinely to get things.
- Create a quiet place within the classroom itself or just outside the door and negotiate the circumstances in which it can be used.
- Designate certain activities as non-vocal activities.
- Use more visual, spatial and kinaesthetic forms of communication.

These suggestions are drawn from the work of many individuals over the last twenty years (Fox Eades 2015; Gathercoal and Gathercoal 2007; Haskins 2010; Lees 2013; Ollin 2008; Lipman 1993; Wingate 1996). It is hoped that in-school teacher assessments will place increasing value on these methods and appreciate the rationale for deploying them.

Concluding comments

Practising positive silence is simple, enjoyable and cost-free; it fosters a sense of equality and forms a platform for democracy that transcends cultural, religious, educational and social barriers (Haskins 2010). The UK government recognises the need for young people to acknowledge their own thoughts and emotions to promote their own mental well-being, and the value of positive silence in achieving this. The earlier these skills are taught, the greater a person's ability to create and sustain silence throughout life (Fox Eades 2015; Haskins 2010).

In the learning environment, thinking and learning flourish; the exercise of democracy enhances the sense of 'citizenship'. From a teacher-training point of view, it is acknowledged that the skills involved are not as easy to record as vocalisations, but observations could also take into account how well the teacher organises the class environment, how long learners work silently for (and how comfortable they are doing so), as well as how sensitive they are to learners who prefer not to participate overtly (Ollin 2008).

More quantitative evidence is needed on the impact of positive silence in different settings and age groups, ideally through large-scale, longitudinal, controlled studies with valid measures of teacher–learner engagement, and outcome measures that are valid indicators of learning, such as age of reading and exam performance, and of behaviour and attitude, such as incidences of disruption, bullying, non-attendance, exclusions and incidence of mental health disorders. Such evidence will make the value of positive silence clear to all relevant stakeholders.

KEY MESSAGES FROM THIS CHAPTER

 Deliberate and regular practise of nothingness allow pupils to slow down and discover their own quiet and inner resources and facilitates balance, renewal and calmness.

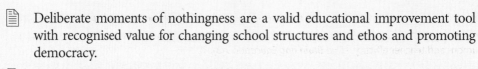

📄 Deliberate moments of nothingness are a valid educational improvement tool with recognised value for changing school structures and ethos and promoting democracy.

📄 Using collaborative, positive silence in groups benefits the group, the wider community and society as a whole.

📄 Democratic principles bring order to classrooms and help learners become effective members of the community.

📄 The skills learnt by children in silence-based practises can be sustained throughout life.

Supporting evidence and further reading

Alerby E (2012) *About Silence. Abstracts of the 40th Annual Congress of the Nordic Educational Research Association (NERA)*. Copenhagen: NERA.

Alerby E, Elidottir J (2003) The sounds of silence: some remarks on the value of silence in the process of reflection in relation to teaching and learning. *Reflective Practice* 4(1), 41–51.

Bathmaker AM, Avis J (2005) Is that 'tingling feeling' enough? Constructions of teaching and learning in further education. *Educational Review* 57(1), 3–20.

Begley S (2009) *The Plastic Mind*. London: Constable and Robinson.

Begley S (2011) I can't think! *Newsweek* 27 February.

Berg D, Corpus JH (2013) Enthusiastic students: A study of motivation in two alternatives to mandatory instruction. *Other Education* 2(2), 42–66.

Buchholz E (1998) *The Call of Solitude*. Available at: www.psychologytoday.com.

Burke CA (2010) Mindfulness-based approaches with children and adolescents: A preliminary review of current research in an emergent field. *Journal of Child and Family Studies* 19(2), 133–44.

Cain S (2011) *Quiet: The Power of Introverts in a World that Can't Stop Talking*. London: Penguin.

Cantor J (2009) *Conquer Cyberoverload: Get More Done, Boost Your Creativity, and Reduce Stress*. Wisconsin: CyberOutlook Press.

Caranfa A (2004) Silence as the foundation of learning. *Educational Theory* 54(2), 211–30.

Corrigan P (2011) Silence in progressive teaching. *Encounter: Education for Meaning and Social Justice* 24(1), 8–11.

Cowan N (2005) *Working Memory Capacity*. East Sussex: Psychology Press.

Delandshere G (2001) Implicit theories, unexamined assumptions and the status quo of educational assessment. *Assessment in Education: Principles, Policy and Practice* 8(2), 113–33.

Dimoka K (2012) How to conduct a functional magnetic resonance (fMRI) study in social science research. *MIS Quarterly* 36(3), 811–40.

Fielding M (2012) *The College of Teachers' Biennial Lecture: Student voice: patterns of partnership and the demands of deep democracy*. Available at: www.collegeofteachers.ac.uk/content/student-voice-patterns-partnership-and-demands-deep-democracy (accessed November 2015).

Fielding M (2013) Whole-school meetings and the development of radical democratic community. *Studies in Philosophy and Education* 32(2), 123–40.

Fielding M, Moss P (2011) *Radical Education and the Common School: A Democratic Alternative*. London: Routledge.

Fine M. (1987). Silencing in public schools. *Language Arts* 64(2), 157–74.

Flint KJ, Peim N (2012) *Rethinking the Education Improvement Agenda: A Critical Philosophical Approach.* London: Continuum.

Flook L, Goldberg SB, Pinger L, Bonus K, Davidson RJ (2013) Mindfulness for teachers: A pilot study to assess the effects on stress, burnout and teacher efficacy. *Mind Brain and Education* 7(3), 182–95.

Fox Eades J (2015) *Silence and stillness in the classroom.* Internet blog, 12 February 2015. Available at: celebratingstrengths. wordpress.com/2015/02/12/silence-and-stillness-in-the-classroom/ (accessed July 2015).

Gathercoal P, Gathercoal F (2007) *The Judicious Professor: A Learner-Centered Philosophy for Teaching and Learning in Higher Education.* San Francisco: Caddo Gap.

Gutmann A (2008) Democracy and Democratic Education. In: R Curren (ed.) *Philosophy of Education: An Anthology. Oxford: Blackwell.*

Hägg HF, Kristiansen A (2012) *Attending to Silence: Educators and Philosophers on the Art of Listening* Kristiansand, Norway: Portal Academic.

Harber C (2009) Revolution? What revolution? Contextual issues in citizenship education in schools in England. *Citizenship, Social and Economics Education* 8(1), 42–53.

Haskins C (2010) Integrating silence practices into the classroom: the value of quiet. *Encounter: Education for Meaning and Social Justice* 23(3), 344.

Hayes R, Matusov E (2005) Designing for dialogue in place of teacher talk and student silence. *Culture and Psychology,* 11(3), 339–57.

Higgins C (2010) The good life of teaching: An ethics of professional practice. *Journal of Philosophy of Education* 44(2/3), 15.

Li H-L (2001) Silences and silencing silences. In: *Philosophy of Education Year Book.* Champaign, IL: University of Illinois Press.

Huppert FA, Johnson DM (2010) A controlled trial of mindfulness training in schools: The importance of practice for an impact on well-being. *Journal of Positive Psychology* 5(4), 264–74.

Hyland T (2009) Mindfulness and the therapeutic function of education. *Journal of Philosophy of Education* 43(1), 119–31.

Kelley P (2008) *Towards Globo Sapiens.* London, Routledge.

Kristiansen A, Hägg H (2012) *Attending to Silence.* Norway: Port.

Leander, K. M. (2002). Silencing in classroom interaction: Producing and relating social spaces. *Discourse Processes,* 34(2), 193–35.

LeClaire A (2009) *Listening Beneath the Noise.* New York: Harper.

Lees HE (2012) *Silence in Schools.* London: Trentham Books.

Lees HE (2013) *Silence as a pedagogical tool.* Available at: www.timeshighereducation.co.uk/comment/opinion/silence-as-a-pedagogical-tool/2006621.article (accessed July 2015).

Lees HE (2013) *The art of being together in schools through silent stillness.* Seminar presented at York St John University, March 2013.

Lees HE (2014) *Can the pause of the child change our understanding of the child?* Paper presented at the Eighth International Conference of Changing conceptions of childhood: Implications for Educational Theory, Research and Practice, Beverley, August 2014.

Lingard L (2013) Language matters: towards an understanding of silence and humour in medical education. *Medical Education* 47, 1.

Lipman M (1993) Promoting better classroom thinking. *Educational Psychology* 13(3), 291.

Lyubomirsky S, King L, Diener E (2005) The benefits of frequent positive affect: Does happiness lead to success? *Psychological Bulletin* 131(6), 803–55.

Miller R (2008) *The Self-Organising Revolution.* Brandon: Psychology Press/Holistic Education Press.

Numminen H, Service E, Ruoppila I (2002) Working memory, intelligence and knowledge base in adult persons with intellectual disability. *Research in Developmental Disability* 23(2):105–18.

Ollin R (2007) *Records of teaching observations: boundary objects between different communities of practice.* Paper presented at Journal for Vocational Education and Training International Conference, Researching Vocational Education Policy and Practice, 6–8th July 2007, Worcester College, Oxford.

Ollin R (2008) Silent pedagogy and rethinking classroom practice: structuring teaching through silence rather than talk. *Cambridge Journal of Education* 38(2), 265–80.

Olson K (2009) *Wounded by School: Recapturing the Joy in Learning and Standing Up to Old School Culture*. New York: Teachers College Press.

Palmer S (2006) *Toxic Childhood: How the Modern World is Damaging our Children*. London: Orion.

Peim N, Flint KJ (2009) Testing times: questions concerning assessment for improvement. *Educational Philosophy and Theory* 41(3), 342–61.

Picard M (2002) *The World of Silence*. Kansas: Eighth Day Press.

Rice Y (2015) *Nothing really matters. A 'moment of silence' to start the school day*. Available at: www.chabad.org/library/article_cdo/aid/492993/jewish/Nothing-Really-Matters.htm (accessed July 2015).

Rowe D (2003) *The Business of School Councils: An investigation into Democracy in Schools* (2nd edn). London: Citizenship Foundation.

Rowe MB (1986) Wait time: slowing down may be a way of speeding up! *Journal of Teacher Education* 37(1), 43–50.

Schultz K (2009) *Rethinking Classroom Participation: Listening to Silent Voices*. New York: Teachers College Press.

Semple RJ, Lee J, Rosa D, Miller LF (2010) A randomized trial of mindfulness-based cognitive therapy for children: Promoting mindful attention to enhance social-emotional resiliency in children. *Journal of Child and Family Studies* 19, 218–29.

Steinbock D (2012) *Making silence together: collaboration in the silent gatherings of Quakers*. PhD dissertation, Stanford University, USA.

Stern J (2012) *Teaching solitude*. Paper presented at the Seventh International Conference on the Social and Moral Fabric of the School, Seattle Pacific University, WA, August 2012.

Stern J (2014) *Loneliness and Solitude in Education: How to Value Individuality and Create an Enstatic School*. Oxford: Peter Lang.

Stern J (2015) *Solitude and enstasy in schools: Reaching within and beyond*. Paper presented at the European *Educational Research* Association (ECER), Corvinus University of Budapest, September 2015.

Stronach I (2010) *Has progressive education a future? The fall and rise of Summerhill School*. Paper presented at the British Educational Research Association Conference, Warwick University, 2010.

Trafford B (2003) *School Councils, School Democracy, School Improvement: Why, What, How?* Leicester: Secondary Heads Association.

von Wright M (2008) *Why is stillness a threat against educational compliance?* Norway: University of Oslo.

von Wright, M. (2012) Silence in the asymmetry of educational relations. In: A Kristiansen, H Hägg (eds) *Attending to Silence*. Norway: Port.

Walton G (2005) Bullying widespread: a critical analysis of research and public discourse on bullying. *Journal of School Violence* 4(1), 91–118.

Wingate J (1996) *Ten ways to achieve silence in the classroom*. Available at: www.etprofessional.com/10_ways_to_achieve_silence_in_the_classroom_2394.aspx (accessed July 2015).

World Health Organization (2012) *The global burden of mental disorders and the need for a comprehensive, coordinated response from health and social sectors at the country level*. Available at: apps.who.int/gb/ebwha/pdf_files/WHA65/A65_R4-en.pdf (accessed July 2015).

Zembylas M, Michaelides P (2004) The sound of silence in pedagogy. *Educational Theory* 54(2), 193–210.

Zenner C, Herrnleben-Kurz S, Walach H (2014) Mindfulness-based interventions in schools—A systematic review and meta-analysis. *Frontiers in Psychology*. Available at: dx.doi.org/10.3389/fpsyg.2014.00603 (accessed November 2015).

Zimmermann AC, Morgan WJ (2015) a time for silence? Its possibilities for dialogue and for reflective learning, *Studies in Philosophy and Education* DOI: 10.1007/s11217-015-9485-0.

Zoogman S, Goldberg SB, Hoyt WT, Miller L (2014) Mindfulness interventions with youth: A meta-analysis. *Mindfulness* 6(2), 290–302.

PART III
The well-being of the leaders of learning

CHAPTER 16

The impact of institutional culture

Stephen P. Day

The prevailing culture within an educational establishment can have a complex influence on both learners and leaders of learning. In educational terms, research indicates that differences in organisational dynamics and culture exist between establishments and different levels within the educational system. This diversity may account for differences in learner attainment and the stress and strain felt by leaders of learning, which in turn can affect morale within an establishment. External factors such as socioeconomics, managerialism and accountability can adversely affect culture, but internal factors such as leadership and student and teacher subcultures can ameliorate or exacerbate stress levels within the cultural confines of the establishment.

The term culture is often used interchangeably with other related terms, such as climate, ethos and environment (FIGURE 16.1). This chapter seeks to clarify, characterise and contextualise how *culture* impacts of the health and well-being of the leader of learning. Contemporary Western society has a tendency to define social, economic, and political issues as problems to be resolved through management. This neoliberal philosophy has driven government concerns to promote efficiency and – by extension – value for (taxpayers') money. This includes redefining the culture of the system under scrutiny from an economic perspective. In recent decades, the UK has seen the introduction of managerialism as a new mode of governance under a restructuring of public sectors (Morley and Rassool 2000; Simkins 2000). This restructuring involves educational reform that shifts the emphasis away from administration and policy, towards management, with managerialism being used as the instrumental means (and legitimising basis) for redesigning educational institutions, bureaucracies and even the policy process.

Successive UK governments, including their devolved administrations across the UK, have tinkered with the education system through a combination of curriculum reform and changes to the structure, examination system and conditions of service of the education workforce. Each wave of reform is usually predicated on the premise that the current curriculum, examination system or management structure are in some way deficient. In addition, Governments tend to be alert to any potential shortfall in the numbers of suitably qualified people exiting the education system and entering employment, where they can make a positive contribution to the economy and society. This increased climate of accountability has led to an increased focus on managerialism within all sectors of education, usually in the form of an increased focus on summative outcome measures and managing their improvement. This ethos of accountability permeates down through the rest of the system. If we take a local-authority secondary school as an example, the chain of management and accountability can flow from the Inspectorate to both local authorities and the headteachers, simultaneously or independently, then to faculty (department) heads or principal teachers, and to the classroom teachers. The pressure on all levels of the system to account for 'their' performance is just one factor among many that affects the health and well-being of leaders of learning and their learners. It is the stress and strain that this ethos of accountability has on leaders of learning – and by extension, the learner – that this chapter will address. Education research has consistently shown that educational reform and the resulting increase in teachers' workloads have a negative influence on the health and well-being of the workforce (Travis and Cooper 1996; Wilson 2002). Further evidence shows that the largest influence on a teacher's decision to leave the profession (other than retirement) is workload (Smithers and Robinson 2003; 2005). The link between educational reform and increased workload is nothing new. Over the last 40 years the education systems across the UK have undergone several major reforms. This level of change places those in control of the system under pressure to account for increased government investment in education and training and, where necessary, to defend any relative lack of improvement in measured outcomes such as those derived from international comparator studies (e.g. TIMSS (Trends in International Mathematics and Science Study) and PISA (Program for International Student Assessment)), while also increasing the burden on teachers to meet quality indicators of teaching and learning, such as exam results and position in league tables. School culture and how it influences the health and well-being of the leaders of learning and the learner is a highly relevant area of education that is contemporary, but under-theorised. The themes that emerge from the research literature can provide an overview of this developing area of academic interest.

Setting school culture within a cultural framework

The main aim of schooling is to create a culture that is hospitable to learning (Barth 2001). Quality learning and teaching is viewed as a major goal that arguably emerges from a complex series of social interactions between the learner and the leader of learning, grounded within a socially constructed context. By placing learning and teaching practice within the sphere of social constructivism, it is possible to critique the quality of teaching and learning and the culture that nurtures them from multiple perspectives.

Culture, climate and ethos

First, it is important to define the key terms. The terms culture, climate and ethos are often used interchangeably and usually without adequate definition (Solvason 2005). School 'culture' is one of the most complex concepts in education, because it is often correlated with school performance in relation to managerialism and accountability. The terms 'ethos' and 'climate' are also commonly used, but the term culture provides:

> *... a more accurate and intuitively appealing way to understand [the] school's own unwritten rules, norms and expectations. (Deal and Peterson 1999)*

The concept of culture can be uncovered by viewing a school's history and by illuminating its shared beliefs and values, choices made and traditions kept. In educational terms, culture may also be referred to as:

> *... the way in which groups of people pass on beliefs and values and the products of human work and thought. (Smidt 2009)*

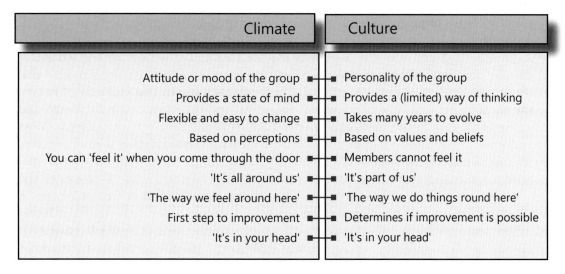

Climate	Culture
Attitude or mood of the group	Personality of the group
Provides a state of mind	Provides a (limited) way of thinking
Flexible and easy to change	Takes many years to evolve
Based on perceptions	Based on values and beliefs
You can 'feel it' when you come through the door	Members cannot feel it
'It's all around us'	'It's part of us'
'The way we feel around here'	'The way we do things round here'
First step to improvement	Determines if improvement is possible
'It's in your head'	'It's in your head'

Figure 16.1: The key characteristics of climate and culture (based on Gruenert 2008).

Edgar Schein (Schein 1985) suggests that the basic essence of an organisation's culture is:

> ... *the deeper level of basic assumptions and beliefs that are shared by [its] members that operate unconsciously, and that define in a basic 'taken-for-granted' fashion an organisation's view of itself and its environment.*

It could therefore be argued that climate and ethos are the products of culture, and climate and ethos are the ambience that is felt in a school as a result of its cultural history – where its presence is fluid and subject to the influence of external and internal forces. Therefore we may comprehend a school's culture, but we physically experience its ethos. School climate (where 'school' refers to the spectrum of establishments from nurseries to universities) is a term that has been used for many decades. Early use related to the ethos, or spirit, of an organisation but it is increasingly thought to represent the attitude of an organisation. The collective mood, or morale, of a group of people has become a greater focus in this new age of accountability. Whenever a group of people spend a significant amount of time together, they develop a common set of expectations, and these evolve into unwritten rules that group members conform to in order to remain in good standing with their peers. A common culture develops in groups so that information can be passed to the next generation, even though that information is a set of beliefs of imperfect humans with personal preferences.

Taking on a new culture

In schools, new teachers arrive with their own ideas about how to do their jobs. Through their education, they have been immersed in theories of best practices. If the culture of their first job does not embrace these new ideas, they soon learn that to compromise and conform to the culture of the establishment in order to fit in. New teachers feel the need to fit in, act like experienced teachers and are therefore vulnerable to the existing culture and all the unwritten rules that have been passed on through the decades.

An organisation's culture dictates its collective personality; if culture is the personality of the organisation, then climate represents that organisation's attitude. It is much easier to change an organisation's attitude (climate) than it is to change its personality (culture). Climate is normally seen to be associated with measurable elements of the school, while the more general features of the atmosphere within a school, sometimes intended (rather than what actually happens), can be said to constitute ethos. Culture as a concept attempts to bring together climate and ethos by offering indicators that can be measured and subjectively evaluated within a framework of practices that may be much more subjective, but can yield objective outcomes (Glover and Coleman 2005). Thus, it is more appropriate to view the term culture as a more complex and dynamic factor than climate or ethos. When viewing culture in this holistic manner, it is important to recognise that subcultures often co-exist within an organisation – for example, student, teacher and leadership subcultures. Culture can be defined by reference to a set of commonly held values and beliefs and unspoken rules, based on history and tradition, which affect how people in the organisation act and interact with each other. On this basis, then it should be possible to measure culture, because it is found within the solidity of the school building and its contents, how it is organised and run, in its staff and how they interact, and in the individual personalities and histories they bring to the mix (Nias 1989). Culture is a tangible entity, whereas ethos is more nebulous and vague.

Internal factors affecting school culture

Internal factors that influence school culture, climate and ethos relate to the subcultures and how they interact with each other. The relevant subcultures are:

- Teacher subculture.
- Leadership subculture.
- Student subculture.

TEACHER SUBCULTURE

Teacher subcultures influence the school culture through the way teachers interact with each other (and their students). Hargreaves (1994) highlights four types of teacher behaviour that influence how teachers interact:

- **Individualism**, whereby the teacher is autonomous, isolated and insulated, and blame and support are avoided.
- **Collaboration**, whereby teachers choose spontaneously and freely to work together without an external controlling agenda, comfortable activities might be the sharing of ideas and materials, and more formal or rigorous forms might include mutual observation and focused reflective enquiry where mutual support is encouraged.
- **Contrived collegiality**, whereby collaborative working relationships are compulsory, with fixed times and places set for collaborative work. Examples are planned meetings where support can be given but there is the potential for conflict.
- **Balkanisation**, whereby teachers are not isolated but they do not work as a whole school; instead, small collaborative groups form, for example, within departments.

LEADERSHIP SUBCULTURE

The leadership subculture within the educational establishment can also have a major influence. For example, the management structure within the school is overseen by a senior manager who adopts a hierarchical 'chain of command' and operates a strict regime of accountability, in which decisions are taken without consultation. Staff morale suffers under the yolk of heavy-handed line management and accountability systems and the feeling of being undervalued, and the net effect on school culture is negative. At the other extreme, when the management of the establishment is highly collegiate, focused on a shared vision and direction, and line management and accountability is rational and measured, then the net effect is positive – the staff feel valued, they share in the decision-making and buy into the vision of the school. Thus the style of leadership employed and enacted within an education establishment can greatly influence its culture.

STUDENT SUBCULTURE

The student subculture impacts heavily on the school culture because the whole enterprise depends on the cooperation and compliance of the students. If a large proportion of the students are non-cooperative or subversive, this conflict within school culture, teacher efficacy and morale can be negative and lead to a change in the teacher subculture, which in turn affects the school culture. In contrast, if most of the students are cooperative and compliant, there is less potential for conflict, less stress at the learning and teaching interface and improved staff morale, and all of these feed back to affect the school culture in a positive manner.

External factors affecting school culture

Educational establishments are not immune to the social context and environmental situation they are in. Factors such as economic and social deprivation, high levels of long-term unemployment, and the devaluing of education through low expectations of the learners within the local community all negatively influence the culture within the school. Other factors such as the threat of school closure, a pending inspection of the establishment by Her Majesty's Inspectorate of Education and the Local Authority may have a deep or a transient influence the culture and, by extension, the ethos.

Stress at the learning and teaching interface

It is widely acknowledged that work-related stress is at epidemic proportions within the UK (Jarvis 2005). Figures from the Health and Safety Executive (HSE) suggest that the annual number of workdays lost due to stress in 2001 was around 13.5 million – double that recorded in 1996. Along with nursing, teaching has the highest rate of stress, depression and anxiety (HSE 2002). This is further evidenced by recent statistics (HSE 2012) on the incidence of work-related stress (FIGURE 16.2):

- For human health and social workers, 2,090 cases per 100,000.
- For workers in education, 1,780 cases per 100,000.
- For workers in public administration and defence, 1,810 cases per 100,000.

These figures are the highest across all industries averaged over 2009/10 and 2011/12.

All schools, colleges and universities have a legal obligation under the Health and Safety at Work Act 1974 and the Management of Health and Safety Regulations 1995 to reduce work-related stress as much as possible. To this end, the HSE (2003) issued benchmarks to which employers are expected to conform, and they provide a standard questionnaire for carrying out organisation-wide stress vulnerability audits, whereby the benchmarks and audit tool are designed to measure (and protect) the rights of the employee. The net effect of these measures has resulted in some high profile legal cases being brought against employers, that muddied the legal position. Then, in April 2004, the House of Lords ruled on a test case by firmly establishing that 'schools' are responsible for the psychological well-being of their employees.

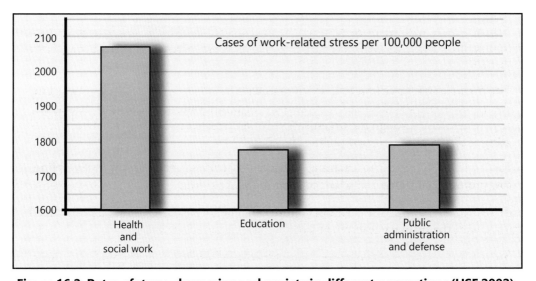

Figure 16.2: Rates of stress, depression and anxiety in different occupations (HSE 2002).

DEFINING STRESS

How work-related stress is defined in relation to education is important because it has become a legal and political issue. The decision to define stress at the individual or organisational level is not politically neutral (Jarvis 2005). At one end of the spectrum, lies the role of the person's perceptual processes and their ability to cope with pressure whereby 'stress occurs when perceived pressure exceeds [the] ability to cope' (Palmer 2001). At the other is the position taken by the National Union of Teachers (NUT 2000) who define stress in the following manner:

> *... stress at work is an organisational problem which employers are required by law to take steps to remove or reduce, and the chief causes of which are inappropriate working patterns, excessive or unnecessary demands on employees and inappropriate or bullying management styles.*

It could be argued that Palmer's definition appeals to a right-wing ideology because it implies that the responsibility for stress management lies with each person, whereas the NUT position appeals to a left-wing ideology because it places the responsibility for stress management on the employer or senior management. Newton (1995) suggests that adherence to the individual approach is rooted in the discourse of traditional managerialism so that what is at stake is not stress as such, but the fitness of the individual to keep their job.

However, the HSE (2003) offers a transactional definition of work-related stress as:

... the adverse reaction people have to excessive pressure or other types of demand placed on them.

This takes into account both individual and the environmental factors but mainly places focuses on the environment, in line with the HSE approach of attributing responsibility to employers. The psychological well-being of educators is arguably related to their ability to cope effectively with a number of stressors. Research identifies dealing with student indiscipline and workload as major stressors (Abel and Sewell 1999; Manassero *et al.* 2006; Wilson 2002). The pattern of stressors that an educator faces are affected by their subcultural context, with some stressors being centred on:

- The educator, such as stress from competing demands of work and family life that interact and sometimes exacerbate work-related stress (often referred to as cognitive factors).

- The organisation environment, which manifests in management practices, including increased accountability, lack of adequate communication, blame and disrespect, which can filter through the organisation (often referred to as systemic factors operating at the institutional and political level).

- Factors that are intrinsic to teaching, such as high workload, poor classroom discipline, low professional status and a lack of support from parents.

Research suggests that a positive school culture can ameliorate the effect of stressors faced by educators, with the primary features of such positive cultures being:

- Supportive colleagues (Brouwers *et al.* 2001; Dussault *et al.* 1999; Gersten *et al.* 2001; Talmor *et al.* 2005).
- Supportive principals or headteachers (Burke and Greenglass 1995; Brouwers *et al.* 2001; Davis and Wilson 2000; Gersten *et al.* 2001).
- Consultative decision-making processes (Ingersoll 1996).
- Greater teacher autonomy (Burke and Greenglass 1995; Ingersoll 1996).
- Shared values and goals (Burke and Greenglass 1995; Dorman 2003).

Support is vitally important for new teachers. Smith and Ingersoll (2004) found that new teachers with mentors (particularly related to collegial support) in their first year were less likely to leave the profession. These aspects of a positive culture relate to some of the environmental and managerial conditions of educational establishments but do not deal with the individual teacher's vulnerability to stress. Factors such as classroom discipline, workload, and evaluation apprehension affect people in different ways. For example, there is great variation in what people consider to be a discipline problem; one might need quiet and become stressed when a class is particularly chatty or one of the pupils is noisy; another might be sensitive to challenges to their authority and feel stressed by pupils who frequently ask searching questions.

Teacher burnout

Research focused on teacher burnout has yielded some interesting findings that influence both the individual and the environmental aspects of work-related stress within education.

They provide useful information that might help make educational establishments more aware of, better able to identify and support vulnerable colleagues. For example, Maslach and Schaufeli (1993) identified three elements of burnout:

- Depersonalisation, whereby the teacher distances him or herself from colleagues, so reducing the quality of contact with colleagues and learners.
- Reduced personal accomplishment, whereby the teacher devalues his or her work.
- Emotional exhaustion, whereby the teacher spends considerably less time in a positive emotional state and is dominated by a sense of weary resignation.

Depersonalisation is an interesting issue since, to a certain degree, it is sometimes seen as a short-term coping mechanism because it allows the person to 'survive' in the profession; in many respects it can be related to Hargreaves' view of individualism as a type of teacher behaviour (Hargreaves 1994). However, in the longer term, it is problematic because the teaching profession involves spending a large part of working life in isolation, in a classroom, and away from the support of colleagues. And teaching is, by definition, an interactive process, where any loss of personal relationships with the learners can quickly result in a decline in performance and satisfaction. Carlyle and Woods (2002) suggest that teacher burnout follows a set process. The teacher's sense of personal identity changes and he or she passes through a number of stages as described below and illustrated in FIGURE 16.3.

- **Organisational stress**: this relates to management practices such as increased accountability, bullying, poor communication, blame and disrespect that cascade through the organisation.

- **Stress in the family**: this entails the competing demands of work and family life.

- **Loss of identity:** This is a downward spiral of loss of prior identity, and a loss of ability to control emotions.

- **Liminality**: this describes the transition from one state to another, where the characteristics of the person in the previous state or stage are lost and not replaced. Teachers who lose their identity through stress tend to hit 'rock bottom' followed by 'cocooning' in which they seek a safe environment to grieve the loss of their old identity and seek a new one. After this, the teacher enters a so-called bridging phase where they begin to make contact with other teachers or a new career or lifestyle.

- **Reconstruction of identity**: the teacher either re-engages successfully with employment having reappraised their goals and attitudes, or leaves teaching either by finding a new career or retiring on health grounds.

Concluding comments

Educational reform has become habitual across Europe, especially within the UK. Over the last twenty years there have been several educational reforms across the home nations, which have led to significant changes in the content of the curriculum, emphasis, management and accountability systems. Such change seems to increase stress within the system as a whole, but is particularly acute at the interface between teaching and learning. Research suggests that the changes usually bring an increased workload, which is one of the biggest

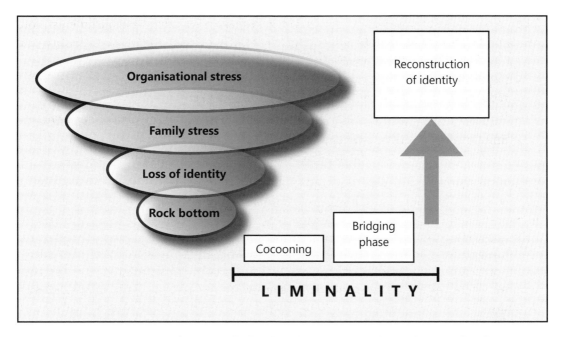

Figure 16.3: The stages of personal identity changes experienced in teacher burnout (based on Carlyle and Woods 2002).

causes of teacher stress, and the main reason for teachers leaving the profession. The term school culture is often conflated with other related terms such as climate, environment and ethos. It is a multifaceted concept that is difficult to define and can be difficult to research, or model and change when it is perceived to be negative in educational terms. How school culture influences the health and well-being of its staff and pupils is mediated through a rich and complex series of social interactions between its component subcultures.

Unfortunately, there is a gap in our understanding of how school cultures, within different settings, form and change over time. Further research is needed with a focus on maintaining the rich complexity of a school culture while mapping and modelling how that culture functions and evolves or emerges over time. This will improve understanding on the best way to implement and evaluate the success (or otherwise) of educational reforms.

A better understanding of the ways in which the subcultural interactions affect stress levels process may help to identify support strategies and even resilience factors that might ameliorate the stress felt by leaders of learning. They may also prevent the increasing incidence of teacher burnout and early retirement.

KEY MESSAGES FROM THIS CHAPTER

 Increased use of managerialism and accountability systems within educational establishments have led to an increase in the levels of stress experienced by staff at all levels of the system.

📄 Recent policy directives in education have exhorted leaders of learning to engage in greater collegiality. However, policy-makers and educational managers within the system have failed to pay sufficient cognisance to factor that affect collegiality (e.g. how the prevailing culture nurtures or militates collegiality).

📄 Culture can be thought of as the personality of an organisation, whereas climate is its attitude. Changing the culture can be difficult and time-consuming but changing the climate is easier because it is affected by small changes in practice.

📄 The prevailing culture within a given setting is composed of a number of subcultures: the leadership subculture, the staff subculture, and the student subculture. They all interact in a complex manner, producing a rich social environment that differs from setting to setting.

📄 All educational settings in the system are subject to extrinsic and intrinsic forces, which act on and influence the culture in any given moment and over time. This adds to the complexity of the prevailing culture, and makes the study of culture in educational settings difficult, from a positivist perspective. Researchers need to shift emphasis to studies on the rich complexity of the setting rather than trying to isolate variables in a linear, scientific manner.

📄 There is a lack of evidence about the effect of the prevailing culture on the physical and mental health and well-being of the workforce and students.

Supporting evidence and further reading

Abel MH, Sewell J (1999) Stress and burnout in rural and urban secondary school-teachers. *Journal of Educational Research* 92, 287–93.

Barth RS (2001) Learning by Heart. San Francisco, CA: Jossey Bass.

Brouwers A, Evers WJG, Tomic W (2001) Self-efficacy in eliciting social support and burnout among secondary-school-teachers. *Journal of Applied Social Psychology* 31, 1474–91.

Burke RJ, Greenglass ER (1995) A longitudinal examination of the Cherniss model of psychological burnout. *Social Science and Medicine* 40, 1357–63.

Carlyle D, Woods P (2002) *Emotions of Teacher Stress.* Stoke-on-Trent: Trentham Books.

Davis J, Wilson SM (2000) Principals' efforts to empower teachers: Effects on teacher motivation and job satisfaction and stress. *The Clearing House,* 349-353.

Deal TE, Peterson KD (1999) *Shaping School Culture.* San Francisco, CA: Jossey Bass.

Dussault M, Deaudelin C, Royer N, Loiselle J (1999) Professional isolation and occupational stress in teachers. *Psychological Reports* 84, 943–46.

Dorman JP (2003) Relationship between school and classroom environment and teacher burnout: A LISREL analysis. *Social Psychology of Education* 6, 107–27.

Gersten R, Keating T, Yovanoff P, Harniss MK (2001) Working in special education: Factors that enhance special educators' intent to stay. *Exceptional Children* 67, 549–67.

Glover D, Coleman M (2005) School culture climate and ethos: interchangeable or distinctive concepts? *Journal of In-Service Education* 31(2), 251–71.

Gruenert S (2008) School culture school climate: They are not the same thing. *Principal* 87(4), 56–59.

Hargreaves A (1994) *Changing Teachers Changing Times.* London: Cassell.

Health and Safety Executive (2002) *Occupational Stress Statistics Information Sheet.* Sudbury, Suffolk: HSE Books..

Health and Safety Executive (2012) *Stress and Psychological Disorders*. Available at: www.hse.gov.uk/statistics/causdis/stress/stress.pdf (accessed July 2015).

Ingersoll RM (1996) Teachers' decision-making power and school conflict. *Sociological Quarterly* 69, 159–76.

Jarvis M (2005) *The Psychology of Effective Learning and Teaching.* London: Nelson Thornes.

Manassero M, Garcia-Buades E, Torrens G, Ramis C, Vazquez A, Ferrer VA (2006) Teacher burnout: Attributional aspects. *Psychology in Spain* 10, 66–74.

Maslach C, Schaufeli WB (1993) Historical and conceptual development of burnout. In: *Maslach C, Schaufeli WB, Marek T (eds) Professional Burnout: Recent Developments in Theory and Research*. Washington, DC: Taylor & Francis.

Morley L, Rassool N (2000) School effectiveness: new managerialism, quality and the Japanization of education. *Journal of Education Policy* 15(2), 169–83.

Newton T (1995) *Managing Stress: Emotion and Power at Work.* London: Sage.

Nias J (1989) Refining the 'cultural perspective', *Cambridge Journal of Education* 19(2), 143–46.

National Union of Teachers (2000) *Proceedings of the Annual Conference.* London: NUT.

Palmer S (2001) Stress management: a masterclass. *Stress News* 13(1).

Schein EH (1985) *Organisational Culture and Leadership. S*an Francisco: Jossey Bass.

Simkins T (2000) Education reform and managerialism: comparing the experience of schools and colleges. *Journal of Education Policy* 15(3,) 317–32.

Smidt S (2009) *Introducing Vygotsky: A Guide for Practitioners and Students in Early Years Education.* London: Routledge.

Smith TM, Ingersoll RM (2004) What are the effects of induction and mentoring on beginning teacher turnover? *American Educational Research Journal* 41, 681–714.

Smithers A, Robinson P (2003*) Factors affecting teachers' decisions to leave the profession.* London: Department for Education and Skills.

Smithers A, Robinson P (2005) *Teacher Turnover Wastage and Movement Between Schools.* London: Department for Education and Skills.

Solvason C (2005) Investigating specialist school ethos ... or do you mean culture? *Educational Studies* 31(1), 85–94.

Talmor R, Reiter S, Feigin N (2005) Factors relating to regular education teacher burnout in inclusive education (original article). *European Journal of Special Needs Education* 20, 215–29.

Travis CJ, Cooper CL (1996) *Teachers Under Pressure: Stress in the Teaching Profession.* London: Routledge.

Wilson V (2002) *Feeling the Strain: An Overview of the Literature on Teachers' Stress (unpublished paper)*. Scottish Executive Education Department.

CHAPTER 17

Expectations of leaders and tensions among staff

Christine Forde, Jim O'Brien and Fiona Patrick

This chapter considers the challenges faced by leaders when leading and managing staff, and the duties and responsibilities associated with planning for and maintaining teacher and headteacher well-being at a time when workforce re-modelling and demands for 'new' professionalism are international concerns. In this chapter, we draw on two recent research studies conducted in Scotland, one exploring why some school managers and potential headteachers do not consider headship as a career step, and the other investigating teachers' working time. These studies and the Scottish context are used to illustrate international issues associated with increasing accountability and performance demands more generally made of the teacher workforce and school leaders. We suggest school leaders should be more aware of the impact that their approach to leadership and management can have on the well-being of their teacher colleagues. We also suggest that school leaders must be able to balance their own workloads without succumbing to the all-consuming demands of headship.

Skakon *et al.* (2010) reviewed over thirty years of research on the relationship between leaders, their behaviours and specific leadership styles, and 'employee stress and affective well-being', as well as providing evidence for a link between them. They did not include research directly associated with schools and teachers. The leadership styles and behaviours, workload, level of demands and incidence of stress among teachers are major concerns for school leaders who have to manage staff effectively to ensure good pupil-learning experiences (Galton and MacBeath 2008; Mulford 2003). The demands on schools and headteachers have multiplied in recent times. Working in an international context, Townsend (2011) confirms that:

The role of the [headteacher] is changing rapidly and seems to be becoming increasingly complex. Change in society towards a more knowledge-based way of looking at the world has been accompanied by changing paradigms of leadership, ranging from organisational leadership, through management, and towards a strong focus on instructional leadership.

School leaders all over the world are faced with considerable challenges (Billot *et al.* 2007; Cranston 2007; O'Brien *et al.* 2008). They must ensure that the increased expectations on schools are realised, at the same time as exercising a duty of care towards the well-being of their staff. They need to be more aware of the impact of their approach to leadership and management, and to balance their own workload despite the all-consuming demands of headship (Gronn 2003). Research conducted in Scotland over the last eight years offers insights into issues related to managing workloads, specifically with respect to teachers' working time (Menter *et al.* 2006) and the experiences of headship (MacBeath *et al.* 2009). These studies provide different perspectives – of teachers and of school managers and leaders.

Scotland's modernisation agenda

Since the Teachers' Agreement (Scottish Executive 2001b), policy developments in Scotland have underlined the primary role of teachers in teaching and learning. This requires a clear commitment to continuing professional development and the wider development agenda of the school. Alongside this, expectations of pupil learning have risen. The reformed curriculum, Curriculum for Excellence (Scottish Executive 2004a; 2006; 2008), emphasises the need for schools to ensure achievement of all pupils and addresses their holistic development and wider well-being (O'Brien and McLeod 2009). Baumfield *et al.* (2010) indicate that the policy outlined in Ambitious, Excellent Schools by the Scottish Executive Education Department (Scottish Executive 2004b) set out:

> *... the modernisation agenda for Scotland's non-selective comprehensive schools. Teachers and schools were afforded greater freedom to tailor learning to the needs of their pupils. Within a framework of national guidance, schools were encouraged to explore flexible, creative and innovative approaches to school improvement.*

Teacher working time

Since the late 1990s there has been an increasing focus on teacher policy in the UK as part of the drive to improve pupil achievement. As Draper and Sharp (2006) indicate:

> *Alterations in the nature of teachers' work frequently come about as unexpected and unplanned by-products of changes elsewhere, for example as consequences of developments in curriculum, the management of schools or local authority reorganisation. Occasionally however there are initiatives which are specifically designed to alter teachers' work.*

They describe the McCrone Inquiry (Scottish Executive 2001a) as a redesign of the professional working conditions of teachers in Scotland. The Teachers' Agreement emerged from concern that not only had teachers' pay fallen behind that of comparative professional groups, but the professional standing of teachers had also gone down, leading to low morale among serving teachers and difficulties in recruiting well-qualified people into the profession. There was a clear sense that what it means to be a teacher should be reconceptualised for the twenty-first century. The set of understandings (Scottish Executive 2001b) underpinning the Teachers' Agreement included:

- Understanding that the current conditions of service for teachers were no longer fully able to support and develop the profession.

- Recognising that this was a unique opportunity to address the question of teachers' esteem, professional autonomy and public accountability in a way that would enhance the capacity of school education to meet the challenges of the 21st century.

Among the key outcomes of the Teachers' Agreement was agreement on: the duties of teachers and those in different promoted posts (Annex B); the activities teachers should not be asked to undertake (Annex E); a 35-hour working week for all teachers including those in promoted posts; the commitment of each teacher to undertaking 35 hours of continuing professional development per annum beyond the working week; a restructuring of the primary school management structures; and a structured induction-year programme for all new entrants into the profession. Five years after the Teachers' Agreement, the Scottish Negotiating Committee for Teachers (SNCT) – responsible for negotiating teachers' pay and conditions of service with representatives from central government, local authorities (the employers) and teacher unions – commissioned a research study of teachers' working time. The study had three main strands:

i. Policy analysis of local policy related to the Teachers' Agreement.
ii. Quantitative study of teachers' working week through a work-time diary including the number of hours worked and the type of activities undertaken.
iii. Qualitative study on the views of teachers through individual interviews, focus group discussions and questionnaires on a number of aspects of their professional lives.

Here we draw on strands (ii) and (iii) to consider the issues related to management of teachers' work and well-being. The purpose of (ii) was to ascertain the number of hours per week that teachers worked routinely and the typical types of activities they engaged in; the purpose of (iii) was to give the teachers a voice and provide an insight into teachers' perceptions of their working lives.

WORKING TIME

Strand (2) aimed to gather robust data via time-use diaries on the number of hours worked by teachers in pre-school, primary, secondary and special school settings, and to gather information on time spent on specific teacher duties. A sample of a representative group of teachers across all sectors in all Scottish local authorities completed a time-use diary. Two 'sweeps' of the time use diary were carried out to see if there was any difference in the patterns of working time and activities at different times during the school year. The two survey weeks were expected to reflect the range of activities typically carried out by teachers. The average number of hours worked for all respondents (including classroom teachers, principal teachers, deputy headteachers and headteachers in all sectors) to the time-use diary was 45 hours per week. The overall average number of hours worked in the sample for Sweep 1 was 45.10 hours and in Sweep 2 the overall average was 44.66 hours. The main conclusion from this national study is that all categories of respondent (teachers and promoted staff) in all sectors worked an average of more than 35 hours per week. FIGURE 17.1 shows the average length of the working week for all teachers and promoted staff combined. Data specifically from classroom teachers gives an average that is above the agreed 35-hour working week. The Teachers' Agreement specified eight professional tasks. FIGURES 17.2 and 17.3 illustrate the breadth of the role of teachers in both primary and secondary schools. This information provides insight into teachers' perceptions of their role following the agreement.

Strand (3) investigated teachers' views about various aspects of their professional role. They reported a number of areas in which they felt there had been a positive outcome, including salary. The Teachers' Agreement resulted in a considerable salary increase for most staff, of 23% staged over a three-year period. The study found that teachers were able to highlight several changes that had resulted in improvements to their working lives and had supported their practice, and their positive response was qualified. Access to continuing professional learning was broadly seen to be positive, particularly those in whom it was recognised and formally recorded. Each teacher was expected to complete 35 hours CPD time in a year in addition to the 35-hour working week and record this in a CPD portfolio. The structured induction year for probationary teachers was also seen as a positive, but it was noted that there were now demands on experienced staff to mentor.

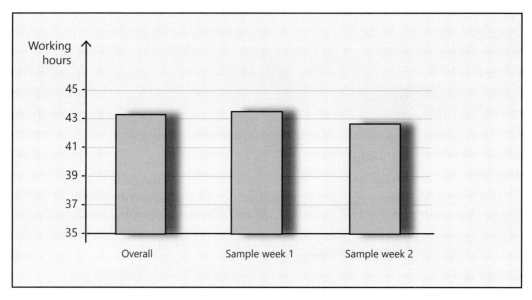

Figure 17.1: Number of hours in the average working week of teachers and promoted staff combined (adapted from Menter *et al.* 2006).

DIFFERENCES AMONG TEACHERS IN PRIMARY AND SECONDARY SCHOOLS

There were some sector differences in the teachers' views about their roles as a result of the agreement. Of those viewed positively by primary teachers were the 'use of classroom assistants' and had previously allowed '2.5 hours allowed per week for non-contact time'. For secondary teachers, preparation time was allowed during the pupil week, but primary teachers were expected to teach for the full 25 hours per pupil week. They also welcomed the introduction of a four-tier promotion structure across all sectors, because it provided primary teachers with a first middle-management promoted post. The situation was different in the secondary sector; for some staff, the restructuring (Anderson and Nixon 2010) had a negative impact. In secondary schools, some tiers were removed – assistant principal teachers and assistant headteacher. Although not part of the agreement specifically, some local authorities used this as an opportunity to remove subject principal teachers and create a smaller number of middle-leader posts to lead faculties of a number of subject areas in one faculty.

Participants in the study indicated that many secondary teachers were deeply concerned about the loss of leadership in certain subjects and the reduction in number of promoted posts. A number of subject principal teachers also lost their status and recognition. Secondary teachers reported that these changes added to their workload, and senior managers reported that their workload had also intensified. There was a mixed response to many of the new structures and practices emanating from the Teachers' Agreement, whereby particular groups perceived themselves as gaining and others as disadvantaged. In relation to wider educational policy, many concerns about extra demands and workload were reported, particularly with respect to curriculum reform, including the Curriculum for Excellence (Scottish Executive 2004a), and to changes addressing the inclusion agenda in Scottish education. So-called innovation fatigue was a common theme, whereby schools were expected to take forward considerable change on a range of initiatives from both central and local government related to teaching,

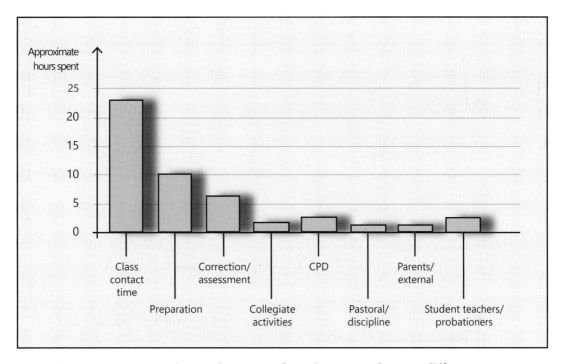

Figure 17.2: Approximate time spent by primary teachers on different activities each week (based on Menter *et al.* 2006).

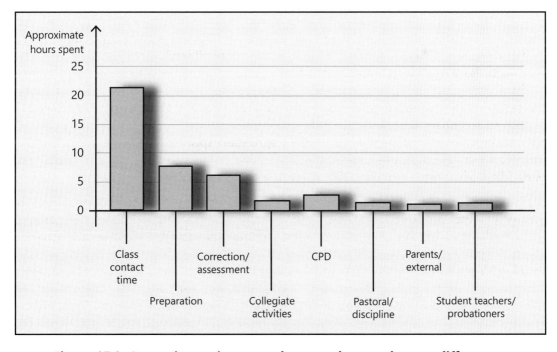

Figure 17.3: Approximate time spent by secondary teachers on different activities each week (based on Menter *et al.* 2006).

learning and the curriculum. The number of initiatives and subsequent workload included paperwork (as distinct from activities, which they conceive of as being more directly related to concerns of learning and teaching); this issue was raised repeatedly. Comments focused on the imposition of a number of initiatives that participants felt they were not fully consulted about, but that they are obliged to implement in their schools. Some staff thought that the number of new initiatives impinged on their own personal sense of professionalism, in that they felt they could not refuse to implement innovation in case they were deemed 'unprofessional'.

SCOTLAND'S SCHOOLS ACT 2000

Alongside this was the impact of the Scotland's Schools Act (2000). This resulted in mainstream schools being responsible for addressing a far more diverse set of learning needs. The issue was not the principle of inclusion – the data show strong teacher support for this – but the resourcing of this fundamental change and its influence on the range of demands they had to meet and their workload. It is against this backdrop of increased expectations that issues related to well-being have to be considered. The Teachers' Agreement was careful to specify the number of hours teachers were expected to work contractually, and the duties they were to undertake (Scottish Executive 2001b: Annex B), as well as the tasks they were not expected to do (Scottish Executive 2001b: Annex E). However, one of the significant tensions revealed by this study was the seemingly impossible task of fitting the range of demands into a 35-hour working week. Specifically, as part of this research, teachers were asked to consider what they deemed essential and non-essential and (notwithstanding their concerns about having to work beyond 35 hours) they found this very difficult to respond to, viewing all activities they undertook as essential in terms of their professional role and the benefits to the pupils. A large number of comments referred to the teachers' views of their own professionalism and the obligations they felt towards the pupils and the teaching profession itself. This sense of obligation leads them to take the approach that they will work whatever hours they need to in order to fulfil their duties to the children. The following comments by a teacher attending a focus group discussion are typical of this standpoint:

> *The feeling in my experience in different sectors is that whatever your contractual hours are, it seems almost irrelevant to when you're working and you're going right through to finish any job that's required. Most staff that we can think of in schools are working nearly all the time and certainly many take work home and go well beyond their contractual hours to get that completed: that seems to be part and parcel of the job. (McPhee and Menter 2006)*

RESEARCH ON TEACHER WORKING TIME

The Teacher Working Time Research study was commissioned by the SNCT and supported by Scottish Executive. The study (Menter *et al.* 2006) found a number of tensions in relation to teachers' perceptions of their workload. What comes across from the data, however, is a strong sense of commitment which needs to be acknowledged when managing teacher workloads. The challenge seems to be about how to manage teachers' work and desire to seek the best outcomes for pupils without exploiting their sense of commitment. The increasingly wide role of the teacher is a significant issue and there seems to be little need to enable teachers to focus on the crucial areas of teaching and learning because they are uniquely prepared for them. Being 'leaders of learning' is something teachers invest themselves in. Consideration of these attitudes should ensure the well-being of teachers and is useful for securing, attracting and retaining committed professionals (McPhee and Menter 2006).

Basically it is a lot of fun. Dealing with kids is a lot of fun. You never, ever get bored. You get frustrated, you get angry – all of these emotions come into it. We are still teachers. We are still here. That is why we came into it. We do enjoy it – I still get a buzz about teaching!

The experiences of headship

It is difficult to recruit teachers into headteacher posts in many national systems (Gronn and Rawlings-Sanaei 2003), an issue that is fuelled by factors such as unrelenting change; increasing pressures; employment stress; a growing work–life imbalance; and work intensification – pithily described as 'greedy work' (Gronn 2003). The Recruitment and Retention of Headteachers study (MacBeath *et al.* 2009) was commissioned and funded by the Scottish Government. Questionnaires and interviews explored headteachers' reflections on their role and sources of satisfaction and tensions. A consistently strong issue was the emotional dimension of leadership, either in negative terms such as 'battles' and the need to 'firefight', or in positive terms such as enjoyment, challenge and satisfaction. Headteachers were asked to estimate the length of their working week and to describe a typical week. A '60 hours plus' week was common (MacBeath *et al.* 2009). Further, the overwhelming message is that, however challenging and stressful headship might be it is 'a privilege and offers a much valued opportunity to make a difference to children's learning' (MacBeath *et al.* 2009); however the price of working long hours can be high 'with an influence health and feelings of loneliness'.

'STRATEGIC LEADERSHIP' AND 'LEADERSHIP OF PERSONNEL

Two distinguishing factors emerge from the data of the study. The first is 'strategic leadership' involving school improvement planning, establishing school priorities, establishing and planning the school budget, reviewing and developing teaching practices and curriculum, and developing the school timetable. The second is 'leadership of personnel', covering development and provision of CPD, supporting new staff and evaluating teachers. Headteachers indicate how much satisfaction they get from working with people, but the study suggests they play a larger role in strategic rather than personnel leadership. Interestingly, they describe themselves in many ways – as problem solvers, politicians, diplomats, police, social workers, therapists and caretakers, 'all of which brought dilemmas and challenges as well as unexpected compensations' (MacBeath *et al.* 2009). Leadership was seen by many as 'emotional work'. Headteachers expressed a high level of confidence in many aspects of their jobs, primarily in their ability to manage teaching and administrative staff. This 'leadership and management confidence' covers various closely related aspects of leadership and management, such as:

- Providing strategic focus and direction to colleagues.
- Leading the development of teaching and learning.
- Managing teaching staff.
- Managing other staff.

This suggests a key focus on managing and dealing with people especially staff colleagues and professional relationships, however, this conflicts with the views of 1,218 teachers in one survey, who underestimate the amount of time that Headteachers reported giving to the people aspects of their job (MacBeath *et al.* 2009).

COPING WITH PRESSURE

Headteachers were also asked how they deal with the many pressures of their role. The data from the study describes five coping strategies that they 'regularly adopt'. These coping strategies:

> *... are significant personally because they affect the health, well-being and sense of professional identity of the individual concerned. (MacBeath et al. 2012)*

'Coping' is a word that carries a sense of struggle, swimming with the current, keeping one's head above water. These were the kind of metaphors used by Scottish heads to depict their situation. Pressure and constant demands 'from above' (in itself a telling metaphor for the hierarchical nature of the relationship between schools, local authorities and government) was a common theme. The strategies are described below.

(i) Dutiful compliance

This reflects the perception of some heads of having little autonomy and minimal latitude for initiative because of concerns about conflict with local authorities. The lack of leadership capacity to delegate often exacerbates the situation. Commitment to the role involving long hours expended on school-related tasks, creates a work–life imbalance so that work often invades their private time and personal life.

(ii) Cautious pragmatism

This strategy does not resist the demands of the workplace but recognises that an open-ended role commitment is detrimental to both private life and well-being. This is evidenced by a clear prioritisation of energy and effort, sometimes matched by a determination to seek to achieve a work–life balance. However such an approach was invested with caution in terms of how their actions/inactions might be interpreted and with what possible consequences.

(iii) Unruffled self-confidence

These heads flourish in their roles through 'an ability to compartmentalise responsibilities and priorities, with non-work time carefully fire-walled from the intrusion of school-related demands'. They have the capacity to discriminate between and determine the importance of various demands and tasks, and carefully protect non-work time.

(iv) Bullish self-assertion

This occurs in people with high levels of self-confidence and self-assurance who also thrive on challenge and are effective problem-solvers and comfortable in a robust relationship with the local authority.

(v) Defiant risk-taking

This is more of a personality trait than a coping strategy, whereby there 'is a sense of fulfilment in rising to the challenge of defending their schools and expressing deeply held educational values'. With respect to managing and leading teachers, the question can be posed about the extent to which any of these five coping strategies or repertoires are effective or counter-productive. Indeed it would be interesting to speculate about the reaction of some school leaders if teachers were to routinely adopt similar strategies, especially those towards the defiant risk-taking strategy end of the spectrum, as a means of coping with the stress they feel when confronted by excessive innovation or demands to meet external requirements.

Flexibility: The McCormac Review

The two studies called the Teacher Working Time Research (Menter *et al.* 2006) and the Recruitment and Retention of Headteachers (MacBeath *et al.* 2009) were conducted at a time when the conditions of service had been set out in the Teachers' Agreement (2001b). Both help to reveal the significant issues related to the management of teachers' work, for teachers and for school leaders. In Scotland, Advancing Professionalism reviewed teacher employment (McCormac 2011) and Teaching Scotland's Future reviewed teacher education (Donaldson 2010), with an increased focus on the development of teachers throughout their careers to realise the ambitions of the Scottish education system in terms of pupil achievement. The McCormac Review (2011) reviewed teacher employment as part of the spending review agreement with the Convention of Scottish Local Authorities (COSLA), the local councils who are also the teacher employers in public sector education (over 95% of provision in Scotland). A key point of this report is 'flexibility', but the focus on prescription was not typical of other professions and was misaligned with the construction of professionalism underpinning this report. The review consistently argues that the arrangements set up through the Teachers' Agreement (Scottish Executive 2001b) reduce rather than enhance teacher professionalism and do not focus on the critical issue of outcomes for pupils. Some consider that the delineation between teachers' duties, and what they should not do, and the working hours allowed for specific duties (e.g. collegiate time, preparation and CPD) focused on inputs that were again at odds with the construction of professionalism. Instead, greater flexibility in the organisation of duties and opportunities for taking on additional duties was endorsed, and the idea of extended professionalism underpinning the report on career-long teacher education, as per the Donaldson Report (2010), is reiterated throughout the review. Teachers are 'leaders of learning' who contribute to the wider learning community and:

> *... teachers must be able to adapt to an ever-changing environment, reflect on their practice and develop their skills as their careers develop. (McCormac Review 2011)*

The studies drawn on in this discussion raise critical issues about the well-being of teachers and school leaders. However, viewing this only in terms of time and intensified demands is limited. Previous studies of their careers and aspirations highlight the importance of motivation in shaping attitudes to work. Wilson *et al.* (2006) found 'a complex mix of factors and variables unique to each' teacher but observed that most have 'a desire to work with children and continue to work with them throughout their career'. Draper *et al.* (1998) noted other aspirations, such as seeking promotion, but also found the intrinsic appeal of working with children and young people was central. This thread runs through the two studies discussed in this chapter. For the headteachers in MacBeath *et al.* (2009), working directly with children and young people was a strong factor, often regarded as an antidote to the bureaucratic demands of school management. Similarly, participants in Menter *et al.*'s (2006) study of working time were reluctant to reduce their range of activities because of the impact that might have on their pupils. At a time of increased expectations on schools to ensure high performance in terms of pupil learning outcomes, coinciding with economic constraints, the demands on teachers and school leaders continues to grow. In Scotland, the previous Teachers' Agreement about conditions of service (Scottish Executive 2001) included not just the duties and responsibilities of teachers but also listed (Annex E) the duties and tasks teachers should *not* be asked to undertake routinely. However, the drive for improvement in national policy has been interpreted as increased productivity. The latest report on conditions of service, *Advancing Professionalism* (McCormac 2011), proposes that 'sensible flexibility within a school – that does not detract from the core educational role of the teacher – should be the norm' and calls for the removal of Annex E. Serious concerns remain about the impact of increased demands on teacher well-being. The challenge is to find ways to reclaim and reify the high level of motivation among teachers and school leaders in the learning lives of children and young people.

Concluding comments

From studying the situation in Scotland, it is clear that improving the learning outcomes of pupils depends not on making teachers work longer hours nor on headteachers driving staff, and themselves, to meet increased expectations. This requires a deeper examination. The Teachers' Agreement tried to bring clarity to issues about duties and the numbers of hours to be worked. However, these two factors – longer hours and the increased number and range of demands made on teachers, headteachers and schools – seem to be irreconcilable. It seems impossible to achieve what is expected within the 35-hour working week. The focus on time remains problematic: Michelson and Harvey (2000) argue that 'time-use measures have been shown to provide valid data on what people do on a chosen day – their activities, the location in which they occur, and the people who are involved', but the emotions of teachers and headteachers should be considered. We should explore how enjoyable or stressful the activities of teachers and headteachers are, particularly when under time pressure. Hargreaves (1990; 1992) and Larson (1980) found that the multiple demands, often in close proximity during the working day, leads to stressful intensification. According to Michelson and Harvey (2000) teachers put in a respectable workday but it is not the sheer number of hours that leads to elevated feelings of time crunch and pressure. The issue now faced in Scottish education is whether greater flexibility in working and focusing on pupil outcomes will alleviate the high level of intensification experienced by teachers and headteachers, and how can they have a meaningful work–life balance that contributes substantially to their individual and collective well-being, at the same time as providing appropriate role models and learning experiences for the young people in their charge. McPhee and Patrick (2009) conclude that despite:

> *... numerous statements from successive government ministers that teachers are hugely valued and should be reprofessionalised ... the rhetoric is not usually borne out in practice. There has been repeated failure at policy level to understand the complexity of the contexts within which teaching is carried out. Combining cultural factors with individual constructs of what it takes to do a job effectively [requires] changing professional practice [according to] changing professionals attitudes and beliefs [and considering both] how policy is implemented [and] who implements [it].*

KEY MESSAGES FROM THIS CHAPTER

 It is against a backdrop of greater political and educational policy expectation that issues related to the well-being of teachers and headteachers should be considered because their workload is increasing and they are experiencing greater accountability.

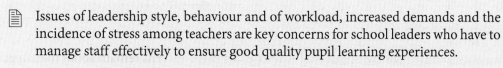 Issues of leadership style, behaviour and of workload, increased demands and the incidence of stress among teachers are key concerns for school leaders who have to manage staff effectively to ensure good quality pupil learning experiences.

A major challenge is how to manage teachers' work while seeking the best outcomes for pupils without exploiting their high level of commitment.

There are limitations in viewing teacher well-being solely in terms of time and intensification of demands. Research on their careers and aspirations highlight the importance of motivation in shaping their attitudes to work.

The appeal of working with children and young people is of great importance to both headteachers and teachers.

The significance of professional identity, or 'being professional', is about building and maintaining relationships.

The authors acknowledge the work of the members of Professor Ian Menter, Dr Margery McMahon, Dr Alison Devlin, Dr John Hall and Dr Alistair McPhee for their work on Teacher Working Time, and Professor Peter Gronn, Professor John MacBeath, Dr Darleen Opher, Dr Mike Cowie and Mr Kevin Lowden for their work on the Recruitment and Retention of Headteachers. They would also like to thank the leaders of learning who readily participated in these projects.

Supporting evidence and further reading

Anderson C, Nixon G (2010) The move to faculty middle management structures in Scottish secondary schools: A case study. *School Leadership and Management* 30(3) 249–63.

Baumfield,V, Hulme M, Livingston K, Menter I (2010) Consultation and engagement? The reshaping of teacher professionalism through curriculum reform in 21st century Scotland. *Scottish Educational Review* 42(2), 57–73.

Billot J, Goddard T, Cranston N (2007) How principals manage ethnocultural diversity: Learnings from three countries, *International Studies in Educational Administration* 35(2), 13–19.

Cranston N (2007) Through the eyes of potential aspirants: Another view of the principalship. *School Leadership and Management* 27(2), 109–28.

Donaldson G (2010) *Teaching Scotland's Future.* Edinburgh: Scottish Government.

Draper J, Fraser H, Taylor W (1998) Teachers careers: accident or design? *Teacher Development* 2(3), 373–84.

Draper J, Sharp S (2006) Continuity or change? The initial impact of the post-McCrone agreement. *Scottish Educational Review*, 37(I), 99.

Gronn P (2003) *The New Work of Educational Leaders: Changing Leadership Practice in an Era of Reform.* London: Sage.

Gronn P, Rawlings-Sanaei F (2003) Recruiting school principals in a climate of leadership disengagement. *Australian Journal of Education* 47(2), 172–84.

Hargreaves A (1990) Teachers' work and the politics of time and space. *International Journal of Qualitative Studies in Education* 3(4), 303–20.

Hargreaves A (1992) Time and teachers, work: an analysis of the intensification thesis. *Teachers College Record* 94(1), 87–108.

HMIE (2007) *Teaching Scotland's children: A report on progress in implementing 'A teaching profession for the 21st century'.* Livingston: HMIE.

Larson, MS (1980) Proletarianization and educated labour. *Theory and Society* 9(1), 131–75.

Galton M, MacBeath J (2008) *Teachers Under Pressure*. London: Sage

MacBeath J, Gronn P, Opfer D *et al.* (2009) *The Recruitment and Retention of Headteachers in Scotland (Main Report)*. Edinburgh: Scottish Government.

MacBeath J, O'Brien J, Gronn P (2012) Drowning or waving? Coping strategies among Scottish headteachers. *School Leadership and Management* 35(5), 421–37.

McCormac G (2011) *Advancing Professionalism in Teaching: The Report of the Review of Teacher Employment in Scotland*. Edinburgh: Crown Publications.

McPhee A, Menter I (2006) *Teachers after McCrone: A new professionalism? Paper presented at Teacher Working Time Symposium*. Scottish Educational Research Association Annual Conference, November 2006, Perth, UK.

McPhee A, Patrick F (2009) The pupils will suffer if we don't work': Teacher professionalism and reactions to policy change in Scotland. *Scottish Educational Review* 41(1), 86–96.

Menter I, Devlin A, Forde C *et al.* (2006) *Teacher working time*. Edinburgh: Scottish Negotiating Committee for Teachers.

Michelson W, Harvey AS (2000) Teachers' work never done? Time use and subjective outcomes. *Radical Pedagogy* 2(1). Available at: www.radicalpedagogy.org/radicalpedagogy.org/Is_Teachers_Work_Never_Done__Time-Use_and_Subjective_Outcomes.html (last accessed July 2015).

Mulford B (2003) *School Leaders: Changing Roles and Influence Teacher and School Effectiveness*. Paris: Organisation for Economic Co-operation and Development.

O'Brien J, Murphy D, Draper J (2008) *School Leadership* (2nd edn). Edinburgh: Dunedin Academic Press.

O'Brien J, McLeod G (2009) *The Social Agenda of the School*. Edinburgh: Dunedin Academic Press.

Scottish Executive (2001a) *A teaching profession for the 21st century: Report (McCrone Report)*. Edinburgh: Scottish Executive Education Department Publications:.

Scottish Executive (2001b) A *teaching profession for the 21st century: Agreement reached following recommendations made in the McCrone Report (Teachers' Agreement)*. Edinburgh: Scottish Executive Publications.

Scottish Executive (2004a) *A Curriculum for Excellence. The Curriculum Review Group*. Available at: www.scotland.gov.uk/Publications/2004/11/20178/45862 (accessed July 2015).

Scottish Executive (2004b) *Ambitious, Excellent Schools; Our Agenda for Action Edinburgh: Scottish Executive*. Available at: www.gov.scot/Publications/2004/11/20176/45852 (accessed July 2015).

Scottish Executive (2006) *A Curriculum for Excellence: Progress and Proposals. A paper from the Curriculum Review Programme Board*. Available at: www.scotland.gov.scot/Publications/2006/03/22090015/0 (accessed July 2015).

Scottish Government (2008) *Curriculum for Excellence: Experiences and Outcomes*. Edinburgh: Scottish Government.

Skakon J, Nielsen K, Borg V, Guzman J (2010) Are leaders' well-being, behaviours and style associated with the affective well-being of their employees? A systematic review of three decades of research. *Work and Stress* 24, 147.

Townsend T (2011) School leadership in the twenty-first century: Different approaches to common problems? *School Leadership and Management* 31(2), 93–103.

Wilson V, Powney J, Hall S, Davidson J (2006) Who wants to be a teacher? The impact of age, disability, ethnicity, gender and sexual orientation on teachers' career aspirations. *Scottish Educational Review* 38(1), 92–104.

CHAPTER 18

Demands of the job, job-related stress and stress burnout

Mick P. Fleming, Stephen P. Day and Colin R. Martin

Several surveys have been carried out that provide evidence of the increasing incidence and prevalence of stress, burnout and physical issues, such as high blood pressure, and mental health issues, such as depression, within the teaching profession. The job demands–resources model is the framework from which to consider the development of longer-term biopsychosocial responses to prolonged, excessive job demands. There is emerging literature that identifies various organisational and personal factors that can mediate the development of burnout arising from excessive job demands. This chapter defines these factors and reviews the relevant empirical supporting evidence. It also discusses the implications for policy-makers, managers of educational organisations and teachers in terms of job performance, absenteeism, presentism, suboptimal performance, premature leaving of the profession, and physical and psychological consequences of stress. Finally, the authors suggest strategies that are aimed at preventing and managing excessive job demands and stress and burnout.

Recent surveys have confirmed earlier findings about the prevalence of stress among teachers (Kyriacou 2001), showing high rates of stress and stress-related responses in teachers and lecturers across the UK (Association of Teachers and Lecturers 2013; National Association of Schoolmasters Union of Women Teachers 2015; Teachers Assurance 2013). In a survey by the Association of Teachers and Lecturers (2014), 55% felt that job-related issues were detrimental to their mental health, involving stress, exhaustion and sleep disturbance, and 38% noticed a rise in mental health problems in their colleagues in the recent past. Among the factors they identified were the pressure to meet targets and the pressure caused by inspections. The findings were consistent with other surveys, such as that conducted by the National Association of Schoolmasters Union of Women Teachers (NASUWT 2015), in which 83–84% of respondents reported the detrimental effect of job factors on stress levels, sleep patterns, and health and well-being throughout the previous year; 67% cited effects on mental health, and 48% saw a doctor for work-related issues.

Both teachers and lecturers have reported issues with depression, stress, insomnia, anxiety, relationship problems, and a loss of confidence in dealing with disruptive and violent learners (Association of Teachers and Lecturers 2013). Increasing use of alcohol, tobacco and caffeine was reported by 25% of respondents in another study (National Association of Schoolmasters Union of Women Teachers 2010). There are important aspects to the finding of these surveys. One is that the teaching profession is becoming highly stressful, and many of the stressors identified are job related, such as pressures of workload and meeting targets, may ultimately lead to burnout. Another is that significant consequences for health and teaching practice arise due to stress and burnout.

Stress

According to the Oxford English Dictionary, stress is a state of psychological and physiological tension and worry caused by demanding circumstances. When the demands in a person's environment outstrip their perceived resources, situations arise where there are perceived threats (Freeman and Freeman 2012). Other recognised definitions relate to the initiation of a stress response.

THE BODY'S RESPONSE TO STRESS

The stress response is a reaction to fear commonly known as the 'fight or flight' response, which has cognitive, emotional and physiological (hormonal and neurological) components. A person experiences a psychosocial stressor in their environment and makes an appraisal or (cognitive) interpretation regarding the level of threat and impact of the stressor. This cognitive process triggers a range of strong unconscious and conscious feelings, which in turn activate the hypothalamus in the brain. This modulates the stress response by stimulating other structures in the body, via the hypothalamic–pituitary–adrenal (HPA) axis, namely the pituitary and the adrenal glands that are part of the sympathetic nervous system. Activation by stress leads to the secretion of adrenaline, a chemical messenger or neurotransmitter that prepares the body to deal with a perceived threat by speeding up the heart rate, contracting blood vessels, tensing the muscles, reducing the flow of saliva, releasing glucose for energy from liver stores, and inhibiting gastrointestinal functioning. The hormone cortisol is released by the adrenal glands; this increases the sensitivity of the heart and other organs to adrenaline and noradrenaline, causing further physiological and psychological arousal and the hyperaroused state that is characteristic of the stress response. There are many mental and physical health consequences of the acute stress response and to prolonged stress.

Burnout

Further negative outcomes arise from a combination of prolonged exposure to stressors, experiencing a continuous stress response, and lacking effective coping strategies; this is called 'burnout' (Brown 2012). Burnout is one specific form of stress response and it occurs most commonly in situations or jobs that involve close working with people where demanding interpersonal and helping/facilitative relationships are a core element of the work. In this respect, burnout is directly related to the type of work, and to specific job- or role-related stressors. Most of the literature considers that the key aspects of burnout are related to the demands of the role over time, when they exceed the internal resources and capacity of the teacher, for example, to fulfil the requirements of their demanding role (Llorens *et al.* 2007; Maslach and Jackson 1981; Maslach *et al.* 2001).

Typical stressors such as high workload, shortages of staff, dealing with difficult students, time pressures, competing demands for time and working to targets (FIGURE 18.1) have been identified by teachers and by people in similar professions (Ahola *et al.* 2014; Buunk *et al.* 2007; Llorens-Gumbau and Salanova-Soria 2014). Striving to achieve the requirements of their role and maintaining an optimal standard of work means teachers have to expend extra emotional energy and invest more and more time and effort. This is in combination with a temporal element, whereby teachers expound this extra emotional investment over a certain period of time.

CONTINUED EXPOSURE TO STRESSORS

Continuous exposure, and reactions, to work-related demands leads to depletion of internal resources, resulting in a state of emotional exhaustion, with feelings of anger, frustration, depersonalisation, cynicism and a lack of confidence in professional ability (Bria *et al.* 2014; Maslach *et al.* 2001).

There may be long-term effects on physical and mental health, including motivation and role performance, and studies have indicated that the characteristics of burnout can last for five to fifteen years (Bakker and Costa 2014). CHAPTER 16 on culture and the health and well-being of leaders of learning discusses the issues of management, work-related stressors and coping more specifically.

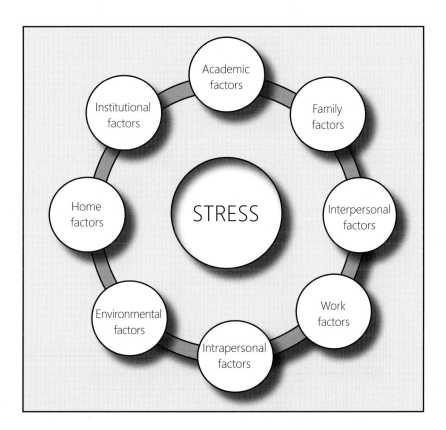

Figure 18.1: Typical stressors in the education environment and their impact on the development of stress.

The job demands–resources model acknowledges that engagement and motivation depend on having a balance in favour of resources over demands (FIGURE 18.3). When the balance favours demands over resources, there is a risk for developing the symptoms of burnout (Llorens *et al.* 2007). There is much empirical support for both the job processes involved in the model, for the correlation between demands and exhaustion, and for the association of job resources with depersonalisation and personal accomplishment (Bria *et al.* 2014).

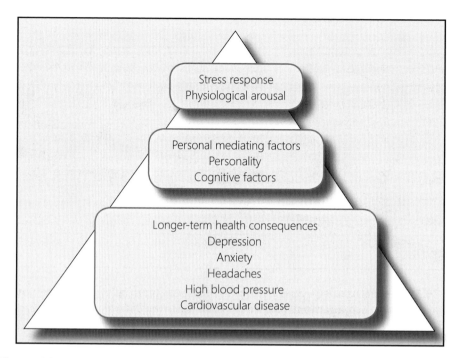

Figure 18.2: Integrated process of burnout and long-term health consequences.

ENGAGEMENT IN THE CONTEXT OF THE JOB DEMANDS–RESOURCES MODEL

Engagement has been defined as the opposite of burnout. It is characterised by three core dimensions, or components: vigour, dedication and absorption, which represent energetic, resilient, motivated and committed teachers, who are engaged emotionally and are cognitively invested and focused on helping to achieve the organisation's goals (Llorens-Gumbau and Salanova-Soria 2014; Llorens *et al.* 2007).

DIMENSIONS OF BURNOUT

Burnout has been conceptualised as a multidimensional syndrome made up of three categories of symptoms (Jansson-Frojmark and Lindblom 2010). In their seminal work, Maslach and Jackson (1981) identified three dimensions:

- **Emotional exhaustion**: chronic feelings of physical and emotional fatigue, loss of energy and tiredness, that emerge from the stress response because of the extra emotional investment demanded by the role (Brown 2012).

- **Depersonalisation**: cynical, indifferent and negative attitudes towards the organisation, colleagues, peers and learners (Buunk *et al.* 2007).

- **Personal accomplishment**: efficacy beliefs characterised by more negative self-evaluative thinking and self-concept, and reduced competence and effectiveness at work (Bakker and Costa 2014; Canadas-De la Fuente *et al.* 2015).

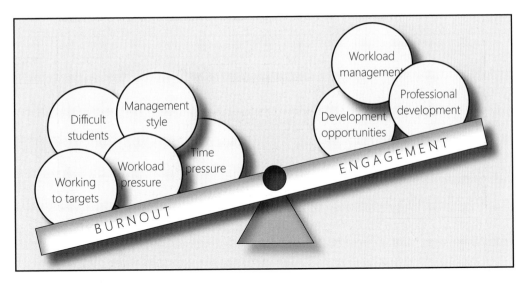

Figure 18.3: Job demands versus job resources and their relation to burnout or engagement (based on Llorens *et al.* 2007).

Psychometric studies measuring the structure of the three dimensions have confirmed their validity in teachers in both primary and secondary schools (Gold *et al.* 1992).

RISK AND MEDIATING FACTORS

The job demands–resources model is useful for gaining insight into the development of burnout. This model has been described as parsimonious by Llorens (Llorens *et al.* 2007) and, as such, provides a useful but sparse understanding of some of the factors associated with work-related stress. In order to understand the interactive elements of the process, it is important to gauge the effects of other organisational and particularly individual psychosocial factors that facilitate or mediate the effects of work-related stress, and prevent the development of burnout (Bakker and Costa 2014). Some of the elements associated with burnout in the literature are *not* dichotomous, and can be seen to contribute to the development of burnout as well as *protect* teachers from the adverse effects of work-related stress, and prevent development of burnout.

Organisational and institutional factors

These can be subdivided into barriers and facilitators. Both are specific – perhaps unique – to the each teacher's own organisation and its particular role. Teachers indicate that working to targets is associated with stress, and the targets come from government policy, and interpretation of and plans for achieving such goals are applied in the context of the particular institution. The targets may effect role definition and workload in a positive or negative way, but the *barrier* is related to the specific management strategy used to interpret and administer the policy target.

Barriers

Barriers are situational factors within an education environment that block teachers, diminish their job performance, and prevent them from achieving the goals that relate to the job's demands. Typical barriers are:

- Management style within the organisation.
- Problems with teamwork.
- Problems with resource allocation.
- Difficult students.
- Difficulties with parents.

Each of these can have an impact on workload, work pressure, role definition and educational outcomes and may influence the balance between job demands and job resources. If a barrier 'tips the balance' in favour of demands, this increases the demands to be met, which causes stress and raises the risk of burnout. In a longitudinal study among 274 secondary school-teachers, structural equation modelling analysis was used to find that barriers experienced at a first time point were significantly correlated with burnout at a second time point, eight months later; these results were statistically significant (Llorens-Gumbau and Salanova-Soria 2014). The authors concluded that there was a causal relationship between the perception of a high number of barriers and the symptoms of burnout relating to emotional exhaustion and aspects of depersonalisation such as cynicism. They also found a mediating role for self-efficacy, which is discussed in more detail below. This study offers novel and interesting findings, as well as identifying a potentially rich area for future research.

GEOGRAPHICAL AND DEMOGRAPHIC FACTORS

One related situational factor may be the geographical area of the educational organisation in terms of sociodemographic profile and their potential to affect outcomes and job demands. Educational organisations in urban areas, for example, are subject to higher levels of deprivation and disadvantage. When combined with policy targets, this has the potential to increase job demands greatly, leading to exhaustion and depersonalisation. In a study of 500 school counsellors in the United States, a strongly significant relationship was found between working in urban areas and emotional exhaustion and depersonalisation compared to suburban and rural areas (Butler and Constantine 2005). While school counsellors have more explicit and defined pastoral roles than teachers, that possibly expose them to more demands of living in an urban area, this factor may have an influence on burnout for teachers.

FACILITATORS

Facilitators are situational factors that relate positively to job performance; they facilitate the achievement of an organisation's goals, overcome certain organisational barriers, offer protection from stress effects, and include policies for effective management of workload and disruptive pupils (Bakker and Costa 2014). Lloren-Gumbau and Salanovo-Soria (2014) developed a list of twelve facilitators from the existing literature and from the content of interviews with teachers at secondary schools; it included 'easy access to information' and 'availability of salient materials during session preparation'. In their longitudinal study, all facilitators were statistically significantly associated with reported levels of engagement.

Other research (unrelated to teaching) using structural equation modelling, found significant support for a model in which job development opportunities increased satisfaction and growth opportunities, and these were related to increased levels of personal accomplishment (Jawahar 2012). Satisfaction with growth opportunities were not related to emotional exhaustion and depersonalisation among this sample of information technologists. These findings provide tentative evidence for the role of development opportunities in personal accomplishment and efficacy of teachers.

INDIVIDUAL (PERSONAL) FACTORS

A number of personal factors are known to influence the effects of excessive job demands and the development of burnout. Among these are motivational personality factors that increase the capacity of people such as teachers to adapt, manage and cope effectively with excessive stressors and demands of their jobs. A number of these so-called resilience factors have been identified in the literature.

PERSONALITY FACTORS

Personality factors have become a strong focus of research for exploring individual differences in burnout among teachers from excessive job demands. High reported scores for emotional exhaustion, depersonalisation and personal accomplishment were associated with personality characteristics of neuroticism and introversion among 99 teachers in a Spanish study, and neuroticism was a statistically significant predictor of emotional exhaustion (Cano-Garcia *et al.* 2005). A strong sense of agency and control was reported to be an effective protective factor in a sample of ten teachers identified as being vulnerable to burnout because of the nature of their work (Howard and Johnson 2004). The teachers in this qualitative study reported having strong thoughts of control in difficult situations, such as dealing with aggression from students or parents.

CONTROL

This issue is worthy of more discussion. Locus of control is a recognised personality concept based on social learning theory and developed by Julian Rotter. It refers to the extent to which people perceive that achievements, goals and events occur as a consequence of their own actions and volition, or from other external forces (Rotter 1966). Based initially on a unidimensional continuum between 'internal' at one end (whereby people strongly believe they have control over events), to 'external' at the other (whereby people believe they have no or limited control over events). People with an external locus of control tend to think that events occur by chance or are controlled by powerful others; they do not believe outcomes depend on their own behaviour or personality characteristics, and are less likely to act in a specific situation. In contrast, people with an internal locus believe their actions have a direct influence on outcomes, and they are more likely to act. This concept has been used to explain motivation to action and to predict human behaviour. Considered as a generalised expectancy of the person in terms of behaviour and outcome (Rotter 1966), is it an artefact of past experience as well as family and other key influences. It might be a mediating factor for increasing job satisfaction among teachers, offering protection from the potential longer-term effects of excessive job demands. Teachers with a more internalised locus of control are more likely to take proactive action because they believe their actions contribute to the management and control of job demands. Those with an external locus are less likely to act and are more likely to experience the adverse effects from excessive demands on them. A study applying locus of control concepts to more than a thousand teachers in China found that the internal locus was positively and significantly associated with psychological empowerment, skills and behaviours within their organisations (Wang *et al.* 2013). In this study, psychological mastery was defined as 'mastery over organisational issues'. In another, smaller study of student 267 teachers in Turkey, small but significant relationships were found between perceived locus of control of students and preferred strategies for coping with stress (Baloglu 2008). The findings from these studies require further testing, but an instrument is now available for measuring locus of control in commercial and educational organisations, and may provide further opportunities to explore the mediation of job-related stress (Martin and Paul 2012).

STATUS AND PERCEIVED POWER

Another aspect of agency – of status and perceived power – may also be a confounding factor in the development of burnout. Loss of status and a sense of defeat were found to predict burnout in a sample of more than 500 teachers from kindergarten, primary and secondary schools in Spain. This longitudinal study revealed a predictive relationship between subjective status, loss of status and sense of defeat at a first time point, irrespective of the stressors experience. It also found that a sense of defeat at that time predicted burnout at a second time point (Buunk *et al.* 2007). Status is not the only influence on identity and level of perceived power, but it can contribute to a sense of agency and perceived power in the teaching profession, whereby the teachers' own perceptions of their status may affect the way the respond to excessive demands.

SELF-EVALUATION

The strategies teachers use to evaluate their own professional performance, and the high standards against which that performance is measured, is implicated in the mediation of both coping styles and burnout. Self-evaluation and concerns about mistakes, pressure to achieve perfection, suboptimal performance and the discrepancy between the ideal and actual performance are associated with maladaptive coping and increased stress and pressure (Stoeber and Rennert 2008). In their study of 118 secondary school-teachers in Germany, Stoeber and Rennert (2008) report feelings of pressure from colleagues, as well as students and parents. Negative reactions to identified imperfection was inversely correlated with active and avoidant coping, as well as emotional exhaustion, depersonalisation, lack of personal accomplishment and total burnout.

COGNITIVE FACTORS

(i) Self-efficacy

Self-efficacy relates to the level of expectancies or beliefs of capabilities, mastery and management of specific tasks in the achievement of explicit goals (Bandura 1997). Self-efficacy is an aspect of social cognitive theory that predicts behaviour and actions in the face of obstacles (Schwarzer and Hallum 2008). It is conceptualised as a unidimensional construct between low and high self-efficacy:

- **Low self-efficacy**: linked to low self-esteem and pessimism about the capability to manage tasks and achieve goals.

- **High self-efficacy:** linked with optimism about the capability to manage tasks and achieve goals.

A systematic review was conducted to explore the strength of the relationship between a teacher's level of self-efficacy and the dimensions of burnout. Of the eleven studies reviewed, taking place between 2000 and 2010, eight provided medium to high overall weight of evidence, and all of them found a relationship between self-efficacy and the three dimensions of burnout (Brown 2012). The majority of correlations were negative, indicating that greater self-efficacy was associated with lower burnout symptoms. The correlations were of fairly low value, however, indicating a smaller association between the two factors (Brown 2012). Schwarzer and Hallum (2008) investigated the role of self-efficacy as a personal resource for mediation of the effects of job stress and the risk of burnout. The sample comprised just over a thousand teachers from Germany and Syria. Analysis revealed a significant positive mediating effect of self-efficacy on emotional exhaustion and depersonalisation, and a negative relation with personal accomplishment. At follow-up one year later (in the German group), a structural equation model was tested and found that self-efficacy at the start of the study predicted the level of job stress experienced as well as burnout. A more recent longitudinal study over eight months, again using structural equation modelling, found a main role for teachers' self-efficacy in what the authors termed a 'positive gain cycle' (Llorens-Gumbau and Salanova-Soria 2014). The model examined cyclical reciprocal causal and reversed relationships between several factors – organisational facilitators, obstacles, engagement, burnout and self-efficacy. Engagement at the first time point was significantly related to self-efficacy at follow-up, and burnout was negatively related to levels of self-efficacy over the same period (Llorens-Gumbau and Salanova-Soria 2014). Consistent results have been found by studies on the strength and the direction of the link between levels of self-efficacy and mediating the effects of job stresses and burnout.

(ii) Emotional avoidance

Specific strategies used by teachers to manage stress by controlling their unpleasant emotions, thoughts and physiological experiences through avoidance appear to be helpful in the short term, because avoidance has the initial effect of controlling anxiety. Strategies involve disengaging from specific activities and using cognition to regulate the distressing thoughts and feelings. In the longer term, however, these strategies are unhelpful because these avoidance behaviours prevent them from goal-setting and problem-solving or the use of other stress management strategies. These techniques are not unique to teachers. Hinds *et al.* (2015) measured emotional avoidance among 529 middle and elementary school-teachers using the Acceptance and Action Questionnaire-II (Bond *et al.* 2011). This instrument assesses two aspects of emotional avoidance: the need for emotional and cognitive control, and the avoidance of action when negative thoughts and emotions occur (Hinds *et al.* 2015). Both high and moderate reports of the three dimensions of burnout were recorded with the following results:

- **Emotional exhaustion:** high 70.8%; moderate 24.4%.
- **Depersonalisation:** high 28.2%; moderate 34.0%.
- **Personal accomplishment:** high 94.4%; moderate not reported.

A hierarchical multiple regression technique was used to test the impact of emotional avoidance on each dimension of burnout, with reported 'stressful student relations' as the predictor variable. They found that emotional avoidance was statistically significantly:

- Greater among teachers reporting higher levels of difficult behaviour by students.
- Positively related to emotional exhaustion and depersonalisation.
- Negatively related to personal accomplishment.

Job performance and health effects

There is evidence that experiencing burnout for a prolonged time has consequences for job performance and the physical and mental health of teachers. There are major implications for managers and policy-makers, too, because of the potential influence on the teaching profession and policy outcomes. Some studies have shown that burnout relates to absenteeism, suboptimal performance and leaving the profession (Bakker and Costa 2014; Bermejo-Toro and Prieto-Uursua 2014).

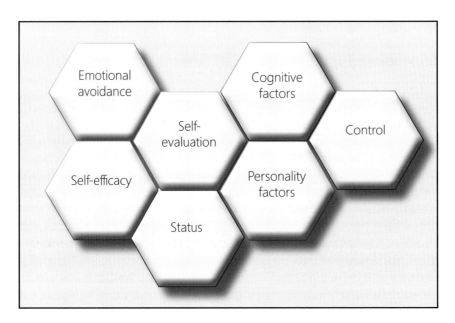

Figure 18.4: Factors that relate positively to job performance and facilitate the achievement of an organisation's goals, overcome barriers, protect from stress, and enable effective management of workload and disruptive pupils.

These outcomes are understandable because these teachers:

- Are exhausted.
- Have difficulty concentrating because of tiredness and anxiety.
- Have limited confidence in personal accomplishment.

The physical health consequences are manifest as headaches, gastrointestinal disturbances and hypertension (Bakker and Costa 2014). The mental health problems experienced depend on each person's age, genetic makeup and other vulnerability factors, as well as the length, magnitude and type of stressor (Schneiderman *et al.* 2005). This was confirmed in the

National Association of Schoolmasters Union of Women Teachers report (2013), in which more than two-thirds of respondents reported anxiety, sleeplessness and reduced well-being. More than a third reported poor health, and nearly half (48%) reported seeing a doctor for a related health problem. A relationship between burnout and depression was found by Hinds *et al.* (2015), who report moderate depression among 8.9% of teachers and severe depression among 2.8%. The National Association of Schoolmasters Union of Women Teachers (2010) analysed the content of interviews with teachers regarding affective, cognitive, behavioural, physical and interpersonal symptoms. The symptom clusters identified were consistent with the symptoms of depression, generalised anxiety, burnout and panic disorders.

Strategies for preventing and managing burnout

The existing literature suggest that preventing the development of burnout in teachers is a priority that requires policy-makers and managers of educational organisations to develop strategies in order to restore the balance between job demands and resources. There are also training programmes to prepare teachers to manage stress effectively.

Management should aim to increase organisational facilitators, such as maximising developmental opportunities, and developing good practice guidelines, protocols and training for managing demanding behaviour in learners. Increasing opportunities for supporting and facilitating team-working and team cohesion increases the potential for effective teams, mentoring and support. Systems of mentorship and supervision of junior colleagues, either in group or individual format, should include dedicated time for shared skill development and problem-solving to facilitate job development and reduce job demands. An open and collaborative management style that values the opinions and experience of frontline teachers can help determine what barriers prevent teachers from achieving their educational goals, and promote strategies that overcome these barriers. Collaborative approaches that empower teachers and provide them with meaningful power to implement change also reinforce a sense of agency. According to Bandura (1997), there are four sources, or influences, on self-efficacy beliefs, and these provide information for trainers, teachers and managers. They are:

- Previous mastery experiences.
- Observation of others successfully completing a task.
- Verbal persuasion from others.
- Interpretation of physiological and affective responses.

Among the factors that increase perceived efficacy, and thus make burnout less likely, are strategies based on reflection and analysis of previous effective performance, observing successful task completion by others, receiving well-constructed positive feedback for task completion and performance, and managing stress responses with time for reflection on those responses. These strategies could be incorporated into initial teacher education programmes for teachers, and might also support developmental processes within specific educational setting. There are several effective stress management techniques that are easy to learn and use; they have a direct effect on the stress response, bringing about deep muscle relaxation, consistent circadian rhythms and daily routines and fostering mindfulness. Others prevent stress by improving problem-solving skills.

Concluding comments

There is an emerging pattern of job-related stress and associated physical and mental health disorders among teachers. This has implications for policy-makers, educational institutions, the teaching profession and wider society. If teachers are exposed to excessive job demands for prolonged periods of time, they are at risk of becoming emotionally exhausted, developing a cynical attitude and becoming less confident in their professional efficacy, and increase their risk of developing a wide range of physical and mental health problems. Recent research has increased our understanding of various organisational and personal factors that can protect teachers from the adverse effects of excessive demands and stress, and may help policy-makers, managers and teacher-training organisations to develop strategies that will prevent and manage job-related stress.

KEY MESSAGES FROM THIS CHAPTER

📄 Job-related stress and has been consistently reported by more than half of teachers in the UK.

📄 Prolonged exposure to excessive job demands can lead to emotional exhaustion, depersonalisation, and a reduced perception of personal attainment and efficacy.

📄 Anyone experiencing emotional exhaustion, depersonalisation and a reduced perception of personal attainment is at increased risk of long-term physical health problems, such as headaches, high blood pressure, gastrointestinal disturbances and cardiovascular disease, and mental health problems such as anxiety, depression and sleep disturbance.

📄 A range of organisational and individual personality and cognitive factors mediate the effects of job-related stress and can prevent the development of burnout.

📄 Policy-makers, managers and teachers have responsibility to develop strategies to reduce excessive demands and stresses of their jobs.

Supporting evidence and further reading

Ahola K, Hakanen J, Perhoniemi R, Mutanen P (2014) Relationship between burnout and depressive symptoms: a study using the person-centred approach. *Burnout Research* 1, 29–37.

Association of Teachers and Lecturers (2014) *Pressures on teachers causing rise in mental health issues.* Press Release ahead of Annual Conference of the Association of Teachers and Lecturers, Northumberland Street, London, 14 April 2014.

Bakker AB, Costa PL (2014) Chronic job burnout and daily functioning: a theoretical analysis. *Burnout Research* 1, 112–19.

Baloglu N (2008) Relationship between prospective teacher strategies for coping with stress and their perceptions of student control. *Social and Personality Behaviour* 36(7), 903–10.

Bandura A (1997) *Self-Efficacy: The Exercise of Control.* New York: WH Freeman.

Bermejo-Toro L, Prieto-Uursua M (2014) Absenteeism, burnout and symptomatology of teacher stress: sex differences. *International Journal of Educational Psychology* 3(2), 175–201.

Bond FW, Hayes SC, Baer RA *et al.* (2011) Preliminary psychometric properties of the Acceptance and Action Questionnaire II: a revised measure of psychological flexibility and acceptance. *Behavior Therapy* 42, 676–88.

Bria M, Spanu F, Baban A, Dumitrascu DL (2014) Maslach Burnout Inventory general survey: factor validity and invariance among Rumanian healthcare professionals. *Burnout Research* 1, 103–11.

Brown C (2012) A systematic review of the relationship between self-efficacy and burnout in teachers. *Educational Child Psychology* 29(4), 47–63.

Butler SK, Constantine MG (2005) Collective self-esteem and burnout in school counsellors. *Professional School Counseling* 9(1), 55–63.

Bunk AP, Peiro JM, Rodriguez I, Bravo JM (2007) A loss of status and a sense of defeat: an evolutionary perspective on professional burnout. *European Journal of Personality* 21, 471–85.

Canadas de la Fuente GA, Vargas C, San Luis C, Garcia I, Canadas GR, de la Fuente EI (2015) Risk factors and the prevalence of burnout syndrome in the nursing profession. *International Journal of Nursing Studies* 52, 240–49.

Cano-Garcia FJ, Padilla-Munoz EM and Carrasco-Ortiz MA (2005) Personality and contextual variables in teacher burnout. *Personality and Individual Differences* 38, 929–40.

Gold Y, Roth RA, Wright CR, Michael WB and Chin-Yi C (1992) The factorial validity of a teacher burnout measure administered to a sample of beginning teachers in elementary and secondary schools in California. *Educational and Psychological Measurement* 52, 761–68.

Freeman D and Freeman J (2012) *Anxiety: A Very Short Introduction.* Oxford: Oxford University Press.

Hinds E, Backen-Jones L, Gau JM, Forrester KK, Biglan A (2015) Teacher distress and the role of experimental avoidance. *Psychology in the Schools* 52(3), 285–97.

Howard S and Johnson B (2004) Resilient teachers: resisting stress and burnout. *Social Psychology of Education* 7, 399–420.

Jansson-Frojmark M, Lindblom K (2010) Is there a bidirectional link between insomnia and burnout: a prospective study in the Swedish workforce. *International Journal of Behavioural Medicine* 17, 306–13.

Jawahar I (2012) Mediating role of satisfaction with growth opportunities on the relationship between employee development opportunities and citizenship behaviours and burnout. *Journal of Applied Social Psychology* 42(9), 2257–84.

Kyriacou C (2001) Teacher stress: directions for future research. *Educational Review* 53(1), 27–35.

Llorens S, Schafeli W, Bakker A, Salanova M (2007) Does a positive gain spiral of resources, efficacy beliefs and engagement exist? *Computers in Human Behaviour* 23, 825–41.

Lloren-Gumbau S, Salanova-Soria M (2014) Loss and gain cycles? A longitudinal study about burnout, engagement and self-efficacy. *Burnout Research* 1, 3–11.

Martin CR, Paul S (2012). *Application of the assessment of locus of control in industry, commerce and education (ALICE) scale in the evaluation of occupational stress.* Abstract from the British Psychological Society Psychobiology Section Annual Scientific Meeting.

Maslach C, Jackson SE (1981) The measurement of experienced burnout. *Journal of Organisational Behaviour* 2, 99–113.

Maslach C, Schaufeli WB, Leiter MP (2001) Job burnout. *Annual Review of Psychology* 52, 397–422.

National Association of Schoolmasters Union of Women Teachers (2010) *Teachers' mental health: a study exploring the experience of teachers with work-related stress and mental health problems.* Rednall, Birmingham: NASUWT.

National Association of Schoolmasters Union of Women Teachers (2015*) A dreadful assault on teachers' mental health and well-being.* Available at: www.nasuwt.org.uk/Whatsnew/NASUWTNews/PressReleases/NASUWT_013973 (accessed July 2015).

Rotter JB (1966) Generalized expectancies for internal versus external locus of control of reinforcement. *Psychological Monographs: General and Applied* 80(1), 1–28.

Schneiderman N, Ironson G, Siegel SD (2005) Stress and health: psychological, behavioural and biological determinants. *Annual Review of Clinical Psychology* 1, 607–28.

Schwarzer R, Hallum S (2008) Perceived teacher self-efficacy as a predictor of job stress and burnout: mediation analyses. *Applied Psychology and International Review* 57, 152–71.

Stoeber J, Rennert D (2008) Perfectionism in school-teachers: relations with stress appraisals, coping styles and burnout. *Anxiety, Stress and Coping* 21(1), 37–53.

Teachers Assurance (2013) *Teachers Assurance stress and well-being research.* Presented at Teachers Provident Society, Bournemouth. Available at: www.teachersassurance.co.uk/money–news/teachers–stress–levels–affecting–performance (accessed July 2015).

Wang J-L, Zhang D-J, Jackson LA (2013) Influence of self-esteem, locus of control and organisational climate on psychological empowerment in a sample of Chinese teachers. *Journal of Applied Social Psychology* 43, 1428–35.

CHAPTER 19

Support for learning-support staff

Deirdre Torrance

This chapter explores the tensions that arise among staff who are engaged with supporting learning – a role that is more complex and diverse than ever, with higher expectations and demands in relation to leadership for learning. A distributed perspective is offered on leadership and management for exploring these increased expectations, the increasingly diverse needs of learners, and the implications for support staff who are able to observe the mental health and well-being of learners. The potential of coaching and mentoring support and ongoing professional development for support staff as leaders of learning is discussed, and recommendations are made for their initial training, ongoing learning and line management.

The roles of staff that work in educational settings continue to evolve, as do expectations of them. Support for learners now extends well beyond academic attainment, with a broader view of achievement and augmented provision in relation to inter-agency working. This can result in 'boundary spanning' (linking of the organisation's internal networks with external sources of information), and challenge conventional notions of remits, as well established cultures (Carroll and Torrance 2013; Stead *et al.* 2007). The roles of staff that support learners have become increasingly complex, but there has been no corresponding recognition of this, or the need for ongoing sustenance.

As discussed in Carroll and Torrance (2013) a range of partners work in education settings, including parent helpers; they are generally referred to as 'teachers' or 'support staff'. The five broad categories and some examples of each are:

- **Learning support staff:** learning assistants, additional support needs (ASN) assistants, peripatetic specialists (e.g. in physical education, drama, music) and ESOL teachers (English for speakers of other languages).

- **Specialist and technical staff:** librarians, ICT (information and communication technology) technicians, AV (audiovisual) technicians, science technicians and food technology technicians.

- **Learner support and welfare staff:** youth workers (Active Break Workers), attendance officers, nurses and counsellors.

- **Administrative staff:** administration and finance assistants, clerical assistants, team leaders (office) and support coordinators.

- **Facilities staff:** caterers, janitors and cleaners.

Depending on their role, staff that support the learning process have contact with learners either directly or indirectly, but this chapter is concerned primarily with those who have direct contact with learners and contribute to leadership for learning. In line with Carroll and Torrance (2013), the title of school support assistant (SSA) reflects various terminologies used across the international literature and should be applied in the widest context. As education systems develop and staff expectations change, the role of SSAs also changes, becoming increasingly complex and diverse. SSAs were originally considered to have an auxiliary role, but now they are more likely to support learners' learning (Mistry *et al.* 2004). Blurring the distinction between their engagement with learners and traditional roles of teachers and lecturers can give great satisfaction but this is accompanied by more challenges. Managers of learning establishments often encourage SSAs to play key leadership and management roles in the supervision and support of learners, particularly within learning establishments (Torrance 2012), in keeping with shared (US) or distributed (UK) perspectives on leadership and management (Bolden 2011).

This chapter explores increased expectations that accompany leadership for learning roles (Spillane and Coldren 2011), drawing from empirical case studies in three primary schools (Torrance 2012), and it addresses the diverse needs of learners in general, and the role of SSAs in their mental health and well-being because they are in a good position for detecting anomalies before class teachers. The lack of initial and ongoing professional support provided for SSAs is discussed (Blatchford *et al.* 2009; Schlapp *et al.* 2001; Stead *et al.* 2007), and coaching and mentoring to support their own mental health and well-being. The chapter concludes by offering recommendations for the initial training, ongoing professional learning and line management of SSAs. In so doing, it is hoped that the chapter stimulates discussion of how the role of SSAs can be utilised to help safeguard the mental health and well-being of learners and SSAs themselves.

Implications for SSAs within a distributed perspective

Leadership assumes a separate and often elevated position, distinct from organisational management, across a range of fields and sectors. It has become associated with transformational change, while management has been downgraded to a maintenance activity (Gunter 2004). One definition of leadership is 'a relationship of social influence' (Spillane and Coldren 2011) which leads to the questions about whose influence and for what purpose? If leadership is perceived as 'a fluid practice that changes with the situation' (Spillane and Coldren 2011), then many things are possible in the work of people focused on supporting learners and learning. When a distinction is made between leadership processes and management approaches of people in formal positions of power and authority, SSAs can have a more influential relationship within and beyond the organisation. Public services face a range of challenges related to modernisation and improvement, which makes engaging staff in organisational improvement more attractive (Hartley and Allison 2000), and this forms the basis of a distributed perspective on leadership and management.

BACKGROUND TO A DISTRIBUTED PERSPECTIVE

Distributed leadership has become a dominant term in educational rhetoric, particularly in the UK (while shared leadership has maintained its standing in nursing, medicine and psychology) (Bolden 2011). Distributed leadership is extending into health and social care through public sector reforms, the drive to revive perceived poor performance in public sector organisations, and efforts to engage staff in collaborative learning and problem-solving (Currie and Lockett 2011), however there is still limited literature on it in the public sector (Brookes 2008); interest in it, and exploration of the concept within education (Fitzsimons *et al.* 2011), are not yet reflected in management and business fields, even though it's role is growing in response to increased complexity and ambiguity (Bolden 2011; Thorpe *et al.* 2011).

In parallel to the move from 'traditional bureaucratic structures to new, flatter forms', new leadership practices are being sought in business management (Ancona and Blackman 2010; Thorpe *et al.* 2011). The potential impact of several informal leaders in an organisation (rather than the authority of a few formal managers) is now being recognised (Pratt *et al.* 2007; Wallace 2011). Moreover, there is 'an imperative within organizations for them to be able to respond ever more quickly and adaptively' to the increased pace of change (Thorpe *et al.* 2011). Both hierarchy (a designed system) and networks (an adaptive system) have been identified as key factors, with greater emphasis on the latter (Currie 2011; Pratt *et al.* 2007).

Although public sector organisations differ from private services in terms of their customers, markets and products (Kinder 2011), they face similar challenges. Public sector professionalism is changing as the work environment becomes increasingly complicated, where quick and creative responses to competing challenges are needed, leading to an 'evolution of professions' which is occurring to some extent 'bottom–up' and is 'grounded in localised practice and learning' (Kinder 2008). These challenges transcend organisational design and learning boundaries across sectors, whereby leadership in education shares many features with other public sector services. Educational leadership is:

> *... located within wider social, economic and political arrangements and has an embedded cultural acceptance of the normality of leaders buttressed by hierarchical remuneration packages. (Gunter 2005)*

Since the beginning of the 1980s, the traditional boundary between public and private sectors, state and market, has shifted dramatically, creating a need to develop networks across the two sectors that:

> *... pursue joint goals in either predictable or ambiguous environments. (Jackson and Stainsby 2000)*

Such networks enable the distribution of information and knowledge (as 'sources of power') and increase 'the probability of successfully solving problems', some of which are 'wicked problems' (outcomes of market failure) that require coordination across agencies and departments (Jackson and Stainsby 2000).

The traditional boundaries between the hierarchies within public and private sectors are now thought inadequate for coping with complex, unpredictable and ambiguous circumstances. In response, there have been efforts to join up localised knowledge sites in the pursuit of improvement, through mutual interest networks based on shared values and joint goals. This requires distribution of power within the network – constellations of centres of power – and of leadership across the network, where network managers have the role of 'sense-makers' (Jackson and Stainsby 2000). These blurred distinctions within and between sectors challenges the concept of educational leadership as a field in its own right. However, there is a distinction between organisational leadership with roots in business management and educational leadership (Gunter and Ribbins 2003). The use of 'educational' here focuses attention on the nature and purpose of leadership, which is 'underpinned by educational values and goals' and 'integrated within teaching and learning' so that 'practice is itself educational' (Gunter 2005). The focus on education, covering aspects such as curriculum, pedagogy and assessment, retains the unique nature of educational leadership (Bush 2008).

Increased expectations placed on SSAs within a distributed perspective

With this perspective, formal and informal leaders have different but complementary roles. Formal leaders focus their efforts on organisational and strategic leadership; informal leaders focus theirs on leadership for learning, either directly or indirectly. Together, the influence of managers at the top of a structured hierarchy is essential for organisational processes and legitimisation of informal leadership roles. Distributed leadership can have a positive effect on the 'softer organisational indicators' such as staff well-being, satisfaction and creativity (Bush 2003), morale (Day et al. 2009) and 'academic optimism' (Hoy et al. 2006), and on the learning experiences and outcomes of learners (Day et al. 2007; Leithwood et al. 2006). It may also capitalise on the strengths and potential of staff to develop the most effective organisation possible, encouraging staff to 'buy into' school improvement measures (Gunter 2004), with some implication of exploitation (Fitzgerald and Gunter 2006). Whether in the interests of democratic principles (Gronn 2009) or in pursuit of workforce reform (Gunter 2012), it becomes more possible for SSAs to have an influence within and beyond the learning organisation.

Although distributed leadership may have a theoretical basis, examples of it in practice are difficult to find, partly because of a gradual shift from vertical to lateral forms of leadership (Harris 2005). Furthermore, 'how leadership is distributed and with what effect is relatively uncharted territory' (Harris and Spillane 2008). In a small-scale empirical study, Torrance (2012; 2013a,b,c; 2014) examined how actors made sense of distributed leadership within and across a small number of primary schools in which a distributed perspective was deliberately being developed. In those settings, SSAs were highly regarded by the headteachers, who believed they made a significant contribution to the leadership of the school, and this was reciprocated, enabling SSAs to act with a degree of autonomy within their remits, particularly in 'whole school' areas.

Teachers are generally positive about the contribution of SSAs, in terms of increased availability of attention for learners and positive influences on teaching effectiveness and classroom management, but they do not always perceive them as having a leadership role (Blatchford et al. 2009; Carroll and Torrance 2013). Torrance found that the headteacher's endorsement and encouragement of SSA leadership roles in 'whole school' areas was not mirrored by other staff; teachers (or SSAs themselves) did not perceive SSAs to have leadership roles in the classroom. There was an exception to this, however, in relation to 'pupil care, welfare and/or personal concerns' whereby SSAs appeared to have a legitimised leadership role, as experts providing longstanding support for 'high tariff' learners. In this respect, SSAs sometimes detect mental health issues of learners before the teachers do. On the whole, the leadership of teachers was considered to be classroom-focused, while that of support staff had more generalised locations; SSAs can be uniquely placed to assess mental health issues in the learning setting.

Despite their unique role in learning settings, SSAs may feel isolated; they have to continuously negotiate their role according to the context and purpose of their work, and the colleagues they are working with. They can feel detached from patterns of teacher leadership influence and support; for instance, they may be in more leader-like roles than many teachers within the public spaces of the school, yet subservient to them in formal learning contexts. Such ambiguity adds to the pressures they experience and can influence their mental well-being. Opportunities to voice and discuss such challenges, as well as strategies for coping with the effects of ambiguity, may be gained from coaching conversations.

Implications for SSAs meeting diverse needs

In recent years, increased expectations have been placed on SSAs meeting diverse needs (Carroll and Torrance 2013), often without attributing them with the status and authority required for executing their role effectively (Stead *et al.* 2007). Negotiating role boundaries can generate a zone of uncertainty (Moran and Abbott 2002) which is amplified when they work with a range of staff, each of whom has different expectations (Wilson *et al.* 2003); or it occurs when SSAs with the same title have distinctive roles that might focus on supporting specific individual learners or on providing more generalised support.

Potential confusions and conflicts arise when the middle-ground is blurred between the prescribed duties of increasingly skilled SSAs (Calder and Grieve 2004).

THE CULTURE OF LEARNING

The enactment of negotiating role boundaries takes place within the culture of a learning organisation. Culture is often implicitly communicated in relation to 'shared norms and values' (Busher 2001), givens and beliefs (Torrington and Weightman 1989), and taken-for-granted assumptions and preconceptions (Busher 2001; Fidler 1998). It is 'the way we do things around here' (Deal and Kennedy 1983) – the patterns of relationships and forms of association (Hargreaves 1994); it is the shared patterns of thought, belief, feelings and values that result from shared experiences and common learning (Schein 1999); it involves passing on, constantly reinforcing shared values and meanings to new group members.

Culture is more permanent than climate or ethos and, as such, far more difficult to influence or change. It is expressed through how people feel or think or act. It presents a potential minefield for SSAs to pick their way through as they negotiate the different facets of their role and the meanings each of their colleagues ascribe to the manifestation of that role. Professional judgement is required, predicated on professional wisdom, thus:

A problem-solving ability involving judgement, evolved by reflection on problems and solutions, informed by codified formal knowledge and instrumentalities and practice which is relevant to situated practice. (Kinder 2008)

It is also 'socially constructed' (Kinder 2008). Professional judgement becomes even more relevant when it is considered in relation to the management of learning organisations such as schools, unique due to high levels of organisational autonomy compared to other public sector organisations (Wiseman 2004).

In the support of learners and learning, much can be taken for granted in relation to implicit assumptions of how adults work together. Within the constraints of the working environment, little time is available to discuss and clarify role expectations. There may also be a lack of understanding of the importance of making time for such discussion, because training for working with adults in support of learning does not form part of initial teacher education (Calder and Grieve 2004) or in-service training for most teachers (Blatchford *et al.* 2009; Mistry *et al.* 2004). Similarly, SSAs generally learn on the job in response to contextual expectations, often having been appointed without training, qualifications for, or experience in, the role. Beyond the induction phase, SSAs often receive little training (Stead *et al.* 2007) and commonly find their continuous professional development needs are not adequately addressed (Blatchford *et al.* 2009). Further, line-management arrangements are often not clearly identified or performed (Mistry *et al.* 2004), which adds to tensions in relationships with colleagues. The distinct needs of support staff may not be considered by colleagues (Burgess and Mayes 2007).

With roles in giving longstanding support to high-tariff learners, and picking up on the mental health issues, coaching and mentoring may be valuable support for SSAs, both in relation to role ambiguity and the challenges they face when supporting learners.

The potential of coaching and mentoring SSAs

SSAs experience many challenges as they respond to the varying expectations of different colleagues, and move between the more private and public spaces of the learning setting, and these are further complicated by the mainstream involvement of learners with increasingly complex needs. Often, SSAs are bestowed the support for learners with more complex needs, who are most demanding of attention and time, such as those of lower-ability, with additional support needs and with pronounced emotional and behavioural needs (Carroll and Torrance 2013). As such, SSAs may find themselves leading learning with or without that leadership role being recognised, without recognition for the complexity of their role and without recognition for ongoing role nourishment. SSAs can find themselves regularly spanning conventional boundaries, challenging established notions of remits as well as organisational cultures. Given the lack of initial and ongoing professional learning generally provided for SSAs (Blatchford *et al.* 2009; Schlapp *et al.* 2001; Stead *et al.* 2007), coaching and mentoring could be utilised in support of their mental health and well-being. It should be acknowledged that to date, the use of coaching in education lacks both a research base (Blackman 2010) and evidence of impact (Davidson *et al.* 2008; Hartley and Hinksman 2003; Jackson 2005). As a result, coaching remains a contested area.

Coaching and mentoring have gained popularity across a range of sectors and settings internationally, in medicine, business, nursing, engineering and education, for general 'experiential methodologies in pre-service and continuing education' (Forde 2011) and specific leadership development methodologies (Hanbury 2009). There is some confusion between coaching and mentoring, but they differ from each other in that mentoring focuses on guidance and advice, while coaching focuses on 'developing capacity within individuals to discover their own solutions in an equal and non-judgmental relationship' (Hanbury 2009). They share a common interest in fostering change in the person and their practice (Torrance 2011).

MENTORING

Mentors require knowledge, understanding and experience of their mentees' roles within the prevailing context and the challenges they encounter; they must be able to determine when more directed support is needed to help the mentee move beyond an obstacle in their practice. Forde (2011) describes mentoring as a structured approach to professional learning and a potentially powerful process, and that formal mentoring in education contexts:

> *... typically has a set duration, is used at key transition points in a ... career, and can include a range of activities such as learner-driven meetings, shadowing of the mentoring by the learner, observation of practice and the use of reflective tools such as journals. (Forde 2011)*

In mentoring programmes, the dynamic relationship between mentor and learner is important as the learner moves from novice to peer. The outcome of the process is the development of an autonomous professional.

COACHING

In contrast, the coaching relationship requires the building of trust, enabling the coachee to reveal their vulnerabilities and areas for further development (Robertson 2009). The coaching role requires the ability to actively listen and provide feedback in a supportive and challenging manner; coaches must challenge underlying assumptions, facilitate visualisation of a future state, enable coachees to identify their own solutions, and agree, set and review goals. Having a defined purpose is important to come up with an agreed agenda between the coach and coachee. The coaching conversations then focus on the desired outcomes and the strategies that might achieve them, and changes in behaviour, with critical reflection on practice and examination of progress towards the desired outcomes. A number of perspectives on coaching exist, some perhaps more appropriate for SSAs. Executive coaching (Feldman and Lankau 2005), for example, relies on the fact that the coach is external to the organisation, which enables dispassionate distancing; other models are more adaptive to professional learning in context. For example:

- GROW (Whitmore 2002) works through a sequence of goals, reality, options and will, and aims to affect action and performance.
- Blended coaching (Bloom *et al.* 2005), with its emphasis on an ethical approach, highlights building trusting relationships and fresh perspectives, uses issues to provide rich learning opportunities and foster adaptability to meet perceived needs, and provides emotional support with a focus on organisational goals.

Both mentoring and coaching have established, but different, purposes for supporting the roles of teachers. It would be valuable to extend them to increase opportunities for support and professional development of SSAs. In order for mentoring to work effectively, line management must be clear and effective; for coaching to work effectively, the quality of the coach is key (Davidson *et al.* 2008; Torrance and Pritchard 2010).

Recommendations on the roles of SSAs

In the changing educational landscape, the role of SSAs continues to develop, partly in response to financial stringencies and partly because of a growing appreciation of the contribution they make to the learning context and to learners' experience. Many organisations are mov-ing towards a distributed perspective on leadership and management, whereby those who direct-ly or indirectly support learners are engaged in the leadership of learning with a social learning system and community of practice. They are constantly engaged in learning as a social process situated in context (Lave and Wenger 1991). Learning and innovation are essential for improving performance, and according to Kinder 'learning-in-organisations' is the 'central resource of pub-lic agencies' (Kinder 2011), with organisations that rely on informal networks and groupings.

> *The organizations that will truly excel in the future will be [those] that discover how to tap people's commitment and capacity to learn at all levels. (Senge 2006)*

For such learning to be enabled, reflection in and on action is vital; through dialogue, members of the organisation (Argyris and Schon 1978; Senge 2006: 9; Schon 1991):

> *Expose their own thinking effectively and make that thinking open to the influence of others. (Senge 2006)*

Critical reflection itself is an intensive form of learning, that emphasises intelligence gathering, experience and experimentation, and organisational learning is an active process that involves reflective inquiry (Argyris and Schon 1978; Garvin 2000). However, critical reflection on practice can be problematic and may be perceived as threatening. Coaching and mentoring offer processes that allow critical reflection on practice to take place in a constructive and safe way. They can also help to build communities of practice (Lave and Wenger 1991; Wenger 1998) or professional learning communities (Stoll *et al.* 2006), and create environments conducive for critical reflection on shared practice. Communities of practice:

> *... connect learners, situations and knowledge with evolving practice and change ... [driving] practice innovation by focusing on contextually relevant problem-solving. (Kinder 2008)*

In this way, learning is viewed as a process of social participation (Houle 1980) rather than individual enterprise. Purposefully embracing all those who support learning in communities of practice requires 'new levels of professionalism' (Hammersley-Fletcher 2005), and changed perceptions of the different roles involved. This will challenge professional boundaries and personal identities, and require:

> *... greater honesty about where authority lies [and] who has a right to exercise it. (Hammersley-Fletcher and Brundrett 2008)*

Clarity is needed to appreciate the locus of each role within a distributed perspective. Coordination and risk management are needed because distributed leadership goes beyond empowerment of the individual (Ancona and Blackman 2010; Malby 2007), with implications for the line management of staff across the learning context. All of this requires commitment to social learning in context because, despite the increasingly complex nature of the SSA role and the expectation that they will take on lead roles within the public spaces of the learning setting, there has been little research on the experiences and perceptions of staff engaged in working co-dependently to support learning. There has been even less research on teachers' perceptions of their roles in relation to developing the leadership role of SSAs, or on SSAs' perceptions of the range of expectations regarding their roles in public and more private spaces. Commitment involves delivery of initial training that is maintained through ongoing professional learning.

Concluding comments

SSAs have an opportunity to help safeguard the mental health and well-being of the learners in schools because they work most closely with vulnerable learners, often on a one-to-one basis. This has implications for their role as leaders of learning, which has not been formally acknowledged in the formal organisational structures or remuneration packages. SSAs experience role ambiguity as they span boundaries to fulfil different expectations of their role in meeting the needs of challenging learners.

The challenges they face are also not well recognised. Coaching and mentoring may be valuable for ongoing support to safeguard the mental health and well-being of SSAs and in their professional development, particularly in the context of a clear and effective line management structure, with accountability for meaningful professional review and development processes. The career structure should recognise both the skills of SSAs and the contribution they make.

KEY MESSAGES FROM THIS CHAPTER

- The roles of staff who support learning is more complex and diverse than ever before, and there are many different expectations of them.

- The increased demands on the staff engaged in leadership of learning are not widely recognised.

- Staff who support the needs of vulnerable learners, by working closely with them, are uniquely placed to review their mental health.

- There are implications for the mental health and well-being of all staff engaged with supporting learning.

- Coaching and mentoring extend the potential for such staff to discuss any challenges they encounter and strategies for coping with them.

- For coaching and mentoring to be valuable, clear and effective, support structures must be firmly in place.

Supporting evidence and further reading

Ancona D, Blackman E (2010) *It's Not All About You. Harvard Business Review.* Available at: blogs.hbr.org/imagining-the-future-of-leadership/2010/04/its-not-all-about-me-its-all-a.html (accessed July 2015).

Argyris C, Schon DA (1978) Organizational Learning: A theory of action perspective. Reading MA: Addison-Wesley.

Blackman A (2010) Coaching as a leadership development tool for teachers. *Professional Development in Education* 36(3), 421–41.

Blatchford P, Bassett P, Brown P, Martin C, Russell A, Webster R (2009) *Deployment and Impact of Support Staff Project. Research Brief.* London: Institute of Education/University of London.

Bloom G, Castagna C, Moir E, Warren B (2005) *Blended Coaching: Skills and Strategies to Support Principal Development.* London: Sage.

Bolden R (2011) Distributed leadership in organizations: A review of theory and research. *International Journal of Management Reviews* 13, 251–69.

Brookes S (2008) *The Public Leadership Challenge: Full Report.* ESRC Seminar Series End of Award Report, RES-451–25–4273. Swindon: ESRC.

Burgess H, Mayes AM (2007) Supporting the professional development of teaching assistants: classroom teachers' perspectives on their mentoring role. *The Curriculum Journal* 18(3), 389–407.

Bush T (2003) T*heories of Educational Leadership and Management (third edn).* London: Sage.

Bush T (2008) From Management to Leadership: Semantic or meaningful change? *Educational Management, Administration and Leadership* 36(2) 271–88.

Busher H (2001) The micro-politics of change, improvement and effectiveness in schools. In: *A Harris and N Bennett (eds) School Effectiveness and School Improvement: Alternative Perspectives.* London: Continuum.

Calder I, Grieve A (2004) Working with other adults: what teachers need to know. *Educational Studies* 30(2), 113–26.

Carroll M, Torrance D (2013) Classroom management: managing abilities, needs and people. In: *TGK Bryce, WM Humes, D Gillies, A Kennedy (eds) Scottish Education (fifth edn).* Edinburgh: Edinburgh University Press.

Currie G (2011) *Leadership in public service networks: antecedents, process and outcome.* Public Administration 89(2), 242–64.

Currie G, Lockett A (2011) Distributing leadership in health and social care: concertive, conjoint or collective? *International Journal of Management Reviews* 13, 286–300.

Davidson J, Forde C, Gronn P, MacBeath P, Martin M, McMahon M (2008) *Towards a 'Mixed Economy' of Headteacher Development: Evaluation Report to the Scottish Government on the Flexible Routes to Headship Pilot.* Edinburgh: Scottish Government.

Day C, Leithwood K, Sammons P, Harris A, Hopkins D (2007) *Leadership and Student Outcomes. DCSF Interim Report.* London: Department for Children, Schools and Families.

Day C, Sammons P, Hopkins D *et al.* (2009) *The Impact of School Leadership On Pupil Outcomes. DCSF Final Report.* London: Department for Children, Schools and Families.

Deal TE, Kennedy AA (1983) Culture: a new look through old lenses. *Journal of Applied Behavioural Sciences* 19(4), 498–505.

Feldman DC, Lankau MJ (2005) Executive Coaching: A review and agenda for future research. *Journal of Management* 31(6), 829–48.

Fidler B (1998) How can a successful school avoid failure? *School Leadership and Management* 18(4), 497–509.

Fitzgerald T, Gunter H (2006) Teacher leadership: a new form of managerialism? *New Zealand Journal of Educational Leadership* 21(2), 43–56.

Fitzsimons D, James KT, Denyer D (2011), Alternative approaches for studying shared and distributed leadership. *International Journal of Management Reviews* 13, 313–28.

Forde C (2011) Approaches to professional learning: coaching, mentoring and building collaboration. In: *C Forde and J O'Brien (eds) Coaching and Mentoring: Developing Teachers and Leaders.* Edinburgh: Dunedin.

Garvin DA (2000) L*earning In Action: A Guide to Putting the Learning Organization to Work.* Boston, MA: Harvard Business School Press.

Gronn P (2009) From distributed to hybrid leadership practice. In: *Harris A (ed.) Distributed School Leadership: Different Perspectives.* London: Springer.

Gunter HM (2004) Labels and labelling in the field of educational leadership. *Discourse: Studies in the Cultural Politics of Education* 25(1), 21–41.

Gunter HM (2005) Conceptualising research in educational leadership. *Educational Management, Administration and Leadership* 33(2), 165–80.

Gunter HM (2012) *Leadership and the Reform of Education.* Bristol: Policy Press.

Gunter HM, Ribbins P (2003) The field of educational leadership: studying maps and mapping studies. *British Journal of Educational Studies* 51(3), 254–81.

Hammersley-Fletcher L (2005) Distributed leadership in primary schools. Education 3–13: *International Journal of Primary, Elementary and Early Years Education* 33(2), 46–50.

Hammersley-Fletcher L, Brundrett M (2008) Collaboration, collegiality and leadership from the head: the complexities of shared leadership in primary school settings. *Management in Education* 22(2), 11–16.

Hanbury M (2009) *Leadership Coaching: An Evaluation of the Effectiveness of Leadership Coaching as a Strategy to Support Succession Planning.* Nottingham: National College for Leadership of Schools and Children's Services.

Hargreaves A (1994) *Changing Teachers, Changing Times: Teacher's Work and Culture in the Postmodern Age.* London: Cassell.

Harris A (2005) *Crossing Boundaries and Breaking Barriers: Distributed Leadership in Schools.* London: International Network for Educational Transformation (iNet).

Harris A, Spillane J (2008) Distributed leadership through the looking glass. *Management in Education* 22(1), 31–34.

Hartley J, Allison M (2000) The Role of Leadership in the Modernization and Improvement of Public Services. *Public Money and Management,* April–June.

Hartley J, Hinksman B (2003) *Leadership Development: A Systematic Review of the Literature.* Report for the NHS Leadership Centre. Warwick: Warwick Institute of Governance.

Houle C (1980) *Continuing Learning In The Professions.* San Francisco, CA: Jossey-Bass.

Hoy WK, Tarter CJ, Woolfolk Hoy A (2006) Academic optimism of schools: a force for student achievement. *American Educational Research Journal* 43(3), 425–46.

Jackson P (2005) How do we describe coaching? An exploratory development of a typology of coaching based on the accounts of UK-based practitioners. *International Journal of Evidence–based Coaching and Mentoring* 3(2), 45–60.

Jackson PM, Stainsby L (2000) Managing public sector networked organizations. *Public Money and Management,* 20(1), 11–16.

Kinder T (2008) *Professional wisdom and innovation in locally delivered public services: The case of West Lothian, Scotland.* Presented at the University of Edinburgh Business School, Edinburgh.

Kinder T (2011) Learning, innovating and performance: New public management of locally delivered public services. *Public Management Review* 14(3), 403-428.

Lave J, Wenger E (1991) *Situated Learning: Legitimate Peripheral Participation.* Cambridge: Cambridge University Press.

Leithwood K, Day C, Sammons P, Harris A, Hopkins D (2006*) Seven Strong Claims About Successful School Leadership.* Nottingham: National College for School Leadership.

Malby B (2007) *How Does Leadership Make a Difference to Organisational Culture and Effectiveness?: An Overview for the Public Sector.* Leeds: Northern Leadership Academy.

Mistry M, Burton N, Brundrett M (2004) Managing LSAs: An evaluation of the use of learning support assistants in an urban primary school. *School Leadership and Management* 24(2), 125–37.

Moran A, Abbott L (2002) Developing inclusive schools: the pivotal role of teaching assistants in promoting inclusion in special and mainstream schools in Northern Ireland. *European Journal of Special Needs Education* 17(2), 161–73.

Pratt J, Plamping D, Gordon P (2007) *Distinctive Characteristics of Public Sector Organisations and Implications for Leadership. Northern Leadership Academy Leadership Summit Working Paper.* Leeds: Centre for Innovation In Health Management, Leeds University Business School.

Robertson J (2009) Coaching leadership learning through partnership. *School Leadership and Management* 29(1), 39–49.

Schein E (1999) *The Corporate Culture Survival Guide*. San Francisco, CA: Jossey-Bass.

Schlapp U, Wilson V, Davidson J (2001) *An Extra Pair of Hands? Evaluation of the Classroom Assistants Initiative*. Interim Report Number 104. Edinburgh: Scottish Council for *Educational Research*.

Schon DA (1991) *The Reflective Practitioner: How Professionals Think in Action*. Surrey: Ashgate.

Senge MP (2006) T*he Fifth Discipline: The Art and Practice of the Learning Organization (second edn)*. London: Random House.

Spillane JP, Coldren AF (2011) *Diagnosis and Design for School Improvement*. New York: Teachers College Press.

Stead J, Lloyd G, Munn P, Riddell S, Kane J, MacLeod G (2007) Supporting our most challenging pupils with our lowest status staff: can additional staff in Scottish schools offer a distinctive kind of help? *Scottish Educational Review* 39(2), 186–97.

Stoll L, Bolam R, McMahon A, Wallace M, Thomas S (2006) Professional learning communities: a review of the literature. *Journal of Educational Change* 7, 221–58.

Thorpe R, Gold J, Lawler J (2011) Locating distributed leadership. *International Journal of Management Reviews* 13, 239–50.

Torrance D (2011) Preparing to lead. In: *Forde C, O'Brien J (eds) Coaching and Mentoring: Developing Teachers and Leaders*. Edinburgh: Dunedin.

Torrance D (2012) *Distributed leadership in Scottish primary schools: Myth or actualities?* PhD dissertation, The University of Edinburgh.

Torrance D (2013a) The challenges of developing distributed leadership in Scottish primary schools: a catch 22. Education 3–13*: International Journal of Primary, Elementary and Early Years Education* 41(3), 330–345.

Torrance D (2013b) Distributed leadership: challenging five generally held assumptions. *School Leadership and Management* 33(4), 354–72.

Torrance D (2013c) Distributed leadership: still in the gift of the headteacher. *Scottish Educational Review* 45(2), 50–63.

Torrance D (2014) *Professional learning for distributed leadership: primary headteachers' perspectives. Professional Development in Education*. Available at: www.tandfonline.com/doi/full/10.1080/19415257.2014.936025#.U_ddsU+1Pwl (accessed July 2015).

Torrance D, Pritchard I (2010) *Developing alternative routes to school headship: Evaluation of the university DARE 2 programme 2009–10*. Edinburgh: University of Edinburgh Centre for Educational Leadership.

Torrington D, Weightman J (1989) *The Reality of School Management*. New Jersey: Prentice Hall.

Wallace M (2011) *Mobilizing public service leaders as change agents through leadership development initiatives in England: Problems and prospects*. Presentation at the Public Management Research Association Conference, Syracuse University, 2–4 June 2011.

Wenger E (1998) *Communities of Practice: Learning, Meaning and Identity*. Cambridge: Cambridge University Press.

Whitmore J (2002) *Coaching For Performance: Growing People, Performance and Purpose (third edn)*. London: Nicholas Brealey.

Wilson V, Schlapp U, Davidson D (2003) An 'extra pair of hands'? Managing classroom assistants in Scottish primary schools. *Educational Management and Administration* 31(2), 189–205.

Wiseman AW (2004) Management of semi-public organizations in complex environments. *Public Administration and Management: An Interactive Journal* 9(2), 166–81.

CHAPTER 20

Meeting the needs of headteachers

Vivienne Grant

I have been in the education profession for over twenty-five years. The first half of my career was spent teaching in the inner city schools of South London. In the ninth year, I was appointed headteacher of a primary school that had recently been placed in special measures; I successfully led it out of special measures, but often there were times when I felt consumed by the role. Support to help with the strategic and operational sides of the roles were never in short supply, but support for the meeting of my mental and emotional needs seemed non-existent, and I often experienced intense bouts of loneliness and isolation. It wasn't until I left headship and went to work on national programmes to support headteachers that I realised I had not been alone in my experience of the role.

The comments in the Personal Reflection below were made be a current headteacher of an inner London primary school. Through listening to accounts such as these it is clear that to be fully effective in their roles, headteachers need to have support that also takes care of their mental and emotional needs. There is something unique about becoming a headteacher. There is a need to learn how to manage both the intense demands of the operational and strategic sides of the role, at the same time as managing the huge range of emotions that are the other side of being a leader.

Personal reflection

I have been working in inner-city schools for 28 years – 14 as a headteacher. Nothing prepares you for headship: the realisation that the buck stops with you, the weight of the responsibility for a community that believes and trusts that whatever the problem, you can fix it. We spend our days surrounded by pupils, staff, parents – their joy, their anger, their fear. We sway from highs to lows, joyous moments to deep sadness, from success to managing failure. We face fear and courage on our own and there are few opportunities to show our own vulnerability. We share different issues with different people in a measured way – we don't want to burden anyone. We are paid to carry the load; it's the responsibility of the job. As a consequence, no one else is the keeper of the whole-school picture. It sets us apart and leads to overwhelming feelings of loneliness – despite being in constant demand. Outwardly we model calm, order, positivity; but as the capacity to cope diminishes, over time we become over absorbed by school life and detached from our own feelings and relationships.

The role of coaching in supporting headteachers

This chapter illustrates the insights I have gained both from my own experience as a headteacher and in the role of a leadership coach providing the type of support for headteachers that was missing when I was a school leader. It describes how deep levels of coaching can help overcome the stresses of their role and maintain their ability to lead and inspire others. Much of what we hear about coaching in the education sector focuses on the 'mechanics' of the process. Coaching is often seen simply as a tool for guiding conversation, where the individual is supported to take ownership of their issue and find an appropriate solution for addressing it. As important as this is, there is so much more to coaching. In the right environment, it supports the growth of the inner self. It helps people to understand and meet themselves on different terms; through questioning, reflection and dialogue, it helps school leaders develop the resilience, insight and courage that are part and parcel of developing their core emotional intelligences.

Understanding the challenges headteachers face

Now, what I want is Facts. Teach these boys and girls nothing but Facts. Facts alone are wanted in life. Plant nothing else, and root out everything else. You can only form the minds of reasoning animals upon Facts: nothing else will ever be of any service to them. (Extract from Hard Times by Charles Dickens 1854)

Today many headteachers face a conflict between their values and those of the current education system. Many are driven by values that support inspiring creativity, awe and wonder in young minds and educating the whole child, but those in recent school policy appear to reflect those alluded to in the opening paragraphs of this Victorian novel. Finding a balance between these different value systems is not easy. Routinely headteachers wrestle with national education directives that oppose their own values and beliefs. This constant wrestling is tiring. It strains the emotions and negatively impacts mental health and well-being.

CHANGING TIMES, CHANGING ROLES

Over the past twenty-five years, the role of the headteacher has changed significantly. It is now fraught with ambiguity and complexity. From day to day, heads find themselves taking on a variety of roles in which, at any given moment, they must demonstrate their leadership prowess as well as show expertise as social workers, counsellors, child psychiatrists, politicians and community workers – all roles for which they have not been trained, yet in which they are expected to be competent. Many heads appear to move seamlessly from one role to another, giving the impression they are at ease with the mental and emotional adjustments needed for each; to a certain degree they are. It is their ability to act that inspires confidence in others, however for each new role they must not only adopt a different psychological perspective, but also process copious amounts of information. The result is mental overload and increased levels of self-doubt. With each performance, the head seeks to illicit a positive response from their audience, and wants to feel they have been listened to, and valued and respected for their leadership. However, for people at the top of an organisation, feedback is not always forthcoming. When it is, the negative tends to override the positive, and not surprisingly they constantly question their reputation in the eyes of others; they struggle to find answers that maintain their self-esteem and promote a sense of well-being. But this struggle clouds their ability to see the really important question that needs to be answered: *'Who do I need to be to get this job done?'*

ANSWERING THE *RIGHT* QUESTION

Before headteachers have a chance to chance to answer this question themselves, the education system forces them to ask *'What do I need to do to get this job done?'*. Having to consider this second question before fully answering the first, headteachers often put themselves on a course – unconsciously – that does not lead to congruent, healthy leadership. When a person's mind is exclusively focused on the job, at the expense of the self, it cannot develop the deep personal understanding that all leaders, particularly heads, need. This level of understanding allows them to:

> *Realise their intellectual and emotional potential and ... fulfil their roles in social, school and working life. (Kinderman 2014)*

When they are constantly required to perform different roles for different audiences, there are emotional and psychological reasons to stop and reflect. When such moments are not available, internal and external fault-lines appear, and their personal and professional lives begin to fracture. During these times they must be encouraged to find ways they can begin to:

> *Weave the slender threads of a broken life into a firm pattern of meaning and responsibility. (Frankl 1946)*

We are all in a continual process of constructing our personal narratives, usually inside our heads. Such internal narratives can be overly critical, leading to anxiety and self-doubt – obviously not conducive to a healthy state of mind. But this is often the shadow side of leadership and, along with increased levels of public scrutiny and personal accountability, it has become a major factor in attrition and early retirement among headteachers.

Learning to step up in a new way

To prevent this situation, headteachers must be supported to 'step up' to their role in a new way, to prioritise not only the emotional intelligences of self-awareness and self-management, but also self-compassion. To fulfil their ambitions for themselves *and* their schools, they need support that helps them face up to and re-frame the way they view their vulnerabilities. This involves being taught how to overcome their limits, frailties, and faulty ways of thinking, and the associated behaviours, so they can consistently show up as they really are and remain connected to their initial vision and passion for the role. Wherever headteachers are in their careers, a new paradigm needs to be introduced to:

> *... address leadership in a more fundamental way and ... attack the foundational belief that we are somehow rational, computer-like beings, and deal with the whole person. (Hamill 2013)*

Support for headteachers must allow them to explore three core aspects of personhood – what it means for them to be human. These are:

- Understanding self.
- Being – not doing.
- Finding meaning in difficult circumstances.

UNDERSTANDING SELF

'Who do I need to be to secure my vision for my school?' This is the question headteachers must be encouraged to ask themselves if they are to fulfil their potential and live mentally and emotionally healthy lives. When someone is asked 'Who do I need to be?' they set in motion an internal process that shifts their mind from the conscious to the subconscious. This enables them to access learning about themselves at a much deeper level. Every headteacher carries with them their own learning history, their own personal story based on their beliefs, emotions and behaviours about who they are, their relationships, their role and the critical events that shaped their lives. These narratives are often hidden from the conscious mind, yet they strongly influence how we engage with the world. Many headteachers do not realise that a time will come when they will have to revisit and rewrite their personal narratives. The habits, thinking processes and behaviours that to that point must be critically reflected upon and analysed; their habits and ways of thinking questioned, and they will need to identify which ways of responding to the world can be kept, adjusted or thrown away in order for them to experience meaningful growth in their roles.

THE SELF AND OUR EMOTIONS

> *What we do is a reflection of who we are, and who we are is the combined total of what we repeatedly do. To see them as separate and distinct is to miss the point. They are both reflections of the same underlying process. (Hamill 2014)*

Our emotions are our 'felt responses' to life's events. Some bring emotions of deep joy, happiness and pleasure, and others the opposite. These felt responses are stored throughout our bodies, in an emotional matrix that runs through every single fibre of our bodies. Every time we experience an event that triggers a specific memory, our mind and body work in synchronicity, causing a particular emotional response. Over time, neural pathways are laid down and connections between synapses become stronger, until certain emotional responses become instantaneous, forming unconscious, conditioned responses. These emotional responses not only shape us, but also influence how we interact with the world and those around us. The mental models we construct are complex; rarely are they conscious, and very often they are based on faulty perceptions about other people's actions towards us and the meaning we attach to them. In the role that headteachers occupy, routinely stressful events trigger emotional responses from the past. It is essential that they are supported to confront their own mental models of the world, to prevent historical emotional and behavioural patterns that undermine their ability to lead from a place of deep inner confidence and self-belief. When such support is available, they start creating new narratives about the challenges they face and can redefine how they respond to the demands of school leadership. This is particularly for people who feel stuck and incapable of seeing their situation from another perspective. As negative emotions are loosened and eventually released, the individual experiences a psychological shift. Their emotions are set free, and their minds are set free, then they can see themselves and how they can approach situations in a more constructive and positive light.

BEING – NOT DOING

The education system needs to recognise that schools are in the process of becoming something better, something greater, and so are headteachers. Their appointment to the post is not the final destination on their leadership journey; rather, it is the beginning – or continuation of – a personal development process for which they need not only strategic and operational support, but psychological and emotional support too. The system continually talks about what headteachers and school leaders should be doing to raise standards, or to tackle underperforming staff, or to build good relationships with their communities. These discussions often take place with little or no regard for how such constant demands impact on the head's sense of self. In education, it is as though we have become:

... hooked on the notion that commitment and activity are inseparable. (Jaworski 1996)

A point has to be reached where commitment and activity can be separated. Constant activity simply sends the body into overdrive, and with it comes a reduction in the mental and emotional faculties that leaders need in order to deliver effectively on his or her commitments. When someone is in a state of constant doing, it is only a matter of time before both mind and the body shout *Enough!* When stress levels rise, the mind plays an acute role in communicating to the body just how to respond.

Psychosomatic illness is well known, where back pain, ulcers [and] high blood pressure can be connected to our mental state. (Hamill 2013)

Physical illness among headteachers, as evidenced by prolonged leave of absence or premature retirement, can lead to a loss of self-worth, a decreased sense of personal dignity, and leaving their school's promise unfulfilled. A truly compassionate and humane system recognises that every school leader is on a journey towards 'self-actualisation' – a term coined by American psychologist, Abraham Maslow. If they are to fulfil their potential, they need help to process deep philosophical and psychological questions, to develop inner tools and see that being:

Has to do with our character, our total orientation to life; it is a state of inner activity. (Jaworski 1996)

Such support enables them to understand that 'inner work' must be done if their experience of school leadership is to be meaningful and fulfilling, and to:

- Talk about what they want as individuals.
- Explore and challenge issues related to their own identity and sense of self.
- Discuss issues related to the fulfilment of their own potential.
- Reflect on the different stages of their own journey of becoming.
- Increase their capacity to be more mindful of themselves and their responses and reactions moment by moment.

When headteachers have support like this as part of their leadership life, then their experience of school leadership takes a different tone. The frenetic nature of the role does not go away, but the way in which they respond changes significantly; they are no longer driven by unconscious emotions and patterns of behaviour, but become more centred and grounded, with a deep connection to who they are and what they stand for.

FINDING MEANING IN DIFFICULT CIRCUMSTANCES

Much of the headteacher's everyday life is spent trying to make sense of myriad difficult circumstances, for which they have ultimate responsibility for resolving. These range from dealing with the collective emotional fallout following an OfSTED inspection, to the death of a child. This extract, from a former head's diary following the death of one of his pupil's, gives

---

Personal reflection

As ever, the management of the fallout, and impact of variables beyond my control has been my leadership challenge this week. Juggling the equally important audiences, communications, risk assessments and contingency planning, along with maintaining good order and clear direction for our school, has required being alert at all times, constantly evaluating and managing risk even more than usual. In amongst these many and multifarious elements, including the wellbeing and grieving of students and staff, has been my own emotional needs which I have never prioritised. My emotional state has been one of high tension in a defensive, protective 'fight' mode in order to protect and ensure the well-being of our staff and students, and safeguard the reputation of the school I have dedicated my life to.

---

insight into the inner turmoil that most headteachers experience when leading a school through difficult times. In circumstances like these, headteachers search for meaning and a way to protect their well-being. With sensitive guidance, they can be brought to a place where they can see how their values provide understanding – even in the most challenging of times. Examination of their values helps them see what options are open to them and what actions they choose to take in order to lead themselves, and others, to 'a better place'. Meaning and purpose are powerful sources of energy, yet mechanisms for exploring them are sadly under-utilised in much of the support that is offered. When people are guided to connect with what matters most to them, their inner resources are fortified and they find within themselves the strength to persist and move forward in pursuit of their goals.

Relationships add meaning

Faced – as they are now – with greater public scrutiny and personal accountability, headteachers find they have fewer professional relationships of mutual trust and respect to draw upon. Increasing competition between schools also causes distrust across the profession. Thus headteachers have become isolated, not only physically – through the breakup of local authorities and the rapid rise of academy chains – but emotionally also. Deep down there is often an unmet need for connection and a desire to find a shared sense of meaning and well-being as part of a community. To ease their inner dissonance and disconnection, heads seek so-called relational leadership to help them make sense of their own humanity and context.

Relational leadership means first and foremost making meaning within a web of relationships, whilst making use of and growing the strengths of those relationships. (De Haan and Kasozi 2014)

Headteachers with few of these relationships find it difficult to extract meaning and validate their roles. However, having relationships that support a 'search for meaning' create a new level of understanding between him or her and the challenges they face. In *Man's Search for Meaning*, Viktor Frank argues from his experiences as a holocaust survivor that if a person is supported to identify their own purpose in life and to connect deeply with it, they will be able to find meaning even in the most difficult circumstances and continue to grow 'in spite of all indignities'. Frankl also points out that the search for meaning, brings many internal conflicts:

Man's search for meaning may rouse inner tension, rather than inner equilibrium.
(Frankl 1946)

Individual headteachers, embarking on their own inner journey, need to be supported so that they do not fall short of their goals or view their inner doubt and confusion as signs of mental weakness or inability to rise to the demands of their role. If the school leadership paradigm can shift, so that vulnerability and struggle are seen as signs of growth rather than personal weakness, headteachers can reclaim their sense of self and well-being. If headteachers are to succeed in fulfilling their visions for both themselves and their schools, then suitable support structures must be in place. Leading a school, getting others to buy into the vision, and transforming the life opportunities of young learners is not just a cognitive process. It is a process that also engages the emotions.

Cultivating a 'deliberate practice'

Peter Hamill, the author of *Embodied Leadership* points out that 'One can have years of experience and not engage in significant deliberate practice'. What our school system should be seeking to do is enable our headteachers to grow wiser and stronger as the years progress, which can only happen when they are engaged in 'deliberate practice'. Deliberate practice is concerned with the 'cultivation of self', which involves developing a deep understanding and awareness of the personal journey that must be undertaken. Deliberate practices for headteachers include having regular 'conscious' moments in their lives when they are supported to stop, pause and reflect, perhaps using 'conscious dialogue", enabling them to explore how to make sense of – and bring deeper meaning to – their leadership life. Greater maturity and wisdom in the thinking process follow, as well as deeper connection with their own intrinsic motivators. When headteachers experience outcomes from coaching in the manner described in this chapter, they experience a relational process that helps them to:

- Feel in greater control of their leadership life and circumstances.
- Identify how to access their own internal resources to bring about personal change.
- Understand the actions they can take to move towards their desired future.
- Know that they are valued for who they are and what they specifically bring to the headteacher role.

Trust: The headteacher's foundation stone

To foster this type of development, headteachers need relationships that are built on trust. When trust is degraded, people do not show up as their best selves. They behave differently and weaken their ability to communicate openly and build relationships that support personal growth. When trust is present, however, they feel a safety and security in the relationship. A non-judgemental space is created in which they can learn to be more reflective and express their vulnerabilities. In developing such deliberate practices and ways of being, they discover a more grounded approach to their leadership practice, and develop an all-round healthier attitude to the challenges of their role. They become better able to protect their own mental health and well-being, and consciously make the connection between their own levels of resilience, mental health and well-being and those of their staff. This way of being with another person involves accepting that their experience of the world is unique and is to be valued and respected. No comparisons with other people or judgements are made. The relationship is solely about how they experience life and what it means for them to be human. It is a journey of self-discovery or, as mentioned earlier, a journey towards 'self-actualisation'.

Concluding comments

Headteachers play a key role in our society. They are the guardians of our children's futures. To succeed in their roles, it is imperative that they are given the emotional and mental support they need to thrive, so they are grounded, confident, emotionally healthy individuals; only then can they a create school environment in which there is a joy and love of learning and the children thrive. For everyone involved in supporting headteachers, this is the ultimate goal.

KEY MESSAGES FROM THIS CHAPTER

 In order to fulfil their key roles in the health of our society, headteachers must be supported emotionally and mentally to manage the intense demands of the operational and strategic sides of their role and the huge range of emotions that leaders experience. When they thrive, so do our schools and our children.

 Headteachers must be given space and support to practise the emotional intelligences of self-awareness, self-management, and self-compassion, to avoid being over-absorbed by school life and detached from their own feelings and relationships, so they can face up to and re-frame the way they view their vulnerabilities.

Supporting evidence and further reading

Arnold K, Turner N, Barling J (2007) Transformational leadership and psychological well-being. *Journal of Occupational Health Psychology* 12(3), 193–203.

Buck A (2009) *What Makes A Great School: A Practical Formula for Success*. London: National College for School Leadership.

De Haan E, Kasozi A (2014) *The Leadership Shadow: How to Recognise and Avoid Derailment, Hubris and Overdrive*. London: Kogan Page.

Frankl, V (1959) *Man's Search for Meaning*. La Jolla, CA: Simon and Schuster.

Goleman D (1996) *Emotional Intelligence: Why It Can Matter More Than IQ*. London: Bloomsbury.

Grant V (2014) *Staying A Head: The Stress Management Secrets of Successful School Leaders*. London: Integrity Coaching.

Hamil P (2013) *Embodied Leadership: The Somatic Approach to Developing Your Leadership*. London: Kogan Page.

Harris B (2007) *Supporting the Emotional Work of School-Leaders*. London: Sage.

Jaworski J (2011) *Synchronicity: The Inner Path of Leadership*. Oakland, CA: Berrett-Koehler.

Lee G (2003) *Leadership Coaching*. London: Chartered Institute of Personal Development.

Lovewell K (2012) *Every Teacher Matters: Inspiring Well-Being Through Mindfulness*. London: Ecademy Press.

O'Conner J, Lages A (2007) *How Coaching Works*. London: A&C Black.

Owen N (2001) *The Magic of Metaphor: 77 Stories for Teachers, Trainers and Thinkers*. London: Crown House.

Pask R, Joy B (2007) *Mentoring–Coaching: A Guide for Education Professionals*. London: Open University Press.

CHAPTER 21

Cognitive–behavioural therapy (CBT)

Jim Gibson, Mick P. Fleming and Colin R. Martin

Cognitive–behavioural therapy (CBT) is often considered to be relevant only to psychiatric clinics and for people experiencing severe mental health problems. This is not the case, however; although the approach has been very successfully applied in severe mental health disorders, its general principles are relevant to mild mental health problems, particularly those associated with stress. Importantly, CBT is an evidence-based approach with a coherent and established theoretical framework comprising both psychological and physical elements, and providing an integrated model of problem identification, intervention and evaluation. It is particularly useful for anxiety-related problems and is effective in depression. The therapy should only be conducted by qualified professionals within a suitable environment, but its general principles and theoretical underpinnings offer great insight into the development of mental health problems in the learning environment and provide a context for identification of problems and intervention. This chapter examines the theoretical framework of CBT and its potential in the learning environment.

The number of teachers taking leave in the UK because of stress has increased by 10% over the past few years. Fifteen local authorities have seen a 50% rise in stress-related absences, according to statistics released under the Freedom of Information Act. Teaching – however rewarding – is a challenging profession and even the greatest teachers can struggle with the stressors they face. The National Association of Schoolmasters Union of Women Teachers (NASUWT) (2008) conducted an extensive study on factors relating to health and safety issues in schools and colleges. Opinions were obtained from nearly 6,000 teachers, school and college leaders and health and safety trade union representatives and published in *Safe to Teach?* in 2008. Most respondents (69%) had suffered from work-related stress, and a third of them had taken time off work. Women and men were equally likely to suffer. In England, only 9% were given access by their employers to occupational health services (and only 8% in Scotland and Wales); similarly, only 9% were given access to an employee assistance programme or teacher helpline (22% in Scotland).

In Scotland, stress is the leading cause of work-related illness in the education sector, according to the newspaper *Scotland on Sunday* (2012), and mirrors the situation across the whole of the UK. Edinburgh City Council, one of the country's largest education authorities, lost the equivalent of 79 months in one year alone (2011) through teacher stress, depression and other mental health issues. In Fife, there were 95 long-term stress-related absences in 2011 – more than several other illnesses combined; fifty-one teachers in Renfrewshire were signed off on long-term sick leave (more than 28 days) for psychological problems including stress, anxiety, depression and chronic fatigue; and in a two-year period, more than 1000 teachers called a specialist phoneline for help dealing with stress. Teacher Support Scotland (2011) cite a doubling of reported issues between 2010 and 2011 – from 675 to 1389.

What is stress?

Stress has different effects on different people. Some are affected more than others, and some thrive in high-pressure environments; something that is stressful to one person may not be to another. However, whatever the trigger is for stress, the person will experience mental and physical tension. This reaction is down to our evolution – if our prehistoric ancestors had not developed this internal alarm, the human race may have become extinct. In those times, the response arose because of acute dangers, such as wild animals. Today, we still face dangers, but tend to use our internal alarm for perceived dangers or threats. It can be activated without conscious thought, through the limbic system which lies deep in the brain. A good analogy is the domestic smoke alarm; while being of undoubted value, they frequently 'go off' when there is no real danger (detecting smoke rather than fire, for example). This might be annoying, but certainly would not warrant a phone call to the emergency services; a quick appraisal of the situation shows that there is no real danger, and simply wafting a towel at the alarm will suffice! Unfortunately, we are not as good at this when it comes to our internal alarms. A worrying thought or physical tension or a churning stomach are not always 'checked out' to determine whether there is any real danger. What often happens – metaphorically speaking – it that the 'emergency services' are called, and the result is stress!

MODELS OF STRESS

Three models of stress are described below (Ratcliffe 2012).

- **The engineering model:** This model presents stress as the load (or demand) placed on a person, which exceeds their 'elastic limit', that is their capacity to adapt to it. In this model, teachers are perceived to be *subjects* rather than *actors*, operating in situations – such as probation, working with children with special needs, or in areas of multiple deprivation – that can give rise to demands that are beyond their adaptive limits.

- **The medical model:** The medical model focuses on physiological and psychological responses, which arise as a consequence of stress. A plethora of symptoms, such as depression, tension, irritability, insomnia, loss of appetite and weight loss, are essential components of the model, although these symptoms are not unique to stress and may be attributed to other medical conditions. Teachers are again portrayed as subjects, on whom pressure is applied, producing stress.

- **The interactive model:** This model perceives stress as interactive and situational, recognising that teaching is a profession, that some schools exert pressures on teachers, and that some teachers react in different ways, using a variety of adaptive resources to help them cope. Importantly, teachers are portrayed as actors rather than subjects, who are not at the mercy of external pressures.

Of these three, the third is helpful because it implies that responsibility for maintaining acceptable levels of stress in teaching is a two-way process. Employers have a statutory duty to ensure that the working environment does not adversely affect their staffs' health, but the staff must apply their adaptive resources to help them cope with the pressures of their chosen profession. Recent appeal-court reductions of awards for stress at work have made it clear that employees who feel they are face undue pressure have a responsibility to inform their employers. Schools and other educational environments are vibrant and challenging places, often with regular pressure-filled events. Pressure is integral to work and can be a factor in maintaining motivation and productivity. However, excessive and prolonged pressure often has a negative effect, with a range of physical and emotional problems that can be debilitating. Stress can be triggered suddenly or arise when a combination of factors accumulate over a long period of time – the so-called 'drip drip' affect).

RECOGNISING STRESS

Stress manifests itself in thinking ability, physical state, behaviour and emotions. It may lead to difficulty in making decisions or concentrating, muscle tension, a churning stomach, disruptive sleep pattern, altered dietary habits, increased alcohol intake, avoidance of actual and perceived situations, depression and guilt – even anger. FIGURE 21.1 lists some of the reactions of teachers to a hypothetical situation involving a disruptive student.

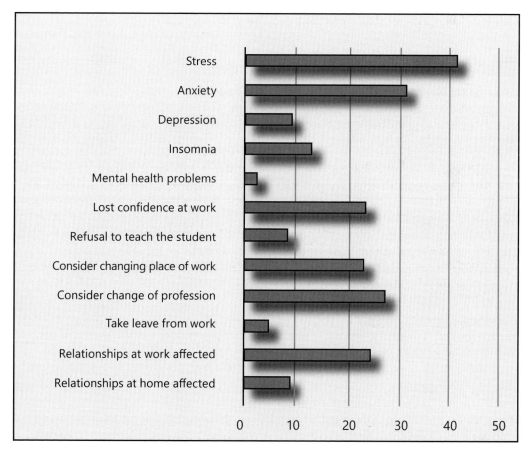

Figure 21.1: Self-reported consequences of dealing with disruptive or violent behaviour from a student in the previous academic year (adapted from Association of Teachers and Lecturers 2013).

What is CBT?

CBT is a commonly used psychotherapeutic method that aims to reduce distress by altering problematic behaviour and unhelpful thinking patterns, which has been shown to be effective in the treatment of depression, anxiety and problematic behaviours (Hepple 2004). The therapy is structured and time-limited (Gibson 2012). The therapist and client work together to identify and understand the client's problems, in terms of the relationship between thoughts, feelings and behaviour (Hawton *et al.* 2004), and the focus is on developing a shared view of such problems. Goals are then identified and strategies to overcome any problems. Much of the treatment is in the 'here and now' and the main objective is to help the clients bring about the desired changes in their lives.

Development of CBT

CBT as a therapy is relatively new, but its origins are much older. Hawton *et al.* (2004) describe the Darwinian view of continuity between man and lower animals that arose in the early twentieth century, whereby the principles derived from animal research might be generalised to man. Two principles of animal learning were identified, namely classical conditioning and operant conditioning.

- **Classical conditioning:** Pavlov famously experimented with dogs. A bell was rung and food was given, and after repeating this a number of times, the dogs began salivating as soon as the bell was rung – before the food was given.

- **Operant conditioning:** This was developed through experiments in which a particular behaviour was consistently followed by a reward. When one behaviour is followed by a particular event, the behaviour becomes reinforced (Hawton 2004), and is more likely to occur again (the Law of Effect).

The development of these two conditioning paradigms was invaluable in the evolution of behaviour therapy. According to Hawton (2004), these same principles are used to help patients: treatments are planned using reinforcers to events that have previously been shown to change behaviours in a desired direction (they are not necessarily intrinsically rewarding). Behavioural therapy fully emerged in the 1970s and numerous new techniques were developed and validated. It became the treatment of choice for many disorders including phobias, obsessions and sexual dysfunctions. Operant and goal-setting techniques were used in rehabilitation (Hawton 2004).

Cognitive aspects of CBT

Discontentment began to arise with respect to the strict behavioural notions of the therapy at that time. It was argued that the majority of behavioural treatments could not be conceptualised in learning theory terms alone. A broader spectrum of behaviour therapy was required, and this led to the inclusion of cognitive components to the techniques, in turn opening the way for the systematic development and application of cognitive approaches (Hawton 2004). Aaron Beck was a psychoanalyst who became involved with the theory of depression when validating psychoanalytical concepts of depression (the need to suffer). His studies showed that depressed people were more likely to elicit responses of acceptance and approval by others, and went on to develop his theory of cognitive therapy (1979). This theory has four elements: schemata, automatic thoughts, thinking errors and the cognitive triad.

- **Schemata**: These contain the assumptions that underpin our views about ourselves, about the world, and about everything that happens in it. Schemata develop by way of our experiences of life and the world, early life events, cultural and social values, and parental and religious teachings.

- **Automatic thoughts**: These are thoughts that pop into our heads about things that happen to us and things we see around us; mostly these are neutral, or positive. However, these thoughts are unspoken and may have a negative effect on our feelings; they derive from our active schema and affect our interpretation of current events.

- **Thinking errors**: Thinking errors enable us to draw conclusions inline with dysfunctional schema, even if there is evidence to the contrary. 'Selective abstraction' focuses on details out of context, while ignoring more salient features of a situation, resulting in comments such as: 'I'm a failure because my paperwork isn't up to date'.

- **Cognitive triad**: This relates to how a person regards him or herself, and the world and the future (Beck 1979), as illustrated in FIGURE 21.2.

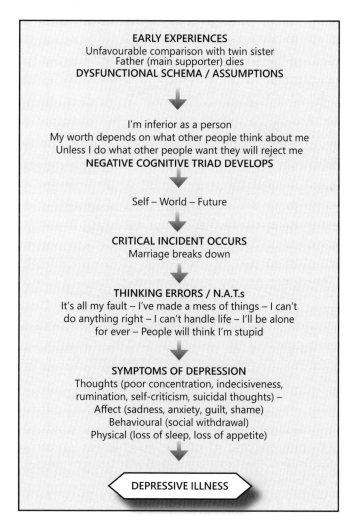

Figure 21.2: The cognitive triad applied to the development of depressive illness.

This 'formulation' shows how the symptoms of depression (or anxiety) can manifest in the way we think and behave, as well as our physiology and emotions. These manifestations should not be viewed in a linear fashion but a circular fashion, because the symptoms 'feed' one another thus maintaining the depression or anxiety, in what is described as a 'vicious circle'. However, the present author suggests that this maintenance of a disorder might be more accurately represented by a 'spiral' because the symptoms actually worsen. FIGURE 21.3 illustrates this alternative relationship. The overarching aim is to intervene in one or more of these areas and break the cycle. According to Laidlaw (2004) the main aim of cognitive therapy is to pass skills on to the client, to enable them to help themselves and deal with their difficulties now and in the future.

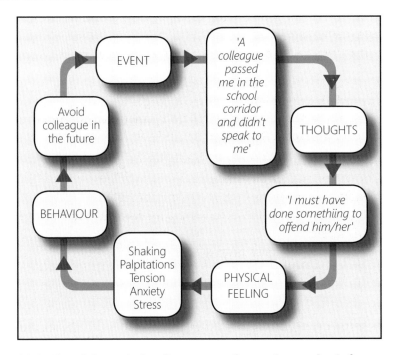

Figure 21.3: The vicious circle of symptom formation and reinforcement.

Application of CBT

CBT is a practical problem-solving approach to treating psychological disorders. It is time-limited, with structured sessions usually lasting for an hour. The number of sessions is negotiated. The goals of therapy should be established early and there should be an atmosphere of collaborative empiricism (engaging, and evidence/theory testing), in which client and therapist are equal partners. This is CBT in a formal sense, where the client has been referred to the therapist by a GP. However, people do not need to engage with CBT in such a formal way; they can employ the principles of CBT in their daily life, and teachers may be well placed to do so. The five areas shown in FIGURE 21.2 appear to be separate entities, but they directly influence each other, for better or worse. According to Williams (2004), the way a person thinks about a situation or a problem affects how they feel emotionally and physically, and alters what they do. These five areas help the person identify clear target areas that can change and make a difference to how he or she feels.

COGNITIONS

Sometimes an event occurs in our lives and we immediately interpret it in a certain manner. If our mood is anxious or depressed, the interpretation will probably be negative. This might be followed by rumination about that particular interpretation, which merely adds to and maintains the original anxiety or depression. If alternative perceptions (thoughts) can be generated about the event, then an opportunity arises to lessen the emotional impact of the event. According to Laidlaw (2004), specific skills can be used for the purpose of challenging unhelpful thoughts. For example, the client might be encouraged to:

- Examine the evidence for and against the thought.
- Imagine how one of their friends would react to the situation or what advice they might give to a friend in a similar situation (cognitive distancing).
- Consider alternative thoughts.
- Review past success and coping methods of other adverse events.

Cognitive distraction is another useful technique. Gibson (2009) suggests it is not used to avoid thoughts as such, but provides the client with cognitive respite. Fennel (2004) suggests that it reduces rumination that can increase distress rather than constructive problem-solving. Some examples of distraction techniques are (Gibson 2009):

- Listening to music, doing word puzzles and exercising.
- Recalling by way of thought and images a favourite holiday or event.
- Counting backwards in sevens from 500 (serial sevens).
- Going through each letter of the alphabet and for each one think of a town, animal, band, type of car, etc.
- Saying 'STOP' when an anxiety-provoking thought pops up and replace it with a more pleasant one (thought stopping).

BEHAVIOUR

When a person's mood changes, they may experience a lack of volition with respect to engaging in previously routine or pleasurable activities. Any reduction in pleasurable activities makes their lives less pleasurable, maintaining the cycle of anxiety and depression. Conversely, if pleasurable activities are prevented from being lost, or if they are re-instated, then life remains pleasurable. According to Lewisham (1980), people can be encouraged to compile a list of the behaviours (activities) that increase or decrease levels of emotional distress, then put the list in a daily activity diary and avoid the distressing ones as much as possible.

PHYSIOLOGY

One technique involves the client setting aside 20 minutes the same time every evening (say around 7PM to sit down, with a pen and notebook or diary – somewhere where the risk of being disturbed is low (Espie and Lindsay 1987). You should encourage the client thus:

- Think about what happened during the day, how events went, and how you felt about the kind of day it was. Write down some of the main points, putting them to rest as you commit them to paper. Write down what you felt good about and what troubled you. Write down anything you feel you need to do on a 'To do' list, with steps you can take to tie up any loose ends or unfinished business.

- Think about tomorrow and what's coming up. Consider the things you are looking forward to as well as the things that worry you. Write down your schedule or review it if it is already there. Write down anything you are unsure about and make a note of a time in the morning when you are going to find out about that. Use this time to make you feel more in control. 'Close the book' on the day.

- At bedtime, remind yourself that you have already dealt with all these things if they come into your mind. If any new thoughts come up when you are in bed, note them down on a piece of paper and leave them at your bedside to deal with in the morning.

EXERCISE

There is increasing evidence about the value of exercise for treating clinical anxiety disorders and more general difficulties with anxiety. Otto and Smits (2011) report on almost 50 studies performed outside the psychiatric clinic, examining the effects of programmed exercise on anxiety as it arises in individuals with medical complaints, among the elderly, after stress, or in the general population. In all cases, regular leisure-time exercise bring about reliable reductions in anxiety at the same time as promoting feelings of wellbeing. There is also increasing evidence for the benefits of exercise for anxiety disorders. In these programmes, 30–40 minutes' exercise was assigned three times per week. As with exercise for a depressed mood, it does not take 10 weeks for the benefits to become apparent; reductions in state anxiety are often found within 10 minutes of completing exercise (Otto and Smits 2011).

Structured problem-solving

Structured problem-solving can play a vital part in preventing or reducing the impact of distressing events. When confronted by an adverse life event (actual or perceived), people very quickly say to themselves 'I'm going to do something about this'. However, little or no time is spent considering what the options are; more often, the result is like a 'bull in a china shop' or simply nothing. These responses may provide a short-term solution to the problem, but in the longer-term may they can make the problem worse. Practical problem-solving can allow more control over life in general, and making decisions (Williams 2004), and this increased sense of control improves self-confidence. Williams (2004) gives seven steps for structured problem-solving for the client (FIGURE 21.4).

Concluding comments

CBT is a useful, evidence-based approach to dealing with mental health problems and issues. It is fundamentally rooted in enduring theoretical positions that provide good explanatory accounts of both normal and maladaptive behaviour. The theoretical underpinning of CBT provides a coherent account of how problem behaviours develop so that, through the use of a theoretically anchored, process-driven approach, an effective and measurable intervention strategy can be found, based on the notion of comprehensive assessment. The application of CBT within the learning environment has not been extensively explored, but there are increasing opportunities to consider and reflect on the general principles for evidence-based problem evaluation, and problem-solving of mental health issues in the classroom using the CBT framework and formulation-focused approach. CBT should only be delivered by suitably qualified individuals in suitably supported environments that permit and advocate its use, in order to facilitate understanding, hope and effective intervention within a structured and theoretically cogent framework.

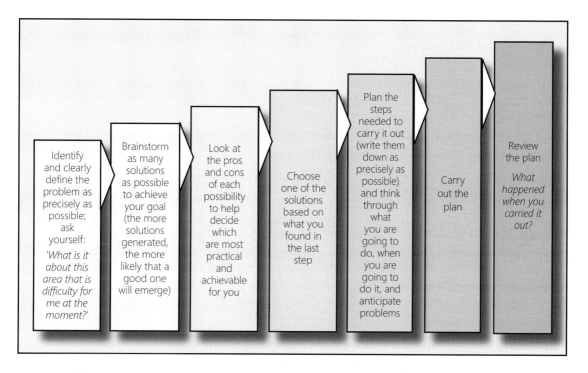

Figure 21.4: Seven steps for structured problem-solving (Williams 2004).

KEY MESSAGES FROM THIS CHAPTER

- CBT is an evidence-based approach to the treatment of a range of mental health problems that may be associated with the challenging classroom environment.

- CBT provides a context and theoretical framework for considering the development of mental health problems within the learning environment.

- Training is essential for the application of CBT.

- CBT may be particularly effective for problems that are often (but not always) associated with occupational stress, specifically anxiety disorders and depression.

Supporting evidence and further reading

Association of Teachers and Lecturers (2013) *Press Release: Disruptive behaviour in schools and colleges rises alongside in children with behavioural and mental health problems*. ATL Annual Conference, Liverpool, 25–27 March.

Beck AT, Rush AJ, Shaw BF, Emery G (1979) *Cognitive Therapy Of Depression*. New York: Guilford Press.

Denholm A (2012) *Teacher Support Scotland* (2012) Available at: wwwheraldscotlandcom/news/education/stressed-scots-teachers-flood-helpline-for/support18807407 (accessed July 2015).

Espie CA, Lindsay WR (1987) Cognitive strategies for the treatment of severe sleep maintenance insomnia: A preliminary investigation. *Behavioural Psychotherapy* 15, 388–95.

Fennel MJ (2004) Depression. In: MJ Hawton, PM Salkovskis, J Kirk. *Cognitive Behavioural Therapy For Psychiatric Problems: A Practical Guide*. Oxford: Oxford University Press.

Gibson J (2012) Cognitive behavioural therapy and the person with dementia. *Mental Health Practice* 14(1), 20–23.

Gibson J (2009) Living with loss. *Mental Health Practice* 12(5), 22–24.

Grant A, Townend M, Mulhern R, Short N (2011) *Cognitive Behavioural Therapy in Mental Health Care*. London: Sage.

Greenberger D, Padesky CA (1995) *Mind Over Mood: Change How You Feel by the Way You Think*. London: Guilford Press.

Hawton K, Salkovskis PM, Kirk J, Clark DM (2004) *Cognitive Behavioural Therapy for Psychiatric Problems – A Practical Guide*. Oxford: Oxford University Press.

Hepple J (2004) Psychotherapies with older people: an overview. *Advances in Psychiatric Treatment* 10(5), 371–77.

Laidlaw K, Thompson LW, Dick-Siskin L, Gallagher-Thompson D (2003) *Cognitive Behavioural Therapy with Older People*. Chichester: John Wiley & Sons.

Lewisham PM, Sullivan JM, Grosscup SJ (1980) Changing reinforcing events: an approach to the treatment of depression. *Psychotherapy: Theory Research and Practice* 17, 322–24.

Marshall C (2012) Scottish teachers take months off in stress epidemic. *Scotland on Sunday* 19 February.

National Association of Schoolmasters Union of Women Teachers (2008) *Safe To Teach*. Edinburgh: NASUWT.

Otto MW, Smits JA.J (2011) *Exercise For Mood and Anxiety: Proven Strategies for Overcoming Depression and Enhancing Well-Being*. Oxford: Oxford University Press.

Ratcliffe R (2012) The rise in teachers off work with stress – and Union warns of more to come. *The Guardian* 26 December.

Turnbull G (2011) *Trauma*. London: Bantam Press.

Williams C J (2003) *Overcoming Anxiety – A Five Areas Approach*. London: Hodder Arnold.

PART IV
Contemporary issues

CHAPTER 22

The principles of mental health intervention in education

Colin R. Martin and Mick P. Fleming

There are myriad evidence-based interventions that may be helpful in supporting both the learner and the leader of learning who is experiencing a degree of mental health distress within the educational environment. However, when considering any intervention it is crucial to identify the boundaries that circumscribe the intervention – the operating parameters under which an intervention is anticipated to be helpful and effective. The evidence base of the intervention itself offers valuable insights into its efficacy and, of course, the precise form to be used, but regardless of the presenting problem and the type of intervention, certain general principles must be recognised. These apply to all interventions and are central to reflecting upon and deciding which one is appropriate. This chapter examines some of the key principles that should be considered before offering any intervention.

Undoubtedly, much can be done to support and help learners and leaders of learning who have compromised mental health. There is also great scope for considering interventions for any-one at increased risk of experiencing such problems in the education setting. Understanding the fundamental principles behind the interventions facilitates decision-making and assessment of their suitability. One critical concept is the nature of an intervention.

What is an intervention?

An intervention is an evidence-based engagement with a specific beneficial effect, that is supported by a cogent evidence base. Interventions are often considered at the personal level, but it is useful to think at an organisational level also. For example, an organisational, evidence-based initiative may be used to reduce levels of stress experienced by learners and leaders of learning in a school. Whether used at a personal or group level, the intervention must be matched to the specific problem and delivered appropriately; it should also be evaluated to determine its efficacy.

Determining the appropriateness of an intervention

Two important considerations are:
- The severity of the identified problem in relation to the appropriateness of an 'in-house' intervention.
- The skills base of the person applying the intervention.

The severity of the presenting problem

One of the most important factors when considering whether an intervention is desirable or suitable is the severity of the presenting problem. Any mental health problem within the educational setting that is regarded to be a clinical problem (in other words, severe) must be dealt with by an appropriately trained and qualified healthcare professional, but it also matters whether the person with the problem is a learner or a leader of learning.

(i) In leaders of learning with mental health problems

This pathway is relatively straightforward because it involves direct engagement with the organisation that is responsible for staff well-being and performance. The route for a clinically relevant problem is likely to be occupational health services or primary care; a human resources route will also probably lead to occupational health services.

(ii) In learners with mental health problems

This pathway is more variable and relies on more complex combinations of service engagement, depending on factors such as the learner's age and legal status (child versus adult), the type of problem, the range of services available in the specific setting, and the support of the learner's family. A child with a clinically relevant mental health problem may have engagement with a school nurse, an educational psychologist, CAMHS, the social services and (occasionally) the criminal justice system.

The skills base of the person applying the intervention

Teachers are in a very good position to recognise the key symptoms of a developing mental health problem in both learners and other members of staff, however it is beyond their scope to carry out interventions for clinically significant problems. This must be left to professionals with appropriate qualifications to engage at the level of diagnosis and treatment. Teachers may only engage at a subclinical level, which relates to someone's psychosocial functioning without symptoms of overt mental illness that must be referred to specialist or statutory services. Understanding the difference between clinical and subclinical issues is important, therefore, and when doubt exists, the default position is to consider any concerns as potentially clinically relevant.

This may sound as if interventions are only considered for clinically relevant problems, whereby a problem is detected but is beyond the scope of the staff member to deal with. This is not the case, however. For example, if a member of the staff recognises that a teacher or a learner is experiencing mild or transitory distress, then simply offering support is an intervention. There is a very convincing evidence base on the benefits of basic support, and if offered at a subclinical stage, it can prevent the development of a clinically relevant problem, or modify the severity of the developing problem. It is therefore incumbent on colleagues to consider their basic skills base for offering support, and to be aware of the efficacy of this basic intervention, even if they might be dismissed as being 'just a friend'.

The efficacy of support may be further enhanced by having increased awareness of the underlying principles relating to their use, such as personal boundaries and competence.

Professional and personal boundaries

It is essential to be aware of professional and personal boundaries when considering an intervention. Boundaries are often defined within the standard operating procedures (SOPs) of specific educational institutions, and some are legally defined as anyone involved in educational practice will know. Boundaries that define relationships well can promote engagement with the person with a problem and promote clarity in terms of the context of the intervention. However, boundaries can be blurred. For example, a teacher might notice that a colleague is distressed but that colleague is also a personal friend. In this case, there may be difficulties in boundary osmosis, even though, ironically, the colleague who is also a friend may be in the 'best place' to offer an intervention. This is where the choice of words becomes critically important: offering support as a colleague and friend is both readily accepted and acknowledged, however, offering an intervention in this context may be seen in a very negative light by the colleague it is aimed at, even if, as was highlighted earlier, they amount to the same thing. By offering an intervention, boundary contamination can result, thus awareness of boundaries is crucial for engagement and communication. Essentially, people are not usually empowered by having something 'done to them', which is how interventions can be perceived if they are presented in an ill-considered manner.

Competence

Some deep soul-searching is common among people working in the education setting about the appropriate level of competence required to offer effective, evidence-based interventions. The interventions outlined in this book are straightforward and evidence-based, but to use them properly requires skill, application and knowledge of the fundamental theoretical tenets of the intervention in question. Anyone considering using them should audit their own skills base and seek additional training or supervision as necessary. There is no doubt that going beyond general advice-giving and collegiate support of the kind described above, requires an enhanced skills set for which supervision would be a requirement.

Ethical practice

The application of evidence-based interventions to help and support someone experiencing a mental health issues requires an engagement that is both evidence-based (in terms of there actually being a problem, and in terms of the theoretical models underpinning the intervention) and ethical. People working in education who consider applying interventions to help people with subclinical mental health concerns must work within an ethical framework, as circumscribed by their professional body. They should also consider general ethical models that offer further insight into the issues involved in applying interventions in mental health. From an ethical perspective, a person with a mental health problem is vulnerable, therefore their well-being must be safeguarded at all times.

Concluding comments

The application of interventions to help and support people within the educational environment who are experiencing mental health difficulties requires a skills set that is rooted in a theoretically robust framework and supported by an evidence base. These must be substantial for all models of intervention, from the simplest to the most sophisticated and complex. When considering the use of an intervention, the teacher or other member of staff needs to be aware of some basic principles, such as understanding his or her own strengths and limitations in terms of knowledge and skills, and they must appreciate the profound issue of boundaries and their potential impact on any encounter, as well as the absolute requirement to conduct oneself in an ethically informed and erudite manner.

To postulate and operationalise an intervention requires competence and additional training beyond the level of basic support and advice-giving, and to facilitate its use in an education setting there must be an awareness of the individual's strengths and weaknesses and an effective supervisory infrastructure.

KEY MESSAGES FROM THIS CHAPTER

- All models of intervention require an underlying theoretical framework and substantive evidence base.

- Additional training is likely to be required to offer interventions beyond advice-giving and general support.

- Competence is essential for the application of effective and beneficial interventions.

- The individual must be aware of the distinction between subclinical and clinical mental health problems and its relevance for determining the appropriateness of an intervention, or referral to a specialist mental health practitioner or relevant part of the organisational infrastructure.

- In addition to having an adequate skills set and theoretical knowledge base, the individual considering applying interventions must subscribe to a code of ethical practice and be aware of the importance, relevance and complexity of interpersonal boundaries.

CHAPTER 23

Mental health and physical illness

Colin R. Martin and Mick P. Fleming

Physical illness, particularly chronic illness, is rarely discussed within the context of the educational process, yet it can present great challenges for those within the educational cycle, irrespective of whether the individual with the burden of illness is the learner or the leader of learning. Moreover, the presence of chronic physical illness in children is often a taboo topic, raising issues about promoting conversation and debate in relation to problem-solving, engagement within education, and support of a child who may have profound needs. The needs of people with a chronic physical illness are accommodated for in the educational system by statutory and legally binding mechanisms, but the relationship between physical illness and mental health within the learning environment is rarely explored. On this issue, both the literature and guidance is sparse. This chapter considers a number of factors relevant to the relation between physical illness and mental health and its impact on the quality of the learning environment from the perspectives of both learners and leaders of learning.

The learning environment is not particularly flexible in accommodating people with physical illnesses, whether they are learners or leaders of learning. Legislation has been introduced that aims to ensure equity of access to education for all. The requirements of this intervention highlight the fundamental issue whereby the traditional learning environment has been designed around the 'average' student – 'average' in terms of intelligence and 'average' in relation to physical health. Such legislation is, therefore, a key that represents access to all. However the notion of access for all may be mis-specified; the conceptualisation of physical illness may be based on the status of the physical illness (which can be acute or chronic), and very importantly, the mental health status of the person experiencing the physical illness, irrespective of its duration. The burden of a physical illness may be accommodated within the learning environment, by providing easy access for a learner with heart disease, for example. However, the emotional and psychological burden of such an illness, and its impact on the person's mental health, is generally not recognised or acknowledged. This is significant because several factors come into play in determining people's emotional responses to physical illness, relating to:

- The acute or chronic nature of the illness.
- The severity of the illness.
- The presence of overt symptoms.
- The feeling of being supported.

Physical illness is generally easy to observe, as in the case of someone with heart disease who may be breathless, or someone who has lost his or her hair during treatment for cancer. In contrast, mental health issues associated with physical health status are less obvious because the symptoms are less readily observed.

What is the relationship between physical illness and mental health?

Traditionally, mental health and physical illness have been considered as two distinct and conceptually divorced phenomena. Consequently the desire to address one of these domains has been considered with scant reflection on the other. However, contemporary research highlights a complex and important relationship between them (Martin *et al.* 2004). More importantly, the research shows this relationship is dynamic, whereby one element can profoundly affect the other (Banks and Martin 2009; Banks *et al.* 2012). The relationship between them has garnered considerable interest within the medical and allied health literature, as it is increasingly acknowledged to be critical to clinical outcomes of a range of physical illness (Glover *et al.* 2012; Muhammad *et al.* 2012).

The literature on this issue within educational settings, in terms of learners and leaders of learning, remains scarce because it is underdeveloped and poorly researched. This may be an artefact of the main performance indicators used in education, which focus on learner performance almost exclusively, with little consideration of their state of well-being except when it has an obviously deleterious effect on performance.

There is also a lack of awareness about the complexity of the interplay between physical limitations, aspirations, support, awareness, facilitation and legal obligations. To address these complex relationships is challenging even for the most proactive leaders of learning trying to accommodate learners with chronic physical illness; there is a confusion about what should be done at the individual, classroom and organisational level, especially with respect to policies of inclusivity and resource allocation. Undoubtedly there is now an imperative to address the vacuum in applied knowledge about the profound, dynamic, interdependent relationship between physical illness and mental health and its significance to the learning environment.

Bringing physical and mental health domains together

An integrative framework that brings together the domains of physical and mental health is highly desirable. It would not only facilitate understanding of the relationship between them, but would also allow identification of the discrete subdomains contributing to the main domains of physical illness and mental well-being. Once the core and dependent components that contribute to this framework are identified, important predictions can be made and hypotheses tested, which are critical to understanding and deconstructing in a meaningful manner the impact of this complex interaction on learner performance and engagement over the course of their studies. The framework would be equally applicable to leaders of learning experiencing physical illness.

A core conceptual framework that brings physical illness and mental health together is the concept of quality of life. Quality of life has emerged as a key concept in the health literature and has provided a number of models that have been used for understanding both disease pathology and psychopathology from a fundamentally holistic standpoint. Within models of quality of life, physical health cannot be considered to be exclusive of mental health. The conceptualisation of quality of life in this manner has led to a step-wise understanding of what well-being means to the individual themselves and the systems within which they function, whether these are social or educational.

The concept of quality of life is found throughout the clinical health literature, so much so that valid quality of life measures and data are central to evaluating the outcome of clinical trials of drug therapies. Quality of life provides a comprehensive, useful and valid conceptual framework with which to consider the impact of the physical illness, and on which to base strategies that might be used to offer appropriate support to the individual.

Quality of life models

Many models have been developed that focus on accurate descriptions of the underlying elements of quality of life and on accurate, psychometrically robust and valid measurements of the key domains and subdomains (Carroll *et al.* 2013, 2014; Lewin *et al.* 2002; Spiteri *et al.* 2013; Tayyem *et al.* 2011, 2014; Yeung *et al.* 2006). Ware and Sherbourne (1992) developed a useful model that provides an easily understood framework for readily identifying the relationship between physical and mental health and its associated subdomains; this is the medical outcomes study Short Form 36 (SF-36) self-report questionnaire. It has become one of the most widely used quality of life measures in the world and has been translated into many different languages. This multipurpose survey of only 36 questions can be used for people of all ages as long as they understand what is being asked of them; they are given a choice of two to five options for questions such as: *The following items are about activities you might do during a typical day. Does your health now limit you in these activities? If so, how much?*

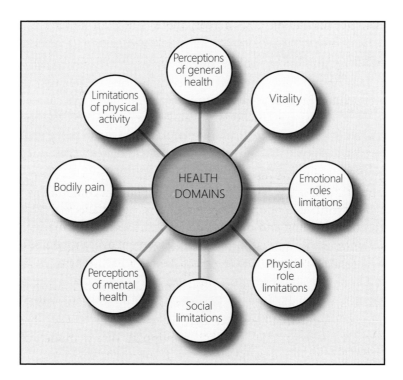

Figure 23.1: Eight health domains addressed in the SF-36.

The questionnaire accurately measures eight distinct health domains as described below:

- **Perceptions of general health**: this is measured in terms of concepts such as excellent or poor, and also involves comparison to other people, such as feeling 'just as healthy as anyone' he or she knows.

- **Perceptions of mental health**: this asks about feeling happy, calm and peaceful, or nervous, worn out and tired.

- **Limitations of physical activity**: this includes vigorous activities such as running and climbing several flights of stairs, and moderate activities such as bending and getting dressed.

- **Bodily pain**: this explores the extent to which pain hinders the performance of activities at work, home or in public.

- **Physical role limitations**: these questions address how their capacity to perform various activities affects their roles on a daily basis.

- **Emotional roles limitation**: this assess whether the respondent's emotional condition, such as depression or anxiety, limits daily functioning and ability to perform roles.

- **Social limitations**: this covers social activities and interactions with significant others such as family members, friends, neighbours and other social relations.

- **Vitality**: this addresses energy levels.

The questionnaire relates to how the individual has been feeling about their health over a certain time period: the previous week, for example, or over a year. The normal version can be reliably re-administered at intervals in cases of chronic illness. The value of frameworks like the SF-36 is that the relationship between domains is circumscribed explicitly, thus the physical health domain is defined by subdomains on physical function, physical role, pain, and health perceptions, all of which are reliably and validly measured; and the mental health domain is defined by general mental health, emotional role, and social function subdomains which are also assessed in a psychometrically rigorous manner. Importantly, the higher-order domains of physical health and mental health are specified as being correlated, revealing statistically significant relationships between the two domains. The value of establishing statistical relationships is that predictions can be made; low scores on specific physical subdomains may be anticipated to correlate with lower scores on specific mental domains.

Generally speaking, when applied across broad clinical groups, such relationships provide 'proof' of the interrelationship between physical and mental health. This is extremely useful for considering the needs of people with physical illness. For example, a teenaged learner with chronic kidney disease may be anticipated to have impaired physical functioning and roles on bespoke measures of quality of life; the relationship between the physical and mental health domains of the quality of life tool can be extrapolated as a template to frame his or her psychological or mental health needs. This is especially useful because the domains of any potential mental health burden are readily identified within the model. Awareness of these quality of life models also provides a simple and straightforward context for engaging with the physically ill person and discussing issues beyond their illness that are personally and practically important to their success or otherwise within the educational environment.

Concluding comments

Chronic physical illness can have a negative effect on a person's mental health. A large body of healthcare research highlights the salience of this relationship, yet this knowledge has not been widely applied in the educational context. In this setting, issues of chronic physical illness and its effect on mental health may be raised by making quality of life assessment tools with standardised models, and further work on this approach is highly recommended, through systematic research and evaluation. This should further our understanding of the fundamental issues, and offer a template for realistic, evidence-based action planning to optimise outcomes for learners and leaders of learning who are affected by a chronic physical illness.

KEY MESSAGES FROM THIS CHAPTER

 Physical illness influences the mental health status of the individual.

 The relationship between physical illness and mental health may be circumscribed within robust and rigorous theoretical models.

 The concept of quality of life provides a coherent framework to consider the relationship between chronic physical illness and mental health in a useful and applied manner of relevance to the educational setting.

 The evidence base for the relationship between physical illness and mental health within the healthcare literature is sophisticated and highly developed, however the application of such evidence to the formal educational setting is currently poor and under-developed.

Supporting evidence and further reading

Banks P, Martin CR (2009) The factor structure of the SF-36 in Parkinson's disease. *Journal of Evaluation in Clinical Practice* 15(3), 460–63.

Banks P, Martin CR, Petty RK (2012) The factor structure of the SF-36 in adults with progressive neuromuscular disorders. *Journal of Evaluation in Clinical Practice* 18(1), 32–36.

Carroll D, Duffy T, Martin CR (2013) Assessment of the quality of life of vulnerable young males with severe emotional and behaviour difficulties in a residential setting. *Scientific World Journal* 2013, 357, 341.

Carroll D, Duffy T, Martin CR (2014) A comparison of the quality of life of vulnerable young males with severe emotional and behaviour difficulties in a residential setting and young males in mainstream schooling. *Journal of Psychiatric and Mental Health Nursing* 21(1), 23–30.

Glover C, Banks P, Carson A, Martin CR, Duffy T (2012) Understanding and assessing the impact of end-stage renal disease on quality of life: a systematic review of the content validity of self-administered instruments used to assess health-related quality of life in end-stage renal disease. *Patient* 4(1), 19–30.

Lewin RJ, Thompson DR, Martin CR *et al.* (2002) Validation of the Cardiovascular Limitations and Symptoms Profile (CLASP) in chronic stable angina. *Journal of Cardiopulmonary Rehabilitation* 22(3), 184–91.

Martin CR, Tweed AE, Metcalfe MS (2004) A psychometric evaluation of the Hospital Anxiety and Depression Scale in patients diagnosed with end-stage renal disease. *British Journal of Clinical Psychology* 43(1), 51–64.

Muhammad, S, Noble, H, Banks, P, Carson, A, Martin CR (2012) How young people cope with chronic kidney disease: literature review. *Journal of Renal Care* 38(4), 182–90.

Spiteri MC, Jomeen, J, Martin CR (2013) Reimagining the General Health Questionnaire as a measure of emotional well-being: a study of postpartum women in Malta. *Women Birth* 26(4), e105–e111.

Tayyem R, Ali A, Atkinson J, Martin CR (2011) Analysis of health-related quality-of-life instruments measuring the impact of bariatric surgery: systematic review of the instruments used and their content validity. *Patient* 4(2), 73–87.

Tayyem RM, Atkinson JM, Martin CR (2014) Development and validation of a new bariatric-specific health-related quality of life instrument "bariatric and obesity-specific survey (BOSS)". *Journal of Postgraduate Medicine* 60(4), 357–61.

Ware JE Jr, Sherbourne CD (1992) The MOS 36-item short-form health survey (SF-36) I. Conceptual framework and item selection. *Medical Care* 30(6), 473–83.

Yeung SM, Shiu AT, Martin CR, Chu KM (2006) Translation and validation of the Chinese version of the Gastrointestinal Quality of Life Index in patients with gastric tumor. *Journal of Psychosomatic Research,* 61(4), 469–77.

CHAPTER 24

Applying psychosocial interventions

Mick P. Fleming and Colin R. Martin

Psychosocial interventions came to prominence within the field of mental health from the 1980s onwards. A range of psychosocial factors have been used to explain the development of stress-related conditions. Evidence is emerging that psychosocial theory and psychosocial interventions can provide a framework of factors that can play a role in understanding learners' behaviour and communication, strategies to manage classroom behaviour, bullying and stress management for leaders of learning as well as the functioning of the learning environment. Within this chapter the authors define psychosocial interventions and then discuss four key underlying principles and their application.

Psychosocial factors such as stress, affect, behavioural patterns and beliefs and can influence mental and physical health and interpersonal functioning. When applied to learners, leaders of learning and the learning environment, psychosocial factors may influence aspects of learner behaviour and communication as well as the role and strategies used by leaders of learning and functioning within the learning environment (Allodi 2010; Alvarez 2008; Smith 2013; Thomas and Anderson 2014). Psychosocial theory provides a framework for understanding psychosocial factors in the development of stress-related conditions, and evidence on the effectiveness of psychosocial treatments for alleviating them.

Defining psychosocial interventions

Psychosocial interventions is an umbrella term for a continuum of evidence-based, systematic and non-pharmacological treatments (Fleming *et al.* 2008). They are based on the principles of social systems, behavioural, cognitive behavioural and interpersonal psychology, and aim to facilitate management of stress and its effects, and enhance coping. Their focus is on individuals, their families and carers. Within the authors' fields of practice, such interventions have been developed and associated with the treatment of serious mental health problems; within the last three decades, for example, a combination of research and training initiatives have led to the development of several specific evidence-based interventions for people with schizophrenia and their families. The interventions are also relevant to and appropriate for people experiencing other long-term conditions such as renal and coronary heart disease and cancer (Thompson 2007; Waghorn 2009).

In the field of education; the literature acknowledges a role for psychosocial factors in school refusal, attention deficit hyperactivity disorder, anxiety, shy and withdrawn learners, victims of conflict, and control of asthma and alcohol use (Foxcroft and Tsertsvadze 2011; Heyne *et al.* 2014; Jordans *et al.*, 2010; Lipp 2011; Maric *et al.* 2013; McKenna *et al.* 2014; McWhirter *et al.* 2008; Schultz *et al.* 2011; Tresco *et al.* 2010). There are many more studies that utilise and evaluate psychosocial interventions among learners from different age groups, but these studies relate to school environments. There is a role for psychosocial factors in changing the physical and mental health of leaders of learning, as well as mental health literacy, coaching and self-efficacy, interpersonal aspects of classroom management, performance, management of bullying and motivation of learners (Almolda-Toma *et al.* 2014; Bogaert *et al.* 2015; Dedousis-Wallace *et al.* 2014; Flook *et al.* 2013; Jing 2008; Piwowar *et al.* 2013; Reinke *et al.* 2014; Whitley *et al.* 2013).

Psychosocial factors such as interpersonal structures and frameworks can have a direct influence on the learning environment, process and – consequently – on educational outcomes. Within primary, secondary and some further educational organisations, families and carers are likely to have a role in their children's education. It is logical that if psychosocial factors play a role in the education process, then psychosocial interventions can be employed to manage and cope with any detrimental effects of these factors.

Underlying principles of psychosocial interventions

Stress caused by change, such as facing new or threatening situations, as part of everyday living or as a direct consequence of a life event, requires the person to adapt. This adaptation or adjustment to stress, and the biopsychosocial aspects of the stress response, as well as longer-term effects of the response, are implicated in the development and maintenance of mental and physical health conditions, and a poorer quality of life. The stress concept is associated with psychosocial interventions in two ways.

STRESS MODELS AND MANAGEMENT

Psychosocial factors can explain aspects of the stress response, the mechanisms by which the change or life event is translated into the stress response, and factors that mediate the effects of the adaptation and the stress response on the individual. Psychosocial factors, such as previous experiences, belief systems, affect, behaviour and interpersonal relationships, often combined with biological factors, have been used to explain the development of stress-related health conditions and the individual's adaptation to the health condition (Falvo 2014). Specific biopsychosocial models have been developed as a way of explaining the development of stress-related conditions over time.

(i) Vulnerability factors

Vulnerability factors are hereditary, in-born and acquired throughout a person's life span, predisposing them to developing specific stress-related conditions. Some studies focus on the activation of these factors through a complex physiological process. Aspects of the central nervous system, particularly the hypothalamic–pituitary–adrenal axis have been implicated in the development of the episodic stress-related conditions (Nuchterlein and Dawson 1984). A combination of vulnerability factors determine the individual's stress threshold or stress tolerance level. When this threshold or tolerance level is breached, a person develops the symptoms of the stress condition. Stress and his or her stress response are the factors that precipitate development of the condition. The relationship between vulnerability factors and stress responses is complex as people are imbued with different degrees of vulnerability, related to hereditary, experiential and environmental factors. In those with a low loading of vulnerability and a high stress tolerance, a large stress response is needed to develop the stress-related condition, while those with a high loading of vulnerability and a low stress threshold require a lower stress response will produce a stress-related condition. This is how individual differences in the general population are explained.

(ii) Mediating factors

The complexity of the relationship is further complicated by factors that mediate or influence the stress response and confound the development of the stress-related condition. Mediating factors work at different stages of the temporal process. Initially a person's vulnerability interacts with their pre-morbid development and functioning; someone with an effective level of pre-morbid functioning, self-confidence, self-esteem and supportive social relationships and network will be protected from developing the stress condition even if they are imbued with a high level of vulnerability (Fleming and Martin 2012; Yank *et al.* 1993). The mediating effect is facilitated by the absorption of stress and by increasing the individual's tolerance to stress. Adaptation and coping are important and effective mediating factors with particular implications for the delivery of psychosocial interventions. These factors include coping effort and coping competence.

- **Coping effort** refers to the energy that someone expends when their initial responses are ineffective in dealing with the stress they experience.

- **Coping competence** is the level of ability and skill utilised by the person to plan coping (Nicholson and Neufeld 1992).

As well as previous effective coping, the number and experience of previous life events, emotional and developmental factors, and the overall level of stress experienced by the individual have a role.

STRESS–VULNERABILITY MODELS

These stress–vulnerability models provide a framework for understanding the temporal process by which psychosocial factors contribute to the onset of certain health conditions (Fleming and Martin 2012). They are not aetiological models, but they identify the factors – or combination of factors – that can cause or affect health (FIGURE 24.1).

Within the field of mental health, the development of psychosocial interventions was prompted by the acceptance of stress vulnerability models, with acknowledgement of the role of psychosocial factors in the development of stress-related health conditions and adaptation. Acceptance precipitates the development and testing of psychosocial interventions to improve problem-solving, stress management and increases coping, which ultimately reduces the risk of developing a stress-related condition by increasing an individual's stress threshold or tolerance level (Baguley and Baguley 1999).

Acknowledgement of previous and competent coping abilities and effort provides important background detail for practitioners who are planning the design and delivery of psychosocial interventions to cope with stress and/or increase the individuals stress threshold (Nicholson and Neufeld 1992).

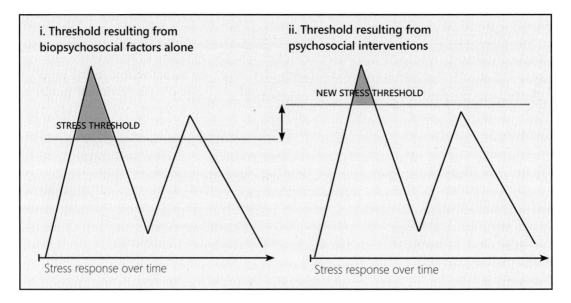

Figure 24.1: Diagram of change in stress threshold, with and without psychosocial intervention, and for the same challenging event depending on vulnerability levels. Grey areas indicate stress-related illness (adapted from Zubin and Spring 1977).

Consequently, these psychosocial strategies can also help people to adapt more effectively to stressful events. Stress management initiatives focus on two aspects of coping.

- **Problem-based coping:** relates to coping with the problem or stress-inducing stimuli, such as coping with workload and work-allocation issues, providing evidence that supports the belief of being in control.

- **Emotion-focused coping:** refers to the development of coping and self-managem -ent of the negative and intrusive emotions that are activated as part of the stress response (Barrowclough and Tarrier 1997). Examples of this are progressive muscle relaxation (PMR), combined cognitive–behavioural therapy (CBT) and yoga and mindfulness, which aim to reduce tension, heart rate, psychological stress and stress behaviour (Granath *et al.* 2006; McCaille *et al.* 2006).

Mindfulness has recently been found to be effective in reducing stress in specific illnesses, such as cancer (Labelle *et al.* 2015), type II diabetes (Rosenzweig *et al.* 2007) and pain from tension headaches (Omidi and Zargar 2014).

Core values

A series of core values underpin the aim and delivery of psychosocial interventions (Davis *et al.* 2006). A number of technical skills relate to the effective administration and delivery of interventions based on behavioural, interpersonal and cognitive–behavioural models. These skills ensure that practitioners delivering an intervention adhere to the fidelity of the particular model that underpins it.

The core values of respect, empathy and collaboration are the foundations from which technical skills are delivered. They work as a guide for practitioners, because they can shape delivery. Failure to consider these values can influence outcomes, and the person undergoing the intervention cannot be a passive recipient; they must play an active role in the process. For example, if the delivery of an intervention based on a cognitive–behavioural model is delivered without engagement of the recipient in identifying stress-inducing scenarios, thoughts, emotions and behaviours, then inaccurate scenarios and thoughts may be used to test out the cognitive–behavioural strategies. These situations are likely to have less beneficial outcomes for the recipient than those in which the practitioner and recipient work in partnership to accurately identify stress-inducing scenarios and the sequence of cognitive, emotional, physiological and behavioural responses (Greenberger and Padesky 1995).

EMPATHY

Empathy refers to the level of understanding of another individual's thoughts and feelings. Sayings such as 'seeing the world through another person's eyes' or 'walking five miles in another person's shoes' reflect the notion of the magnitude of understanding required to demonstrate empathy, and acknowledge the process of gaining understanding from other person's perspective. This is the defining characteristic of empathy, as distinguished from sympathy. Demonstrating empathy is another key value that guides the practitioner in the delivery of psychosocial interventions. It facilitates accurate insight into a person's inner world, aids collaborative empiricism, and facilitates planning of suitable and effective psychosocial interventions.

GOAL ACHIEVEMENT

Many psychosocial interventions are based on goal achievement. The process involves engagement, assessment, case formulation, intervention and relapse prevention. Case formulation provides the opportunity to apply a theoretical model to a particular clinical case and to build a picture of an individual based on that model; it becomes the practitioners 'compass' in terms of directing the design and delivery of the intervention (Persons 1989). Within the process, the level of joint understanding that arises is used to collaboratively set a problem and goal statement, from which the intervention is planned.

PERSONAL STRENGTHS

Most psychosocial interventions focus on a person's existing strengths in terms of coping skills and abilities, but some focus on a wider range of strengths such as attitudes, motivation, knowledge and networks of relationships. Carer interventions particularly focus on the combined strengths of different family members. Once identified these strengths are employed to assist in goal and need achievement.

Evidence-based interventions

A closely related principle is that of psychosocial interventions being based on evidence. The last three decades have seen increasing scientific evidence supporting the efficacy of these interventions. Adequately powered, double-blind randomised controlled trials provide the best standard of evidence. The quality of studies varies, but more sophisticated and larger studies have reported on the efficacy of interventions. Most studies use manuals to guide practitioners when delivering the intervention and support uniform application of skills and techniques. Researchers also supervise practitioners to monitor fidelity of skills, techniques and models underpinning the intervention. Thus, researchers protect the internal validity of the study. When studies are comprehensively reported in peer review journals, practitioners in practice can review them and consider application of the intervention. The Cochrane database of systematic reviews is a dynamic source of evidence, comprising randomised controlled trials and key trends within the existing evidence. These and other relevant peer-reviewed journals help practitioners consider the evidence on efficacy, suitability and applicability of a specific intervention. It is their responsibility to update their knowledge with the latest studies and critically appraise them, in terms of outcomes, suitability for use in specific populations, applying the skills and techniques in their own practice. In doing this, practitioners may obtain the same outcomes as those reported. Randomised controlled trials are the best type of study for evaluating cognitive behavioural, behavioural and carer interventions. Consistent with the principles of experimental designs, they incorporate measurable factors such as number of sessions, time of sessions, and specific objective and uniform techniques. Less systematic and uniformly applied interventions are inconsistent with these principles, as evidenced by case studies.

Interventions for engaging carers and the family

Interventions for carers are another defining principle of psychosocial interventions. Mental health support for families and carers is prioritised in recognition of the key role they have in supporting individuals receiving mental health treatment. It has been estimated that having a family member as a carer of someone diagnosed with schizophrenia has enormous savings for tax payers – amounting to £1.24 billion per year (Schizophrenia Commission 2012). Carers have active roles in the recovery process and often support treatment aims and goals. Support for carers, including providing information and training them in problem-solving skills, contribute to the achievement of goals and help reduce relapses. There is strong evidence that families and carers adopt maladaptive coping mechanisms in response to the stresses involved in caring for someone with schizophrenia; this can have an adverse effect on the emotional environment, which in turn impacts on the course of relapses (Barrowclough and Hooley 2003).

Psychosocial interventions based on goal-setting, communication training, problem-solving and stress management have proved value in engaging families and carers in the collaborative process, improving their problem-solving abilities, and goal achievement, with the wider effect of preventing hospitalisation, reducing relapses and improving family functioning. Multiple family interventions have been successful in achieving the same goals. Some are helpful to educational organisations in terms of engaging families and carers in supporting specific educational strategies. These family interventions are behavioural, based on the principles of social learning theory, and with the aim of changing the behaviour of the family members through coaching to develop communication and problem-solving skills (Falloon *et al.* 1993). Other interventions are based on cognitive behavioural theory, and aim to alter the attributions of family members – their ability to manage and control behaviour through provision and collaborative testing of concrete evidence arising from goal-setting, constructive problem solving and stress management (Barrowclough and Tarrier 1997).

SCHOOL-BASED PARENTAL INTERVENTIONS

These issues are relevant in the educational field because young learners live with their families, and families can support their educational aims and goals; specific learning and developmental problems influence the family and the emotional environment and conversely the emotional environment influences the learner's behaviour and progress. There is some evidence of benefit to parental stress levels and children's behaviour when parental training is included within interventions to reduce the symptoms of ADHD (Zwi *et al.* 2011). Behavioural family therapy was found to have no more effect on the symptoms of ADHD than routine treatment (Bjornstad and Montgomery 2004). Other school-based studies have evaluated the effect of parental education as part of a wider package to support learners with learning disabilities. The scope is wide, as illustrated by the following studies:

- Mishna and Muskat (2004) found changes in the attributions of parents regarding the behaviour of the learners; there were changes in the learner's behaviour, but it was not possible to determine whether they were associated with those changed attributions.

- Thomas *et al.* (2014) conducted a review of eight combined school- and family-based interventions reduced the risk of smoking in learners classed as children and adolescents compared to school intervention only.

- Quinn *et al.* (2014) used a multiple family group approach in a combined school and family intervention for parents of sixth-grade learners in the US who were labelled aggressive. Nearly half (48.3%) of the 643 families attended eleven or more sessions, indicating their level of commitment. Factors such as child–parent bond predicted attendance and engagement, and provided evidence of the potential for the involvement of parents in school- and family-based interventions.

- Reinke *et al.* (2008) reviewed the potential of combined school and family interventions as an early intervention to prevent disruptive behaviour. They identified the benefits of separate interventions for both the school environment and the family environment, acknowledging the potential efficacy of combining the interventions for bringing behaviour change in school into the family environment.

Concluding comments

The three key elements of the educational process – leaners, leaders of learning and the learning environment – and the relationships between them are based on verbal and non-verbal interpersonal communication and behaviour, group behaviour, individual behaviours, home–institution relationships, attitudes, social cognition, social influences and affect and emotions. Educational outcomes include psychosocial factors such as increased self-esteem, confidence and improved social and interpersonal skills and communication. Psychosocial theory can be employed to understand the nature of these relationships as well as the factors within each element that influence the education and the well-being of learners and leaders of learning. Evidence also suggests that psychosocial interventions can be used to improve their well-being, mental health and functioning.

Joint working between departments of education, psychology and mental health in higher education institutions will contribute to the development of collaborative training initiatives, and promote the delivery and evaluation of psychosocial interventions within educational organisations. Psychosocial interventions are particularly relevant where stress and stress management contribute to the well-being of learners and the leaders of learning. School-children are likely to live with their families, and families are part of the wider learning environment, and can therefore support the achievement of learning and educational outcomes. A wealth of family and carer intervention is available on communication, information giving and collaborative goal-setting that may be directly applied in educational organisations.

KEY MESSAGES FROM THIS CHAPTER

📄 Psychosocial factors were initially related to mental health theory, but are also relevant to the functioning and behaviour of learners and leaders of learning, and interpersonal aspects of the learning environment.

📄 Psychosocial interventions are non-pharmaceutical interventions based on psychological theory and social theory relating to people in groups and individuals and a combination of both.

📄 There is an emerging, dynamic evidence base in support of psychosocial interventions.

📄 The delivery of psychosocial interventions is based on the core values of empathy and respect.

📄 Stress management and involvement of families and carers are underlying principles of psychosocial interventions.

Supporting evidence and further reading

Allodi MW (2010) Goals and values in school: A model developed for describing, evaluating and changing the social climate of learning environments. *Social Psychology of Education 13*(2), 2070–35.

Almolda-Toma FJ, Sevill-Serano J, Julian-Clemente JA, Aborca-Sos A, Aibar-Solana A, Garcia-Gonzalez L (2014) Application of teaching strategies for improving student's situational motivation in physical education. *Electronic Journal of Research in Educational Psychology* 12(2), 391–417.

Alvarez HK (2008) Teachers thinking about classroom management: The explanatory role of self-reported psychosocial characteristics. *Advances in School Mental Health Promotion* 1(1), 42–54.

Baguley I, Baguley C (1999) Psychosocial interventions in the treatment of psychosis. *Mental Health Care* 2(9), 314–16.

Barrowclough C, Hooley JM (2003) Attributions and expressed emotion: A review. *Clinical Psychology Review* 23(6), 849–80.

Barrowclough C, Tarrier N (1997) *Families of Schizophrenic Patients.* Cheltenham, Stanley Thornes.

Bjornstad GJ, Montgomery P (2004) *Family therapy for attention-deficit disorder or attention-deficit/hyperactivity disorder in children and adolescents.* Cochrane Library. Doi: 10.1002/14651858. CD005042.pub2.

Bogaert I, De Martelaer K, Defarche B, Clarys P, Zinzen E (2015) The physically active lifestyle of Flemish secondary school teachers: A mixed-methods approach towards developing a physical activity intervention. *Health Education Journal* 74(3), 326–39.

Davis E, Velleman R, Smith G, Drage M (2006) Psychosocial developments. Towards a model of recovery. In: R Velleman, E Davis, G Smith, M Drage (eds) *Changing Outcomes in Psychosis.* Oxford: Blackwell.

Dedousis-Wallace A, Shute R, Varlow M, Murrihy R, Kidman T (2014) Predictors of teacher intervention in indirect bullying at school and outcomes of a professional development for teachers. *Educational Psychology* 34(7), 862–75.

Falloon IRH, Laporta M, Fadden G and Victor-Hole G (1993) *Managing Stress in Families: Cognitive and Behavioural Strategies for Enhancing Coping Skills.* New York: Routledge.

Falvo DR (2014) *Medical and Psychosocial Aspects of Chronic Illness and Disability* (5th edn). Burlington, Jones & Bartlett Learning.

Fleming M, Savage-Grainge AP, Martin CR, Hill C, Brown S, Miles JNV (2008) The role of intrinsic factors in the implementation of psychosocial interventions into routine clinical practice. *Journal of Mental Health Training, Education and Practice* 3(2), 32–41.

Fleming M, Martin CR (2012) From classical psychodynamics to evidence synthesis; the motif of repression and a contemporary understanding of a key mediatory mechanism in psychosis. *Current Psychiatry Reports* 14(3), 252–58.

Flook L, Goldberg SB, Pinger L, Bonus K, Davidson RJ (2013) Mindfulness for teachers: A pilot study to assess the effects on stress, burnout and teacher efficacy. *Mind Brain and Education* 7(3), 182–95.

Foxcroft DR, Tsertsvadze A (2011) Universal school-based prevention programmes for alcohol misuse in young people. *Cochrane Library* Doi: 10.1002/14651858. CD009113.

Granath J, Ingvarsson S, von Thiele U, Lundberg U (2006) Stress management: A randomised study of cognitive behavioural therapy and yoga. *Cognitive Behaviour Therapy* 35(1), 3–10.

Greenberger D, Padesky, C (1995) *Mind Over Mood: Change How You Feel by Changing the Way You Think.* New York: Guildford Press.

Heyne DA, Sauter FM, Ollendick TH, Van Widenfelt BM, Westenberg PM (2014) Developmentally sensitive cognitive behavioral therapy for adolescent school refusal: Rationale and case illustration. *Clinical Child and Family Psychology Review* 17(2), 191–215.

Jordans MJD, Komproe IH, Tol WA *et al.* (2010) Evaluation of a classroom-based psychosocial intervention in conflict-affected Nepal: A cluster randomised controlled trial. *Journal of Clinical Psychology* and Psychiatry 51(7), 818–26.

Jing L (2008) Faculty's job stress and performance in the undergraduate educational assessment in China: A mixed-method study. *Educational Research and Review* 3(9), 294–300.

Labelle LE, Campbell TS, Faris P, Carlson LE (2015) Mediators of mindfulness-based stress reduction (MBSR): Assessing the timing and sequence of change in cancer patients. *Journal of Clinical Psychology* 71(1), 21–40.

Lipp A (2011) Universal school-based prevention programmes for alcohol misuse in young people. *Journal of Evidence Based Healthcare* 9(4), 452–453.

Maric M, Heyne DA, MacKinnon DP, van Widenfelt BM, Westenberg M (2013) Cognitive mediation of cognitive–behaviour therapy outcomes for anxiety-based school refusal. *Behavioural and Cognitive Psychotherapy* 41(5), 549–64.

McCaille MS, Blum CM, Hood CJ (2006) Progressive muscle relaxation. *Journal of Human Behaviour in the Social Environment* 13(3), 51–66.

McKenna AE, Cassidy T, Giles, M (2014) Prospective evaluation of the pyramid plus intervention for shy withdrawn children: An assessment of efficacy in 7-to-8 year old school-children in Northern Ireland. *Child & Adolescent Mental Health* 19(1), 9–15.

McWhirter J, McCann D, Coleman H, Calvert M, Warner J (2008) Can school promote the health of children with asthma? *Health Education Research* 23(6), 917–30.

Mishna F, Muskat B (2004) School-based group treatment for students with learning disabilities: A collaborative approach. *Children & Schools* 26(3), 135–50.

Nicholson I, Neufeld W (1992) A dynamic vulnerability perspective on stress and psychosis. *American Journal of Orthopsychiatry* 62(1), 117–29.

Nuchterlein KH, Dawson ME (1984) A heuristic vulnerability/stress model of schizophrenic episodes. *Schizophrenia Bulletin* 10, 300–12.

Omidi A, Zargar F (2014) Effect of mindfulness-based stress reduction on pain severity and mindful awareness in patients with tension headache: A randomised controlled clinical trial. *Nursing and Midwifery Studies* 3(3), 1–5.

Persons J B (1989) *Cognitive Therapy in Practice: A Case Formulation Approach.* New York: Norton & Company.

Piwowar V, Thiel F, Ophardt D (2013) Training in-service teachers' competencies in classroom management: A quasi-experimental study with teachers of secondary schools. *Teaching and Teacher Education: An International Journal of Research and Studies* 30, 1–12.

Quinn WH, Hall DB, Smith EP, Rabiner D (2014) Predictors of family participation in a multiple family group intervention for aggressive middle school students. *Journal of Community Psychology* 38(2), 227–44.

Reinke WM, Splett JD, Robeson EN, Offutt CA (2008) Combining school and family interventions for the prevention and early intervention of disruptive behaviour problems in children: A public health perspective. *Psychology in the Schools* 46(1), 34–43.

Reinke WM, Stormont M, Herman KC, Newcomer L (2014) Using coaching to support teacher implementation of classroom-based interventions. *Journal of Behavioural Interventions* 23(1), 150–67.

Rosenzweig S, Reibel DK, Greeson JM *et al.* (2007) Mindfulness-based stress reduction is associated with improved glycaemic control in type 2 diabetes mellitus: A pilot study. *Alternative Therapies* 13(5), 36–38.

Schultz BK, Storer J, Watabe Y, Sadler J, Evans SW (2011) School-based treatment of attention deficit/hyperactivity disorder. *Psychology in the Schools* 48(3), 254–62.

Smith PR (2013) Psychosocial learning environments and the mediating effects of personal meaning upon satisfaction with learning. *Learning Environments Research* 16(2), 259–80.

Thomas GP, Anderson D (2014) Changing the metacognition orientation of a classroom environment to enhance students metacognition regarding chemistry learning. *Learning Environments Research* 17(1), 139–55.

Thomas RE, McLellan J, Perera R (2014) Schools-based programme for preventing smoking. *Cochrane Database of Systematic Reviews* 2013; 4:CD001293.

Thompson, D (2007) Psychosocial interventions in cardiovascular nursing. *European Journal of* Cardiovascular Nursing 6(3), 165–66.

Tresco KE, Lefler EK, Power TJ (2010) Psychosocial interventions to improve the school performance of students with attention-deficit/hyperactivity disorder. *Mind Brain* 1(2), 69–74.

Yank GR, Bentley KJ, Hargrove DS (1993) The vulnerability–stress model of schizophrenia: Advances in psychosocial treatment. *American Journal of Orthopsychiatry* 63(1), 55–69.

Waghorn J (2009) Depression in chronic medical illness. *Mental Health Practice* 12(9), 16–20.

Whitley J, Smith DJ, Vallancourt T (2013) Promoting mental health literacy among educators: Critical in school-based prevention and intervention. *Canadian Journal of School Psychology* 28(1), 56–70.

Zwi M, Jones H, Thorgaard C, York A, Dennis JA (2011) Parent training interventions for attention deficit hyperactivity disorder in children aged 5–8 years. *Cochrane Library.* Doi: 10.1002/14651858. CD003018.pub3.

Zubin J, Spring B (1977) Vulnerability-A new view of schizophrenia. *Journal of Abnormal Psychology* 86(2), 103-126.

CHAPTER 25

Mindfulness

David McMurtry and Graeme Nixon

In this chapter, the authors introduce the concept of mindfulness in education. An initial introduction to mindfulness and its origins as a secular approach to health and well-being is followed by a consideration of the broad educational context and the challenges and opportunities associated with introducing mindfulness into education. Mindfulness is then considered as a means to enhance both well-being and learning. The chapter concludes with a consideration of the potential benefits of mindfulness for learners and leaders of learning. In helping us to let go of the often mindless and restless striving that lies at the heart of our mental processes and habit-driven behaviour, mindfulness prepares the way for genuinely rich and deep learning and the journey from self-obsession to a fuller engagement with life and with others. There can be few worthier educational ideals (Hyland 2009).

Mindfulness is the capacity for observing our thoughts and experiences moment by moment, without judgement or preference, and with an attitude of kindness, curiosity and openness (Kabat-Zinn 2002). It is becoming an established technique in all sorts of professional and life settings, including education. Improving the health and well-being of children and young people is also a growing part of educational policy. In the face of recommendations and evidence, governments are developing educational programmes and curricula that increasingly focus on the well-being of school-children, giving schools and teachers a central role. In the UK, there are a several initiatives aimed at introducing mindfulness to young people. The benefits of mindfulness affect mental, emotional, social and physical health, touching on stress, behaviour, sleep patterns, metacognition and self-image. It has positive effects on thinking and attentional skills, as well as creativity and memory (Keare 2012). These benefits are clearly of relevance to teachers and students, and while research is ongoing in this area, samples sizes are small and standardised measures still need to be developed.

The emergence of mindfulness

Before discussing the benefits of introducing mindfulness to teachers and school-children, it may be helpful to say a little more about the emergence of mindfulness and the nature and origins of this practice. It is widely acknowledged that Jon Kabat-Zinn, a long-term meditator, is largely responsible for the process by which secular mindfulness meditation became established in the West as a contemporary practice and therapy. Working within the University of Massachusetts, Kabat-Zinn was interested in the potential of mindfulness for alleviating stress and contributing to holistic healing processes. In 1979 he developed an eight-week course known as Mindfulness-Based Stress Reduction (MBSR). MBSR is a group programme in which participants undergo a number of mindfulness 'practices'. The sessions allow them to observe physical experience, perceptions, emotions, thinking and images in a non-evaluative way, thereby creating a sense of distance and space from mental and physical phenomena, which in turn gives rise to a more responsive, compassionate and accepting perspective on experience. Such ingredients are core to the range of mindfulness-based approaches that have emerged in subsequent years.

THE ROLE OF BUDDHISM

It is necessary to stress the influence of Buddhism in a historical sense as a primary originator of the mindfulness approach. Mindfulness has recently emerged, however, as a secular approach to meditative practice, with no reference to metaphysical, enchanted or supernatural beliefs. Given the (often unreflective) antipathy to 'religion' in increasingly secular developed countries, this is perhaps worth emphasising. Interestingly, such antipathy is not directed towards Buddhism, as shown by the range of Buddhist images in places as diverse as garden centres and restaurants. Reasons for this apparent immunity to antireligious sentiment may lie in its philosophically pragmatic, non-theistic approach, and in its appeal to individual experience rather than any institutional or theistic hegemony (Bruce 2002). Having said that, mindfulness simply involves paying attention to our experiences without judgement, and although this is something that happens to be found in a range of spiritual and mystical traditions, it is more of an interesting coincidence rather than causal significance.

THE NATURE OF MINDFULNESS

Another common assumption about mindfulness is that it is about somehow stopping thought, and settling the mind. Mindfulness is instead about acknowledging the unsettled nature of our minds and simply observing its behaviour without 'buying in' to the various storylines, ruminative tendencies and habitual patterns. Attempting to stop the flow of thoughts is a little like trying to dam a river – impossible and dangerous; it is better to watch the flow, to recognise the patterns of the currents, and avoid falling in quite so much!

FROM MINDFULNESS-BASED STRESS REDUCTION TO MINDFULNESS-BASED COGNITIVE THERAPY

During the 1980s, Kabat-Zinn's MBSR programme yielded promising results relating to stress, and it was broadened to include people suffering from a range of conditions – terminal illness, chronic pain, anxiety disorders, autoimmune disorders and drug addiction (Grossman 2004). In the 1990s, interest in the success of MBSR led to the development of Mindfulness-Based Cognitive Therapy (MBCT), which focuses on mindfulness as a means of developing psychological resilience among people who suffer from depressive relapses (Williams *et al.* 2007). MBCT aims to develop metacognition and acceptance relating to ruminative patterns of thought, thereby producing a degree of cognitive and emotional control. Positive results led MBCT to be adopted as a recognised treatment by the NHS (National Institute for Clinical Excellence 2009).

EXPANDING ROLES OF MINDFULNESS

Mindfulness is a burgeoning field with mindful-based programmes or approaches including dialectical behaviour therapy, acceptance and commitment therapy, mindfulness-based eating, and mindfulness-based parenting. A corollary of the growth of mindfulness approaches is the emergence of postgraduate programmes in mindfulness in a number of British universities.

The universities of Oxford, Bangor, Exeter and Aberdeen offer courses mindfulness and its theoretical underpinnings. In the main, these flow from the clinical genesis of secular mindfulness (principally based on MBCT), but the MSc courses at Bangor and Aberdeen also offer students the chance to study the potential of applying mindfulness to a range of personal and professional contexts. This reflects the fact that mindfulness is now being applied to fields as diverse as sports coaching, business management and education. It is to this latter application that we now turn.

Mindfulness in education: Contemporary context

Contextual factors have a significant bearing on the relevance and impact of mindfulness within and on learning and teaching. Within a contemporary context, education systems are being transformed in countries like China, Slovenia, Croatia, Scotland, England and Singapore. Educators, of course, face multiple challenges. Developments in information technology, particularly the internet, mean that teachers no longer have a monopoly on knowledge; it can be accessed by anyone, anywhere, at any time. Technology is also transforming how, where and when we learn, yet many learners are not able to fully reap the benefits and potential of new technologies within school, resulting in inequalities and a perception that much of the learning in school is outmoded or irrelevant.

At a time when attainment standards and expected educational outcomes were being raised, the global economic downturn in the 2010s meant that many institutions had to do more – with significantly fewer resources. In 2000, the European Commission agreed benchmarks for educational achievement. These included better literacy, fewer early school-leavers, and proficiency of all students in at least two languages. Yet, in 2006 limited progress was reported and member states and educators were encouraged to 'redouble efforts', to 'increase the efficiency of investment', and to create new initiatives (Commission of the European Communities 2006).

In response to these challenges and opportunities, educators and policy-makers began reforming their education systems and practice – devising new curricula, revisiting pedagogy and enhancing the culture of schools as learning communities (for examples, see Organisation for Economic Co-operation and Development; Executive Agency Education, Audiovisual and Culture). The roles and professional identities of teachers are changing as a consequence of, and in response to, such developments in education. New ways of working bring with them professional opportunities, as well as challenging issues.

Until relatively recently, due to its individual nature and contextual complexity, it has not been possible to say much with certainty about the learning process. However, there is a growing consistency of opinion about the nature of intelligence and the key elements of successful learning, pertaining to most learners and most learning contexts. Evidence is drawn from several sources – neurology, psychology, pedagogy, longitudinal studies and professional practice and experience. Many educationalists have identified the character-istics of intelligence, of successful learning and of effective teaching (see for example Bransford *et al.* 2000, Brown *et al.* 1996, Claxton 2001, 2007, Costa and Kallick 2007 and Perkins 2009). Lucas and Claxton (2010) link what they argue are the characteristics of intelligence and learning (see FIGURE 25.1).

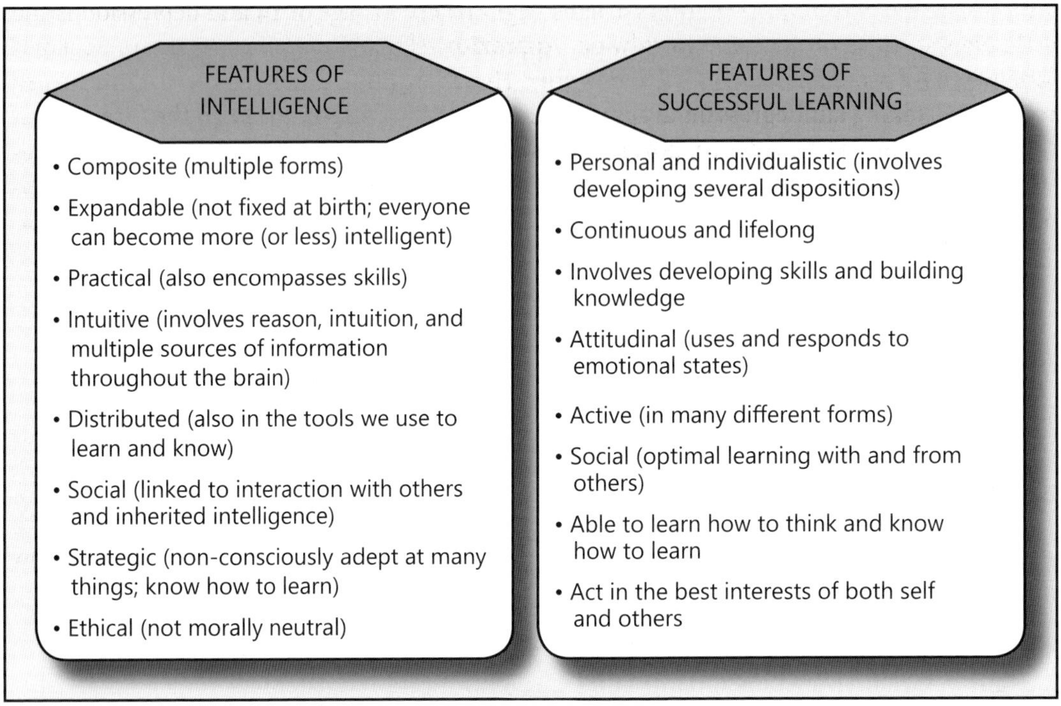

Figure 25.1: Features of intelligence and successful learning (adapted from Lucas and Claxton 2010).

The relevance of mindfulness in learning and teaching, and receptivity towards it is informed by (perhaps even determined by) the contemporary context in which learning and teaching occurs. This is so in a number of ways. For it to be valued by the individuals, the wider educational community and culture, it has to be in harmony with the aims and objectives of those involved, including learners, carers, educators and policy-makers. To what extent do the perceived benefits of mindfulness contribute to the successful implementation of policy objectives and priorities? Does it lead to better learning, higher attainment and happier, more fulfilled people? Mindfulness ought to enhance or ameliorate contextual and environmental influences and effects on individual people and communities. It should help teachers engage with learners more effectively or to deal better with stress. It should enable learners to focus more. For it to be a sustainable aspect of learning and teaching it must contribute to and enhance strategies for learning, and make a positive contribution to what we know about intelligence, to effective teaching and to successful learning. Does mindfulness enhance social skills? Are mindful people more mindful?

Mindfulness, well-being and learning

Improving the health and well-being of young people is an increasingly important part of educational policy. International guidance, such as that from the World Health Organization (WHO), suggest that poor mental health correlates closely with poor physical health and that there is a pressing need to address mental health problems and related issues such as stigmatisation and the human rights of people with mental illnesses (WHO 2012). According to WHO, over half of mental health problems begin before the age of 14 and depression is the single biggest cause of disability worldwide. Approximately 20% of young people in Scotland alone will have a mental health problem (Public Health Institute of Scotland 2003) leading to around 14% taking antidepressant drugs in adulthood (ISD Scotland 2012). In the face of such recommendations and evidence, governments are developing educational programmes and curricula that increasingly focus on this issue, giving schools and teachers a central role in its development. Arguably education has taken a 'therapeutic turn' (Hyland 2009), recognising that the aims of education and therapy are to:

> *... involve the development of knowledge, values, emotions, understanding, reason, skill, experience and insight [that] are equally necessary for accessing work, social relationships and the wider communities of practice that constitute the good life.*

It is recognised that not only is there 'no health without mental health' (WHO 2010) but that good mental health is essential for participating and flourishing within society (Lyubomirsky *et al.* 2005). Within the *Curriculum for Excellence* in Scotland (Education Scotland 2013), health and well-being is an area of responsibility for all teachers. The main purpose is to allow children and young people to:

- Make informed decisions in order to improve their mental, emotional, social and physical well-being.
- Experience challenge and enjoyment.
- Experience positive aspects of healthy living and activity for themselves.
- Apply their mental, emotional, social and physical skills to pursue a healthy lifestyle.
- Make a successful move to the next stage of education or work.
- Establish a pattern of health and well-being that will be sustained into adult life and help to promote the health and well-being of the next generation.

These objectives show a clear recognition of the foundational nature of mental health. The outcomes specify, for example, that young people should develop the abilities to articulate their emotions and thoughts; recognise the variety of thoughts they have; acknowledge that their well-being can depend on internal and external factors; and develop lifelong skills and strategies for good mental health. These aims correlate closely with the qualities developed by mindful awareness, whereby learners are encouraged to recognise thoughts and emotions. Discussions about these experiences that can follow mindfulness practice are a powerful way to bring about such aspirations.

In the UK, an increasing numbers of initiatives aim to introduce mindfulness to young people. Two examples are the Mindfulness in Schools Project (MISP) and Be the Change. Both have developed materials and inputs for introducing teachers and school-children to mindfulness attentional training. At the time of writing, over 200 teachers in the UK have been trained, and a suite of mindfulness curricula have been developed for primary and secondary schools and adult learners. Working in association with the MISP, Keare (2012) summarised two systematic reviews and twenty other studies of mindfulness-based approaches in children of various ages at school and in clinical and community contexts.

The study concluded that mindfulness:

- Is a cost-effective, accessible and enjoyable intervention.
- Is beneficial for mental, emotional, social and physical health, and stress, behaviour, sleep patterns, metacognition and self-image.
- Has positive effects on thinking, attentional skills, creativity and memory.
- Improves blood flow to areas of the brain associated with attention, emotion, self-awareness and compassion.
- Has positive effects on children with attentional and behavioural problems, enhancing sustained attention and self-regulation.

Brown, Ryan and Cresswell (2007) examined evidence from empirical and clinical studies including trait measures, psychometric tests, randomised clinical trials, self-report co-relational research and brain scans, and highlighted various cognitive and affective indicators of mental health and well-being that are positively linked to mindfulness. They also reported reductions in psychopathological symptoms. The changes they noted include:

- Lower levels of depression or anxiety and an increased ability to self-prevent relapses.
- Higher levels of subjective well-being (e.g. increased satisfaction with life).
- Higher levels of eudamonic well-being (e.g. more vitality and enhanced self-actualisation).
- Stronger affect regulatory tendencies (e.g. greater acceptance of emotions and improved ability to change unpleasant mood states).
- Less reactivity and emotional volatility.
- Faster recovery from negative emotional states.
- Reduced burnout.

Brown *et al.* (2007) state that:

The receptively observant processing of internal and external information that characterizes mindfulness, facilitates the healthy regulation of action through the provision of choice that is informed by abiding needs, values, and feelings and their fit with situational options and demands.

In other words, practitioners of mindfulness, it is claimed, make choices that are more appropriate for themselves, for others, and for the contexts in which they are situated. The 'observant stance, perceptual flexibility and relative freedom from conceptualisation' that characterise mindfulness when practised over time, result in a de-centred perspective that may have positive behavioural and psychological consequences. These include less habitual thought patterning (such as rumination and obsession), a willingness to be with and observe unpleasant thoughts and emotions, and greater choice in behaviour:

Thoughts become 'just thoughts', feelings 'just feelings' rather than necessarily accurate reflections of reality'. (Brown et al. 2007)

These benefits are clearly of relevance to both teachers and students. Stress and being overwhelmed by demands that are perceived to be beyond their control are common causes of teacher and student ill health and lack of well-being. Stress can lead to the breakdown of relationships and a failure to learn and flourish, thus being able to make informed choices and engage in more effective and sustained action is key to health and well-being, and effective teaching and successful learning. Schoeberlein (2009) discusses ways in which being mindful can have a positive influence on teachers and teaching, and learners and learning. It has the potential to develop or enhance a wide range of skills, attributes and dispositions. In schools, it involves explicit activities as well as implicit ways of acting, behaving and being. According to Schoeberlein (2009), mindful teachers:

- Are self-aware.
- Are attuned to their students.
- Are compassionate and empathetic.
- Are inclined towards healthy relationships.
- Have greater perspective.
- Have an enhanced sense of choice.
- Model desirable qualities, characteristics and dispositions.

Napoli (2004) reported that a small group of teachers who undertook a mindfulness training programme used mindfulness to great benefit as an aspect of the curriculum, using it as a tool to deal with anxiety and conflict in the classroom, and to make changes in the classroom as well as in their personal lives. Meiklejohn *et al.* (2012) reported that:

School-based mindfulness training appears to offer a means for students to cultivate attentional skills [and] other aptitudes that may enhance their capacity to cope with their psychosocial as well as academic challenges.

They list several potential benefits:

- It encourages 'pro-social behaviour' by strengthening self-regulation and control of impulses.
- It alleviates the effects of stress that impact negatively on learning.
- It provides skills that promote 'brain hygiene' and physical and emotional well-being for life.

HOW MIGHT PUPILS LEARN AND ENGAGE IN MINDFULNESS IN THE CLASSROOM?

There are a number of initiatives that encourage sustained practice of mindfulness among school-children. Common techniques include using a support such as the sound of breathing, counting and body awareness to remain mindfully aware of the present and gently return to full awareness when the mind wanders, making use of techniques such as mindful walking, visualisations, and the body scan. Ritchhart and Perkins (2000) argue that:

It is not enough to simply overlay a series of discrete instructional practices on teachers' existing repertoires.

Practice of mindfulness in the classroom must not only be meaningful but should also deeply engage the students and teachers, and it:

... must be more than a set of instructional techniques. It must take hold in classrooms in ways that permeate the lives of both students and teachers. Only by developing a disposition toward mindfulness can we alter substantially the educational landscape of students.

Mindfulness can be enhanced through direct and explicit practices, and indirectly through activities that implicitly aim to increase awareness of the present. This is the case with many other classroom approaches to learning. Ritchhart and Perkins (2000), propose three 'high-leverage practices that can be used in developing students' sensitivity, inclination and ability with regard to mindfulness'. These are:

- Seeing and being open to new information or adopting a 'beginner's mind' as described in Zen Buddhism.

- Exploring possibilities and perspectives, and ways of seeing and being.

- Introducing ambiguity and viewing knowledge as something conditional that is gained through autonomous activity (rather than passively).

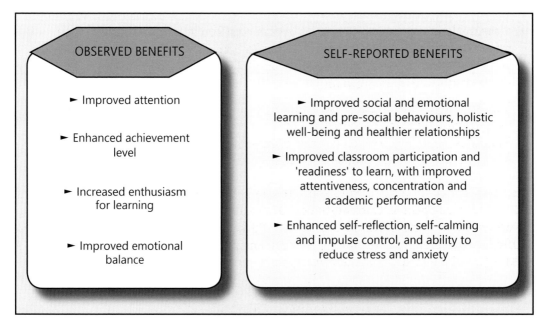

Figure 25.2: Benefits of mindfulness among students (adapted from Napoli 2004).

Langer (1993) has brought a broad understanding of the relevance of mindfulness to education. She argues that mindfulness has the potential to radically change certain ideas about what learning involves, to develop practice and to contribute to our understanding of (and justification for) practice and policy. She agrees that mindfulness allows practitioners to see:

> ... any situation or environment from several perspectives ... there is not a single optimal perspective, but many possible perspectives on the same situation.

Four key arguments made by Langer (1997) are based on observations and evidence drawn from psychological research, and can be summarised as follows:

- Teachers and schools often encourage learning by rote – unthinking learning – but with mindful, conscious learning, students access their own strengths and weaknesses and apply them in different contexts. Learning and remembering information mindfully allows that information to be used sensitively; when accepted without awareness or unquestioningly, information is often de-contextualised and has limited utility.

- Focusing or paying attention involves being able to change context and seek variety. When we are distracted it is because we are thinking about something else! Traditional schooling often forces students to concentrate to little effect or benefit. Mindfulness, however, can lead to a more focused mind as well as a joyful and creative engagement with a variety of stimuli to learning. Langer (1997) uses the term 'soft vigilance' to describe a mindset that is focused and also open to noticing and novelty. She also suggests that in addition to giving drug therapy to pupils with ADHD), the perspective should shift to understanding the role of context and variety in maintaining attention. Varying perspective mindfully (rather than mindlessly) may be more effective for many learners.

- Pleasurable engagement is a critical feature of effective learning, but teachers and schools often base learning on delayed gratification, along the lines of 'Learn this and you'll get good grades and a good job'. Mindfulness brings pleasure to learning and intrinsic motivation and reward.

- Valuing mindfulness and present-moment attention changes how problems are viewed and solved, and encourages people to step back from their perceived problems Situations are more likely to be seen as novel and of interest rather than part of a linear process which the problem-solver aims to move through as quickly as possible.

Some caveats should be mentioned about research into mindfulness and introducing it to children and young people. Current studies have small numbers of participants, and outcome measures need to be standardised. Saying that, Burke (2010) reviewed fifteen papers on the mindfulness-based approaches among children and adolescents, focusing mainly on MBSR and MBCT, and concluded that there was:

A reasonable base of support for the feasibility and acceptability of mindfulness meditation practices with children and young adults.

However, Burke noted the lack of empirical evidence on efficacy of the interventions, as well as the use of weak methodology and design of the studies, and an over-reliance on self-reporting. There are broader ethical issues in introducing mindfulness to young people relating to voluntarism and inadequate delivery. Introducing practices, for example, from mindfulness-based cognitive therapy may be problematic for certain vulnerable children. If it is used in a clumsy manner, it can encourage rumination, self-attack, and low mood; telling children to try to silence their thoughts can be counter-productive (and impossible), leading to a sense of failure and low self-esteem. This is, of course, an incorrect application of mindfulness which should be about accepting a thought as it arises rather than attempting to subjugate it.

Lees' concept of silence

Mindfulness, meditation, 'stilling' and 'pausing' are being used increasingly in schools. Lees (2012) offers a range of evidence for this, and a lexicon by which we can distinguish the various forms 'silence' can take in schools. She argues for the currency of, and appetite for, silence, referring to social theory as well as case studies in schools to suggest that there is a pressing need in such a stimulating (some would say toxic) social climate for childhood, to have some form of pause or silence (Palmer 2006; Williams and Penman 2011). Lees describes mindfulness as a form of 'techniqued' silence. However, any teacher considering the use of this approach should properly understand the aims of mindfulness, and have their own experiential grounding in its practice. Lees (2012) provides evidence that mindfulness is an effective way to democratise learning, as a means:

... for children to appreciate their own natural inner resources in a world of mainly media-driven externalising tendencies of the self.

In the modern 'sociotechnological panopticon', mindfulness provides an intimate freedom – a seed-bed for original thought, a means to develop respect for others with whom we publicly are silent and to develop an empathetic awareness of the internal experiences of others, and thus a more intimate knowledge of our own. In the face of government policy that appears to encourage discussion, collaboration and successful contributions in education, it could be argued that mindfulness is necessary to accommodate young people for whom such modes of learning and expression are not best fits. More broadly there is a cultural climate whereby noise is privileged over silence, particularly evident in the perpetual audience of social media. Children are continually forced to consider how they exist in the minds of others, when there is instead a need for them to rest in, and appreciate, their own experiences.

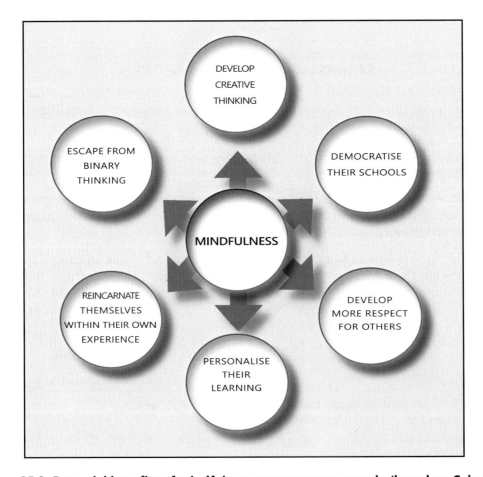

Figure 25.3: Potential benefits of mindfulness among young people (based on Cain 2011).

Cain (2011) believes that there is a tyranny of group work and social collaboration in education that ignores the right to individual counsel and silence. Perhaps it is not only introverts that are sidelined in contemporary education. Arguably, the very possibility of introspection and space for creative engagement with ourselves lacks emphasis and is under-valued. Mindfulness is thought to present three key benefits for young people. It allows them to:

- Escape from binary thinking and develop more creativity.
- Democratise their schools, personalise their learning and develop more respect for others.
- 'Re-incarnate' themselves within their own experience.

Concluding comments

Mindfulness encourages learners and teachers to become students of themselves, and provides a powerful means for schools to develop genuine metacognition. Mindfulness nurtures spaciousness and enables rational autonomy. It dissolves dichotomous thinking, develops trust, respect and sensitivity and heightens powers of observation and attention. It also develops clarity of thought and ultimately leads to improved academic performance.

KEY MESSAGES FROM THIS CHAPTER

📄 Mindfulness encourages people to observe their thoughts and experiences moment by moment, without judgement or preference, and with an attitude of kindness, curiosity and openness (Kabat-Zinn 2002).

📄 Mindfulness is becoming an established technique in all sorts of professional and life settings, including learning and teaching environments.

📄 The relevance of mindfulness in learning and teaching – and receptivity towards it – is informed by (and possibly determined by) the contemporary context in which learning and teaching occurs.

📄 Within the outcomes and experiences for health and well-being' in many school curricula, there is a clear recognition of the foundational nature of mental health. The outcomes of 'emotional and mental well-being' include allowing young people to develop their ability to articulate their emotions and thoughts and recognise the variety of thoughts they have, to acknowledge that their well-being relates both internal and external factors, and develop lifelong skills and strategies for good mental health.

📄 The benefits of mindfulness practice are clearly and obviously of relevance to teachers and students. Stress and being overwhelmed by demands that are perceived to be beyond their control, commonly lead to ill health among teachers and students, to the breakdown of effective relationships and failure to learn.

Using mindfulness to increase awareness of the present is an element of many classroom approaches to learning (Ritchhart and Perkins 2000).

Online resources

- Be Mindful
  www.bemindful.co.uk/about–mindfulness/

- Be the Change
  www.be-the-change.org/

- Ten facts on mental health: World Health Organisation
  www.who.int/features/factfiles/mental_health/mental_health_facts/en/index9.html /

- Executive Agency Education, Audiovisual and Culture
  www.eacea.ec.europa.eu/education/eurydice/

- Mindfulness in Schools Project (MISP)
  www.mindfulnessinschools.org/

- Organisation for Economic Co-operation and Development
  www.oecd.org/pisa/pisaproducts/46581016.pdf

Supporting evidence and further reading

Bransford J, Brown A, Cocking R (eds) (2000) *How People Learn. Brain Mind Experience and School.* Washington: National Academy Press.

Brown A, Metz K, Campione J (1996) Social Interaction and Individual Understanding in a Community of Learners: The Influence of Piaget and Vygotsky. In: Tryphon A, Voneche J. (eds) Piaget-Vygotsky: *The Social Genesis of Thought.* Hove: Psychology Press.

Brown KW, Ryan RM, Creswell JD (2007) Mindfulness: theoretical foundations and evidence for its salutary effects. *Psychological Inquiry* 18(4):211–37.

Bruce S (2002) *God is Dead: Secularization in the West (Religion in the Modern World).* Oxford: Blackwell.

Burke C (2010) Mindfulness-based approaches with children and adolescents: a preliminary review of current research in an emergent field. *Journal of Child and Family Studies* 19, 133–44.

Cain S (2011) *Quiet: The Power of Introverts in a World that Can't Stop Talking.* London: Penguin

Claxton G (2001) *Wise Up: The Challenge of Lifelong Learning.* Stafford: Network Educational Press.

Claxton G (2007) Expanding young people's capacity to learn. *British Journal of Educational Studies* 55(2), 134.

Commission of the European Communities (2006) *Commission Staff Working Document Towards The Lisbon Objectives in Education and Training. Report Based on Indicators and Benchmarks.* Brussels. Available at: ec.europa.eu/education/policies/2010/doc/progressreport06.pdf (accessed July 2015).

Costa A, Kallick B (2007) *Describing 16 habits of mind.* Available at: ftp://download.intel.co.jp/education/Common/au/Resources/EO/Course_Resources/Thinking/Habits_of_Mind.pdf (accessed July 2015).

Education Scotland (2013) *Principles and practice: Health and well-being.* Available at: www.educationscotland.gov.uk/learningteachingandassessment/curriculumareas/healthandwell-being/principlesandpractice/index.asp (accessed July 2015).

Grossman J (2004) Mindfulness-based stress reduction and health benefits: a meta-analysis,. *Journal of Psychosomatic Research* 57(1), 35–43.

Holyoak K, Morrison R. (2005) *The Cambridge Handbook of Thinking and Reasoning.* Cambridge: Cambridge University Press.

Hyland T (2009) Mindfulness and the therapeutic function of education. *Journal of Philosophy of Education* 43(1), 119–31.

ISD Scotland (2012) *Prescribing and Medicines: Medicines for Mental Health.* National Health Services Scotland.

Kabat-Zinn J (2002) Commentary on Majumdar *et al.* Mindfulness Meditation for Health. *Journal of Alternative and Complementary Medicine* (8(6), 731–35.

Keare K (2012) *Evidence for the Impact of Mindfulness on Children and Young People.* Exeter: Mindfulness in Schools Project/University of Exeter Moods Disorder Centre.

Langer E (1993) *A mindful education. Educational Psychologist* 28(1),43–50.

Langer E (1997) *The Power of Mindful Learning.* Cambridge, MA: Da Capo Press.

Lees HE (2012) *Silence in Schools.* London: Trentham.

Lucas B, Claxton G (2010) *New Kinds of Smart. How The Science of Learnable Intelligence is Changing Education.* Maidenhead: Open University Press/McGraw Hill.

Lyubomirsky S, King L, Diener E (2005) The Benefits Of Frequent Positive Affect: Does Happiness Lead To Success? *Psychological Bulletin* 131(6), 803–55.

Meiklejohn J, Freedman M, Griffin M *et al.* (2012) Integrating mindfulness training into K-12 education: fostering the resilience of teachers and students. *Mindfulness* 3, 291–307.

Napoli M (2004) Mindfulness training for teachers: a pilot program. *Complementary Health Practice Review* 9(1), 31–42.

National Institute For Health and Clinical Excellence (2009) *Depression: The Treatment and Management of Depression in Adults.* London: NHS.

Palmer S (2006) *Toxic Childhood How the Modern World is Damaging our Children.* London: Orion.

Perkins D (2009) *Making Learning Whole. How Seven Principles of Teaching Can Transform Education.* San Francisco, CA: Jossey Bass.

Public Health Institute of Scotland (2003) Needs Assessment Report on *Child and Adolescent Mental Health.* Edinburgh: National Health Services, Scotland.

Ritchhart R, Perkins D (2000) Life in the mindful classroom: nurturing the disposition of mindfulness. *Journal of Social Issues* 56(1), 27–47.

Ritchhart R, Perkins D (2005) Learning to think: the challenges of teaching thinking. In: *Holyoak K, Morrison R (eds)* The Cambridge Handbook of Thinking and Reasoning. Cambridge: Cambridge University Press.

Schoeberlein D (2009) *Mindful Teaching and Teaching Mindfulness. A Guide For Anyone Who Teaches Anything.* Boston, MA: Wisdom.

Warren Brown K, Ryan R, Cresswell J (2007) Mindfulness: theoretical foundations and evidence for its salutary effects. *Psychology Inquiry: An International Journal for the Advancement of Psychological Theory* 18(4), 211–37.

Williams M, Penman D (2011) *Mindfulness: A Practical Guide to Finding Peace in a Frantic World.* London: Piatkus.

Williams M. (2007) *The Mindful Way Through Depression: Freeing Yourself from Chronic Unhappiness.* New York: The Guildford Press.

World Health Organisation (2010) *Factsheet 220. Mental health: strengthening our response.* Available at: www.who.int/mediacentre/factsheets/fs220/en/ (accessed July 2015).

World Health Organisation (2012) *The global burden of mental disorders and the need for a comprehensive, coordinated response from health and social sectors at the country level.* 65th World Health Assembly Available at: apps.who.int/gb/ebwha/pdf_files/WHA65/A65_R4-en.pdf (accessed July 2015).

CHAPTER 26

Faith and conviction in educational settings

Stuart Blythe and James Gordon

In many learning and teaching environments there are people who hold various beliefs. These beliefs as convictions shape their identity and behaviour. In this chapter we are concerned specifically with people who articulate their beliefs as religious faith. The primary categories of convictions and faith discussed here can be related to belief systems that may not necessarily be classed as religious.

Faith and identity

From the perspectives of inclusion, equality and diversity, all learners have a right to have a good experience, which includes promoting their mental health and well-being as they participate in the learning and teaching environment. For people of faith this creates particular challenges and opportunities. Faith is part of a person's identity, significantly shaping who they are. Their faith is not something that can simply be left 'off campus'. To understand this we can use the language of 'convictions'. People of faith are people who hold certain convictions. Theologian James Wm. McClendon and philosopher James M. Smith (McClendon and Smith 1994) described such convictions as follows:

> *A conviction (as we use the term) means a persistent belief such that if X (a person or community) has a conviction, it will not easily be relinquished and it cannot be relinquished without making X a significantly different person (or community) than before.*

Convictions defined this way are 'beliefs' – a 'special form of belief' or category of beliefs that 'bear a special relation to the rest of our beliefs and ourselves as well' (McClendon and Smith 1994). Accordingly, convictions are both 'persistent' and 'significant'; persistent, because they sustain 'the capacity to resist, attack, to overcome, to continue in the face of difficulties'; and significant, because they 'exercise a dominant or controlling role over a number of other beliefs held by their believers, or those that govern (or correspond to) broad stretches of their thought and conduct' (McClendon and Smith 1994).

Convictions

Faith convictions support the mental health and well-being of people in a variety of ways, by building a sense of meaning for a person in relation to issues of life and death. For example, beliefs and practices such as prayer and meditation provide inner resources for dealing with crisis and difficulties, and faith can provide a perspective from which to understand and negotiate the world. Owning such convictions can bind a person into a supportive community of shared values. Healthy human development is dynamic and organic, so that a person's identity develops and is discovered throughout life. While convictions can change, the nature of convictions are so woven through a person's identity that if a person changes their convictions it evokes language such as the term conversion.

In contexts of learning and teaching, beliefs, ethics, and values are often at stake. At times this is explicit and at others, implicit. Whenever they are at stake there is the possibility of challenging the beliefs – or convictions – of people of faith in a way that creates dis-ease at a personal and existential level, as they seek to hold together what they are experiencing and learning with their existing convictions based on faith beliefs. Stated more positively, education involves creativity and risk, because it is a quest, whose steps are questions and whose goal is personal transformation.

Education assumes that there is always more to life than meets the eye; that life itself always exceeds our grasp; that wisdom is not found through our measure of conceptual control, but through our measure of openness to that which always exceeds and surprises our current take on things (Veling 2005). This is not to say that only people who own faith in some religious sense are likely to experience such challenges – people who hold non-religious convictions and convictional communities may have similar experiences. However, the focus of this chapter is people of owned faith, who consciously associate their religious and spiritual convictions with their identity. The question is how best to support this group of learners as they negotiate existential challenges in the learning and teaching environment.

Supporting people of faith and the role of chaplains

One prominent resource for supporting the mental health and well-being of staff and students of faith in the learning and teaching environment are religious chaplains. They are often provided as part of the welfare provision in settings such as hospitals and higher education institutions. The book *Being a Chaplain* discusses the reflections of Christian chaplains in a range of educational and other settings (Threfall and Newitt 2011). Some chaplains are paid by institutions, some are paid by their supporting religious body, and others act voluntarily by virtue of their religious role in society. Often they function as part of multifaith spiritual care teams. Their presence is usually advertised and noted in the official documents of the institution. Sometimes they facilitate, directly or by management, religious acts of observance for different faith traditions, and their activities are often related to 'welfare'. Stephen Fagbemi, chaplain at Sunderland University writes (Fagbemi 2011):

> *As a team of chaplains our responsibility is to provide pastoral, religious and social support for all people in the university. In other words, we are primarily concerned about people's well-being.*

In this role, chaplains may be an alternative to or complement other university welfare resources. They may provide a perceived independence from institutional structures, which may be particularly important if the institution is regarded by those seeking help as a cause of their stress, or they are concerned that their problems may affect their educational outcome (an argument in favour of the independent nature of chaplaincy teams; Fagbemi 2011).

Furthermore, people seeking support can also be 'signposted' to the other services (McBeath 2011). Chaplains provide a specific faith-based resource and caring experience and skills as part of the support offered within educational institutions both to people of faith and of no faith.

The presence of chaplaincy teams in educational institutions can reinforce the validity of having and holding faith in this context. Most educational establishments are publicly accountable, the general ethos is secular and faith may be treated with attitudes ranging from indifference to open hostility. The presence of chaplains, whether accessed or not, can reassure people that holding faith is a valid perspective, especially if they are from a minority group. This is particularly the case for international students or those staying away from home for the first time, whereby the chaplain may direct them to relevant local faith communities or faith-based groups.

Chaplaincy teams offer support for people of faith who face the challenges of living away from home and in a completely new social environment. In this respect, Bailey (2002) recognises the intellectual and social challenges faced by people of faith particularly when studying in higher education; she talks about chaplaincy as offering a context in which people can reflect on their experiences and deal specifically with issues that may directly relate to their faith, such as 'guilt' in relation to new behaviours over and against their faith traditions. Chaplaincies also provide teaching staff with a resource to which they can refer students who are people of faith, when they feel that providing spiritual care will promote their sense of mental health and well-being. While chaplaincy provides useful and general support, it does not address the issue of the learning and teaching process itself, or the challenges this creates, and the strategies that can be adopted to promote well-being among people of faith. This can be discussed in terms of delivering theological education in higher education.

Theological education in higher education

The context here is Christian theological education in a progressive and supportive British university, and is used to illustrate the ways in which the existential challenges faced by people of faith can be negotiated creatively in the learning and teaching environment. This means exploring and developing effective strategies that might be adopted in supporting people of faith, so enhancing their learning experience in ways that are creatively transformative. Theological education in higher education requires people not simply to know, describe and discuss their beliefs and practices, but to explore their beliefs and practices critically. Critical engagement is required by the progressive, credit-bearing, quality-assured educational framework in which we operate. It can be argued that it is also required by academic theological study as a life discipline and practice. Accordingly, theology involves:

> *... the discovery, understanding, and transformation of the convictions of a convictional community, including the discovery and critical revision of their relation to one another and to whatever else there is. (McClendon 2002)*

Not all beliefs, however, have the status of convictions, and not every class in theological education is directly engaging with convictional identity. At any one time what might be at stake is nothing more than matters of opinion to be debated and discussed, laid and lifted in the flow of conversation. Yet some students feel that exploring a particular opinion threatens the foundations of their faith; this may not be totally unwarranted because in terms of internal coherence to change, one opinion may have ramifications for others and, in turn, for convictions themselves. The nature of theology, therefore, is to explicitly enquire and explore faith convictions which essentially define the personal identities of people with faith. Students may not be prepared for this and it may create mental and emotional dis-ease, and the existential challenge it creates is intensified by a number of factors. Faith can be conceived as something to be trusted or held on authority, not something to be critically examined. In this respect, the work of Michael Jacobs is particularly helpful (highlighted by Bailey in a discussion of *Faith and Spirituality in Students Mental Health* in 2002). Jacobs (1998) offers a 'psychology of belief' in which he describes the different ways in which people can hold faith, religious or not:

- Trust and dependency.
- Authority and autonomy.
- Competitive and cooperative.

He makes the point that these modes are not stages, because people might hold faith in different ways at different times over different issues. In turn, and importantly, he wants to defend the validity of each. This said, he describes them with a clear developmental aspect, whereby the third mode is advanced as more 'healthy' than the first two for dealing with the complexities and challenges of life. The developmental aspect is significant here.

- The first mode – *faith as trust and dependency* – relates to complete trust and dependency on God. It can be imaginative, playful, illogical, ignoring questions and contradictions. It appears to have 'little need for explanation, proof, or the quest for truth' (Jacobs 1998).

- In the second mode – *faith as authority and autonomy* – pressing questions and contradictions are managed by looking to external authorities to bring answers and control. In the Christian faith creeds and statements of faith, 'authority figures' such as authors can serve such a validating purpose.

- The third mode – *competitive and cooperative faith* – involves people working their own understanding of faith with and against the opinion of others; it may not result in changing beliefs or convictions, but can lead to personal ownership of them. This owned faith can hold its own position while open to the diversity of other views. Interestingly, in this mode, the significance of imagination and symbols may be rediscovered (Jacobs 1998).

All of the above is significant because in our experience most young people who come to study at undergraduate level hold faith in the first and second modes. Theological study encourages them to the third mode because that is its nature and purpose. The problem from the perspective of modes one and two, with their emphasis on trust and certainty, the third mode can broker a variety of opinions and live with contradictions and can seem like unfaithfulness. A sense of unfaithfulness is contrary to a sense of well-being.

The existential challenges of theological study are intensified for the learner because their faith convictions are formed and held in communities. When they come to study theology, they come from (and frequently continue to belong to) their church communities, who provide supportive and reinforcing authorities for their beliefs. During study, the learner may develop independent views, apart from their established communities, and as they progress from mode one or two to mode three, they may feel at odds with them. Some church leaders warn potential students that studying theology can damage their faith; and some students complain that exploring the practices of the church, such as worship, 'spoils' the services for them because they begin to analyse them rather than participate freely. More seriously, this can lead to damaged and strained relationships within their faith communities; moving to the third mode, as Jacobs indicates, can be very lonely (Jacobs 1998).

Facing loneliness requires courage, but also accompaniment and support in the learning experience, in the quest where footsteps are questions. Thomas Merton encourages questions to be asked because spiritual insecurity is the fruit of unasked and unanswered questions. Questions cannot go unanswered unless they first be asked. And worse anxiety and worse insecurity come from being afraid to ask the right questions – because they might turn out to have no answers. One of the moral diseases we communicate to one another in society comes from huddling together in the pale light of an insufficient answer to a question we are afraid to ask (Shannon 1993).

This fear may make some students resist the 'discovery, understanding and transformation' of their convictions and the move to the more contested, cooperative mode of believing. It can create its own existential and relational problems; it can set a student against their cohort on what are seen as matters of great importance. This in turn can lead to loneliness in the classroom setting, or a barrier (real or perceived) to rise at a convictional level between student and staff. Additional angst might follow because teachers have power and can influence grades. In situations like this, the student may feel that what matters most to them is under attack in the classroom. This has various effects: some withdraw from engagement, some do what is required in order to 'pass' without owning the learning, and some become combative, especially when staff and other students feel that their own convictions are being constantly challenged, undermined and tested. All of this has intensity precisely because what is at stake are convictions, related to faith, that are integral to the identity of the people involved. Complexity is compounded because not only are identifiable ideas, beliefs and convictions involved, but also the less obvious issue of different modes of holding faith.

Given the nature of convictional faith, these factors may have a negative influence on the mental health and well-being of the learner negotiating such challenges and changes resulting from their learning. Not every learning setting involves this sort of explicit, direct analysis and critique of faith convictions. Yet people of faith participate in a wide range of roles and learning and teaching contexts; any context in which beliefs, ethics and values are at stake has the potential to create the sort of complex existential dis-ease in relation to peoples' convictions. This is particularly intense when their convictions are the specific focus of the learning and teaching experience.

CREATING A HEALTHY LEARNING AND TEACHING ENVIRONMENT

Here we highlight some features that may help create a healthy learning and teaching environment, in which people of faith can engage in a healthy way not just with the convictional content of their studies, but also with the process of becoming deep learners, moving from one mode of faith to another. To this end, we have identified a number of important practices.

(i) Provide a safe space for the exploration of ideas

The first is creating opportunities for 'safe space' discussion. This can relate to the general culture of the total learning and teaching environment, or involve creating opportunities during the delivery of specific subjects. Father Timothy Radcliffe (Radcliffe 2005) discusses the problems of searching for 'truth' in a surveillance society when and where 'one would never know when one's words might be used as evidence against one'. He continues:

> *... how can we ever think about anything if we never had the freedom to try out crazy ideas, float hypotheses and make mistakes? Meister Eckhart maintained that no-one can attain the truth without a hundred errors on the way. We need the freedom for words for which we are not going to be held eternally responsible. Seeking the truth requires time of protected irresponsibility.*

In the learning and teaching environment, safe spaces should have a number of dimensions, and should be a declared and agreed open and safe space, where general rules of equality, diversity and mutual respect apply. Critically, the opinions given and questions asked will not to be regarded as anyone's last word on any subject, but nothing more than a present reflection of thinking that is being offered for consideration. No-one's discussions or contributions will be recorded by manual or electronic means, and the conversations will not be used to influence summative assessments, although they may result in informal formative conversations with a student. This said, these conversations will not be reported to others in order to indicate particular things about his or her beliefs. The rules that apply to learners also apply to the leaders of learning, the teachers who have an important facilitatory role. There is a paradox in creating such a safe place: on the one hand, the significance of what people say is being downplayed because what is said is not being treated as anyone's last word; on the other, the safe space allows students to own questions and doubt and have their own positions contested.

Accordingly, such an approach models mode three, and may be a stimulus for convictional change. It can be reassuring for students to be told they are not being asked to change their opinions, but to consider how and why they hold them. Jacobs writes that people who go through the process of assessing their views do not necessarily change them dramatically, but in mode three faith opinions are developed and adapted as they are made 'their own' (Jacobs 1998).

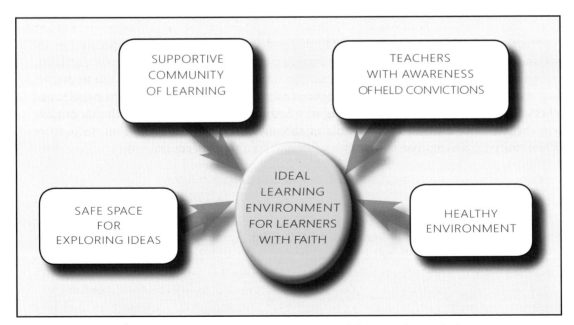

Figure 26.: Factors that support people of faith and conviction in the learning environment.

(ii) Foster a supportive community of learning

A second strategy involves developing the student body as a supportive community of learning – this cannot be assumed to happen when a disparate group of people meet in a room to discuss something together. It should represent a range of faith beliefs, opinions, convictions, and modes of holding faith, even in an institution that belongs to a particular religious tradition and a specific grouping within that. The goal is to form a learning community that is supportive of the sort of learning and existential engagement that theological study creates. The development of ecologies of support, in which the student body evolves into a supportive learning community, adds relational respect and care to the provision of safe space. It can be advanced in several ways.

- First, the value of learning together with others can be emphasised (it is one thing for educators to believe this, but another to communicate this to learners who may be very much focused on their 'own' learning). In our context, the value of learning by engagement with others is given theological and pedagogical significance. The life of the mind is not an indulgence or an inconvenience – it is an expression of faith – and collaborative learning can become a true companionship, a sharing of bread in mutual nourishment, an exploration of convictions in the context of respect for each other, and a transformative encounter with truth that may challenge existing convictions and lead to personal change.

- Second, deliberate use of learning activities can encourage collaborative exchanges in learning as students negotiate contested positions. We do this by encouraging diverse set reading tasks before class meetings where students critically discuss their reading with one another.

- Third, collaborative activity can be rewarded in relation to assessments.

These are all concerned with class-based learning experiences. Beyond this, wider collaborative, social (and in our case, faith-based) activities relating to acts of shared corporate worship can be organised. These activities help build relationships which move people's perceptions of one another away from simply opinions stated in class to develop common ground and trust. The goal is to create the sort of learning community in which the students learn to contest their own ideas and that of others in a context of respect for the different faith positions of others. This process is directly in keeping with helping to form the type of faith that can live with diversity and difference, while holding to convictions. It seeks to develop methods of communal engagement that students may adopt in their future leadership roles.

(iii) Encourage teachers to be attentive to the nature of faith convictions

A third feature of developing a healthy learning and teaching environment relates to the role of the teacher, in recognising that people of faith often hold their convictions in very different ways, but that each of mode of faith is valid. Accordingly, the opinions and views of students should not be diminished or dismissed in an unhelpful way. For people of faith, beliefs and opinions may be related to convictions that are 'personal' and freighted with personal identity. Thus theological education requires critical engagement with the personal. It is the nature of the discipline and a goal in higher education. It requires teachers to behave in ways appropriate to the level of learning, and to encourage the sort of questions that allow students to develop their critical analytical skills. When students move from a trusting faith to an authorised faith, and from an authorised faith to a competitive and cooperative faith, the teacher may for a time have to become an authority figure, to provide stability while the student challenges other authorities. The goal of the teacher here is not to gather their own 'band of disciples' but to help educate them to think for themselves about the views and convictions they hold – including the positions they hold over and against the teacher. To help students progress in their learning and faith to this position, teachers should model such faith by their willingness to lay open to critique, and to challenge and change their own convictions. In practice this may include articulating thoughts such as:

'This is my opinion. It is an informed opinion, and I think it is right, but it is only my opinion'

- or -

'I am open to be convinced differently'.

Teachers will model this approach in terms of the way they respond to positions of difference articulated during classroom discussions. If done authentically and with humility, and always being alert to issues of power in the class setting, this can be both uncomfortable and rewarding for teachers as their own convictions and ways of holding them may be challenged and changed. Teaching theology – like learning theology – is personal and personally rewarding and transformative. At the very least, attention should be given to these three areas to create a healthy learning and teaching environment for exploring faith convictions in a way that promotes rather than hinders mental health and well-being.

Other teachers and other subjects

Not all subject areas involve the same sort of explicit engagement with faith convictions that are required during theological education, when values, ethics, and beliefs are part of the subject matter and problems encountered during the learning process can lead to mental dis-ease. Their values, ethics, and convictions may also be at variance in relation to studies of science and economics, for example, and in relation to personal morality, expectations of professional conduct, and the nature and value of human life. It is important therefore that all teachers are aware of this dynamic and put in place the sort of strategies we suggest, so that learners of faith have a learning experience that is as personally fulfilling as that of other students.

Virtual learning situations

So far, we have assumed teaching and learning takes place in a classroom situation. In higher education, however, there may be a 'virtual' environment. This context may involve less direct challenge to a student's position because of the mediated, less direct nature of the interaction. Trying to replicate a good classroom experience is met with specific challenges: for example, creating a 'safe space' when material may be recorded in some way; or creating a sense of a supportive learning community without physically meeting each other. Then there is the issue of how a teacher facilitates challenging learning through virtual presence. None of these are insurmountable, but they raise pedagogical and formative issues in relation to how people of faith can be encouraged to critically engage with their faith convictions in a supportive and healthy way.

Concluding comments

People of faith have various roles in learning and teaching environments. Faith shapes their identity at a convictional level, and this can mean they face particular challenges to their mental health and well-being, as they encounter new lifestyle opportunities and learning experiences. Faith-based chaplaincy, usually in tertiary learning centres, offers learners and leaders of learning a general resource to help them negotiate changes and challenges in a healthy manner. Chaplaincy support does not, however, deal with any learning and teaching strategies; yet this is the most likely place for learners to meet the sort of challenges to their convictions that can create dis-ease at the level of identity, particularly when ethics, values, and beliefs are part of the subject matter. In the university setting we participate in, faith convictions are actively explored; students negotiate changing opinions and changing their ways of believing. We advocate that learning and teaching strategies that are cognisant of the challenges faced by faith students are included in the delivery of all educational programmes. These strategies include the intentional creation safe spaces for discussing contested areas, the development of supportive communities of learning, and employing leaders of learning who are sensitive to the convictional nature of faith dynamics.

KEY MESSAGES FROM THIS CHAPTER

- Convictions are a category of beliefs that relate to a person's other beliefs.

- Faith convictions may, in a variety of ways, support mental health and well-being by building a sense of meaning to issues of life and death.

- Whenever beliefs, ethics and values are at stake, there is the potential to challenge the beliefs and convictions of people of faith.

- Faith can be conceived as something to be trusted or held on authority rather than some-thing to be critically examined.

- In the learning and teaching environment, safe spaces for discussion can generate general rules of equality and diversity, and mutual respect.

- Learners who evolve in a supportive learning community, add relational respect and care to the provision of a safe place for discussion.

- Creating a healthy learning and teaching environment requires a safe place for the exploration of ideas, as well as a supportive learning community and leaders of learning who are aware of the nature of faith conviction.

Supporting evidence and further reading

Bailey A (2002) Faith and spirituality in students mental health. In: N Stanley, J Manthorpe (eds) *Student's Mental Health Needs: Problems and Responses*. London: Jessica Kingsley.

Fagbemi S (2011) Sunderland University. In: M Threfall Holmes, M Newitt (eds) *Being a Chaplain*. London: SPCK.

Jacobs M (1998) Faith as the 'space between'. In: M Cobb, V Robshaw (eds) *The Spiritual Challenge of Health Care*. Edinburgh: Churchill Livingston.

McBeath C (2011) A further education college. In: M Threfall Holmes, M Newitt (eds) *Being a Chaplain*. London: SPCK.

McClendon JWm, Smith JM (1994) *Convictions: Defusing Religious Relativism*. Eugene: Wipf & Stock.

McClendon JWm (2002) *Ethics: Systematic Theology*. Nashville, TN: Abingdon Press.

Radcliffe T (2005) *What is the Point of Being a Christian?* London: Burns & Oates.

Shannon WH (1993) T*he Silent Lamp*. London: SCM Press.

Threfall Holmes M and Newitt N (2011) *Being a Chaplain*. London: SPCK.

Veling TA (2005) *Practical Theology: On Earth as it is in Heaven*. Maryknoll: Orbis.

CHAPTER 27

Clinical supervision for leaders of learning

Graham Sloan

This chapter gives a brief overview of the factors contributing to 'less than helpful' teaching, presenting them as a foundation for the consideration of a resource that has been embraced by some of the healthcare professions. A detailed explanation of clinical supervision is outlined, highlighting the many potential benefits it may bring, and one particular guiding framework from the healthcare literature is described. Recommendations are also made on the way in which the practice of clinical supervision in teaching can be taken forward.

In modern day culture, teaching is a highly valued occupation. Leaders of learning are in a privileged position when they embark on making a significant and pivotal contribution to the education of children and young people. Not only are they key to the coverage of essential educational curricula, but they are important role models for how we think and feel about learning. We can all recall a favourite teacher from our primary or secondary schools, whom we still hold in high regard for the information they passed on to us. These cherished teachers conveyed so much more than the content of the standard curricula. They had many personal attributes worthy of note: warmth, enthusiasm, interest in the children, energy for teaching, time available and made space for creativity. These aspects were all as important as the written syllabus – if not more so.

However, our memories of 'less than helpful' teachers can be just as readily accessible. Many children passing through the system regard their education as disappointing; some have a sense of being short-changed. Children subjected to unhelpful teaching experiences are unable to take the perspective of the teacher or give any thought to the multitude of factors contributing to their suboptimal practices. Adults can also find it difficult to create enough emotional distance from their early life experiences to give themselves the space and time to understand the teacher's frame of reference. It is now appreciated that emotional labour is inextricably linked with teaching (Kinman *et al.* 2011). On a day-to-day or minute-to-minute basis, teachers experience a broad range of emotions in response to the varied roles they engage in during teaching. Continuous experience of negative emotions such as anxiety, anger, frustration and guilt – in the absence of emotional regulation or coping strategies – can result in emotional exhaustion (Chang 2009).

There is a plethora of research evidence informing that teaching is a stressful occupation (Antoniou *et al.* 2009; Bowers 2004; Rothi *et al.* 2010). Some consider it to be one of the most stressful professions in the UK (Miller and Travers 2005). Sadly, exposure to prolonged stress can result in a negative impact in the physical and psychological health of anyone, resulting in emotional exhaustion and burnout (Chang 2009; Rothi *et al.* 2010). For teachers, this can affect the quality of their teaching. All too often, the stressed teacher becomes so dissatisfied that they leave the profession (Rothi *et al.* 2010). Forlin (2001) divided sources of teacher stress into three clusters:

- **Administrative**: workload, role conflict, role ambiguity, etc.
- **Classroom-based**: classroom environment, teacher-to-pupil ratio, disruptive pupils, etc.
- **Personal**: relationship issues with colleagues, working environment, etc.

Richards (2012) cites the teaching of high-need students without adequate work-based support as a particular stressor in the USA. The potential emotional labour involved in providing an effective educational environment for students with mental health difficulties, and its contribution to teacher stress has also been recognised (Milkie and Warner 2011; Smith 2008).

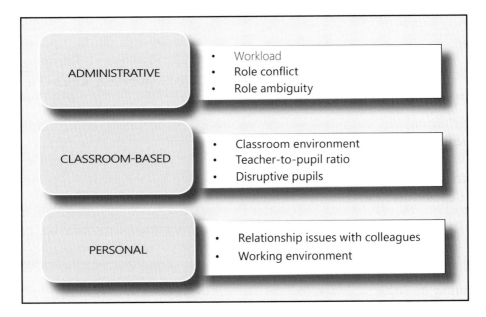

Figure 27.1 Sources of teacher stress according to Forlin (2001).

What can help?

Chang (2009) presents a number of options to help with the emotional labour of teaching. These include appreciating that emotions are an integral aspect of this role, being able to identify the range and intensity of their emotional experiences, adopting reappraisal strategies to adjust goals and understanding of pupil behaviours, and using effective and multiple coping strategies.

TEACHER SUPPORT TEAMS

Teacher support teams provide a forum for reflection and the potential for continuous professional development (Bedward and Daniels 2005). They consist of a small group of teachers who encourage reflection and problem-solving among peers on an issue by the 'referring teacher'. The issue may focus on concerns about the class as a whole, a group of students, or a single pupil, and there may be follow-up meetings. Further options for teacher support have been recommended

– importantly, including the need for psychological intervention via counselling. It was also recommended that schools should offer confidential in-house support, advice and guidance to teachers and headteachers, possibly through trained mentors (Rothi *et al.* 2010).

CLINICAL SUPERVISION

The use of clinical supervision in teaching dates back to the 1950s. Since then, a range of models guiding practice have been developed and presented in the literature. Clifford *et al.* (2005) describe the University of Oregon's model of clinical supervision, influenced by the principles of five existing models. These are:

- Original clinical supervision model.
- Artistic model.
- Developmental model.
- Technical/didactic model.
- Reflective model.

Goldhammer (1969) produced the original model of clinical supervision, which described a series of special methods for the supervision of teachers:

- Pre-observation.
- Observation.
- Analysis and strategy.
- Conference.
- Post-conference analysis.

Expanding on this, Cogan (1973) presented an eight-item framework, comprising:

- Establishing the teacher–supervisor relationship.
- Planning with the teacher (lessons, units, objectives).
- Planning the strategy of observation (collection of data).
- Observing the instruction.
- Analysing the teaching–learning process.
- Planning strategies for the conference.
- Having the conference.
- Renewed planning.

Combined instructional supervision and staff development provided by the school's principal teacher is described by Colantonio (2005), who emphasises the preference for hierarchical provision of such supervision. Conversely, a recent study showed that supervisor support represented authority, whereby supervisors did not interact with teachers on an equal basis. It was implied that the supervisors were insensitive to teacher-related problems, and judgemental and critical. Not surprisingly, supervisor support did not appear to be a useful preventative measure for burnout (Bataineh and Alsagheer 2012). Bearing this in mind, there may be a role for the style of clinical supervision found in healthcare settings, particularly that used in mental health settings, and specifically psychological therapy (Cornforth and Claiborne 2008). In the context of the emotional labour that is inextricably linked to teaching when working with troubled children, the value of clinical supervision seems obvious.

Clinical supervision in psychological therapies

Clinical supervision has an essential role in facilitating the provision of effective psychological therapies (NHS Education Scotland 2011). It facilitates the supervisee's experiential learning, particularly in relation to case conceptualisation, psychological therapy skills competence and therapeutic relationship qualities. It also contributes to establishing the necessary competence of the supervisee to practise, maintaining competency standards, and facilitating professional development generally (Milne and James 2000). Ultimately, it guides the supervisee to provide effective therapy to their patients (Milne 2009). The following definition underpins a recently developed psychological therapy supervision competency framework, and helps to clarify its fundamental intention. Supervision is a 'formal but collaborative relationship' in an organisational context, forming part of the overall training of the supervisee and guided by 'some form of contract' between supervisee and supervisor (Roth and Pilling 2008).

The expectation is that the supervisee offers an honest and open account of their work and that the supervisor offers feedback and guidance which has the primary aim of facilitating the development of the supervisee's therapeutic competencies but also ensures that they practise in a manner which conforms to current ethical and professional standards.

Following publication of the UK-wide competency framework, NHS Education Scotland (NES) developed a training portfolio for implementation throughout NHS Scotland to enable achievement of these competencies (Bagnall *et al.* 2011). A two-stage training model is adopted. First is a three-day generic course on supervision across all psychological modalities; second, is a supplementary specialist courses for individual therapeutic modalities that expand on specific supervision issues (and related competencies), such as cognitive behavioural psychotherapy, interpersonal psychotherapy and psychodynamic psychotherapy.

Conceptual frameworks

One topic covered in the three-day NES training course is conceptual frameworks. These can be used as guiding frameworks for clinical supervision; some already exist and are in use by teachers in education. There has been a gradual increase in the number of conceptual models in the literature, but research on their utility and effectiveness is scarce. Many generic guiding frameworks for clinical supervision are available. Among them are:

- Heron's six-category intervention analysis (1989).
- Hawkins and Shohet's process model (2006).
- Stoltenberg and McNeill's developmental model (2010).
- Kolb's experiential learning (1984).
- Holloway's systems model (1996).

PROCTOR'S FRAMEWORK FOR CLINICAL SUPERVISION

Possibly the most popular supervision framework – applied at least in nursing in the UK – was developed by Brigid Proctor (Buus and Gonge 2009). This three-function interactive model has been implemented in a diverse range of nursing contexts, including mental health nursing (Walsh *et al.* 2003), practice nursing (Styles and Gibson 1999) and medical and surgical nursing (Bowles and Young 1999). Initially this framework was described as having three functions (Proctor 1987). A formative function, with the aim of developing skills and increasing knowledge; a normative function, with the aim of maintaining professional standards and delivering a high-quality healthcare service; and a third function that focuses on restoration from the stress and emotional labour inextricably linked to healthcare provision by way of emotional support. The original three-function interactive framework, has been subjected to empirical evaluation (in studies by Butterworth *et al.* 1997, Dunn 1998, Malin 2000, Nicklin 1997 and Teasdale *et al.* 1998 among others). Previously it was argued it lacked essential guidance on what to offer when working within each of its functions (Sloan 2006), but Proctor amended the framework and described it as the supervision alliance model (Proctor 2001). This model has much to offer those engaging in clinical supervision. It incorporates a number of valuable features and offers a rich description so that users of the framework have a solid foundation on which to base their supervisory practice. The key features include clarity on the essential values and assumptions when engaging in clinical supervision, emphasis on the adoption of a collaboratively negotiated supervision agreement, and the integration of others' work which helps with focusing and doing clinical supervision.

Values and assumptions

Proctor (2001) makes clear the values and assumptions on which the supervision alliance model are founded, as follows:

- Practitioners are keen to work well and are self-monitoring.
- Practitioners have the ability to reflect on their experience and practice.

It seems that clinical supervisors who choose to be guided by this model appreciate the notion of working in alliance – rather than hierarchically – and that clinical supervision is a cooperative enterprise. Proctor therefore recommends that clinical supervision is distinguished and detached from formal managerial assessment procedures (Proctor 2001). Moreover, it is acknowledged that working in an alliance requires the foundation of a working agreement that is personal and particular to each supervisory relationship.

WORKING AGREEMENT

Beinart (2012) advised that when a detailed, co-constructed, rigorous contract (or supervision agreement) is established, and renegotiated when necessary, the quality of the supervisory relationship is enhanced and deepened; both the supervisor and the supervisee report increased satisfaction with outcomes. Supervision is an interpersonal process, and its success owes much to the quality of the relationship between both parties (Lawton 2000; Loganbill *et al.* 1982; Termini and Hauser 1973). The supervision agreement serves as a solid foundation for an effective supervisory relationship. It facilitates the sharing of desires and expectations of clinical supervision, and promotes a shared understanding on the work to be undertaken. It also helps to foster a style of working that is structured and collaborative, and to minimise problems later in clinical supervision. There are a range of supervision agreement templates (e.g. Scaife 2010). The agreement developed by Howard (1997) provides a thorough account of issues that may contribute towards establishing an effective supervisory relationship (FIGURE 27.2). Proctor's (2001) supervision alliance model provides additional details about the doing of clinical supervision and includes supervision skills, focusing and the learning cycle. Some existing frameworks on interpersonal skills are integrated into the supervision alliance model. One of these, the six-category intervention framework (Heron 2001), has a plethora of helpful interventions for supervisors to consider.

Purpose	☐
Professional disclosure statement	☐
Practical issues	☐
Goals	☐
Method/framework	☐
Evaluation	☐
Accountability and responsibility	☐
Confidentiality	☐
Documentation	☐
Dual relationships	☐
Problem resolution	☐
Statement of agreement	☐

Figure 27.2: Howard's (1997) supervision agreement.

SIX-CATEGORY INTERVENTION ANALYSIS

This was developed between 1974 and 1976 to help delivery of interventions within a helping relationship. It consists of two domains, authoritative and facilitative, each with three categories (see FIGURE 27.3). The interpersonal framework model has been helpful for mental health nurses in interactions with patients (Ashmore 1999; Chambers 1990; Hammond 1983). It has been suggested that nurses who develop competence in all six categories could be effective in a wide range of interpersonal contexts (Burnard 2002). The system describes the basic kinds of intention a helper can have when working with someone – the teacher – who is seeking help. Here are four of them:

- **Prescriptive** interventions aim to influence and direct his or her behaviour and include offering advice and making suggestions.

- **Confronting** interventions directly challenge the rigid and maladaptive ways that limit people from seeking help currently; they bring into awareness an uncomfortable truth 'with kindness, in order that the client concerned may see it, fully acknowledge it' (Heron 1989).

- **Supportive** interventions validate or affirm the worth of the person seeking help, their qualities, attitudes and actions (Heron 1989).

- **Cathartic** interventions help to process difficult emotions such as grief, fear and anger, and encourage further self-exploration.

Johns and Butcher (1993), Chambers and Long (1995), Fowler (1996), Cutcliffe and Epling (1997) and Driscoll (2000) described a standalone clinical supervision model for nursing based on Heron's (1989) six-category intervention analysis framework, perhaps highlighting its

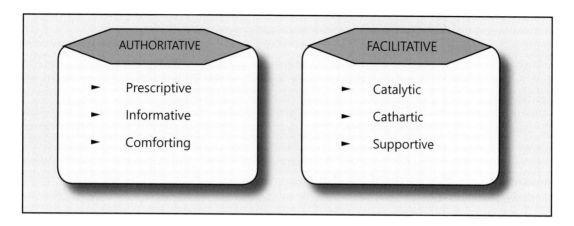

Figure 27.3: The range of interventions.

significance and relevance to clinical supervision. FIGURE 27.4 (overpage) gives examples of prescriptive, catalytic and cathartic interventions in teaching and education contexts, addressing the same issue throughout to highlight the perspectives of the different categories.

FOCUSING: BASED ON THE PROCESS MODEL (HAWKINS AND SHOHET 2006)

Another framework brought into the supervision alliance model is that of Hawkins and Shohet (2006). Their well-known process model is a double matrix or seven-eyed supervisor model, focusing on the processes of the supervisory relationship. Hawkins and Shohet propose that to carry out effective supervision of any deep therapeutic work, supervisors should be able to use all seven modes of supervision and suggest it is particularly applicable to the supervision of counsellors, psychotherapists and other helping professionals who supervise indepth clinical work. They developed the process model essentially to provide a frame of reference for the range of potential foci for supervision, such as:

- Supervisee's client.
- Strategies (e.g. educational approaches).
- Client–supervisee relationship.
- Supervisee.
- Supervisor–supervisee relationship.
- Supervisor.
- Wider organisational, family and cultural influences.

The learning cycle

This is an aspect of Proctor's alliance model which most educators are familiar with. It reaffirms the fundamental purpose of clinical supervision as an educational enterprise, which provides an almost infinite range of learning cycles and opportunities during the clinical supervision session, following through on discussions when back in the classroom.

(i) Cognitive therapy in supervision

Here we give an overview of one of the modality-specific supervision frameworks covered in one of the NES supplementary specialist courses in cognitive therapy supervision (Padesky 1996). Briefly, clinical supervision, which is guided by the cognitive therapy model, is similar to the therapy process in that it aims to be focused, structured, educational and collaborative. Clinical supervisors aim to help supervisees to apply cognitive therapy to a high standard, and develop their assessment, conceptualisation and treatment skills; they also facilitate the supervisees' reactions to the therapy process. In cognitive therapy supervision, a supervision mode is the means by which supervisee learning and discovery occur; it can include case discussion, review of audiorecordings of a therapy tape, role play, clinical observation and providing relevant educational material. The focus of supervision can include the mastery of new skills, developing conceptualisation skills and progressing the supervisee's understanding of the therapy relationship and processes integral to both therapy and supervision (Sloan *et al.* 2000).

(ii) Formats for the provision of clinical supervision

Reports of how clinical supervision has been introduced to a broad range of clinical settings have been published by Styles and Gibson (1999); Ashmore and Carver (2000); Clough (2001) and Spence *et al.* (2002), among others. Descriptions of its implementation highlight that, regardless of the conceptual model guiding it, clinical supervision can be delivered in a variety of formats. The most common form in the UK (in nursing) is individual supervision (Edwards *et al.* 2000; Ho 2007; Sines and McNally 2007); group and triad formats are less common (Price and Chalker 2000; Sloan *et al.* 2000). There is a lack of evidence supporting one type over another, but their use depends on practitioner preferences, organisational needs and availability of supervisors who are competent in a particular form.

(iii) Barriers to the implementation of clinical supervision

Potential barriers to clinical supervision are experienced in many professions. In the UK, it is common for supervisory arrangements to be hierarchical (Davey *et al.* 2006; Rice *et al.* 2007; Sines and McNally 2007). While there is some support for a management-led model of delivery (e.g. Darley 2001), there are many suggestions that managerial supervision should exist parallel to – not concomitant with – clinical supervision (Cutcliffe and Hyrkas 2006). When provided in this fashion, management agendas infiltrate and overwhelm clinically focused discussions during clinical supervision (Duncan-Grant 2000; Kelly *et al.* 2001; Sloan 1999; 2006). Hierarchical delivery can have a negative influence on how nurses, for example, engage in clinical supervision. According to O'Riordan (2002), staff withdrew from clinical supervision because the supervisor was an insider to the unit and a manager.

Clinical supervision is viewed negatively if feedback reaches the management, or it is associated with a sense of being watched, or appears to be unimportant to management (Rouse 2007). From one study on clinical supervision in mental health nursing, the discussions were filled with talk about performance appraisals, professional development planning, annual leave and off-duty and staff relations. Such hierarchical provision is predetermined and therefore contrary to the notion, supported conceptually and empirically, that the supervisee should have some choice about the supervisor (Bond and Holland 1998; Cowie 2011; Driscoll 2007; Davys 2005; Edwards *et al.* 2000; Sloan 1999, 2006; van Ooijen 2000; Winstanley and White 2003).

The definition of clinical supervision cited earlier is appropriate for those delivering psychological therapies, but may jar with the expectations of general nursing staff and physiotherapists. There is a plethora of alternative definitions, and this lack of consensus on a standard definition is a serious obstacle to developing the field (Buus and Gonge 2009) and the successful implementation of effective clinical supervision. Absence of such clarity may continue to influence how clinical supervision is applied, the frameworks guiding its delivery, the expectations on what it can achieve and, ultimately, the training programmes for its participants.

PRESCRIPTIVE INTERVENTION	► *Supervisee (sounding anxious)*: I feel like I'm letting wee Joe down, not making the sessions interesting enough for him. ► *Supervisor*: You should ask for feedback, not just from wee Joe but all of the class – what they enjoyed and also what could be improved on.
CATALYTIC INTERVENTION	► *Supervisee (sounding anxious)*: I feel like I'm letting wee Joe down, not making the sessions interesting enough for him. ► *Supervisor*: I'm really sorry to hear this and can hear it's causing you anxiety. It's really hard making the content of teaching of interest to everyone. It's something I struggle with too. Can you tell me what makes you think that the sessions aren't interesting enough for Joe?
CATHARTIC INTERVENTION	► *Supervisee (sounding anxious)*: I feel like I'm letting wee Joe down, not making the sessions interesting enough for him. ► *Supervisor*: And that's causing you some anxiety? ► *Supervisee*: Yes, it does. I am anxious ... because they should be interesting. It's hard work preparing the sessions. I'm up all night sometimes, making sure everything is perfect – just right. You know I've been working late to prepare some of the sessions but for several months I've also been having to continue on them at home. It's all I've been doing! ► *Supervisor*: I'd really like for us to spend some time on this anxiety. See if we can figure it out a bit more. Would that be okay? ► *Supervisee*: Yes, I know it's getting to me. If only I was better at teaching, I'd be fine. ► *Supervisor*: Tell me some more about the things that trigger your anxiety at work?

Figure 27.4: Examples of prescriptive, catalytic and cathartic interventions in an educational context.

Training practitioners for their engagement in clinical supervision

There is limited available training in clinical supervision, particularly for clinical supervisors of teaching professionals (Wright *et al.* 2012). Developing such opportunities should increase the numbers of available adequately trained clinical supervisors and make delivery of clinical supervision more effective and competent. Ultimately, the provision of effective training may lead to useful practice-focused outcomes, but decisions must be made about who to train and what to include.

Some argue that the success of clinical supervision is highly dependent on the supervisor (Gilmore 2001), thus training opportunities are often confined to clinical supervisors. Importantly, clinical supervision is not something that is done to the supervisee; it is something that both super-visor and supervisee contribute to. Therefore, training opportunities should perhaps be made available to both supervisors and supervisees. The method and approach to training can be flexible.

Ideally trainee supervisors should be introduced to the educational material using a variety of teaching aids. Having cognisance of learning styles and adult experiential learning principles is essential. Teaching sessions should be highly interactive, to facilitate discussion and engagement in experiential exercises. They should also create thinking space for participants to reflect on their supervision experiences before training began, and forward planning for subsequent engagement in supervision.

For clinical supervisors, training should include a variety of media, including DVD footage, role play, and information and reflective exercises that are cognisant of different learning styles and adult experiential learning principles. Sessions should be highly interactive, facilitating discussion and engagement in experiential exercises, with thinking space provided for trainees to reflect on their experiences before training and forward planning. The potential components of specific sessions for supervisees and supervisors are shown in FIGURES 27.5, 27.6 and 27.7.

TRAINING PROGAMME FOR SUPERVISEES

- Introduction
- InIdentifying aims for the session
- Defining and clarifying the purposes of clinical supervision
- Key drivers for clinical supervision
- Potential benefits of clinical supervision
- Getting the most from clinical supervision
- Supervisee contribution

Figure 27.5: Potential components of half-day training session for supervisees.

TRAINING PROGAMME FOR SUPERVISORS

SESSION 1

GETTING THE MOST FROM CLINICAL SUPERVISION

Introduction • Establishing the aims of sessions • Clarifying and defining
clinical supervision • Key drivers for introducing clinical supervision
Getting the most from clinical supervision – supervisee contribution
Homework aims for the session • Defining and clarifying the purposes of
clinical supervision • Key drivers for clinical supervision • Potential benefits
of clinical supervision • Getting the most from clinical supervision
• Supervisee contribution

SESSION 2

GIVING YOUR BEST – PROVIDING EFFECTIVE SUPERVISION

The supervision agreement • Establishing agreement on the purpose
of supervision • The supervisory relationship – getting to know each
other • Practical arrangements • Identifying learning objectives
and goals • Evaluation of processes and outcomes • Confidentiality
Accountability, responsibility and ethical practices • Documentation
and supervision records • Dual relationships • Problem resolution
• Homework

SESSIONS 3 & 4

GIVING YOUR BEST – PROVIDING EFFECTIVE SUPERVISION

Supervision models and methods • Supervision frameworks • Frameworks guided
by psychotherapy models • Models of reflection • Learning theory
Discussion of supervision-related issues • Homework

SESSION 5

PROVIDING EFFECTIVE SUPERVISION

The empirical literature – good enough supervision • Discussion of
supervision-related issues • Homework

SESSION 6

PULLING IT ALL TOGETHER AND MOVING FORWARD

Discussion of supervision-related issues • Action plans to move forward
with clinical supervision

**Figure 27.6: Potential components of six half-day training sessions
for supervisors.**

Supervisors should be encouraged to provide clinical supervision that incorporates their learning from the training programme, and they should be allowed time to contemplate their action and learning plans. A follow-up session can be negotiated, usually after six months, and the provision of supervision can be nurtured with opportunities for supervision of their supervision and through supervisor's support groups.

Concluding comments

This chapter has outlined the potential factors contributing to 'less than helpful' teaching, as a foundation for the resource known as clinical supervision, which has been embraced by the healthcare profession. Some potential benefits have been presented, with descriptions of Proctor's (2001) supervision alliance model and particular benefits it may have for the teaching profession. Clinical supervision requires considerable investment and commitment, but it is a golden opportunity, when provided effectively, to facilitate high-quality teaching. All stakeholders, supervisees, supervisors, management and educators in the learning and teaching environment can (and must) contribute.

KEY MESSAGES FROM THIS CHAPTER

- Teaching can be emotionally demanding and is regarded as one of the most stressful occupations.

- Clinical supervision has been applied to teaching for several decades.

- Clinical supervision provides a safe space to reflect on, and process, the emotional labour inherent in the role of teaching.

- Clinical supervision facilitates the development of teacher competence.

- Ideally, clinical supervision should be separated from managerial supervision.

- Proctor's supervision alliance model can be used to guide the clinical supervision of teachers.

Supporting evidence and further reading

Antoniou AS, Polychroni F, Kotroni C (2009) Working with students with special educational needs in Greece: teachers' stressors and coping strategies. *International Journal of Special Education* 24(1), 100–11.

Ashmore R (1999) Heron's intervention framework: an introduction and critique. *Mental Health Nursing* 19(1), 24–27.

Ashmore R, Carver N (2000) Clinical supervision in mental health nursing courses. *British Journal of Nursing* 9(3), 171–76.

Bagnall G, Sloan G, Platz S, Murphy S (2011) Generic supervision competencies for psychological therapies. *Mental Health Practice* 14(6), 18–23.

Bataineh O, Alsagheer A (2012) An investigation of social support and burnout among special education teachers in the United Arab Emirates. *International Journal of Special Education* 27(2), 5–13.

Bedward J, Daniels HRJ (2005) Collaborative solutions. Clinical supervision and teacher support teams: reducing professional isolation through effective peer support. *Learning in Health and Social Care* 4(2), 53–66.

Beinart H (2012) Models of supervision and the supervisory relationship. In: Fleming I, Steen L (eds) *Supervision and Clinical Psychology Theory Practice and Perspectives* (2nd edn). London: Routledge.

Bond M, Holland S (1998) *Skills of Clinical Supervision: A Practical Guide for Supervisees, Clinical Supervisors and Managers.* Buckingham: Open University Press.

Bowers T (2004) Stress, teaching and teacher health. Education 3–13: *International Journal of Primary Elementary and Early Years Education* 32(3), 73–80.

Bowles N, Young C (1999) An evaluative study of clinical supervision based on Proctor's three-function interactive model. *Journal of Advanced Nursing* 30(4), 958–64.

Burnard P (2002) *Learning Human Skills: An Experiential and Reflective Guide for Nurses and Health Care Professionals.* Oxford: Butterworth Heineman.

Butterworth T, Carson J, White E, Jeacock J, Clements A, Bishop V (1997) *It Is Good To Talk: An Evaluation Study in England and Scotland.* Manchester: University of Manchester.

Buus N, Gonge H (2009) Empirical studies of clinical supervision in psychiatric nursing: a systematic literature review and methodological critique. *International Journal of Mental Health Nursing* 18(4), 250–64.

Chambers M (1990) Psychiatric and mental health nursing: learning in the clinical environment. In: Reynolds W, Cormack D (eds) *Psychiatric and Mental Health Nursing: Theory and Practice.* London: Chapman and Hall.

Chambers M, Long A (1995) Supportive clinical supervision: a crucible for personal and professional change. *Journal of Psychiatric and Mental Health Nursing* 2(5), 311–16.

Chang ML (2009) An appraisal perspective of teacher burnout: examining the emotional work of teachers. *Educational Psychology Review* 21(3), 193–218.

Clifford JR, Macy MG, Albi LD (2005) A model of clinical supervision for preservice professionals in early intervention and early childhood special education. *Topics in Early Childhood Education* 25(3), 167–76.

Clough A (2001) Clinical leadership: turning thought into action. *Primary Health Care* 11(4), 39–41.

Cogan M (1973) *Clinical Supervision.* Boston: Holt Reinhart Wilson.

Colantonio JN (2005) On target: combining instructional supervision and staff development. Principal Leadership 5(9), 30–34.

Cornforth S, Claiborne LB (2008) When educational supervision meets clinical supervision: what can we learn from the discrepancies. *British Journal of Guidance and Counselling* 36(2), 155–63.

Cowie C (2011) *Conceptualising the Foundation of an Effective Clinical supervision Cycle in Mental Health Nursing.* MSc Thesis, University of Otago, New Zealand.

Cutcliffe JR, Epling M (1997) An exploration of the use of John Heron's confronting interventions in clinical supervision: case studies from practice. Psychiatric Care 4(4), 174–80.

Cutcliffe J, Hyrkas E (2006) Multidisciplinary attitudinal positions about clinical supervision: a cross-sectional study. *Journal of Nursing Management* 14(8), 617–27.

Darley G (2001) Demystifying supervision. Nursing Management 7(10), 18–21.

Davey B, Desousa C, Robinson S, Murrells T (2006) The policy–practice divide: who has clinical supervision in nursing? *Journal of Research in Nursing* 11(3), 237–48.

Davys A (2005) Supervision: Is what we want, what we need? In: Beddoe L, Worrall J, Howard F (eds) *Supervision Conference 2004: Weaving the Together the Strands of Supervision.* Auckland: University of Auckland.

Driscoll J (2000) *Practising Clinical Supervision: A Reflective Approach.* London: Bailliere Tindall.

Driscoll J (2007) *Practising Clinical Supervision: A Reflective Approach for Healthcare Professionals* (2nd edn). London: Elsevier.

Duncan-Grant A (2000) Clinical supervision and organisational power: a qualitative study. *Mental Health Care* 3(12), 398–401.

Dunn C (1998) *Implementing and Evaluating Clinical Supervision at the Royal Berkshire and Battle Hospital NHS Trust*. Reading: Battle Hospital.

Edwards D, Burnard P, Coyle D, Fothergill A, Hannigan B (2000) Stress and burnout in community mental health nursing: a review of the literature. *Journal of Psychiatric and Mental Health Nursing* 7(1), 7–14.

Forlin C (2001) Inclusion: Identifying potential stressors for regular class teachers. *Educational Research* 43, 235–45.

Fowler J (1996) Clinical supervision: what do you do after you say hello? *British Journal of Nursing* 5(6), 382–85.

Gilmore A (2001) Clinical supervision in nursing and health visting: a review of the UK literatures. In: J Cutliffe *et al.* (eds) Fundamental Themes of Clinical Supervision. London: Routledge.

Goldhammer R (1969) *Clinical Supervision: Special Methods for the Supervision of Teachers*. New York: Holt, Reinhart and Winston.

Grant A (2000) Clinical supervision and organisational power: a qualitative study. *Mental Health Care* 3(12), 398–401.

Hammond J (1983) A clutch of concepts. *Nursing Mirror* 5(1), 34–35.

Hawkins P, Shohet R (2006) *Supervision in the Helping Profession*s. Milton Keynes: Open University Press.

Heron J (1989) *Six Category Intervention Analysis*. Guildford: University of Surrey, Human Potential Resource Group.

Heron J (2001) *Helping the Client: A Creative Practical Guide* (5th edn) London: Sage.

Holloway EL (1996) *Clinical Supervision: A Systems Approach*. Thousand Oaks, CA: Sage.

Ho D (2007) Work discussion groups in clinical supervision in mental health nursing. *British Journal of Nursing* 16(1), 39–46.

Holloway EI (1995) *Clinical Supervision: A Systems Approach*. California: Sage.

Howard FM (1997) Supervision. In: Love H, Whittaker W, Wellington W (eds) *Practice Issues for Clinical and Applied Psychologists in New Zealand*. Auckland: New Zealand Psychological Society.

Johns C, Butcher K (1993) Learning through supervision: a case study of respite care. *Journal of Clinical Nursing* 2(2), 89–93.

Kelly BA, Long A, McKenna H (2001) A survey of community mental health nurses' perceptions of clinical supervision in Northern Ireland. *Journal of Psychiatric and Mental Health Nursing* 8(1), 33–44.

Kinman G, Wray S, Strange C (2011) Emotional labour, burnout and job satisfaction in UK teachers: the role of workplace support. *Educational Psychology: An International Journal of Experimental Educational Psychology* 31(7), 843–56.

Kolb DA (1984) *Experiential Learning: Experience as the Source of Learning and Development*. San Francisco, CA: Jossey Bass.

Lawton B (2000) 'A very exposing affair': explorations in counsellors' supervisory relationships. In: Lawton B, Feltham C (eds) *Taking Supervision Forward: Enquiries and Trends in Counselling and Psychotherapy*. London: Sage.

Loganbill C, Hardy E, Delworth V (1982) Supervision: a conceptual model. *Counselling Psychology* 10(1), 3–42.

Malin NA (2000) Evaluating clinical supervision in community homes and teams serving adults with learning disabilities. *Journal of Advanced Nursing* 31(3), 548–57.

Milkie MA, Warner CH (2011) Classroom learning environments and the mental health of first-grade children. *Journal of Health and Social Behaviour* 52(1), 4–22.

Miller GVF, Travers I (2005) Ethnicity and the experience of work: job stress and satisfaction of minority ethnic teachers in the UK. *International Review of Psychiatry* 17(5), 317–27.

Milne D (2009) *Evidence–Based Clinical Supervision: Principles and Practice*. West Sussex: Wiley.

Milne D, James I (2000) A systematic review of effective cognitive–behavioural supervision. *British Journal of Clinical Psychology* 39, 111–27.

NHS Education for Scotland (2011) *The Matrix: A guide to delivering evidence-based psychological therapies in Scotland*. Edinburgh: NHS Education for Scotland.

Nicklin (1997) *Clinical Supervision: Efficient and Effective*. York: University of York.

O'Riordan B (2002) Why nurses choose not to undertake clinical supervision: the findings from one ICU. *Nursing in Critical Care* 7(2), 59–66.

Padesky C (1996) Developing cognitive therapist competency: teaching and supervision models. In: Salkovskis M (ed.) *Frontiers of Cognitive Therapy*. London: Guilford Press.

Price AM, Chalker M (2000) Our journey with clinical supervision in an intensive care unit. *Intensive and Critical Care Nursing* 16(1), 51–55.

Proctor B (1987) Supervision: a co-operative exercise in accountability. In: Marken M, Payne M (eds) *Enabling and Ensuring: Supervision in Practice*. Leicester: National Youth Bureau and the Council for Education and Training in Youth and Community Work.

Proctor B (2001) The supervision alliance model. In: Cutcliffe JR, Butterworth T, Proctor B (eds) *Fundamental Themes of Clinical Supervision*. London: Routledge.

Rice F, Cullen B, McKenna H, Kelly B, Richey R (2007) Clinical supervision for mental health nurses in Northern Ireland: formulating best practice guidelines. *Journal of Psychiatric and Mental Health Nursing* 14(5), 516–21.

Richards J (2012) Teacher stress and coping strategies: a national snapshot. *The Educational Forum* 76(3), 299–316.

Roth A, Pilling S (2008) *A competence framework for the supervision of psychological therapies*. Available at: www.ucl.ac.uk/clinical-psychology/CORE/supervision_framework.html (accessed July 2015).

Rothi D, Leavey G, Loewenthal K (2010) *Teachers' Mental Health: A Study Exploring the Experiences of Teachers with Work-Related Stress and Mental Health Problems*. Birmingham: NASUWT/Teachers Union.

Rouse J (2007) How does clinical supervision influence staff development? *Journal of Children's and Young People's Nursing* 1(7), 334–40.

Scaife J (2010) *Supervising the Reflective Practitioner: An Essential Guide to Theory and Practice*. London: Routledge.

Sines D, McNally S (2007) An investigation into the perceptions of clinical supervision experienced by learning disability nurses. *Journal of Intellectual Disabilities* 11(4), 307–28.

Sloan G (1999) Good characteristic clinical supervision of a clinical supervisor: a community mental health nurse perspective. *Journal of Advanced Nursing* 30(3), 713–22.

Sloan G (2006) *Clinical Supervision in Mental Health Nursing*. London: Wiley & Sons.

Sloan G, White C, Coit F (2000) Cognitive therapy supervision as a framework for clinical supervision in nursing: using structure to guide discovery. *Journal of Advanced Nursing* 32(3), 515–24.

Smith H (2008) Mental health in school-aged children. *British Journal of School Nursing* 3(6), 285–86.

Spence C, Cantrell J, Christie J, Samet W (2002) A collaborative approach to the implementation of clinical supervision. *Journal of Nursing Management* 10(2), 65–74.

Stoltenberg CD, McNeill BW (2010) *IDM Supervision: An Integrative Developmental Model for Supervising Counselors and Therapists* (3rd edn). London: Routledge.

Styles J, Gibson T (1999) Is clinical supervision an option for practice nurses? *Practice Nursing* 10(11), 10–14.

Teasdale K, Thom N, Brocklehurst N (1998) *The Value of Clinical Supervision in Nursing: A Research Study Commissioned by The NHS Executive in Trent*. Boston, Lincolnshire: South Lincolnshire Training and Development Partnership.

Termini M, Hauser MJ (1973) The process of the supervisory relationship. *Perspectives in Psychiatric Care* 11(3), 121–25.

Van Ooijen E (2000) *Clinical Supervision: A Practical Guide*. London: Churchill Livingstone.

Walsh K, Nicholson J, Keough C (2003) Development of a group model of clinical supervision to meet the needs of a community mental health nursing team. *International Journal of Nursing Practice* 9(1), 33–39.

Winstanley J, White E (2003) Clinical supervision: models, measures and best practice. *Nurse Researcher* 10(4), 7–38.

Wright SC, Grenier M, Channell K (2012) University supervision within physical education teacher education. *Education* 132(4), 699–707.

CHAPTER 28

Engagement of stakeholders in learning and teaching

Amanda McGrandles

Globalisation, a competitive market, and limited resources have significantly influenced how organisations manage their businesses. Sustainable survival of all organisations – including educational institutions – depends on meeting the needs of its stakeholders. Both the public and the media are interested in the relationship between organisations and their stakeholders at a time when such relationships are critical and must be carefully managed. Review of the literature across business, health and educational arenas has led to the identification of a number of contemporary issues, and the aim of this chapter is to explore some of issues relating to stakeholder analysis, engagement and management in the context of the teaching and learning environment. The benefits of a collaborative approach are discussed, along with innovative practice and the interface between mental health and education.

Freeman's (1984) stakeholder theory has provided a platform from which to explore relationships between organisations and their stakeholders (Beach 2008; Friedman and Miles 2006). In our changing global climate, however, there are many more factors to consider than those covered in Freeman's (1984) early work, such as power, levels of interest, and methods to add value for customers. More and more stakeholders are choosing to invest in organisations that are more socially responsible, and organisations that choose to ignore this, do so at their peril. It is a particularly exciting time for stakeholders at the interface of mental health and education, because there are numerous possibilities for collaboration and joint ventures. The frameworks and tools outlined in the chapter aim to facilitate the integration of theory and practical application.

The stakeholder concept

Freeman's (1984) seminal text defines stakeholders as:

> *Any group or individual who can affect or is affected by the achievement of the organisation's objectives.*

This is an 'all-encompassing' definition. The literature reveals at least another 66 definitions (Beach 2008; Bryson 2004; Buchholz and Rosenthal 2005; Friedman and Miles 2006; Pesqueux and Damak-Ayadi 2005). There are some differences between them, but also many common themes. Mainardes *et al.* (2011) highlight that the abundance of literature on stakeholder theory can be criticised because of the often simplified definitions used, which are often vague and ambiguous. Many researchers using the term make no attempt to define it in context or achieve any sort of consensus, thus there is no single definitive and generally accepted definition. Furthermore, Mitchell *et al.* (1997) suggest that Freeman's original definition is very broad; limits must be established in order to define more specifically the extent of the stakeholders. From analysis of the definitions, three main components of the stakeholder concept emerge (Clarkson 1995):

- The organisation.
- Other actors.
- The nature of the company–actor relationships.

This focus on the nature of the relationship between organisations and stakeholders is supported by Clarkson (1995), Friedman and Miles (2006) and Frederick *et al.* (1992). Frooman (1999) considers that the company–stakeholder relationship is dyadic and mutually independent, while Freeman and Evan (1990) consider the organisational environment to have multilateral agreements with its stakeholders.

Context and development of stakeholder theory

The origin of the stakeholder concept is the literature of business science (Freeman 1984), however it has been suggested that stakeholder theory has clear links with four of the social sciences, namely sociology, economics, politics and ethics, and that it is particularly relevant to corporate planning and corporate social responsibility (Mainardes, Alves and Raposo 2012). Due to a rise in public interest and greater coverage by the media, the term has increased in popularity among policy–makers, regulators and non-governmental organisations (Friedman and Miles 2006), as well as in education and mental health (HM Inspectorate of Education 2007; Scottish Government 2012a, 2012b). In the context of rising competitiveness, globalisation and the growing complexity of company operations, Freeman's definition (1984) highlights to business organisations that they should be concerned not only with the interests of shareholders, but also with those of stakeholders when considering stakeholder decisions (Friedman and Miles 2006). A review of stakeholder theory would not be complete without mentioning the following three approaches (Donaldson and Preston 1995):

- **Descriptive approaches:** focus on how the organisation operates in terms of stakeholder management.

- **Instrumental approaches:** focus on how to attain organisational objectives through stakeholder management.

- **Normative approaches:** focus on how businesses should operate, especially in relation to moral principles.

Following Freeman's initial work, several authors were instrumental in developing the original theory over the years. Clarkson (1995), Donaldson and Preston (1995), Mitchell *et al.* (1997) and Rowley (1997) and Frooman (1999) all reiterated the importance of including a broad range of people to include groups that were not always considered when thinking in the formal sense of a stakeholder. These groups included employees, suppliers and other interested parties (Clarkson

1995) as well as clients, parents, children, teachers and nurses (Donaldson 2010; HM Inspectorate of Education 2007).

Who are the stakeholders?

Stakeholders are most commonly considered as groups of people. A selection are listed in FIGURE 28.1. Shareholders, employees, suppliers, clients and other parties potentially interested in a company's activity are most frequently quoted in the literature (Ayuso *et al.* 2011; Clarkson 1995; Mainardes *et al.* 2011, 2012). The preferred definition of stakeholder will influence the groups that most aptly fit. Freeman's broad definition from 1984 would support the fact that most groups of people are affected in some way by the many things that a corporation might do in order to achieve its objectives (Friedman and Miles 2009; Mainardes *et al.* 2011). In an attempt to clarify how organisations should deal with stakeholders in each segment, it is suggested that they are divided into two main groups (Clarkson 1995; Friedman and Miles 2009):

- **Primary stakeholders**: have a formal, official contractual relationship with the company, such as clients and employees.

- **Secondary stakeholders**: do not have such contractual relationships with the company (e.g. governments and local communities).

Donaldson and Preston (1995) suggest the importance of distinguishing between the influencers and the stakeholders – for example, some may have stakes but no influence (e.g. job applicants) and others may have influence but no stakes (e.g. the media). More recently, there has been a growing interest in the groups who seamlessly span the internal and external environments, who may have explicit or implicit relationships with the company (Forray and Goodnight 2010).

Independently within mental health services and education settings there are stakeholders who are actively involved with their respective organisations. However, the interface of mental health and education is an area that is still developing. Policy drivers support the direction of 'partnership working' and the need for a collaborative approach (Children and Young People's Mental Health Coalition 2013; Donaldson 2010; HM Government 2011; HM Inspectorate of Education 2007). Jones and Wicks (1999), Savage *et al.* (2004) and Philips *et al.* (2010) summarise some core assumptions of stakeholder theory (see FIGURE 28.2), addressing the interests of stakeholders, their levels of influence, their relationships in terms of processes and results, managerial decision–making, and the need to balance the interests of participants (Mainardes *et al.* 2012).

Meeting the expectations of the most important stakeholders will be a valuable part of organisational effectiveness. However, reaching agreement on which groups are most important to the company's survival and success may not be straightforward (Friedman and Miles 2006). The most popular model for this is that of Mitchell *et al.* (1997). Their 'stakeholder salience' model addresses power, legitimacy and urgency, and relates to the stakeholders' powers of negotiation, their relational legitimacy with the organisation, and the urgency applied to attending their requirements. This model is highly influential in stakeholder theory literature (Friedman and Miles 2009; Mainardes *et al.* 2011). Recent research supports the view that senior managers are influenced by stakeholder credibility in relation to power, legitimacy and urgency (Aaltonen *et al.* 2008).

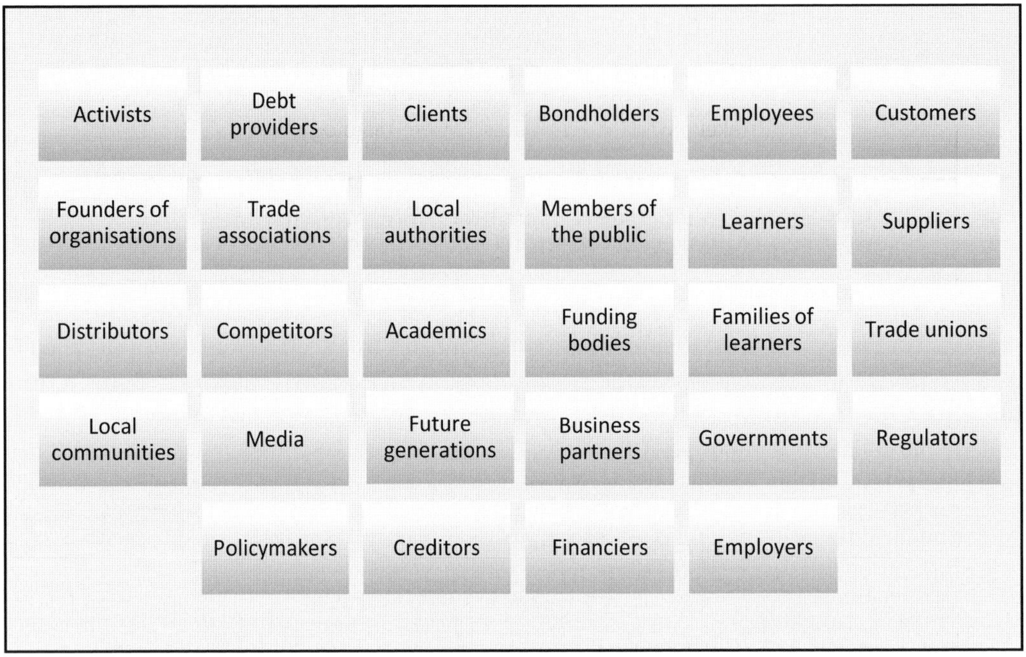

Figure 28.1: A selection of stakeholders (groups of people) in an organisation.

Limitations of stakeholder theory

Criticisms of stakeholder theory focus on the variation of definitions and approaches that lead to a diverse range of evidence and contradictory arguments (Mainardes *et al.* 2011). Beyond the definitions, stakeholder theory does not elaborate on processes or provide understanding about the complex system in which companies operate. There is also a requirement for deeper analysis of the internal and external variables, as well as a more complete evaluation of the environment, with greater consideration given to the dynamic (changing) factors (Mainardes *et al.* 2011).

Ladder of stakeholder engagement

Arnstein (1969) originally developed a 'ladder' of public involvement in relation to policy creation. This was later adapted by Friedman and Miles (2009) (FIGURE 28.3) who suggest that a number of factors influence the level at which management practices take place. These include the characteristics of the stakeholders, different stages in organisational life cycles and different strategies pursued by stakeholders (Friedman and Miles 2006; Frooman 1999; Mitchell *et al.* 1997; Savage *et al.* 1991). The lower levels on the ladder are suggestive of the organisation simply informing stakeholders of decisions that have already been reached, and are reflective of an autocratic style of stakeholder management. Midway up the ladder are gestures of participation, whereby views are heard but there are no guarantees that they will have any influence. At the higher levels, engagement is defined with active attempts at empowering stakeholders in corporate decision-making, and this involves trust and a degree of control over outcomes.

■ Organisations engage in relationships with many groups that either influence or are influenced by them ('stakeholders" in Freeman's 1984 terminology)
■ Theory focuses on these relationships in terms of processes and results for the company and the stakeholders
■ Interests of all legitimate stakeholders are of intrinsic value and no single set of interest prevails over all others
■ Theory focuses on managerial decision-making
■ Theory identifies how stakeholders seek to influence organisational decision-making processes so they become consistent with their needs and priorities
■ Organisations should strive to understand, reconcile and balance the various interests of participants

Figure 28.2: Core assumptions of stakeholder theory (adapted from Jones and Wicks 1999, Philips *et al.* 2010, Savage *et al.* 2004 and cited in Mainardes *et al.* 2012).

Stakeholders and competitive advantage

Strategic management is considered to be complex and fascinating with straightforward underlying principles – but no 'right answers' (Thompson 2003). Companies are more likely to succeed if the 'fit' is right between the organisation's resources and the market it targets, and the ability to sustain this fit over time in changing circumstances. A considerable part of this strategy involves the stakeholders. Companies fail when their strategies fall short of the expectations of their stakeholders. The stakeholders generate contributions and significant resources and so successful identification and careful management of those who are important to organisational survival is essential (Mainardes *et al.* 2012).

The more recent literature refers to the development of new communication technologies and reinforces the powerful role that the media, corporate communications and public relations have in organisational survival (Luoma-aho and Vos 2010). Stakeholder analysis and mapping considers stakeholders in terms of their level of interest and power. Their position on the grid (FIGURE 28.4) will influence the extent of communication required with them.

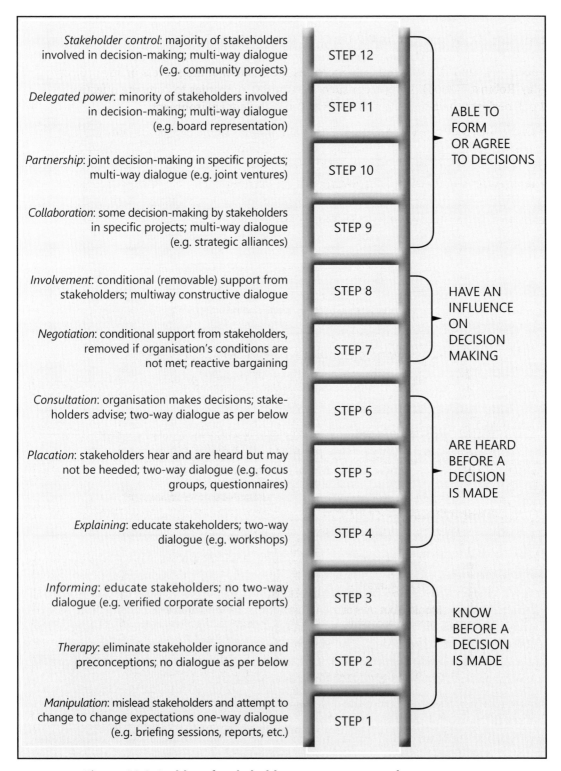

Figure 28.3: Ladder of stakeholder management and engagement (adapted from Friedman and Miles 2009).

Several authors suggest that this process of stakeholder engagement and evaluation is fundamental to success – it should never be completed simply as a 'tick-box' exercise. This is because it helps to ensure that the best plan is in place, for which strong support has been won, and this subsequently increases the chances of the success of any project (Finlay-Robinson 2009). Long-term success requires companies to compete effectively and out-perform their rivals in a dynamic, often turbulent environment.

To achieve this, they must find ways to create and add value for their customers. Adding value can be enhanced with a value chain analysis (Thompson 2003). This is a systematic way of studying the direct and support activities undertaken by a company. Completion of the analysis results in greater awareness concerning costs and the potential for lower costs and for differentiation (i.e. products of services that have distinctive properties that set them apart from competitors).

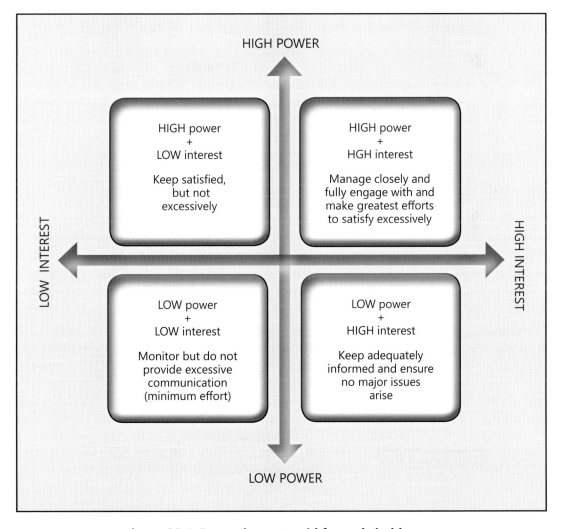

Figure 28.4: Power/interest grid for stakeholders.

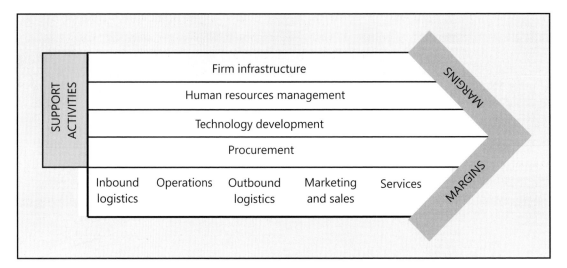

Figure 28.5 Porter's generic Value Chain (based on Porter 1985).

Porter's (1985) Value Chain (FIGURE 28.5) assists in demonstrating the value chain moving from left to right through primary and support activities. Competitive advantage may be achieved when performing the company's essential functions, either more cost effectively, or better than their competitors (Johnson and Scholes 2002; Thompson 2003). Furthermore, the strengthened stakeholder relationships themselves may become a source of competitive advantage in terms of trust, reputation and innovation (Rodriguez *et al.* 2002).

Corporate social responsibility (CSR)

In our global society, contemporary investors are revisiting their definition of 'value' and their expectations of companies. This will have a significant effect on organisations, governments and economic theorists, because 'value' for some has much more of a moral undertone. In a changing climate, sustainability or business commitment to sustainable economic development means working with employees, their families and local communities, and society in general to improve quality of life (World Business Council for Sustainable Development 2006).

Quite simply, some stakeholders are choosing to invest in organisations that are considered to be more socially responsible (Maharaj 2007). Reputation is becoming increasingly important for operating in the new media environment where online information about most organisations is readily available (Luoma-Aho and Vos 2010). Is this so far removed from the early work of Bowen (1953), who believed that individuals had a right to earn a reasonable profit but also had a duty to conduct business with a concern for all affected parties? Perhaps not. But the abundance and multifaceted nature of the CSR literature since then suggests that any company who chooses to ignore it will be regarded unfavourably. The principles identified in to-day's literature are conceptually linked to management thought from the twentieth century in rel-ation to recognising external environment and collaboration and development of shared understanding, however Evans *et al.* (2013) suggest collaboration and shared understanding are not always evident in practice. There is an expectation that organisations will conduct their operations responsibly. This is largely based on the need to align the social, environmental and economic responsibilities of business, so that the financial position of an organisation is considered alongside other important factors. There is a wealth of literature on CSR and stakeholder theory, which was reviewed by Laplume *et al.* (2008). The relationship between the organisation and stakeholders is recognised as a two-way process, with responsibilities on both sides, therefore any expectations regarding CSR should apply to stakeholders as much as they do to company members. Fassin (2012) suggests this is the case and that loyalty and responsibility are key features of their roles.

Stakeholder governance

An increasing number of companies recognise the value of engaging proactively with their stakeholders, but there is still room for improvement to ensure that the voices of all stakeholders are heard in the corporate decision-making processes and governance arrangements (Spitzeck *et al.* 2011). There is evidence of early success with joint management–stakeholder committees (JMSCs) – and innovative practice (Spitzeck *et al.* 2011). One recent study highlighted that outcomes from JMSCs were better than those of focus groups for demonstrating how dialogue with stakeholders directly influenced corporate decisions through the adoption of policies and performance indicators. Most significantly, the process of the collaboration created trust and transparency in decision-making (Spitzeck *et al.* 2011).

Stakeholder engagement—research, sustainable innovation, knowledge transfer

It is recommended that all stakeholders, including leaders of learning, refer to the latest scientific research when making decisions, but this tends to be published in peer-reviewed journals, making it less accessible to non-academic audiences. So-called knowledge transfer has many benefits because it increases the use of research evidence by non-research audiences or stakeholders in their decision-making; the process also builds relations and develops communication so that the translation of research findings into action is improved. This can be optimised by providing opportunities for direct interactions between researchers and relevant audiences, with collaboration from the earliest opportunity (Keown *et al.* 2008). The most successful mechanisms for this currently are life-long learning activities, such as Masters-level study and research; these build the knowledge and skills required for a more qualified and research-capable public sector workforce. Future prosperity will be influenced by the ability to compete in a global economy that is driven by research and innovation (UWS 2012a, 2012b). These have become international endeavours and are at the centre of the Coalition Governments Agenda (Department for Business Innovation and Skills 2011), and developing these skills will be essential for survival in a competitive market.

Collaboration with stakeholders brings limitless opportunities for generating new creative solutions, and is beneficial for all involved (Ayuso *et al.* 2011). Several qualitative studies have focused on stakeholder engagement, CSR and innovation (Holmes and Smart 2009: MacGregor and Fontrodona 2008), and according to Ayuso *et al.* (2011) the main ingredients in the creation of organisational capabilities are 'knowledge and learning'. Several authors have identified the importance of relationships and interactions for knowledge transfer both within and across organisational boundaries. Examples of these include alliances, joint ventures (such as collaborative interfaculty programmes and conferences) and networks with organisations to acquire new knowledge for innovation processes (Chang 2003). Knowledge translation (KT) and the closely related concepts of knowledge exchange, knowledge transfer and knowledge mobilisation have been widely embraced as mechanisms for facilitating the uptake of research-derived knowledge into a range of practice settings including health and education (Reimer-Kirkham *et al.* 2009). In their review of the literature on the subject, Reimer-Kirkham *et al.* (2009) identify the following that refer to 'some of the most noteworthy' recent cultural shifts (Reimer-Kirkham *et al.* 2009):

- A shift to acknowledge the complexity of knowledge translation as other than a linear rational process.
- A shift in how evidence is viewed, from preference for context-stripped evidence to the integration of context-sensitive knowledge, with recognition of the diverse ways of generating knowledge that counts as legitimate evidence.
- An acknowledgement of the contributions of non-instrumental uses of knowledge.
- A shift from silos of practice and research to university–community and clinical partnerships and exchanges.
- A shift in the responsibilities of researchers, from detached scientists to involved collaborators, negotiators and communicators of knowledge.
- Recognition that knowledge translation occurs at many levels, and is aimed not only at healthcare practitioners but actively involves policy and decision-makers.

These points highlight the progress that has been made to date, although there is still room for improvement.

Higher education and sustainable development

Universities have for some time been drivers of regional economic development (Drucker and Goldstein 2007). Although there may be variations between universities, at least 40% of all academic staff members currently interact with the private sector (Blewitt 2010) and there is general agreement on the need to cooperate, collaborate and network. In response to the changing global environment, new learning requires a new approach to university education and considerable levels of participation, engagement, autonomy, trust, cooperation and collaboration with all stakeholders including those in professions, trades, academic disciplines and various communities of practice. New graduates need to be equipped during their education so they can:

- Build capacity for community-based decision-making by promoting practical citizenship (Fien and Wilson 2005).
- Develop higher-order thinking skills and be comfortable using a variety of pedagogical techniques to promote participatory learning (UWS 2012a).
- Address global issues and local priorities (UNESCO 2005).
- Consider sustainability in terms of the environment, society and the economy (Organisation for Economic Co-operation and Development 2009).
- Understand the needs and perspectives of others, and explain, justify and negotiate ideas and plans (Blewitt 2010).
- Develop their interprofessional and intercultural manner (UNESCO 2005).

Learning around sustainability can be an open-ended and transformative process. Meaningful learning can occur when there is constructive dissonance and increased social cohesion. 'Difference' and 'diversity' can assist in creating change and building resilience in complex situations where there are varying degrees of uncertainty (Wals *et al.* 2009).

The interface of mental health and education

The recent Leadership for Learning Report (HM Inspectorate of Education 2007) clearly states that:

No establishment can work in isolation. We all operate within a context that involves groups of stakeholders including learners, their families, the broader community, employers, local authorities and funding bodies. All of these groups, and others, have an interest in education and can have something to give to the quality of the learners' experience.

The report explains the significance of this:

Where this interest develops into an effective partnership, with two or more establishments working together with a common purpose, there can be major contributions to the well–being and progress of learners.

The recommendation for greater collaboration between stakeholders at the interface of mental health and education is also highlighted in a number of other key documents (Donaldson 2010, Scottish Government 2012; Children and Young People's Mental Health Coalition 2013). In broad terms, the potential benefits include increased knowledge and competency, synergy and a stronger global presence in new markets utilising new technologies, sharing expertise, resources and good practice. At a time when cost-effective strategies have never been more important, this can only result in win–win situations. Among the innovative ideas to be considered are establishing closer links between schools and universities, incorporating a 'teaching hospital' model, and joint appointments to address the perceived theory–practise gap. The creation of a network of 'hub school' partnerships is in its infancy and closer links with Child and Adolescent Mental Health Services (CAMHS) are being explored. Programmes that promote interprofessional learning within faculties, across disciplines and across statutory and third-sector organisations create opportunities to develop a shared understanding and allow for creative solutions as a result of facing challenges together. Ideas can be developed using shared resources to maximise outputs, and using a range of tools and checklists for project management facilitates a structured approach to the process.

STAKEHOLDER ENGAGEMENT CHECKLIST (based on Revit 2007; www.revit–nweurope.org)

- **Scoping process**: clear evidence of purpose, scope, context, stakeholder identification and desired outcomes.
- **Purpose**: clearly defined aims and objectives agreed by all parties involved in commissioning, and clarity on use of outputs to achieve desired outcomes.
- **Scope**: specific boundaries for tasks and definition of engagement, identifying elements that can or cannot be changed, with thoroughly identified and evaluated risks.

- **Context**: detail and communicate wider issues to participants early (historical, political, physical and cultural contexts), link with past/present related activities, organisations, consultations, legal policy and decision-making parameters, timescale constraints, participant characteristics and capabilities.

- **Stakeholder identification**: transparent and documented, using a contacts database, based on coherent understanding of purpose and context, including all stakeholders and hard-to-reach groups at each part of the process; complete stakeholder analysis in relation to interest/power, and discuss and agree communication strategy.

- **Desired outcomes**: define exactly what is wanted from the process, and consider the most appropriate methods to achieve this.

- **Institutional buy-in**: key decision-makers in the organisation are fully informed and supportive of the engagement plan.

- **Engagement plan**: base on results of the scoping process, with backing from institutional support; clearly document all main components of the engagement process, outline organisational logistics, review schedule and evaluate plan.

- **Methods**: research and select appropriate methods for each issue and their stakeholders, carefully plan complementary methods for overall success.

- **Resources**: allocate sufficient budget for desired outcomes, and clearly detail and time-line roles and responsibilities for all involved; allocate appropriate skills and training for specific tasks.

- **Time schedule**: realistic timings, including time between events to complete work and taking to the next stage; specify key dates, actions and decision deadlines, and create Gant chart.

- **Outputs**: agree clear, tangible outputs before engagement activities, aligned with methods for achieving desired outcome of engagement process.

- **Engagement process**: flexible approach needed to help respond to unpredictability, informed by ongoing review.

- **Review process**: structured so that all involved in the engagement process are able to judge whether the process is likely to be, or was, a success, to manage risk and make responsive amendments to the process.

- **Final evaluation**: qualitative and quantitative criteria needed to evaluate achievement of outcomes using appropriate methods, outputs, stakeholders, budgeting, staff resource use, and effective response to feedback; include log of lessons learnt.

Concluding comments

This chapter has explored a number of issues in relation to stakeholder engagement. Previous stakeholder theory has paved the way for valuable developments in terms of identifying stakeholders and what is needed to establish effective relationships between them and organisations, with consideration given to levels of interest and power. In our changing global environment, many stakeholders choose to invest in organisations that are more socially responsible. Evidence is building that suggests loyalty and responsibility are becoming recognised as essential components of the relationship between stakeholders and organisations. It is an exciting time, especially for stakeholders at the interface between mental health and education, because there are so many possibilities, and sustainable innovations, knowledge transfer and collaborative ventures will further facilitate the sharing of resources and expertise to maximise outputs within the confines of limited budgets.

KEY MESSAGES FROM THIS CHAPTER

- The public and media have an increased interest in the relationship between organisations and their stakeholders.

- Careful analysis of, engagement with and management of stakeholders is essential for sustainable survival of organisations and company success.

- Companies have to out-perform their rivals in a dynamic environment, and find creative ways to add value for their clients.

- Stakeholders are increasingly investing in companies that demonstrate CSR in their activities.

- The interface of mental health and education offers wide scope for innovative practices, including knowledge transfer, interprofessional learning and joint ventures.

- Meaningful partnership and collaboration facilitate sharing of resources and expertise, and thus enhance knowledge, competency and synergy, as well as a stronger global presence in new markets.

Supporting evidence and further reading

Aaltonen K, Jaakko K, Tuomas O (2008) Stakeholders salience in global projects. *International Journal of Project Management* 26(1) 509–16.

Arnstein, SR (1969) A ladder of citizen participation. *American Institute of Planners Journal* 35, 216–24.

Ayuso A, Rodriguez MA, Garcia-Castro R, Arino MA (2011) Does stakeholder engagement promote sustainable innovation orientation? *Industrial Management and Data Systems* 111(9), 1399–417.

Beach S (2008) Sustainability of network governance: stakeholder influence. In: *Proceedings of Contemporary Issues in Public Management: The 12th Annual Conference of the International Research Society for Public Management.*

Blewitt J (2010) *Higher education for a sustainable world Education and Training* 52(6/7), 477–88.

Bowen HR (1953) *Social Responsibilities of the Businessman.* New York: NY: Harper and Row.

Bryson J (2004) What to do when stakeholders matter? *Public Management Review* 6(1), 21–53.

Buchholz R, Rosenthal S (2005) Toward a contemporary conceptual framework for stakeholder theory. *Journal of Business Ethics* 58(1), 137–48.

Chang YC (2003) Benefits of co-operation on innovative performance: evidence from integrated circuits and biotechnology firms in the UK. *Taiwan Research and Development Management* 33(4), 425–37.

Children and Young People's Mental Health Coalition (2013) *Resilience and results: How to improve the emotional and mental well-being of children and young people in your school.* Available at: www.cypmhc.org.uk/media/common/uploads/Final_pdf.pdf (accessed July 2015).

Clarkson M (1995) A stakeholder framework for analysing and evaluating corporate social performance. *Academy of Management Review* 20(1), 92–117.

Department for Business Innovation and Skills (2011) *Innovation and Research Strategy for Growth.* London: Department for Business, Crown Copyright.

Donaldson G (2010) *Teaching Scotland's future: report of a review of teacher education in Scotland.* Edinburgh: Scottish Government.

Donaldson T, Preston LE (1995) The stakeholder theory of the corporation: concepts, evidence and implications. *Academy of Management Review* 20(1), 65–91.

Drucker J, Goldstein H (2007) Assessing the regional economic development impacts of universities: a review of current approaches. *International Regional Science Review* 30(1), 20–46.

Evans W R, Haden S Clayton R, Novicevic M (2013) History-of-management-thought about social responsibility. *Journal of Management History* 19(1), 8–32.

Fien J, Wilson D (2005) Promoting sustainable development in TVET: the Bonn declaration. *Prospects* 35(3), 273–88.

Finlay-Robinson D (2009) What's in it for me? The fundamental importance of stakeholder evaluation. *Journal of Management Development* 28(4), 380–88.

Evans W R, Haden S, Clayton R, Novicevic M (2013) History-of-management thought about social responsibility. *Journal of Management History* 19(1), 8–32.

Fassin Y (2012) Stakeholder management, reciprocity and stakeholder responsibility. *Journal of Business Ethics* 109, 83–96.

Forray J, Goodnight J (2010) Think global, act local: a methodology for investigating international business curriculum priorities using stakeholder feedback. *Organization Management Journal* 7, 56–64.

Frederick W, Post J, St Davis K (1992) *Business and Society: Corporate Strategy Public Policy Ethics (seventh edn)* New York: NY: McGraw-Hill.

Freeman RE (1984) *Strategic Management: A Stakeholder Approach.* Boston, MA: Pitman.

Freeman RE, Evan WM (1990) Corporate governance: a stakeholder interpretation. *Journal of Behavioural Economics* 19, 337–59.

Friedman A, Miles S (2006) *Stakeholders: Theory and Practice.* Oxford University Press, Oxford.

Frooman J (1999) Stakeholders influence strategies. *Academy of Management Review* 24(2), 191–205.

HM Government (2011) Health without Mental Health. Available at: www.gov.uk/government/uploads/system/uploads/attachment_data/file/135457/dh_124058.pdf (accessed July 2015).

HM Inspectorate of Education (2007) *Leadership for Learning: The Challenges of Leading in a Time of Change.* Livingston, HMIE.

Holmes S, Smart P (2009) Exploring open innovation practice in firm-nonprofit engagements: a corporate social responsibility perspective. *Research and Development Management* 39(4), 394–409.

Husted BW, Allen DB (2011) *Corporate Social Strategy: Stakeholder Engagement and Competitive Advantage.* Cambridge: Cambridge University Press.

Johnson G, Scholes K (2002) *Exploring Corporate Strategy.* Essex: Prentice Hall.

Jones T, Wicks A (1999) Convergent stakeholder theory. *Academy of Management Review* 24(2), 206–21.

Keown K, Van Eerd D, Irvin E (2008) Stakeholder Engagement Opportunities in Systematic Reviews: Knowledge Transfer for Policy and Practice. *Journal of Continuing Education in the Health Professions* 28(2) 67–72.

Laplume AO, Sonpar, K, Linz RA (2008) Stakeholder theory: reviewing a theory that moves us. *Journal of Management* 34(6), 1152–89.

Luoma-Aho V, Vos M (2010) Towards a more dynamic stakeholder model: acknowledging multiple issue arenas. *Corporate Communications: An International Journal* 15(3), 315–31.

Maharaj R (2007) Critiquing and contrasting 'moral stakeholder' theory and 'strategic stakeholder': implications for the board of directors. *Corporate Governance* 8(2), 115–27.

MacGregor SP, Fontrodona J (2008) *Exploring the fit between CSR and innovation. Working paper WP-759*. Barcelona: IESE Business School Center for Business in Society/University of Navarra.

Mainardes EW, Alves H, Raposo M (2011) Stakeholder theory: issues to resolve. *Management Decision* 49(2), 226–52.

Mainardes EW, Alves H, Raposo M (2012) A model for stakeholder classification and stakeholder relationships. *Management Decision* 50(10), 1861–79.

Mitchell R, Agle B, Wood D (1997) Toward a theory of stakeholder identification and salience: defining the principle of who and what really counts. *Academy of Management Review* 22(4), 853–58.

Organisation for Economic Co-operation and Development (2009) *Sustainable manufacturing and eco–innovation: framework practices and management*. Available at: www.oecd.org/innovation/green/toolkit/48661768.pdf (accessed July 2015).

Pesqueux Y, Damak-Ayadi S (2005) Stakeholder theory in perspective. *Corporate Governance* 5(2), 5–22.

Philips R, Berman S, Elms H, Johnson-Cramer M (2010) Strategy, stakeholders and managerial discretion. *Strategic Organization* 8(2), 176–83.

Porter M (1985) *The Value Chain*. Available at: www.mindtools.com/pages/article/newSTR_66.htm (accessed July 2015).

Porter M (1985) *Competitive Advantage: Creating and Sustaining Superior Performance*. New York: Free Press.

Reimer-Kirkham S, Varcoe C, Browne A, Lynam M, Khan KB, McDonald H (2009) Critical inquiry and knowledge translation: exploring compatibilities and tensions. *Nursing Philosophy* 10, 152–66.

Revit (2007) *Working towards more effective and sustainable Brownfield revitalisation policies: Stakeholder engagement a toolkit*. Available at: www.revit-nweurope.org/selfguidingtrail/27_Stakeholder_engagement_a_toolkit-2.pdf (accessed July 2015).

Rodriguez MA, Ricart JE, Sanchez P (2002) Sustainable development and the sustainability of competitive advantage: a dynamic and sustainable view of the firm. *Creativity and Innovation Management* 11(3). 135–46.

Rowley T (1997) Moving beyond dyadic ties: a network theory of stakeholder influences. *Academy of Management Review* 22(4), 887–910.

Savage GT, Nix TW, Whitehead CJ, Blair JD (1991) Strategies for assessing and managing organizational stakeholders. *Academy of Management Executive* 5(2), 61–75.

Savage G, Dunkin J, Ford D (2004) Responding to crisis: a stakeholder analysis of community health organisations'. *Journal of Health and Human Services Administration* 6(4) 383–414.

Scottish Government (2012a) *Getting it Right for Children and Families: Engagement with Stakeholders and Partners*. Available at: www.scotland.gov.uk/Resource/0040/00408494.pdf (accessed July 2015).

Scottish Government (2012b) *Report of the Review of Further Education Governance in Scotland*. Available at: www.scotland.gov.uk/Resource/0038/00387255.pdf (accessed July 2015).

Spitzeck H, Hansen EG, Grayson D (2011) Joint management-stakeholder committees: a new path to stakeholder governance? *Corporate Governance* 11(5), 560–68.

Thompson J (2003) *Strategic Management (4th edn)*. London: Thomson.

UNESCO (2005) *United Nations decade of education for sustainable development (2005–2014)*. Available at: unesdoc.unesco.org/images/0013/001393/139369e.pdf (accessed July 2015).

University of the West of Scotland (UWS) (2012a) *Research and Knowledge Exchange Strategy*. Ayrshire, UWS.

University of the West of Scotland (UWS) (2012b) *Internationalisation and Global Citizenship Strategy and Action Plan 2012–2015*. Ayrshire, UWS.

Wals AEJ, der Hoeven N, Blanken H (2009) *The Acoustics of Social Learning: Designing Learning Processes that Contribute to a More Sustainable World.* Wageningen: Wageningen Academic Publishers.

World Business Council for Sustainable Development (2006) *Corporate Social Responsibility.* Available at: www.wbcsd.org (accessed July 2015).

PART V
The way forward

CHAPTER 29

A comprehensive, integrated framework for evaluation

Mick P. Fleming, Jean Rankin and Colin R. Martin

The integration of mental health theory with educational theory and practice has resulted in the application of biopsychosocial interventions and strategies among learners, educators and the learning environment as a whole, and new application of interventions provides novel opportunities for evaluation. Evaluation is important to ensure such interventions are associated with beneficial outcomes for learners and educators, and in the learning environment and wider community. Political decisions must also be made by educational organisations and policy-makers about efficient use of resources, especially of public money raised from taxation. Data from evaluation studies also provide evidence about effectiveness of interventions and associated costs, to help support managers of educational organisations and policy-makers make decisions about biopsychosocial interventions. This chapter considers the nature of evaluation and the design of evaluative studies, and describes aspects of knowledge development through qualitative methodologies based on observation and theory generation (inductive), as well as quantitative methodologies based on hypothesis testing (deductive). Ethical principles, which protect study participants from harm, are considered in the context of evaluation of education interventions.

Recent reports by the National Association of Schoolmasters Union of Women Teachers (2010), Teachers Assurance (2013), and Department FOR Education (2015), and the wider literature suggest that there is some rationale for integrating the theory and practice of mental health with that of education, in order to confer benefits on learners and educators, and ultimately the management and functioning of the learning environment and the wider community. This is a recent recommendation, with pragmatic and political implications for practitioners and policy-makers in terms of operationalising and administering interventions and programmes. If mental health theory is to influence educational practice, training and practice interventions/programmes will be needed. Not all educational institutions are public bodies, but most are financed by public monies. Future mental health interventions are likely to cost money and influence allocation of resources within educational organisations, and implementing them into such organisations may mean diverting money away from other important areas. For policy-makers and managers, this is a further responsibility to taxpayers. Bodies that allocate public monies rely on detailed information about spending and societal benefits, thus clearly designed evaluation processes are needed.

The emerging discipline of mental health and education and public financing of educational organisations means that research – particularly evaluation of mental health interventions within education – is an important part of the process. Detailed review of planning and delivery of these combined strategies is important for understanding the elements of and processes involved, their effectiveness, and their suitability for learners, educators and policy-makers. They will also provide important information for development and adjustment required.

The nature of evaluation

Evaluation is a specific type of applied research and function of research methods. Pure research is open-ended and contributes to the knowledge base, while evaluation involves systematic investigation of the aims, delivery and outcomes of specific interventions. The process is similar to auditing, but audit focuses on professional practice, while audit and evaluation monitor interventions or programmes against pre-defined standards (Bowling 2004). Evaluation is an empirical process that follows scientific method, using standard research methods and processes to appraise interventions. Here, there is a strong association between evaluation and research methods.

Types of evaluation

There are two types of evaluation – formulative and summative.

- **Formative evaluation:** This occurs while the intervention is being delivered, and focuses on the processes of and application of the intervention, aiming to provide data that improves the administration and implementation of the intervention (Hartas 2010a). For example, review of the processes involved in preparing and training educators to deliver stress management interventions to their peers as part of a stress management programme; or review of the suitability of a stress management intervention for those delivering and those receiving the intervention.

- **Summative evaluation:** This occurs at the end of an intervention or programme. It is primarily concerned with the outcomes and ant effects on the recipients, providing data on the effectiveness of the intervention in relation to its stated aims. An example is evaluation of the outcomes on stress and anxiety levels of educators after undergoing a peer-led stress management intervention.

Nevo's three-phase framework is a rough guide to planning evaluation studies, rather than strict instructions for evaluators to follow (Hartas 2010a). The phases are:

- **Defining** the aims and purpose of the evaluation, which generally include evaluating all mechanisms and processes, providing evidence for development of the intervention, and providing new knowledge about it.

- **Describing** dimensions of the evaluation, such as components of its implementation, and the human, social, cultural and political environments within which the evaluation takes place.

- **Formulating** the key questions for evaluation, selecting the most capable methodology and outcome measures, and measuring the impact.

Methods of evaluation

Evaluation research is a clear and sequential process. It is planned in a way that is consistent with a series of pre-defined research rules and conventions, which govern the planning and delivery of methods used in studies to identify and organise the requirements of the participants, study design, data collection and analytic methods (Robson 1999). The methodology is the conceptual and philosophical framework that provides the rules, conventions and guidelines that prescribe the design of the study (Polgar and Thomas 2008). Epistemological theory relates two paradigms, or world views, within research; each one relates to one of two methodologies that shape the practice of evaluation research and knowledge development (Cook and Garratt 2005). They are based on different beliefs about the ways that knowledge and theory are developed, and each prescribes different rules and conventions for the study design.

QUALITATIVE METHODS

Qualitative methodologies are based on theories that knowledge develops by understanding people's interpretations of phenomena (Bowling 2004). Theory is generated through observation of people and phenomena in their natural settings, and to identify themes and patterns and draw principles, knowledge and theory from them (Brink *et al.* 2011). Development of general theories of explanations – as opposed to specific and universal conclusions – distinguishes the methodologies from each other. The strategies or study methods are classed as inductive because the process involves drawing inferences from data obtained from the observations in order to develop a general theory that explains them.

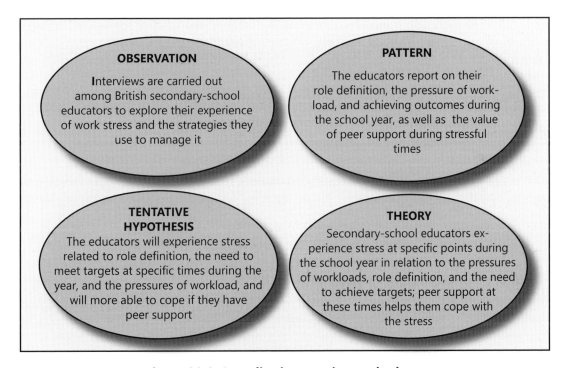

OBSERVATION

Interviews are carried out among British secondary-school educators to explore their experience of work stress and the strategies they use to manage it

PATTERN

The educators report on their role definition, the pressure of work-load, and achieving outcomes during the school year, as well as the value of peer support during stressful times

TENTATIVE HYPOTHESIS

The educators will experience stress related to role definition, the need to meet targets at specific times during the year, and the pressures of workload, and will more able to cope if they have peer support

THEORY

Secondary-school educators experience stress at specific points during the school year in relation to the pressures of workloads, role definition, and the need to achieve targets; peer support at these times helps them cope with the stress

Figure 29.1: A qualitative enquiry method.

QUANTITATIVE METHODS

Quantitative methods are deductive; they start with a theory from which a testable hypothesis is deduced. This hypothesis makes predictions about the expected patterns of relationships between two or more variables, and its falsifiability is then tested by observation to see whether the evidence supports the prediction. The process of hypothesis testing allows theories to be developed and refined. The findings confirm or disconfirm the existing theory, thus leading to the modification of the theory (Polgar and Thomas, 2008). Quantitative methodologies are based on rationality and the assumption of a universal and objective reality. The rules and conventions used in such evaluation studies aim to support validity and reliability, and protect the process from bias that may influence findings. Internal and external validity measures are used to judge the objectivity and meaningfulness of the findings (Bowling 2004). Specific systematic sampling and randomisation procedures and control of confounding variables improve the internal validity of these evaluation studies (Clark-Carter 2010). The selection of the methodology depends on the aims and questions of the evaluation. Choosing the correct method is essential for designing the study and achieving the aims of the evaluation (Clark-Carter 2010). The wrong methodology results in the adoption of incorrect rules and conventions and would not achieve the aims of the evaluation.

INDUCTIVE METHODS

These are associated with qualitative research (Silverman 2010) which broadly focus on the use of subjective data to explore issues, understand phenomena and answer questions, making sense of unstructured data through analysis and evaluation (see FIGURE 29.3 overpage). Ind-uctive approaches reverse the processes characteristic of deductive research (Lancaster 2005). Qualitative research involves numerous paradigms, approaches, schools of thought, and ontological, epistemological and methodological assumptions (Robson 2011). This is the same for evaluation research approaches that differ in their ideology, philosophy or method-ology. The wide range of strategies underlines the importance of observation, the need for retaining phenomenological quality, and the value of subjective human interpretation (Silverman 2010). Examples include naturalistic evaluation approaches, interpretive and constructive qualitative approaches, and critical theory approaches. The main philosophical approaches used to inform mental health research are interpretive and critical humanism paradigms. These emphasise the importance of understanding the meanings of human actions and experiences, and on generating accounts of their meaning from these viewpoints, representing different ways of looking at the world, and using different approaches to observe and measure various phenomena. The interpretive approach increases understanding of the world from an individual perspective, while critical humanism – a subtype of the interpret-ive paradigm – uses data gathered from the study population for social change.

INTERPRETIVE METHODS

These mainly focus on understanding and accounting for the meaning of human experiences and actions, and emphasise inherent meanings in human experience and action, regardless of their individual or collective origin. Ethnography, phenomenology and narrative approaches are often adopted in mental health context, whereby each method addresses the same issue from a different standpoint (Silverman 2010).

CRITICAL METHODS

The critical paradigm concerns awareness of how our thinking is socially and historically constructed. It emphasises the social and historical origins and contexts of meaning, regardless of the individual or collective forms of expression. The focus is on critiquing and transformation of current structures, relationships and conditions that shape and constrain

T H E O R Y

By reviewing the literature, an association between increased stress levels and increased workload pressures in secondary schools educators is identified, and peer support shows a beneficial effect on stress levels

H Y P O T H E S I S   T E S T I N G

H$_1$
There will be a significant association between measured stress levels and reported increases in workload pressure

H$_1$
There will be a significant difference in stress levels of educators who receive formal peer support and those who do not

H$_0$
There will be *no* significant association between measured stress levels and reported increases in workload pressure

H$_0$
There will be *no* significant difference in stress levels of educators who receive formal peer support and those who do not

O B S E R V A T I O N

Investigate reported stress levels and objective measures of workload pressure by conducting a survey, and analyse the strength and direction of any association

Conduct a trial to compare reported pre-/post-test stress levels of two equal-sized, randomly allocated groups, one receiving formal peer support, and the other none

T H E O R Y   C O N F I R M A T I O N

Increased workload pressure is associated with higher levels of stress in secondary school educators

Peer support reduces the level of stress in secondary school educators

Figure 29.2: A quantitative enquiry method.

the development of social practices in organisations and communities. Critical review is not directed towards understanding for its own sake, but towards understanding as a tool to be used in the ongoing process of practical transformation of society. Methodologies informed by this perspective foster self-reflection, mutual learning, participation and empowerment (Kindon *et al.* 2007). Participatory action research is a one example; it engages relevant client groups and key stakeholders as participants (Kindon *et al.* 2010). The approach has been used in psychiatry to amplify the voices of consumers and carers in mental health research and strengthen their role in mental health service evaluation and development (Davidson *et al.* 1997; Nelson *et al.* 1998). The process involves people of unequal power and status, and aims to bring about change in a practice setting (Kindon *et al.* 2010; Mertens 2005). These are more explicit features than found with other qualitative methodologies.

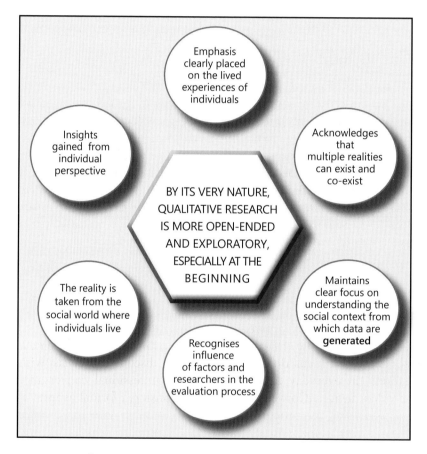

Figure 29.3: Key factors in qualitative research.

Types of study

Each study should address the aims and objectives of the evaluation, and take into account any underpinning philosophy, with careful consideration and planning of the evaluation process. Various approaches are used in mental health evaluation.

PHENOMENOLOGY

This qualitative approach explores the lived experiences of individuals, the way they experience their world and what it is like for them, and how best to understand their experiences. It acknowledges that a person's 'life world' is a social, cultural and historical product, as well as individual subjectivity. The approach has origins in philosophy but is now used across all disciplines to formulate meaning-oriented descriptive knowledge of human experience (Wertz *et al.* 2011). The aim is to consistently conceptualise the processes and structure of mental health, and the way situations are meaningfully lived through as though they are experienced 'with nothing added and nothing subtracted' (Giorgi 2009). Phenomenology is the science of phenomena; it does not relate to things, but the way they manifest; it deals with the nature of the appearance, rather than interpretation, and allows individuals to speak for themselves (Lewis and Staehler 2010). Two key approaches are Heidegger's interpretive phenomenology and Husserl's descriptive phenomenology. The latter is commonly used in evaluation research and requires researchers to set aside their own experiences and assumptions before the research begins. Interviews are the main method of data collection (Silverman 2010).

ETHNOGRAPHY

Ethnography is driven by the concept of 'being there' and observing events as they occur (Borneman and Hammoudi 2009). It does not exclusively focus on talk, but includes activities and events (Flick 2014), and acknowledges that communities are comprised of individual people, each with their own subjective experiences. The method involves participant observation whereby the researcher becomes part of 'the field' for some time to observe what goes on, describing phenomena within societal and cultural context. It also explores the way in which phenomena are constituted within the community. Over time, the researcher collects data through various methods including observation, participation in activities, field notes and talking to individuals and groups. The qualitative ethnographic approach is prominent in local and disciplinary contexts for focusing on other peoples' experiences.

ETHNOMETHODOLOGY

This analyses the methods used by people to organise their everyday lives in a meaningful and orderly way (Flick 2014). It involves observation of mundane or institutional routines, for example to examine the steps involved in admitting mental health patients into a psychiatric hospital. There is a focus on conversations and discourse analysis, with analysis of verbal interactions, in everyday talk, institution or professional conversations collected with audio or video devices. Conversation analysis considers formal aspects of talk where rules can be identified in the process (Flick 2014). This is a growing form of qualitative research into the content of conversation and the impact on everyday issues.

ACTION RESEARCH

Action research is a popular approach used for improving conditions and practices in healthcare (Lingard *et al.* 2008). It is also known as Participatory Action Research (PAR), community-based study, co-operative enquiry, action science, and action learning. It involves researchers conducting systematic enquiries to improve their own practices and working environment, and ultimately patient and user care. The aim is to bring about change in specific contexts, through observation and communication with other people; healthcare workers are continually making informal evaluations and judgements about what it is they do

(Reason and Bradbury 2008). The strength of the approach is its focus on generating solutions to practical problems and its ability to empower practitioners by getting them to engage with research and any subsequent development or implementation activities (Cresswell 2013).

GROUNDED THEORY

The premise of this approach is that theories should be developed from empirical material and analysis (Flick 2014), and are the end-point of such research. It is a general research method (not owned by either quantitative or qualitative methods) and is now considered as a constructive approach. It enables researchers to conceptualise social patterns and structures in a specific area of interest through the process of constant comparison. An initial, detailed inductive approach to data analysis results in a deductive phase of the final process (Wertz *et al.* 2011). Both qualitative and quantitative data can be collected from video-recordings, images, text, observation, and the spoken word, and analysed following a detailed and strict procedure.

Data collection

The key methods in evaluation research relate to verbal data, obtained through interviews, focus groups and narratives of personal stories and conversations, or through observation, field-notes and documentation. These often involve digitally audio- and video-recordings, but the chosen method should support the research design. Data selection, interpretation and analysis must be rigorous in terms of reliability and validity so that the quality of research is not compromised (Silverman 2006).

INTERVIEWS

A range of interview techniques is used to gain rich and detailed information. Interview schedules should be well planned and appropriate in content and duration, and should be conducted by an experienced interviewer. Semi-structured interviews are based on a series of planned, mostly open-ended questions that guide the interview and interviewer, with sufficient flexibility built in to allow the interviewee to add their own perspective (Robson 2011). Face-to face interviews are conducted in a quiet, private environment. Online interviews are gaining popularity, providing computer-mediated communication. Narrative interviews focus on a specific process of development in the life of the interviewee, with little input from the interviewer. Most semi-structured interviews and narration-orientated interviews focus on an individual. In focus groups, verbal data is provided from several people in a group situation, with the expectation that their discussions will yield more data than individual interviews (Silverman 2010); a moderator should oversee the quality of the process. Interviews continue until sufficient information is gathered to fully develop or saturate a model. In ethnography, interview opportunities arise spontaneously, with a more informal schedule, whereby the interview is co-constructed by interviewer and interviewee.

Data analysis

A systematic and structured approach to data analysis is essential. Qualitative research methods in the field of evaluation are controversial, so this improves the quality and detail of the overall findings. Interviews and focus groups are normally digitally recorded and transcribed for manual analysis. Phenomenological analysis is descriptive, and does involve a theoretical model as in grounded theory. Thematic analysis for phenomenology is normally conducted using one relevant frameworks, or transcripts are analysed online using relevant software. Manual analysis involves a structured step-by-step approach of reading and re-reading transcripts to identify significant statements, from which meanings are formulated into clusters, then themes and emerging themes (Cresswell 2013). This process should be clear and transparent, with final themes being member-checked by the participants.

Grounded theory interviews proceed in detailed stages (Flick 2014). First there is open coding, whereby researchers form categories of information about the phenomenon under study. Next is axial coding, whereby researchers assemble data in new ways, presenting them in a visual model in which researchers identify the central phenomenon, explore causal conditions, identify context and intervening conditions, and delineate consequences of the phenomenon. In selective coding, researchers often write a story line to connect the categories. Finally a matrix of factors influencing the central phenomenon may be produced. The process produces a theory that is close to the specific problem or population (Wertz *et al.* 2011).

Documentary analysis uses a similar systematic and detailed approach to identify recurring and interesting content. Well-planned checklists and criteria are set for systematically analysing other data, such as video-recordings and field-notes. As the role of qualitative research in evaluation is expanding in healthcare, rigorous planning of the process is essential to minimise limitations.

DEDUCTIVE METHODS OF EVALUATION

Deductive methods are associated with a positivist philosophy and rationality, which considers all aspects of human behaviour as measurable and objective discrete or continuous variables, with numerical values applied to the measurable variables (Coolican 2009; Robson 1999). Validity and reliability are indicators of the robustness of the study and its findings. Evaluations are based on clear questions or hypotheses, with statistical analysis of data from which conclusions are drawn (Robson 1999). There are three categories of deductive study.

(i) Descriptive studies

These types of studies explore the characteristics and experiences of specific groups or populations (Coolican 2009), such as learners aged 12–14 years attending secondary schools who display self-harming behaviour. The studies are limited because it is not possible to make inferences about the relationships between different variables, thus, in the example above, the data cannot explain why the learners of that age and at that school display those behaviours. However, they can help identify trends and patterns within specific populations.

(II) Exploratory studies

Exploratory studies usually test a set hypothesis as well as a research question, and explore the relationships between variables, such as the association between self-harming in 12–14-year-old learners at secondary school and stress levels. It is then possible to draw inferences about the strength of relationship for predictive purposes; for example, a certain amount of stress may be indicated by a value on measurement instrument and thus predict self-harming behaviour. Such findings may then influence future observations of stress in that population to facilitate early recognition and intervention.

(iii) Experimental studies

Experimental studies measure cause and effect relationships between variables. True experiments have good internal validity because they follow strict rules. Then exploring the effect of manipulating or changing an independent variable to establish cause and effect. In most cases, manipulation or change means allocation of study participants to one of at least two groups, where the only difference is that one group receives an intervention or is exposed to a specific stimulus, while the other group does not. Group equivalence is crucial, that is they must have the same characteristics, so that any difference between them can be related to the intervention or stimulus. There are also dependent variables in these studies, which are affected by manipulation of the independent variable; for example, in a study designed to evaluate the effectiveness of a cognitive behavioural stress management intervention among secondary school teachers, the independent variable is the population of secondary school teachers. A smaller sample representing the characteristics of the population would be selected to participate in the experiment. Then participants are divided into two equivalent groups, with one receiving the cognitive intervention and the other receiving another intervention (such as peer support). The value of the dependent variable (i.e. the level of stress reported by the participants) is caused by the independent variable (i.e. cognitive behavioural intervention or peer support), and is usually measured by an established instrument such as a stress and anxiety scoring system.

(iv) Group equivalence and randomisation

The results of the experiment are only accurate if there was group equivalence. Any differences in the participants' characteristics can affect the results, for example, if one group was more experienced, with more stress exposure, coping strategies and resilience. Results favouring that group might reflect these factors rather than the effect of the intervention. Randomisation is used to create group equivalence, whereby each participant has an equal chance of being allocated to either group. Various paper- and software-based strategies are available for ensuring true probabilistic random assignment (Portney and Watkins 2009).

Randomisation and manipulation of the independent variable are characteristic of true experiments, but some naturally occurring phenomena prevent random assignment. It would be impossible (and unethical) to randomly allocate 14–15 year olds into groups of those expected to display self-harming behaviour and those who are not. When random allocation is not possible, non-random groups can be used. These so-called quasi-experiments yield less definitive results than true experiments, and results may be influenced by group differences, thus internal validity is not robust.

Study design and methods

Methodology refers to the overarching philosophical framework that guides studies to generate and develop knowledge and theory, but study design and methods involve the processes and procedures used and how they are organised (Coolican 2009; Polgar and Thomas 2008). The design of deductive approaches ensures that collected data are relevant, and that the goals and aims of the evaluation are achieved. The study might be cross-sectional (with data collected only once to capture a point in time), or longitudinal (with data collected several times over specified time periods). The number of times data are collected relates to the goals and aims of the evaluation and the research question.

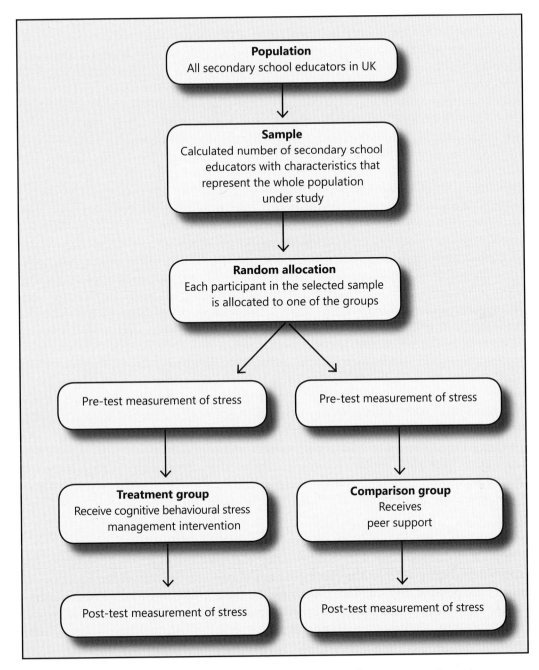

Figure 29.4: Diagrammatical example of a true experiment.

SURVEYS AND CENSUSES

Surveys are common in education and health research as they allow researchers to collect a large volume of accurate data relating to opinions, attitudes, personality factors, thoughts, emotions, behaviours and other mental health factors (Watson and Coombes 2009) and usually involving face-to-face interviews, specific measurement tools and self-report measures. The data are used to increase understanding of trends and population characteristics, as well as relationships between factors such as stress levels and workload. The approach can be used for descriptive and exploratory studies, among individuals or institutions, and can answer research questions and test hypotheses. Surveys explore factors in a sample of a population of interest, unlike censuses that explore entire populations (Bowling 2004). When exploring factors within a sample, it is important that the sample truly represents the characteristics of the entire population in order to generalise results from the study.

COHORT STUDIES

There are two defining characteristics of cohort studies. First is the notion of inquiry into a specific group, that is a group of individuals that share a characteristic such as year of birth or attendance at the same university (Portney and Watkins 2009). Second is that participants are followed together over time to explore identified outcomes or conditions that develop. Thus they include a temporal element and are longitudinal as there are often several data collection points over time (Cohen *et al.* 2007). The time points are pre-determined according to the factors being studied, such as annual checks of developmental milestones in pre-school-children. Birth cohort studies help identify the incidence or prevalence of a specific condition, whereby babies born in a certain year are entered into a national register and monitored over a specified period of time to see if they develop the condition and the outcomes of that condition. Data can be collected retrospectively, from past events, or prospectively, from future events (Adetunji *et al.* 2009), using face-to-face or telephone interviews, medical notes, or measurement instruments. The data can be used to answer research questions and to test hypotheses relating to specific groups, but they are only observational so cannot establish cause and effect (Adetunji *et al.* 2009). Their strength is in providing rich information about trends and changes within specific groups, and have particular value in educational studies where they can identify changes. Examples might be groups entering educational institutions in a specific year, groups entering secondary schools in a specific local authority area, or age groups in which specific learning needs are identified.

(i) Randomised controlled trials (RCTs)

These are the 'gold standard' design for determining cause and effect between two or more variables, and for investigating the effectiveness of an intervention. Participants are randomly allocated to one of two groups, one receiving the intervention and the other receiving an alternative intervention that is already in use or no intervention. Strict inclusion and exclusion criteria and robust randomisation procedures help create equivocal groups for comparison, to minimise confounding variables and maximise validity. Outcomes and dependent variables are measured before and after the intervention using a validated and reliable instrument.

Where an intervention is based on a psychosocial model, such as cognitive behavioural therapy, researchers must ensure that each therapist delivers the intervention to participants in exactly the same way, to maximise the internal validity of the study. Inconsistent delivery is a confounding factor that might influence outcome. Trials of psychosocial interventions use manuals that specify the intervention, the skills required and manner of delivery with training and supervision as required. These strategies are common in RCTs investigating the effectiveness of psychosocial interventions and are especially relevant to mental health interventions within educational institutions.

Single blinding means that participants are not informed whether they are receiving the tested intervention or the control intervention; in double-blinded trials, the data collectors also do not know which intervention the participants are receiving. This lack of awareness is important for reducing bias as they assess or interview participants. These trials are the most expensive to set up but have the highest internal validity. There are four designs based on the function of the groups in the study.

- **Within groups:** here, the same participants are in each comparison group. Allocation to different groups is the equivalent of manipulating the independent variable. Outcome measures are the dependent variable. Such a design is suitable for testing two interventions consecutively, or the effect of one intervention on a consequent second intervention (Martin and Thomson 2000). For example, participants may receive deep muscle relaxation therapy to increase coping ability, and this may then be used as a coping strategy within a systematic desensitisation intervention, thus multiple outcomes can be measured.

- **Between groups:** in these studies, the sample is randomly divided into two separate or independent groups for comparing outcomes (Martin and Thomson 2000). Randomisation levels out any differences between the groups and allows the researcher to control some of the confounding variables. Each group then receives a different intervention, usually the experimental intervention or an existing intervention, with outcomes used to compare efficacy and effectiveness of each, and before and after effects. Studies can be conducted over months or years to reveal any long-term benefits. In a study of motivation in physical education, participants from a selected sample would be randomly allocated to a group receiving motivational intervention before physical education sessions, or a group preparing for sessions in the usual manner. Baseline measures, before the intervention, might comprise attendance at sessions and the time spent in sessions. These would be measured again after delivery of the intervention, at agreed time points. To minimise confounding factors within each group, participants would either receive the same motivational intervention or undergo the same preparation. Manuals, training and supervision are usually provided to ensure uniform delivery of the intervention and hence maximise internal validity (Cohen *et al.* 2007).

- **Mixed groups:** these integrate elements of within groups and between groups designs to investigate both within-group and between-groups factor (Clark-Carter 2010). There are two independent variables, one relating to the within-groups factor and the other to the between-groups factor (Martin and Thomson 2000). In a study in which a stress management intervention is expected to be most effective for 14-year-olds three days after delivery, measures would be needed before intervention and at, for example, at two, three and five days after. This would be the within-groups factor, with overall efficacy and effectiveness as the between-groups factor at different time points.

(ii) Crossover trials

These are used to clarify the full effect of an intervention. Participants are randomly allocated to one of two independent groups. One receives the experimental intervention, and the other the standard or established (control) intervention. On completion of the intervention, the participants of the control group are then given the intervention, while those in the experimental group then receive the control intervention (Portney and Watkins 2009). However, the effects of the first intervention on will confound the effects of the second intervention. Cross-over designs are not appropriate for medium or long-term studies, such as cognitive behavioural therapy. In the short-term, they might be used to investigate the effects of specific dietary elements on the classroom behaviour of 8–10-year-olds. The diets of participants could be manipulated, first by removing certain elements, then re-introducing them. Behavioural outcome measures would be made before and after both stages.

(iii) Cross-cultural studies

These are used to systematically investigate variations and similarities between different cultures or ethnic groups, or the efficacy of educational or psychosocial interventions (Coolican 2009; Hartas 2010b). Educational organisations often deal with learners from many different cultural and ethnic backgrounds, so decision-makers need to understand any variations that exist in the effectiveness of an intervention as a consequence of cultural variation, in order to make adaptations and maximise benefit across the board.

(iv) Single-subject designs

These investigate the effect of a specific intervention on one person, where the single subject is also the control. The design is flexible and can include many variations in the types and sequence of interventions and timings of outcome measures. However, the findings have limited applicability to the wider population. This kind of study might be used to investigate the delivery and impact of a specific communication intervention on a learner with a sensory impairment.

(v) Case–control designs

These are useful for epidemiological studies, for example to explore risk factors for a specific health or psychological condition (Adetunji et al. 2009). They can be retrospective (e.g. at exposure to risk factors) or prospective (to investigate outcomes of a particular health condition) (Portney and Watkins 2009). Participants (or cases) are selected through diagnosis of various clinical criteria or treatment. Comparison is made with controls, that is participants who do not have the condition. For comparison to be meaningful, all participants should be from the same population and have the same characteristics (Portney and Watkins 2009). Stratified sampling is used to recruit a suitable control group. Within educational research, groups are likely to be matched for age range, gender distribution, geographical area, and similarity of education and educational attainment.

(vi) Cross-sectional studies

Unlike longitudinal studies, only one observational measurement is taken in these studies (Cohen et al. 2007; Hartas 2010c); Portney and Watkins 2009). Choosing between a cross-sectional or longitudinal design depends on the research question and aims. Cross-sectional designs are useful for identifying the prevalence and incidence of health conditions, and for collecting data on different variables, to explore, for example, the relationship between age and academic development. Longitudinal studies are better suited to investigate changes over time, for example the changes in stress levels of first year undergraduate students throughout the academic year.

Ethical issues

In the current context, ethics relates to the moral principles guiding research on human participants. Studies must be safe and participants protected from harm (Bowling 2004). Higher education institutions have various processes in place for monitoring and advising researchers, with specific ethics committees who independently scrutinise all proposed studies. These committees are usually made up of academics and have the power to grant or withhold permission for a study to commence, for example if they perceive some risk to participants. The researchers may then re-design the study to address those concerns. There are four common ethical principles that human studies should adhere to (Johnson and Long 2010; Portney and Watkins 2009; Robson 1999).

AUTONOMY AND SELF-DETERMINATION

This ethical issue is commonly linked to the concept of informed consent. Researchers must respect the potential participant's decision to participate or not in a study. The voluntary nature of the study should be clearly communicated to participants before they make a decision. Researchers also respect the decision of a participant to withdraw from a study at any later point. Clear and unambiguous information must be provided, therefore, so participants have the full knowledge, as well as capacity and time, to make an informed decision (Johnson and Long 2010; Lindsay 2010). The capacity to provide consent may be an issue for participants under the age of 18 years, with learning disabilities or mental ill-health, who must be protected from potential exploitation; in these cases their parents or guardians must be contacted or objective assessment made of their capacity. Ethics committees can be a source of valuable advice and guidance for researchers, so it is better to contact them at an early stage of planning.

NON-MALEFICENCE

Non-maleficence is a principle that guides researchers to develop methods that protects participants from harm while they are participating in a study (Boulton 2009). As well as eliminating risk to participants from the intervention under evaluation, the identity of participants is protected to maintain their privacy and dignity. Ensuring all data are secure reduces the chance that harm will result from divulgence of personal details, for example about education status and health conditions, especially in mental health related studies where participants may report sensitive data on stressful conditions, emotions and specific work or life events (Cohen *et al.* 2007).

BENEFICENCE

Beneficence involves acting to benefit others – particularly participants in a study and the wider population. In terms of evaluation studies, it relates to providing benefits for the population under scrutiny and contributes to the development of knowledge (Portney and Watkins 2009). Evaluation studies are designed to focus on interventions with potential benefits for participants and the wider population.

PRINCIPLE OF JUSTICE

The principle of justice guides the researchers regarding fairness and equitable treatment of all participants and ensures that their rights are respected, so that the needs of the researcher and the study are not given priority over the needs and rights of the participants (Lindsay 2010).

Concluding comments

There is a rationale that supports the evaluation of mental health interventions within educational organisations, or application of psychosocial interventions to educational practice, to learners or educators, whereby educationalists need to have confidence in the interventions they use in their work and environment. The systematic application of mental health interventions in learning environments is relatively new, so researchers need to provide meaningful evidence on the effectiveness and suitability of these interventions in this context. To this end, they must design a range of systematic, robust studies to evaluate the delivery of interventions, using inductive and deductive methodologies that impose rules and conventions relevant to the research question. The methods described in this chapter are available to researchers in this area, although they may need to combine elements of both inductive and deductive methods to achieve their aims. Mixed methods studies allow researchers to consider suitability issues as well as efficacy of interventions, which is particularly important bearing in mind the novelty of applying mental health theory to educational practice and organisations.

KEY MESSAGES FROM THIS CHAPTER

- The systematic delivery of mental health interventions within educational practice and organisations is novel and provides a rationale for robust evaluation of these interventions.

- Evaluation is a specific type of applied research and a function of research methods.

- Evaluation research is a clear and sequential process that is planned according to a series of pre-defined research rules.

- The two distinct methodologies (qualitative and quantitative) have an epistemological basis and provide researchers with rules and conventions for designing evaluation studies.

- There are a range of inductive (qualitative) and deductive (quantitative) research methods for designing evaluation studies.

- Ethical principles must be applied to all planned evaluation studies.

Supporting evidence and further reading

Adetunji HA, Neale J, Wheeler N (2009) Cohort studies. In: J Neale (ed.) *Research Methods in Health and Social Care\.* Basingstoke: Palgrave Macmillan.

Borneman J, Hammoudi A (eds) (2009) *Being There: The Fieldwork Encounter and the Making of Truth.* CA: California Press.

Boulton M (2009) Research ethics. In: Neale J (ed.) *Research Methods for Health and Social Care*. Basingstoke: Palgrave McMillan.

Bowling A (2004) *Research Methods in Health. Investigating Health and Health Services* (2nd edn). Berkshire: Open University Press.

Brink H, Van der Walt C, Rensburg G (2011) *Fundamentals of Research Methodology for Health Care Professionals* (2nd edn). JUTA: Cape Town.

Clark-Carter D (2010) *Quantitative Psychological Research* (3rd edn). East Sussex: Psychology Press/Taylor & Francis,.

Cohen L, Manion L, Morrison K (2007) *Research Methods in Education* (6th edn). London: Routledge/Taylor & Francis.

Cook C, Garratt D (2005) The positivist paradigm in contemporary social science research. In: B Smoekh, C Lewin. *Research Methods in Social Sciences*. London: Sage Publications.

Coolican H (2009) *Research Methods and Statistics in Psychology* (5th edn). London: Hodder-Education.

Creswell JW (2013) *Research Design: Qualitative, Quantitative and Mixed Methods Approaches* (4th edn). London: Sage Publications.

Cresswell JW (2007) *Qualitative Inquiry and Research Design: Choosing Among Five Approaches* (2nd edn). London: Sage Publications.

Davidson L, Stayner DA, Lambert S, Smith P, Sledge WH (1997) Phenomenological and participatory research on schizophrenia: recovering the person in theory and practice. *Journal of Social Issues* 53, 767–84.

Department for Education (2015) *Mental Health and Behaviour in Schools: Departmental Advice for School Staff*. Available at: www.gov.uk/government/publications/mental-health-and-behaviour-in-schools—2 (accessed July 2015).

Flick UWE (2014) *An Introduction to Qualitative Research* (5th edn). London: Sage.

Giorgi A (2009) *The Descriptive Phenomenological Method in Psychology*. Pittsburgh, PA: Duquesne University Press.

Hartas D (2010a) Evaluation research in education. In: D Hartas (ed.) *Educational Research and Enquiry: Qualitative and Quantitative Approaches*. London: Continuum.

Hartas D (2010b) Doing a literature review. In: Hartas, D (ed.) *Educational Research and Enquiry: Qualitative and Quantitative Approaches*. London: Continuum.

Hartas D (2010c) Survey research in education. In: Hartas, D (ed.) *Educational Research and Enquiry: Qualitative and Quantitative Approaches*. London: Continuum.

Johnson M, Long T (2010) Research ethics. In: K Gerrish, A Lacey (eds) *The Research Process in Nursing* (6th edn). Oxford: Blackwell.

Kindon S, Pain R, Kesby M (2010) Participatory action research: Origins, approaches and methods. In S Kindon, R Pain, M Kesby (eds) *Participatory Action Research: Connecting People, Participation and Place*. London: Routledge.

Lancaster (2005) *Inductive Approach: Research Methodology*. Available at: www.research-methodology.net/research-methodology/research-approach/ind/ (accessed August 2015).

Lewis H, Staehler T (2010) *Phenomenology: An Introduction*. London: Continuum.

Lingard L, Mathieu A, Levinson W (2008) Grounded theory, mixed methods, and action research. *British Medical Journal* 337, a567.

Lindsay G (2010) Ethical considerations and legal issues in educational research. In: D Hartas (ed.) *Educational Research and Enquiry: Qualitative and Quantitative Approaches*. London: Continuum.

Martin CR, Thomson DR (2000) Design and Analysis of Clinical Nursing Research Studies. London: Routledge/Taylor & Francis.

Mertens DM (2005) *Research Methods in Education and Psychology: Integrating Diversity with Quantitative and Qualitative Approaches* (2nd edn). London: Sage.

National Association of Schoolmasters Union of Women Teachers (2010) *Teacher's Mental Health: A Study Exploring the Experience of Teachers with Work-Related Stress and Mental Health Problems*. Rednall, Birmingham: NASUWT.

Nelson G, Ochocka J, Griffin K, Lord J (1998) 'Nothing about me, without me': Participatory action research with self-help/mutual aid organizations for psychiatric consumer/survivors. *American Journal of Community Psychology* 26, 881–912.

Polgar S, Thomas SA (2008) *Introduction to Research in the Health Sciences* (5th edn) London: Churchill Livingstone/Elsevier.

Portney LG, Watkins MP (2009) *Foundations of Clinical Research: Applications to Practice* (3rd edn). Upper Saddle River, NJ: Prentice Hall.

Reason P, Bradbury H (2008) *The SAGE Handbook of Action Research: Participative Inquiry and Practice* (2nd edn). London: Sage.

Robson C (1999) *Real World Research. A Resource for Social Scientists and Practitioner Researchers*. Oxford: Blackwell.

Robson C (2011) *Real World Research* (3rd edn). Chichester: John Wiley & Sons.

Silverman D (2006) *Interpreting Qualitative Data Methods for Analysing Talk, Text and Interaction* (3rd edn). London: Sage.

Silverman D (2010) *Qualitative Research* (3rd edn). London: Sage.

Teachers Assurance (2013) Stress and Well-Being Research. Bournemouth, Teachers Provident Society.

Watson M, Coombes L (2009) Survey design. In: J Neale (ed.) *Research Methods in Health and Social Care*. London: Palgrave Macmillan.

Wertz FM, Charmaz LA, McMillen LM, Ruthellen J, Anderson R, McSpadden (2011) *Five Ways of Doing Qualitative Analysis*. New York: Guilford Press.

CHAPTER 30

Editors' reflections

Colin R. Martin, Mick P. Fleming and Hugh Smith

This book has presented an overview of key aspects relating to the synthesis of mental health and well-being within education. The intention was to provide a broad prospective with insight into the interrelationships between mental health, well-being, learning and teaching, and to show how such interrelationships rely and impact on each another. Moreover, the book was designed to empowering its readers to engage with wider discussions in formulating meaningful strategies for anyone encountering mental health difficulties within the learning and teaching environment. Practical engagement with any topic can only be considered through subsequent acquisition of knowledge, and a main focus of this book has been to present underlying knowledge to its readers in an accessible manner, without superfluous jargon. This approach should contribute to the process of identifying emerging practical applications to issues that present themselves.

Demystifying, deconstructing and contextualising evidence-based information encourages the reader to reflect, consider, discuss and – where necessary – to intervene in a relevant, non-reactive fashion. In considering the complexity of the interrelationship and subsequent interaction between concepts within mental health and education, it is not possible to present both a comprehensive overview and cover all areas of synthesis because there are many unique interactions that would warrant numerous whole volumes.

It is the editors' and authors' hope that the chapters within the book provide an informed overview of key issues for non-specialists that will contribute to what might develop as an individual 'one-stop shop' for a range of learning and training organisations. If the reader feels they may have grasped a fundamentally better understanding of key aspects of the interrelationship between mental health and education and feel empowered to engage in discussion and formulation of strategies that will subsequently support students and colleagues, then the aspirations of all who have contributed to this book will have been achieved.

Index

M

T